EVERYDAY:

GETTING CLOSER TO
BUDDY HOLLY

SPENCER LEIGH

saf publishing

Also by Spencer Leigh:

The Cavern:
The Most Famous Club in the World

SAF Publishing

Price; £12.99

ISBN: 978-0-946719-90-7

EVERYDAY:

GETTING CLOSER TO
BUDDY HOLLY

SPENCER LEIGH

saf publishing

saf publishing

First edition published in 2009 by SAF Publishing Ltd

SAF Publishing Ltd
149 Wakeman Road,
London. NW10 5BH
ENGLAND

www.safpublishing.co.uk

www.spencerleigh.demon.co.uk

ISBN 978-0-946719-31-0

Cover design: © Anthony Brown. www.emso.co.uk

All lyrics quoted are for review, study or critical purposes.

A CIP catalogue record for this book is available from the British Library.

Printed in England by The Cromwell Press Group, Trowbridge, Wiltshire.

Contents

INTRODUCTION...7

ACKNOWLEDGEMENTS 9

TAKE YOUR TIME: A BUDDY HOLLY TIMELINE 11

1. NEVER MIND THE LUBBOCKS.. 15

2. TIGHTEN UP YOUR BIBLE BELT 23

3. LEARNING THE GAME 28

4. SHOCK OF THE NEW 38

5. THE TEX—NEW MEX SOUND 48

6. RHYTHM METHOD 55

7. HERE I GO, BREAKING ALL OF THE RULES.........................81

8. BROKEN WINGS 116

9. BUDDY HOLLY LIVES 134

10. GRAVE ON.. 142

11. LISTEN TO ME 147
    Soundalikes
    Influencing The 60s
    Cover Versions—It's So Easy, Or Is It?
    Family Connections

12. WHAT'S GONNA BECOME OF ME? 160
    The Buddy Holly Story
    Buddy
    Buddy On The Box
    From Lubbock To Liverpool

13. THE CRICKETS AND THEIR BUDDIES.............................170

14. NOW AND FOREVER TILL THE END OF TIME 184
    I. Those Who Really Care
    II. What If...

APPENDICES 189

UK DISCOGRAPHY 190

US DISCOGRAPHY.. 193

SOME BUDDIES—DISCOGRAPHY...................................... 195

BIBLIOGRAPHY 196

CONTRIBUTORS... 199

INTRODUCTION

In 1984, Ian Dury made an album called *4000 Weeks Holiday*. The title scared the hell out of me because I realised that's all the time we've got on earth—if we're lucky. Ian Dury was unlucky, and Buddy Holly was especially unlucky as he was only alive for 1,169 weeks, or 8,184 days. Buddy Holly packed a lot into those days and what he did resonates today and should endure for decades to come. But just exactly what did Buddy Holly do? Could the fact that he was rock'n'roll's first major casualty have something to do with the way that we approach his legacy today? Time and again, interviewees said to me that they think of his death every time they hear one of his records, and I wonder if it clouds our judgement.

I thought it would be irritating, it not patronising, to convert monetary amounts into today's terms. America still has dollars and cents and roughly speaking, $1 in 1960 would be worth $8 today. The UK currency has changed and there used to be 12 pence in a shilling and 20 shillings in a pound. A UK £1 in 1960 would be worth £12 today.

The industry giant, Decca, owned both the Coral and Brunswick labels. Tracks from Buddy Holly's Nashville sessions of 1956 were issued on Decca in the US and Brunswick in the UK. In 1957/8, the Crickets had releases on Brunswick in the US while Buddy was on Coral, but all these releases were issued on Coral in the UK. Nowadays, "Buddy Holly" is a brand name that is used indiscriminately and frequently the Crickets' "That'll Be The Day" is released under the name of "Buddy Holly" or "Buddy Holly and the Crickets". Even the Crickets' version of "Love's Made A Fool Of You", which was recorded without Holly, has been released on an official compilation under his name. It's shambolic and it highlights the lack of care over his catalogue.

Around 1965, Jerry Allison of the Crickets started calling himself J.I. For simplicity, he is called Jerry Allison throughout, except in some direct quotes.

ACKNOWLEDGEMENTS

My friend, Glenn Frankel of the *Washington Post* tells me that there are two valid ways to approach the writing of a biography: you either discover information that hasn't been made public before or you attempt to tell the story better than it has been told before.

Because of the conscientious and diligent work of several Buddy Holly completists—John Beecher, Jim Carr, John Firminger, John Goldrosen, Bill Griggs (who even moved to Lubbock!), Ian Higham, John Ingman—there can't be much more of significance to be discovered, especially as anyone who could talk effectively about knowing Buddy Holly would have to be at least 65 years old. Their research has been invaluable and so, in different ways, have been the biographies by Ellis Amburn and Philip Norman. In addition, there have been specialist books about his tours and his final days. The various sources are acknowledged in the Bibliography: plagiarism is stealing from one author, but good research is stealing from lots of them. One thing is certain: outside of Elvis Presley, no rock'n'roller has been under such close scrutiny, and as the majority of the ultra-keen scrutineers are British, I knew I would have to find out why. Although I hoped

to find some new information (and I think I did), the thrill of writing this book would be in trying to tell the story in a fresh and hopefully enlightening way.

You can, I think, learn from bad examples. Normally a very sound author, Philip Norman in his 1996 biography states at the outset that Holly, compared with Presley, "was a pioneer and a revolutionary, a multidimensional talent that arrived fully formed in a medium still largely defined by fumbling amateurs." I would question that on several counts, but Norman is asserting this at the beginning. Hopefully, I have started with no assumptions or conclusions, and only, when appropriate, will I draw conclusions about Holly, bringing things together at the end.

Everyday—Getting Closer To Buddy Holly tells the story of Buddy Holly's life and times and assesses his musical contribution, but it is an oral history as well as a biography. I have spoken to people who knew and worked with Buddy as well as numerous musicians and fans, and I've enjoyed collecting different takes on his music. My thanks to everybody who has spoken to me, whether for this book or as part of an interview for a magazine or for BBC Radio Merseyside. All the contributions are numbered and you can find out about the speakers in the final section of the book.

Most of the speakers are not collectors and so I have corrected them when they have given the wrong B-side or put a track on a wrong album. However, I left their memories intact even if it does not accord with the acknowledged facts. This is partly because this is of interest in its own right and secondly, that they might just be right. However, I have tried to make the text around these quotes as accurate as I can. There are differences in many of the old press stories (sometimes quite deliberately!) and hopefully, I've used a little logic to determine what really happened.

In a way, there has been too much to look at, let alone analyse. Only the other week, I bought the complete back issues of *Rolling Stone* on DVD. This is a wonderful collection but when I looked up "Buddy Holly", I came up with 571 features or news items. The last time I spoke to Peter Carlin, who is writing a biography of Paul McCartney, he said that he was going to go through all the references to him on Google. There are 15 million references to Macca, and if Peter only spends a minute on each item, his lifetime would be over. You can see how easy it is to get paralysed by information overload. Similarly, there are 5 million references to Buddy Holly on Google and some of the less familiar sites may glean unusual titbits or insights, but life is too short, as Buddy himself would testify.

My thanks to Dave Barnes (British Archive of Country Music), John Beecher (Rollercoaster Records), Els Boonen (BBC Written Archives), Geoffrey Davis, John Firminger (Crickets File), Ian Higham, Roger Hill, Anne Leigh, Mark Lewisohn, Jim Newcombe, Mick O'Toole and Denny Seyton. My special thanks to Mike Brocken for allowing me to access the remarkable collection of Holly magazines, records, tapes and memorabilia, which has been left to the Institute of Popular Music at Liverpool University by the family of the late David Friedman.

It's been a pleasure and a privilege to write this book.

Spencer Leigh

TAKE YOUR TIME

A Buddy Holly Timeline

Monday 7 September 1936,
Days left—8,184
Birth of Charles Hardin Holley, known as Buddy, in Lubbock, Texas.

Friday 14 October 1955,
Days left—1,208
A Nashville talent scout recognises Buddy's talent when he opens for Bill Haley.

Saturday 15 October 1955,
Days left—1,207
Elvis Presley and Buddy Holly cruise around Lubbock.

Wednesday 7 December 1955,
Days left—1,154
Buddy records demos for Nashville.

Thursday 26 January 1956,
Days left—1,104
Buddy records his first single in Nashville.

Monday 16 April 1956,
Days left—1,023
First Buddy Holly single released in US; "Blue Days—Black Nights".

Monday 2 July 1956,
Days left—946
UK release for "Blue Days—Black Nights".

Sunday 22 July 1956,
Days left—926
Buddy records first versions of "Rock Around With Ollie Vee" and "That'll Be The Day" in Nashville.

Thursday 15 November 1956,
Days left—810
Second version, with saxophone, of "Rock Around With Ollie Vee" in Nashville.

Wednesday 9 January 1957,
Days left 755
Hank Thompson's country and western tour includes Buddy Holly and the Two-Tones.

Monday 25 February 1957,
Days left—708
Second version of "That'll Be The Day" at Norman Petty's studio in Clovis.

Monday 8 April 1957,
Days left—666
Double-tracking of "Words Of Love" in Clovis.

Monday 27 May 1957,
Days left—617
"That'll Be The Day", the first single as the Crickets released in the US.

Wednesday 29 May 1957,
Days left—615
"Everyday" and "Not Fade Away" recorded in Clovis.

Saturday 29 June 1957 and next two days,
Days left—584 to 582
"Peggy Sue", "Listen To Me" and "Oh Boy!" recorded in Clovis.

Sunday 28 July 1957,
Days left—555
The Crickets leave for tour with black R&B performers.

Friday 16 August 1957,
Days left—536
The first day at the Apollo Theatre, New York.

Sunday 1 September 1957,
Days left—520
Start of two month tour with Paul Anka, Chuck Berry and the Everly Brothers.

Tuesday 10 September 1957,
Days left—511
UK release for "That'll Be The Day".

Saturday 21 September 1957,
Days left—500
End of week statistics put "That'll Be The Day" at top of US *Billboard* chart.

Tuesday 1 October 1957,
Days left—490
That'll be the day that their single sells a million.

Saturday 2 November 1957,
Days left—458
End of week statistics put "That'll Be The Day" at top of *New Musical Express* chart.

Sunday 1 December 1957,
Days left—429
The Crickets on *The Ed Sullivan Show* with "That'll Be The Day" and "Peggy Sue".

Wednesday 8 January 1958,
Days left—391
First day of *The Everly Brothers Show* with Paul Anka, and Danny and the Juniors.

Saturday 25 January 1958,
Days left—374
Holly records "Rave On" in New York.

Thursday 30 January 1958,
Days left—369
Start of Australian dates with Paul Anka and Jerry Lee Lewis.

Friday 14 February 1958,
Days left—354
Buddy Holly spends Valentine's Day recording "Take Your Time", "Fool's Paradise" and "Think It Over" in Clovis.

Wednesday 19 February 1958,
Days left—349
Using his middle name, Ivan, Jerry Allison, backed by Holly, cuts "Real Wild Child" in Clovis.

Thursday 20 February 1958,
Days left—348
First day of tour with the Everly Brothers, Bill Haley and Jerry Lee Lewis.

Saturday 1 March 1958,
Days left—339
Start of UK tour with compère Des O'Connor.

Sunday 2 March 1958,
Days left—338
The Crickets on *Sunday Night At The London Palladium*.

Friday 28 March 1958,
Days left—312
Start of *Alan Freed's Big Beat Show* with Chuck Berry and Jerry Lee Lewis.

Sunday 25 & Monday 26 May 1958,
Days left—254 & 253
Buddy records "It's So Easy" and "Heartbeat" in Clovis.

Thursday 19 June 1958,
Days left—229
Buddy Holly records "Early In The Morning" in New York.

Friday 4 July 1958,
Days left—214
Start of *Summer Dance Party* with Tommy Allsup's Western Swing Band.

Friday 15 August 1958,
Days left—172
Buddy marries Maria Elena Santiago in Lubbock.

Wednesday 10 September 1958,
Days left—146
Saxophonist King Curtis joins Holly in Clovis and they cut "Reminiscing".

Tuesday 30 September 1958,
Days left—126
Buddy Holly and Phil Everly produce Lou Giordano in New York.

Friday 3 October 1958,
Days left—123
Start of *The Biggest Shows Of Stars For 1958— Autumn Edition* with Frankie Avalon, Bobby Darin and Dion and the Belmonts.

Tuesday 21 October 1958,
Days left—105
A string session in New York for "True Love Ways" and "It Doesn't Matter Anymore".

Wednesday 3 December 1958,
Days left—62
Buddy starts recording at his apartment in New York.

Saturday 27 December 1958,
Days left—38
Back in Lubbock, Buddy is challenged to write a song on the spot.

Monday 5 January 1959,
Days left—29
US release for "It Doesn't Matter Anymore".

Friday 23 January 1959,
Days left—11
Start of *Winter Dance Party* with the Big Bopper and Ritchie Valens.

Monday 2 February 1959,
Days left—1
Day 11 of *Winter Dance Party* at the Surf Ballroom, Clear Lake, Iowa.

Tuesday 3 February 1959
The day the music died.

1

NEVER MIND THE LUBBOCKS

"Everybody gives Lubbock a hard time."
(Joe Ely, 2008)

In 1957, Frank Sinatra recorded his exotic collection of travelling songs, *Come Fly With Me* where he sang about magical nights in Brazil, Capri, Hawaii, Vermont, London and Paris. A couple of years later, he revisited "Let's Get Away From It All" and, in a version which was never released, he paid tribute to Lubbock, a devout city in the Bible belt which banned alcohol. Sinatra sang:

"Let's go to Lubbock or Clovis
I'll get a real Southern drawl
We could get lost in
Somewhere like Austin
Let's get away from it all.

A city that's drier than Texas
You'll find no booze there at all
You better believe it—
Lubbock or leave it—
Let's get away from it all.

My compass points to roadside joints
Where coffee's just a dime,
The waitress thinks she's Monroe,
The music's '59.

We're heading out on the highway,
Buddy just gave me a call.
Hey wind, blow my hat back,
I'll start a new rat pack
Let's get away from it all."

I've made that up, or at least, I've made it up with my friend, Andrew Doble: I don't want to do a Norman Petty here. Sinatra would never have considered Lubbock his kind of town. In fact, very few outsiders, and precious few insiders, would have sung Lubbock's praises. It was in the middle of nowhere and there was nothing to see once you got there. It is so flat that you wonder what driving instructors do for a hill start.

Richard Wootton (1): "While researching my book *Honky Tonkin'—A Travel Guide To American Music* in the late seventies I tried to visit as many of America's musical cities as I could, but I never got to Lubbock. It is nowhere near anywhere else, but the main reason I avoided it was because it sounded like the dullest, flattest place on earth. The flatness reminded me of my home county of Suffolk, which I was so glad to escape from when I was 18. Lubbock musicians always talk about 'the flat lands' and it was Terry Allen who told me that if you stood and stared into the distance on a clear day you could sometimes see the back of your own head."

Terry Allen (2): "There's barely a tree in the city and it's flat, totally flat, in every direction. Looking back, I'm sure that's helped me and some other writers as it has made imagery and story-telling highly significant."

Any city wanting to put itself on the tourist map needs to sound as appealing as possible. It's self-evident that any tourism officer who wants a challenge should settle in Lubbock. I love their adverts: "Get blown away" and "Hot…Windy… Dry". It strikes me immediately that Buddy Holly didn't wear contact lenses because the grit would have got under the hard surfaces and been most uncomfortable.

Lubbock wasn't on the tourist route and it wouldn't be now if it weren't for Buddy Holly. Okay, don't write in: I know some people go to see windmills and tractors and for all I know, some may be obsessed with prairie dogs. The city receives 100 requests a day from potential tourists and the majority relate to Buddy Holly.

Joe Ely (3): "Lubbock's a big city in the middle of a cotton field. There are a lot of people living there but it's like a small town because it is so spread out. The main things are just cotton and boredom. I spent most of my time in high school thinking of how to get out. Lubbock is a musically creative area, and maybe that's because there's nothing else to do. Making music is something that has been passed down. There are songs that have been passed down from generation to generation that you won't hear anywhere else."

One of Lubbock's most famous residents, Waylon Jennings, said in 1975: "It's like they say sport is to black dudes: it's a way to get up and get away from something that's bad. You'll do any-thing to get out of West Texas. I'll tell you what it is: it's either music or pull cotton for the rest of your life. You'll learn to do something else if you've ever been to a cotton patch." Waylon also commented, "Anyone who spends his life in the cotton patch is going to end up weird or unique." And he should know.

Terry Allen (4): "There was nothing happen-ing in Lubbock while I was there. I would stand

under the Great Plains Life Building and look straight up and imagine that I was in New York."

You've got to travel a long way to get out of Lubbock, but it's easier to escape now. In Buddy Holly's time, you had to go to Amarillo for a plane and now there is the Lubbock International Air-port, although in keeping with the times, it can't be long before it becomes the Buddy Holly Inter-national Airport. No, no, hang on, they must have thought of that already, and it wouldn't inspire confidence to name an airport after someone who had died in a plane crash. Indeed, the authorities in Liverpool probably called it the John Lennon International Airport because John had written "Above us only sky" whereas Paul McCartney had gone "All the way a paper bag was on my knees, Man, I had a dreadful flight."

Lubbock is part of West Texas, a huge isolated region with vast, featureless plains. You would need to travel 100 miles to find another town or city with over 25,000 people. Oklahoma City is 300 miles north-east: Fort Worth and Dallas 300 miles south-east and travelling even further you hit Austin, Houston, San Antonio and, on the coast, Corpus Christi. Is this the way to Amarillo? Well, yes it is if you go 100 miles due north. There's not too much heading west: Clovis, New Mexico is 100 miles away; the ultra-spooky Roswell 150; and it's 250 to the West Texas town of El Paso. By the time you got to Phoenix you would have travelled 700 miles and seen a lot of mountains, and it's another 300 miles to the Cali-fornia girls and Los Angeles.

In his song, "Wheatfield Lady" (1974), John Stewart sings, "Laying out before me, the end-less highway lies." Spot on, mate, and we're talk-ing distances here: I don't know where you come from but I live in Liverpool and going the 200 miles to London and back would take all day and I put off my visits until I can do several things at once. However, in Lubbock, in the 1950s, nobody appeared to be concerned about travel-ling: I didn't find anyone who said, "God, I hated the trip from Lubbock to Clovis." (Oh, they wouldn't say "God" either: even slight profani-ties are out. Buddy never swore—he said "barf" when he was irritated—so there are no fucks in this book: whoops, just said one.) The journeys passed the time and got them out of Lubbock, and they just accepted it: you had to travel to get anywhere. Buddy Holly and his cohorts were perpetually in motion, and as they're writing songs as they went, it's also poetry in motion.

Tim Whitnall (5): "Texas is sprawling. If you go to Lubbock, Dallas, Austin or Fort Worth, you will find that the business districts are very small and the rest is a great big suburb. I like the roads in Texas and I think of the Crickets and the others travelling through the nights in their sedans and station wagons, sometimes doing two gigs a night in clubs or gymnasiums."

Butch Hancock (6): "I've both loved and hated Lubbock, but I was born with a big rubber band around me. I can get away from there but sooner or later, the band goes boing!, and I'm back in Lubbock. I was born in Lubbock, and we lived on farms in the area. I drove tractors for my dad around Lubbock and that's very good for songwriting as there's not much else to think about while you're driving a tractor. Nearly everybody in Lubbock is aware of the climate. In a city, you have to look up to see the sky. In Lubbock, you could see right across to the horizon."

Jimmie Dale Gilmore (7): "I like the sense of humour in Lubbock. We're always making fun of the place and it's really because we love it so much."

All the cities in that Texas Panhandle area, including Lubbock, are young. There may have been human life in the area for 10,000 years, but none of the cities was there in 1850. The very name, Fort Worth, tells you what happened as the soldiers were garrisoned in forts across the country. The lands belonged to the Indians (then called the Red Indians and now, with political correctness, the American Indians). They were fighting with the American army, the miners and the white settlers for many years but things came to a head with the Battle of Little Bighorn in 1876. The Indians won the battle but the American public was appalled that one of its heroes, General George Custer, had been killed. The campaign against the Indians intensified and they were bullied, broken and beaten, not just by the white man's military might and superior weaponry but also by the slaughter of their prime source of meat, the buffalo. Nobody cared about the Indians, and General Sheridan, in keeping

with the times, coined the infamous phrase, "The only good Injun is a dead Injun."

The last big Buffalo Hunt took place in 1878 and lots of hunters came to take part. Two hunters were singing around a campfire. When one of them sang, "Where seldom is heard a discouraging word", the other added, "Home, home on the range", and Kansas had its state song. I'm uneasy about the provenance for that story but it is cited in "What to see, What to do", a leaflet published by the Lubbock Chamber of Commerce.

Lubbock County was founded in 1876 and named after Thomas Saltus Lubbock, a Confederate colonel and founder of the Texas Rangers, and indeed, Buddy Holly attended the Tom S. Lubbock High School. Fabulous surname, isn't it? Lubbock sounds like a Lancashire town: "Ee, he sounds like a right lubbock."

The first settlement was established by some Quakers from Indiana in 1879. The threat from the Indians had disappeared, but the combination of appalling winters and rattlesnakes soon made them head home. However, one couple, Paris and Mary Cox, remained, partly because Mary was pregnant and, all in all, it was safer to stay. In June 1880, their daughter, Bertha, was the first white person to be born in north-west Texas. Then Hank Smith established a cattle farm and discovered that the land was good for grazing. Things didn't exactly happen fast, but, getting the priorities right, a post office was established in 1884; the first wedding took place in 1889; then George and Rachel Singer opened the first store, and in 1891, there were enough children for a teacher and a schoolroom. There were attempts to grow cotton but nobody got it right until 1904 and then West Texas became a major centre for cotton production, and still is. Lubbock is surrounded by cotton fields, oil fields and cropland.

In the UK, a city is a large town and has, until recent times, had to have a cathedral. Americans think differently and the city of Lubbock was incorporated on 16 March 1909 when its population was barely 2,000 (people, that is; there were a lot more rattlesnakes). The railway played its part in helping the region to grow, and so did the motor car. In 1914, all the ten cars in the region came together for a group photograph. Whatever, the population was on the rise, hitting 20,000 in

1930; and then, thanks to the oil boom, 72,000 in 1950, and 130,000 in 1960 (sadly, minus one by that time.) By then, West Texas produced 15% of all the US oil.

Covering spiritual, physical and mental strength, a combination of God, guns and guts made the west. The way that Lubbock developed from the pioneering spirit is reflected in the city today. The average Joe would never think of choosing a new life out west. These were violent, lawless places and you had to be tough to withstand treacherous conditions. The survivors would be the toughest of the bunch, and their children and their children's children and so on passed on their spirited genes to current generations.

The forefathers of the city were mostly male; there was a marked shortage of females. Not that it bothered the good ol' boys too much until it came to dances. Then the men would take it turns to put a cloth on their arm to signify that they were the females for the next waltz, but probably not the last waltz. These counterfeit women were, in the terminology of the day, "heifer branded", and many a dance ended with a fight.

After all, who was the most famous person to come from the region before Buddy Holly? Billy the Kid! William Bonney was born in New York in 23 November 1859 and after his father died, his mother moved with a prospector to the optimistically named Silver City in New Mexico. The Bonney boy killed a bully in Silver City when he was 12 and got involved in fighting over grazing land in Lincoln County, indeed, Billy, a right-handed gun for hire incidentally, fought and killed for both sides.

When the going got hot, Billy made a deal with Governor Lew Wallace of New Mexico (then writing "Ben Hur" in his spare time) that he would shop others in exchange for a pardon. He was arrested but he suspected that Wallace would betray him and escaped. Pat Garrett, the sheriff of Lincoln County, trapped him and put him in jail in Santa Fe. He was condemned to be "hanged by the neck until you are dead, dead, dead" to which the Kid replied, "May you rot in hell, hell, hell." When Garrett went to supervise the gallows, the Kid escaped from his deputy, but Garrett, his reputation damaged by the jailbreak, tracked him down to Fort Sumner. On 14 July 1881, the Kid

had gone to see his friend Pete Maxwell and in the dark, he asked, "¿quién es? (Who is it?)" (Not bad, huh: a psychopathic gunman but he learned a second language.) Garrett couldn't take any chances—he wasn't even sure it was the Kid—and he replied by firing two shots into him.

There is a glorious moment in Sam Peckinpah's 1973 western, *Pat Garrett And Billy The Kid*, where Garrett (James Coburn) shoots Billy the Kid (Kris Kristofferson) and seeing his own reflection in a mirror, puts a bullet through the glass. The implication is that the death of his adversary also marked his own end. Because his killing of the Kid had been as barbaric as the Kid's own deeds, he lost his job and tried unsuccessfully for other posts. Haunted by the death of Billy the Kid, he renounced violence and went into ranching, but he died in a gunfight in 1908. His grave in Las Cruces, New Mexico is unmarked but the site of Billy the Kid's death and his tombstone in Fort Sumner are tourist attractions. The gunslinger was nearly 22 when he died: the fun singer had just passed his 22nd birthday when he died.

Clovis is less than 100 miles from Lubbock in the badlands of New Mexico, outlaw country, Billy the Kid country. Not a place for the innocent in the 1850s: maybe, not a place for the innocent in the 1950s.

The official guide to Lubbock says that it has an excellent climate with over 3,550 hours of sunshine every year: "The summers are dry and not extremely hot, and the winters are dry and moderate." That is putting the best picture on things: the songs tell a different story. You don't get many weather reports in English songs, but it's a preoccupation with the songs from the Texas Panhandle. Ian Tyson writes about a rodeo rider in "Someday Soon", which has the line, "So blow, you old blue norther, blow my love to me."

There is little that ties down a time or a place in Buddy Holly's song lyrics, but had he lived, he may well have written about his adolescence. **Richard Wootton (8)**: "Buddy Holly had fond memories of Lubbock, as did the other musicians like Joe Ely and Butch Hancock, but all used music as a means of escape from having to live there. There is nothing like the dull boredom of a small town to stimulate ambition and Buddy was one of the first musicians of the rock'n'roll era to emerge from a small town and amaze the world. I recently rediscovered his cover of the Roy Orbison and Norman Petty song 'An Empty Cup (A Broken Date)' which is a terrific piece of small-town teenage angst."

Andy Wilkinson (9): "All of Buddy's music says 'Lubbock' to me, because what makes Lubbock music is the same for all of us from this place, and that is that we all take a variety of musical influences and create something else from them. You can hear that in Waylon Jennings, Mac Davis, Butch Hancock, Jimmie Dale Gilmore, Joe Ely, Terry Allen, Cary Swinney, and on and on. Very few of us write about Lubbock *per se*, but I think you can hear the Lubbock wind in all our music."

Joe Ely has recorded "Windy Windy Windy", "Because Of The Wind" and "Wind's Gonna Blow You Away", so you get the picture.

The weather is unpredictable and you can experience both summer and winter on the same day. Summers are arid with clear blue skies and temperatures over 90 degrees, even, on exceptional days, 110 degrees: autumns are breezy with some rain: winters can be mild and sunny but it can snow, briefly and heavily, and temperatures can fall to well below zero, and as for springs, beware of high winds and thunderstorms. Twenty-six people were killed when a tornado hit Lubbock in May 1970 and enormous structural damage was done. Despite taking a direct hit, the Great Plains Life Building (now the NTS Tower) survived but it was built to withstand the storms.

In various combinations, Joe Ely, Jimmie Dale Gilmore and Butch Hancock (who first worked together as the Flatlanders) have made careers out of singing and writing about the weather. Joe Ely is at his best in the 'Because Of The Wind', a song which resonates with the charm of Bob Dylan's "Girl Of The North Country". After pointing out that the trees bend because of the wind, Ely sings: "Now if she is like the breeze that blows from Corpus Christi, Then I must be like the trees 'cause Caroline blows through me."

Butch Hancock's farming song, 'West Texas Waltz', celebrates life in Lubbock County and finding happiness in hardship: "The tractor's been acting up, And the sewer line's a-backing up, But I'll be dancing tonight anyway."

And it concludes with innuendo: "Only two things are milk shakes and malts, And one is dancing like the dickens to the West Texas Waltz."

Because of its climate and man-made irrigation, Lubbock has fared well with cotton and crops but it also has had success with its much respected university, Texas Tech. It opened in 1923 and now, with the addition of its health sciences centre, offers higher education to over 20,000 students a year.

In 1951, the first sighting of the Lubbock Lights was seen. The UFO sightings were considered credible (though not by me) because they were witnessed by several science professors at Texas Tech and were photographed by one of its students. The likelihood is that plovers looked sinister in the glow of Lubbock's new street lights.

Another possibility is that the whole thing was faked. Only four years earlier, the media reported the bizarre happenings at Roswell, New Mexico, and maybe some of the citizens in Lubbock wanted some of the action. It was suggested that an alien craft had landed at Roswell and the Government and the military had hushed it up. I doubt that and I doubt too that sightseers would have been attracted to the real deal. If you really thought an alien craft had landed in Roswell, wouldn't you get the hell out of the place?

Lubbock is part of the Bible Belt, maybe even the buckle of the Bible Belt. There are many religions in the area, but the prime one is Baptist. The Protestants in America objected to the many evolutionary theories of the 19th century and at a conference in Niagara in 1895, they agreed the five tenets of fundamentalism: the total acceptances of the Scriptures, the divinity of Jesus Christ, the Virgin Birth, the Resurrection and the need for Atonement. Within a few decades, the Baptists had split into fundamentalist and modernist groups. The Holley family, and Buddy himself, belonged to a fundamentalist Baptist church.

Scientists believe, say, the theory of natural selection because they have studied the evidence. Fundamentalists have not subjected the Biblical narrative to any scientific scrutiny. The Bible is a holy book that's historically accurate, and that's the end of the matter.

The Baptists maintains that, despite its many contradictions, everything in the Bible is true, but how come? If the baby Jesus received gold, frank-incense and myrrh, why was the family so poor? Where did Noah find the polar bears and pen-guins for his Ark? Richard Dawkins' infamous book, *The God Delusion* (2006), is much more an attack on fundamentalism than on Christian-ity *per se*, and he would be ill-advised to make a personal appearance in Lubbock. The Baptists are very God-fearing people: in the UK, we accept free speech much more readily than in America and hence, nobody here took much notice of what John Lennon said about the Beatles being more popular than Jesus. The burning of Beatle records was in the Bible Belt and if a performer from Lubbock had made such a remark, his career would have been over.

As I writing this, there was a news report that 1 in 10 people in the UK now believe in some form of fundamentalism, whether Christian or some other religion. I find the rise of Christian fun-damentalism hard to accept, but maybe fanciful computer games have given youngsters a distorted view of the world where anything is possible.

The Bible Belt can be a formidable place for a young, impressionable child. Willie Nelson has said that when he was 10, he already thought he was destined for Hell and, as you can't go to Hell twice, he continued in that vein.

Butch Hancock (10): "Life in Lubbock was full of contradictions. You learn that God loves you and that you're going to burn in hell. You learn too that sex is the most awful, filthy thing on earth, and that you should only do it with somebody you love."

The country singer and crime novelist, **Kinky Friedman (11)** had a hard time in Texas and he now says, "There's nothing wrong with Southern Baptists except they don't hold 'em under long enough." To be fair to his opponents, Kinky was so unorthodox and so cynical that he would have had a hard time anywhere. Later in the book, there is a story about Little Richard in Lubbock which Richard interprets as being racial but his camp demeanour was way outside the norm in Lubbock in the mid-50s.

Members of the Baptist church would tithe their earnings as a matter of course. Some books say the four Crickets gave 40% of their earnings to the church: total nonsense. A tithe is, by defi-nition, 10% and so it was 10% of their total earn-ings. Their manager, Norman Petty, also tithed his income, and it seems to me, none of them ever questioned this. An English equivalent is unthink-able. Imagine someone asking John Lennon to donate 10% of his earnings to the church.

On a daily basis, it wasn't aliens in Roswell or encounters with the Devil that bothered the good people of Lubbock. It was alcohol. During Buddy Holly's time, Lubbock was dry, which meant that you could not officially purchase alcohol within the city limits, so bootleggers made a good living. Lubbock remained dry until 1972 when alcohol by the glass could be served in restaurants and bars, but liquor stores were still forbidden. Out-side the city limits, a batch of stores opened on the Strip on Highway 87. In 2006, the Lubbock City Council allowed liquor stores inside the city, but as it added a considerable sales tax, this has not caught on.

Joe Ely (12): "Lubbock was dry and so you had to go outside the county line to this place called the Strip. It was a whole line of liquor stores out in the cotton fields."

Michael Gray (13): "As for Lubbock, it's famously a complete dump, an absolute nothing, and in Buddy Holly's day, it was a dry town in a dry county, so that all the good ol' boys would jump in their pick-up trucks and roar out beyond the county line to buy their booze; and it's very flat, in every sense."

And sometimes those good ol' boys would stay out there. There have been strange events to rival Roswell when carloads of residents headed out to the cotton fields, put their cars in a circle and turned on the headlights. They danced in the middle of this ring of lights, or if they wanted something more macho, indulged in bare knuckle boxing.

Jimmie Dale Gilmore (14): "Lubbock was totally dry when I started performing and I could either play at little coffee houses in the city or at bootlegging joints. I would sing Willie Nelson songs as he was popular around Lubbock long before he was famous. One of my first composi-tions was 'Treat Me Like Saturday Night' which I wrote when I was 20 and I'd been very inspired by Terry Allen."

But being dry gave young musicians the opportunity to play. There was no reason to exclude them from the clubs. Jerry Allison was drumming in Lubbock clubs from the age of 14, but whether he got his homework done is another matter.

Jesse "Guitar" Taylor (15): "It was quite common to see chicken wire at those out-of-town clubs. Some of those places get very rough and rowdy. I've been on both sides of the chicken wire but I've never thrown a bottle at anybody. If it gets real rowdy, you're sure glad it's there as you don't have to duck." Surely the best way to avoid getting bottles thrown at you is to play really well. "No, no, it's pretty indiscriminate, just a bunch of drunk cowboys."

Joe Ely (16): "Lubbock was an agricultural area. People worked hard during the week and then wanted entertainment on Saturday. There were only the honky tonks and the high school football games. You could tell a good show by the number of fights. If the band played really good, there would be a lot of fights afterwards."

Snuff Garrett (17): "I was born and raised outside of Dallas and I grew up with a lot of the country stars of the day like Hank Thompson and Lefty Frizzell, and Willie and I go back to the same era and he is a great, great guy. If you didn't want to grow up, you went to some of the clubs he played. You could almost die on the spot."

Jimmie Dale Gilmore (18): "I was 19 or 20 when I started going out and playing gigs. Lubbock was totally dry, there was no legal alcohol and so the little clubs that had it were illegal, bootleg joints, and the age limit didn't apply as everybody was breaking the law anyway. Joe Ely and I were doing solo gigs and we got to be fans of each other in those bootleg joints. They were never raided while we were there, but it meant we were involved with the outlaw crowd of the time. The bootleg clubs were in town but they would be hidden away down dark streets. They certainly didn't advertise—it was all word of mouth!"

And it's not just the wild clubs. Lubbock appears to be a hell of a dangerous place with youngsters driving cars and vehicles going at up to 130mph on the desert highways. Buddy himself loved to make tyres squeal. Thank God the city was dry or there'd be no one left alive.

Maybe the best example of Lubbock's anonymity comes with the liner notes for the Crickets' first LP, *The Chirping Crickets*, in 1957. It said that the group came from Bullock, Texas and Holly does not appear to have insisted on a correction. **Ian Higham (19):** "The first US pressing of *The Chirping Crickets* refers to Bullock as does an EP with the same name. The following year, *The Sound Of The Crickets* EP in the US does correctly say Lubbock. On the other hand, I have 11 copies of the UK pressing of *The Chirping Crickets* LP from March 1958 to October 1960 and even though the date of the reprint is noted on the sleeves, 'Bullock' is never changed. Similarly, with the UK release of *The Sound Of The Crickets* EP from May 1958 to November 1963, the notes all refer to Bullock."

Texas was a melting pot of cultures as European immigrants swarmed the area looking for opportunities. There were English, French, Germans and Swedes and they brought skills in building trains and mines. They brought their own customs and crafts which included brewing beer and dancing the polka and the waltz. They brought their instruments like horns, fiddles, accordions and harmonicas. There was a crossbreeding of their cultures and so we got the Tex-Mex of accordion and polka sounds.

Jimmie Dale Gilmore (20): "I still love Buddy Holly's music and anytime one of his songs comes on the radio, I am likely to turn it up. It is still amazing to realise how young he was, the strength of his voice and how those melodies endure. Part of his originality was that his songs blended different backgrounds that hadn't been put together before. It had something folky to it, a little bit of blues to it, and definitely a Tex-Mex flavour. Of course, it wasn't Tex-Mex like Doug Sahm and some of those guys, but that Mexican influence is there. Of course, it need not have come from Lubbock as Latin-American rhythms had affected the American popular music of the day."

The Mexicans were called "wetbacks" as they had often come illegally into the Southern States looking for work. There was cheaply paid work available at harvest time.

Joe Ely (21): "My father had a used clothes store in Lubbock and I used to work there when I was 12 or 13. We had Mexican wetbacks coming in from across the Rio Grande. They'd come in to chop cotton. Thousands of them would come down the East Broadway part of Lubbock. They'd come into town at weekends to buy old clothes and I would pick up some Spanish and some Mexican songs."

Andy Wilkinson (22): "The Mexican and Mexican-American influences here in Lubbock are huge, and Buddy lived near those neighborhoods and went to school with kids from that culture. The curious thing is that the young Mexican-Americans who were doing music in those years were playing rock'n'roll themselves. Indeed, their contributions to American rock are much overlooked."

Maybe the term, Tex-Mex, music has some validity for Buddy's music, although you are scratching around to find that Mexican component: a bit of "Heartbeat", perhaps. **Flaco Jiminez (23)**: "I wouldn't really call Buddy Holly Tex-Mex. Tex-Mex is more Doug Sahm and Augie Meyers

with the Sir Douglas Quintet and it is a happy go lucky music, a blend of Mexican songs, polka beats and rock'n'roll. There was a time when even Mexicans didn't want to hear accordion music, but now people really go for the groove and it appeals to young and old."

Look at the longitude and you will see that Lubbock is on the same band as Casablanca, Jerusalem, Delhi and Shanghai. All that heat can affect you and maybe that's a reason why there are so many colourful characters in this story. Maybe the sun makes everybody a little crazy. In 1978, one of Waylon Jennings' country hits attempted to explain his wild behaviour and was called "I've Always Been Crazy": "I've always been crazy but it's kept me from going insane, Nobody knows if it's something to bless or to blame."

Buddy Holly never got as personal or as confessional as that, but he would have endorsed the sentiment.

2

TIGHTEN UP YOUR BIBLE BELT

*"That's my life to the present date, and even though it may
seem awful and full of calamities,
I'd sure be in bad shape without it."
(Buddy Holly writing an essay, June 1953)*

On Valentine's Day, 1959, just 11 days after the crash which killed her son, Ella Holley wrote to the families of the other performers who had died, the Big Bopper and Ritchie Valens. They are beautifully composed letters, revealing her bewilderment and grief, but they also show her strong faith that they will all be reunited in Heaven. However, what makes her action extraordinary is that she wrote a similar letter to the widow of the pilot, Roger Peterson. She did not cast any blame, although the accident was largely due to his inexperience, and she said, "We are crushed by this terrible tragedy and the loss of our son, and we know you are suffering the same. We have never known before the grief and suffering from the death of a loved one but we do know now, and our hearts go out to you because we know what you are going through. We will keep you in our prayers."

Fifty years on, this letter is incredibly touching and is the most noteworthy artifact to have been preserved about Buddy Holly. It shows what a remarkable woman Ella Holley must have been. It indicates how Buddy Holly had been raised and how his parents had shaped his personality. Indeed, it is often said that rock'n'roll was the music of rebellion, a response to the dull, conventional lifestyles of the singers' parents. There is none of that in the Buddy Holly story: his parents supported him all the way and he, in turn, loved and supported them.

Like most Americans, the Holley family had a colourful background and there are English and Welsh antecedents. They would have come to America for a new start and one of Buddy's relations on his mother's side had a child with a Cherokee, which added Indian blood to the mix. The same can be said of Elvis Presley, who has Morning Dove White on his family tree. On his mother's side, the family claimed to have been related to Sir Francis Drake, though I can find no evidence for this. Indeed, I went "Oh, please!" when I saw this just as when my Dad said we were related to Jane Austen which turned out to be rubbish.

Norman Killon (24): "I think there are several indications that Buddy Holly was linked to the UK. He had a Protestant work ethic, and he really liked it over here. There is also an English feel throughout his work. Little Richard, on the other hand, was totally outrageous and you wouldn't have found anyone remotely like him in England in the 1950s."

Buddy Holly's father, Lawrence Odell Holley, was born on a small farm in Honey Grove, Texas on 4 November 1901. Honey Grove is close to Paris, Texas and if you've seen the film, you'll know how desolate the area is. Ry Cooder's score for *Paris, Texas* brilliantly captures the location and how one town is isolated from another. Buddy Holly's mother, Ella Pauline Drake, was born in Bridgeport, Texas on 29 August 1902. This is close to Fort Worth and 150 miles from Honey Grove.

Both Lawrence and Ella had moved west to Vernon, Texas where they met and were married on 8 June 1923. Buddy's father was known as L.O., so he must have been sick of everyone going "Hello, L.O.", especially as he was working in a diner.

The creation of Texas Tech promised employment in Lubbock and so Mr and Mrs Holley moved there. Lawrence found regular work with L.D. Thomas—he was known as L.D. and then Little Dog and finally as Pup. Pup tried his hand at many things and took L.O. with him. He was the timekeeper when Pup presented the one-time heavyweight champion of the world, Max Baer, in Lubbock. At the time of Buddy Holly's birth, L.O. was earning $12 a week from Pup at Thomas Custom Tailors on Main Street, and he was more fortunate than some as he had worked throughout the Depression. Nevertheless, the white-framed bungalow they lived in was only one-up from a shack and had few mod coms: certainly not a telephone: just a couple of rooms with no electricity and lit by oil lamps.

The Holleys had three children in four years: Lawrence Odell Jr (known as Larry), born 7 October 1925; Travis Don, born 10 July 1927, and Patricia Lou (known as Pat), born 7 March 1929. You faced the extremes of weather in Lubbock and a huge dust storm blew through the region early in 1935. Woody Guthrie, who lived 150 miles away in Pampa, Texas, wrote about it. His original title for "So Long It's Been Good To Know You" was "Dusty Old Dust".

Their fourth child, Charles Hardin Holley, was born seven years later at 3.30pm Labour Day, Monday 7 September 1936. He was named after his grandfathers, John Hardin Holley and Charles Wesley Drake, but his mother considered

Charles Hardin Holley a big name for a little boy and nicknamed him "Buddy". Just as well as Charlie Holly doesn't have the right ring about it, and "Buddy" was the perfect, friendly name for him. The baby, who weighed six and a half pounds, was born at home at 1911 6th Street in Lubbock.

Being poor is nothing to be ashamed about, but in later years, the Holleys did not discuss their humble upbringings and Ella Holley was relieved that their original family home had not been saved.

Ellis Amburn (25): "The Holley home was dragged out beyond the city limits and demolished. Mrs. Holley told fans not to try to save it as she was embarrassed at how modest it was. There is now a larger than life statue in the town centre, which is a ghetto, in my opinion. Before the movie, *The Buddy Holly Story*, came out, there was nothing there. It tells me that those people in Lubbock were more impressed with Hollywood's reaction to their own native son than with Buddy Holly himself."

On 8 September 1936, Lubbock's *Evening Journal* ran a short announcement about Buddy's birth, or did it? There are five mistakes in one short listing: I know newspapers like that.

"A daughter weighing 8½ pounds was born at 6.10 Monday afternoon at Clark Key Clinic to Mr and Mrs Lawrence O. Holley of 1913 Sixth Street."

When Buddy's birth certificate was completed, his surname was spelt as "Holly", so you get the impression that no one was concerned about accuracy.

In 1937, the Holley family moved to Wolforth, a small suburb south-west of Lubbock, but they returned to Lubbock itself a year later. Their new address was 612 Avenue O. The Holleys were to move several times, and Buddy lived in 17 different addresses in Lubbock, but this is symptomatic of American life, especially for families on low income. The historian, William Manchester in *The Death Of A President* reveals that 90 per cent of American families had moved home in the 10 years prior to 1963.

All the Holley addresses make dull reading: 2711 28th Street was the next faceless address in

1942. There are no Menlove Avenues or Arnold Groves here, and, following the lead from New York, Lubbock was built on a grid system with the roads at right angles to each other. By and large, the numbered streets are east/west and the lettered avenues are north/south. Although the house numbers increase as you walk down the street, they do not follow sequentially: 1, 2, 3, 4 and so on. The numbers refer to their place within the grid and the fact that the Holleys lived at 1911 6th Street does not mean that there were 1910 other buildings in the street: far from it. Check it out on Google Earth.

There's a similar anonymity with the names of radio stations. Under international agreements, every station is given a coded identification and in the US, the stations tend to use these codes as their public names. In the US, the first letter, K, is generally given to stations on the west and W for those on the east, and the stations around Lubbock, which is roughly in the middle, had four letters with the first one K. One of the key ones in Lubbock was owned by Dave Stone and with a little originality, he named it KDAV, but the names give no clue as to what the station is broadcasting, in his case, country music.

Both Larry and Travis Holley enjoyed singing and playing country music together and, in June 1939, they appeared on KFYO in Lubbock. Soon, Pat was singing with them. Buddy wasn't a child prodigy, but a local newspaper carried news of a birthday party for four-year-old Maria Kay Fortenberry in April 1940. Pat and Buddy were amongst the guests and the paper reported that "Buddy sang a song."

It was a musical, happy household and Ella would sing as she did the housework. Larry and Travis had guitars, a violin and an accordion and when he was five, Buddy joined them for a talent contest at a school hall in County Line, a town 30 miles north-west of Lubbock with a population of 400. Larry and Travis were confident of winning, but they reckoned without Buddy and his toy violin. Buddy sang, or rather hollered, a gospel song, "Did You Ever Go Sailing", and won the first prize of $5. The song is more suited to an old salt like Willie Nelson than a five-year-old Buddy:

"Did you ever go sailing down the river of memories
To the little log cabin that's nestled among the syca-
more trees,
Where the sunshine is cheery
And nothing in the world grows dreary,
That's my cabin at the end of my river of memories."

Buddy's win was regarded as a fluke, and although he had some piano lessons, he lost interest and what talent he had for playing was picked up by ear. Buddy secured a second hand Harmony guitar from a pawn shop when he was 12 and with Travis's help, he picked up the chords quickly. He also had some help from Wayne Maines from the first generation of the Maines Brothers. The big hit of the day was Hank Williams' "Lovesick Blues" and Buddy would entertain his classmates, yodelling and all. (In 1975, the UK music magazine, *Let It Rock*, reprinted an interview with Buddy Holly from the US magazine *Hit Parade*, in January 1959. He spoke at length of his love for Hank Williams, but the interview, although no doubt accurately conveying his feelings, was faked.) However, Holly did have a great love for Williams and he stretched syllables just the way Williams did on "Lovesick Blues".

Jerry Naylor (26): "In Lubbock, we now have the Buddy Holly Centre which depicts every influence on his music including the black side. We also have the Holley's home which is very telling. They were humble Christian people, not affluent at all and it is furnished in typical 40s/50s style in keeping with their financial status."

Jimmie Dale Gilmore (27): "Buddy Holly's parents were wonderful people, very much a one-generation-off-the-farm type of people. Lubbock wasn't a small town, it was a city with 150,000 people, but most of the population were people just newly off the farm and were salt of the earth people."

Surprisingly, there is a home recording of Buddy in 1949 singing a country favourite, written and recorded by Hank Snow, "My Two Timin' Woman", and later cut by Johnny Cash for Sun. By then, Buddy was living in his eighth address and it was probably recorded at his home of 3315 36th Street. It is not known how the recording came to be made or whose equipment was being used. The performance is no disgrace: Buddy's voice hasn't broken but he is already proficient on his guitar.

The first verse is badly recorded but there is some skill in the way Buddy sings and then speaks the line "She blossoms in the spring, then she's gone in the fall." However, the recording quality improves during the first instrumental break as someone has repositioned the microphone. The lyrics are typical of country music of the time and would be seen as politically incorrect today: "If I ever find her, gonna chain her to the floor, Then tell her, 'Now sit here, woman, you ain't leaving no more.'"

And all this is being sung by a 13 year old boy! Still, Sonny Curtis made his performance début when he was 10 singing about getting drunk on "Good Ol' Mountain Dew" and making love in Frank Sinatra's "Five Minutes More".

In June 1949, Buddy and Barbara Denning appeared as the King and Queen of the Sixth Grade at Roosevelt Elementary School, and assuming that they chose the best photograph, Buddy wasn't thrilled about it. One of Buddy's first assignments at his next school, J.T. Hutchinson Junior High School, was to write about himself. He told of his dog, Lonzo and a grouchy rabbit: there are photos of Buddy and Pat with Lonzo from 1945. He wrote, "My father is in construction work. My mother keeps house if you want to call that work. My sister and one of my brothers are married." It was at this school that he met his first musical partner, Bob Montgomery.

In September 1950, Travis bought a .22 calibre rifle in a barroom for $20. When he arrived home, his mother asked him if he had bought a present for Buddy's birthday. He thought for a moment and then said, "Yes". It was hard to get Buddy up early for anything but rabbit hunting.

In November 1951, Buddy and his classmates were entertained by a mixture of comedy and music from Erman Gray, a musician from New Mexico noted for his marimba playing. Buddy was involved with the school newspaper but although he was bright enough, he lacked the discipline to be an outstanding student.

In 1951, Larry Holley founded his own company, Lubbock Ceramic Tile, which became a family business with Travis and, on occasion, Buddy himself and his friend, Bob Montgomery.

In 1952, Travis was laying a floor at West Texas State College and he had a young helper, another Buddy, Buddy Knox.

Lawrence Holley was still working for Pup Thomas, this time as a carpenter. In 1952, he could afford to move to a bigger property at 4211 41st Street. Rather than renting, he bought it with a 90% mortgage. Buddy went on the family holiday to Colorado in August 1952.

The whole family attended the Tabernacle Baptist Church, which at the time was at the corner of 15th Street and Avenue N. Its first pastor was Ben Johnson in 1933 and he remained there until 1961. Lawrence Holley was a deacon, teaching in the Sunday School and taking the Young Married People's Class.

In September 1952, Buddy enrolled at the Lubbock High School on 19th Street. His voice had broken and he sang first tenor in the acappella choir, although his voice was to change again. When asked to write about common errors in speech, he cited starting sentences with "Well", soon, however, to be essential for rock'n'roll singers. Buddy's six-syllable "Well" the start of "Early In The Morning" is his finest and other great introductions can be heard on Gene Vincent's "Be-Bop-A-Lula" and Lulu's "Shout".

The Beach Boys' song, "Be True To Your School" (1963), seems alien to us in the UK, but its sentiments rang true for young Americans. Lubbock High School Westerners played and beat the San Angelo Bobcats at the Jones Stadium in Lubbock, and, get this, 13,000 attended. Buddy went again in December 1952 and the Westerners completed a run of 25 straight wins. Buddy was not heavy enough to be good at sports and anyway, he preferred reading adventure stories and later, science fiction. He had few bad habits, although he did smoke a little and his mother tried to wean him off cigarettes with toothpicks soaked in cinnamon.

The petite Echo Elaine McGuire had been born in Lubbock on 29 January 1937 and her father owned a dry cleaners. She met Buddy in school when she was eight. While she was growing up, she often dated Buddy on the Friday and Bob Montgomery on the Saturday. Buddy took her hiking, skating and to football matches. She had a black horse and sometimes she would borrow another for Buddy so that they could ride together. Echo was a member of the Church of Christ, a sect that thought little of entertainers. When she and Buddy were at the Tabernacle Baptist Church, the preacher once said, "What would you do if you had $10?" and Buddy muttered, "If I had $10, I wouldn't be here." (We will be making comparisons between Buddy Holly and Bob Dylan later, but there's another Echo in their girlfriends as Dylan dated Echo Helstrom.)

Buddy was driving from a young age, being allowed to use the family car when he was 16. At various times, he had both a bicycle and a motor scooter. He had played various instruments in his youth but he took a leap forward with a gold-top Gibson acoustic guitar, made in 1945, which he purchased for $35 on 10 October 1953, although he always felt it was heavy. He was skilled in leatherwork and he made a case for the guitar. The instrument with its casing was subsequently bought by the actor Gary Busey for $200,000.

Many of Buddy Holly's most dedicated fans are blinkered and will hear nothing bad about their idol. Some of the Holly biographies have included distasteful stories about him, which are dismissed by his fans as being out of character. However, there are rather too many of them for this argument to hold good every time. A key issue is: was Buddy Holly a racist? By the time he was adult and had settled in New York, I am sure that the answer is "No". Okay, there are incidents such as a bust-up with the singer LaVern Baker, but she was argumentative and always looking for trouble.

Before then, I'm not so sure. Everyday life in Texas was full of endemic, institutional racism. Lubbock was no exception and the black community was effectively ghettoised. The population of Lubbock was 10% black, but Buddy could have gone many a day without meeting any of them. He went to white schools and the equivalent high school for Negroes was Dunbar on 23rd Street. It was a poor area, but the black singer, Virgil Johnson, describes how his family moved from Cameron to Lubbock for a better life. Apparently, they picked cotton in East Texas but they pulled it in West Texas, which meant that they gathered the entire boll: this involved some danger and you could be scarred as you gathered the crop.

Until the mid-1950s, it appeared that both the black and white population in Lubbock accepted this situation, that there would, for example, be separate toilets and drinking fountains in the shopping areas and that some clubs would be "whites only". Buddy's parents, who were extremely good natured, nevertheless accepted the *status quo*, and Buddy would have done the same as he would have been a very enlightened and unusual adolescent to think any differently. Buddy wouldn't have met many people who thought more liberally about the issues until he reached New York in 1957.

In June 1953, the 16-year-old Buddy wrote an essay about his life. It contained this telling passage: "I am behind with my biology work and will probably fail every course I'm taking. At least, that's the way I feel. But why quit there? I may as well go ahead and tell all. My father's out of town on a fishing trip, and he is really going to be proud of my latest accomplishments when he gets back. When I was driving our pick-up on Sunday afternoon against a hard wind, the hood came unfastened and blew up and now it's bent so that it won't fasten down good. Before I got home, I stopped at a boy's house and he knocked a baseball into the front glass, shattering it all over me. As if that wasn't enough, I had an appointment to apply for a job with a drafting firm yesterday afternoon and my mother let me drive on towards town. I had brought a picture of the choir and she was looking at it. She asked where I was and I pointed to my picture. Just as I looked back up, we hit the back of a Chrysler and tore the front end of our car up. So you see, I hope my father gets to catching so many fish that he will forget to come back for a little while."

After listing his hobbies as hunting, fishing, leatherwork, reading, painting and playing western music, Buddy wrote, "I have thought about making a career out of western music but I will just have to wait to see how that turns out." Indeed.

3

LEARNING THE GAME

"Buddy Holly was doing his best to be an Elvis Presley imitator but it became his own thing."
(Bob Montgomery)

If you went on the British streets and asked passers-by what they thought of country music, most would pull faces and say it held no interest for them. Its image of dead dogs, sickly narrations, false sentiments and steel guitars is somewhat unfortunate as it was crucial to the development of rock'n'roll as well as being socially significant in its own right. What's more, the best country artists—Hank Williams, Patsy Cline, Johnny Cash—were wonderful.

Kinky Friedman (28): "I was in a country band with a social conscience and looking back, I can see that it was a ridiculous notion. Country music is not an area for intellectuals in general, although Roger Miller and Hank Williams were bright lights. There are two types of people in America: people who read books and don't know anything about country music, and people who don't read books and listen to country music."

In 1986, the ultimate outlaw country artist, David Allan Coe released the single, "A Country Boy (Who Rolled The Rock Away)". It described how going from country music to rock was a good career move. The three verses were about Hank Williams (whose "Move It On Over" could be described as the first rock'n'roll record), Elvis

Presley (who brought a beat, a pelvic thrust and male magnetism to country music) and Buddy Holly (who started in country music but found his expression elsewhere). The musicians all came from poor backgrounds, and so did their own heroes. There are no doctors or lawyers in Buddy's family tree: it is a background of farmers and labourers and it is Buddy, not John Lennon, who was the working class hero.

Buddy Holly took a whole raft of people with him in his expedition into rock'n'roll. Rather like the Beatles in Liverpool, he was surrounded by talented musicians and their journey is as enthralling as Buddy's and yet relatively unknown. Buddy didn't do it on his own.

Buddy's first radio appearances were with Jack Neal. Jack Neal is usually presented as an older man who became a mentor to Buddy but he only had a couple of years on him. He was an electrician who worked with Lawrence Holley, and Lawrence told him of his son's interest in music. Jack was a competent country singer, guitarist and pianist and soon they were playing together, mostly Jack on guitar and Buddy on mandolin. As if to accentuate the difference in their ages, Jack would call Buddy "boy". They also went fishing, hunting and riding together and Jack tells how Buddy once shot a coyote.

Bob Montgomery was born on 12 May 1937 in Lampasas, Texas, nearly 300 miles south-east of Lubbock. His father was a construction worker and the family moved to Lubbock in 1949. He met Buddy Holly in the J.T. Hutchinson Junior High School when he was 12 and Buddy was 13. By 1951, they had started performing together, generally with Bob taking the lead vocals and playing guitar and Buddy the harmony vocals and tenor banjo, mandolin and sometimes second guitar. Overall, they sounded like an adolescent Flatt and Scruggs or, even better, the new kids on the chart block, Johnnie and Jack. Indeed they performed Johnnie and Jack's 1951 hit, "Poison Love".

Three home recordings from 1952/3 have survived—Flatt and Scruggs' "I'll Just Pretend" (virtually a rewrite of Hank Williams' "There'll Be No Teardrops Tonight", with Buddy's mandolin to the fore), Pee Wee King's "Take These Shackles From My Heart" and Bill Monroe's "Footprints In The Snow". "Footprints In The Snow" is short, quick and intense and shows that they meant business

At a school assembly, Buddy and Bob sang the Ernest Tubb and Red Foley duet, "Too Old To Cut The Mustard", and dedicated it to one of the teachers: similar to what John Lennon did when he rewrote "Puttin' On The Style" about his headmaster, Mr. Pobjoy.

Bob Montgomery (29): "We met at Junior High. We had a common interest in music and we were both learning to play guitars and whatever. Buddy had a musical family; his two brothers, Larry and Travis, both played, and so it was a natural transition for him. When we started out, we were doing the Lester Flatt and Earl Scruggs songs, and Buddy played banjo and mandolin for a while. There were lots of duet harmony records that we liked, all bluegrass stuff. We started playing in school talent shows and we eventually had our own little radio show on KDAV through Pappy Dave Stone. Pappy featured local talent every Sunday afternoon, and Buddy and I ended up with our own radio show every week." And did you get paid? "(Laughs) Are you kidding?"

David Pinkston, who was born in 1913, came to Lubbock in 1931 and attended Texas Tech. He settled in Lubbock in 1946 and worked as a DJ on KSEL for some years. He became known as "Pappy" Dave Stone, "the man with the smile in his voice", and, on 19 September 1953, he started his own, country music station, KDAV, although the licence only covered daytime programming. He also acquired KPEP in San Angelo, KZIP in Amarillo and KPIK in Colorado.

Jerry Naylor (30): "KDAV in Lubbock and KPEP in San Angelo, which were both owned by Dave Stone, were the first full-time country music radio stations in America, and have been honored by the Country Music Association. The stations only played country music, but that did include rockabilly, so they played Elvis Presley, Carl Perkins, Roy Orbison and Buddy Holly. Each of the stations also featured live performances from local bands, and these included Buddy and Bob as well as my own group in San Angelo, the Cavaliers. We were on air in 1956 and 1957 and we also did commercials for the station. I was 14 and a disc jockey on KPEP from the time it began broadcasting in 1953. Joe Treadway, who was one of Dave Pinkston's partners, was my mentor, and he and his wife, Matilda, became my foster parents in late 1955, after the death of my mother. KDAV and KPEP also promoted live concert performances from the country stars of the era and other great acts from West Texas and New Mexico. Buddy Holly, Buddy Knox, Roy Orbison, Waylon Jennings and myself got the opportunity to perform on these shows."

KDAV's other key presenter was William Joseph Duncan who had been born in Haskell County, Texas in 1914. He had seen action in the Second World War and been injured. When he saw a radio station being built in Amarillo, he asked if he could help. Henry Clay's Food Store wanted a country show so he devised *Hi Pockets Hank's Hillbilly Hop*. From then on, he was known as Hi Pockets Duncan and he worked on one radio station after another. When Dave Pinkston secured him for KDAV, they determined to feature live music from local musicians where quality permitted. Both of them were involved in cross-promotions with the Cotton Club in Lubbock. When Nashville-based country stars appeared there,

Buddy, perhaps with Bob Montgomery, perhaps with Jack Neal, might be an opening act.

From September 1953, Hi Pockets established the 15 minute segment, *The Buddy And Jack Show*, which was part of his afternoon entertainment, *Sunday Party*. Buddy and Jack responded to requests and dedications—Jack still has the fan letters including one from another Lubbock musician, Tommy Hancock—and the repertoire was country and gospel. There was "Your Cheatin' Heart" (Hank Williams), "I Couldn't Keep From Crying" (Marty Robbins), "Midnight" (Red Foley), "Somebody's Stolen My Honey" (Ernest Tubb), "Crying In The Chapel" (Darrell Glenn) and "I Forgot More Than You'll Ever Know" (Davis Sisters). Buddy's childhood favourite, "My Two Timin' Woman", was still around.

Sometimes they featured Don Guess on bass or on that most complicated of instruments, the steel guitar—well, have you ever seen a steel guitarist look up? He had been born on 14 May 1937 in Aspermont, Texas, 100 miles south-east of Lubbock. The family have moved to Clovis in 1943 and Lubbock in 1951. The family would soon be on the move again, this time to El Paso, but until then Don played steel guitar for Buddy and Jack. Their instrumentals included "Rhumba Boogie" (Hank Snow) and the standards, "Under The Double Eagle" and "Sugar Foot Rag". They appeared on a local TV talent show on Channel 13, which was sponsored by a dairy and hosted by Jack Hubble, whom we'll meet later. Although no entire programmes have survived, Jack Neal kept an acetate of himself singing and Buddy playing guitar on "I Hear The Lord Callin' For Me" and "I Saw The Moon Cry Last Night", both recorded at KDAV on 10 November 1953. Don Guess had suggested the titles to Neal, who then wrote the songs. They are decently recorded and "I Hear The Lord Callin' For Me" shows how church-minded even the youngsters were back then.

Don McCalister (31): "There's quite a beat in bluegrass bands—a driving off beat, a mandolin beat—very much a delta blues thing. We did some novelty bluegrass in the Flaky Biscuit Boys and we had a song called 'Zen Gospel' about a feller who was a Baptist and turned into a Zen Buddhist and the one thing he missed was the singing as you don't get that in the Zen temples."

Early in 1954, the Holley family (just Lawrence, Ella and Buddy as the others had married and left) moved to 2304 1st Street. Always bursting with enterprise, Buddy sent a circular to high schools in the vicinity. He wrote it on behalf of himself and Jack as well as the 580 Ranch Hands, who also had a Sunday show on KDAV, the "580" being a reference to the tuning. They were offering their services for stage shows, which could be advertised on the radio. The shows would be for school funds, but, according to the letter, their own fee would help pay their way through high school. Jack, however, had got married (everybody marries young in our story) and as he was working six days a week and playing some nights, he wanted to spend Sundays with his wife. This brought an end to *The Buddy And Jack Show*, though he still played on stage with Buddy from time to time.

So, *The Buddy And Jack Show* became *The Buddy And Bob Show* as Buddy returned to playing with Bob Montgomery, and they would open their shows with Buddy's instrumental, "Holly Hop", then presumably "Holley Hop". The fact that Buddy's name was coming first doesn't imply supremacy: it sounded better that way and they wanted a name like the hit duo of the day, Johnnie and Jack.

Buddy and Bob asked Larry Welborn to play double-bass. Larry, who was only 15, had been born on 13 April 1939 in Pleasant Hill, Oklahoma—the place names, if not the street names, are often colourful. He had met Buddy in Tommy Hancock's Danceland club on the east side of Lubbock. The best-known photo of the three of them has Larry in the centre, staring at the camera like a young Dustin Hoffman. Their visiting card showed that they played "western and bop".

Also, Buddy and Bob befriended another musician, Sonny Curtis. He had been born on 9 May 1937 and raised in Meadow, 30 miles south-west of Lubbock. His older brothers, Pete and Dean, had played on local radio and appreciated that Sonny was truly musical. In 1952, Sonny won a talent contest and had a regular spot on Bernie Howe's TV show, which led to several gigs. He sang Slim Whitman's "Northwind" and Tommy Collins' novelties. He was writing songs in school exercise books: he recorded the first song he wrote,

"Moon, Moon, Silvery Moon", in the 80s. There is a recording of Sonny in Fort Worth performing at a convention in 1953 when he was the president of the local branch of the Future Farmers of America. When the country star, Webb Pierce, cut his song, "Someday", in 1953, not only did he want to publish the song, he also wanted a composing credit. "I didn't mind," said Sonny, "I wanted to see my name on a record label." The song is owned by Donkey Music, but that doesn't mean Sonny was a bit of an ass as this malfeasance was established practice.

Sonny was influenced by his uncles, the Mayfield Brothers—big stout guys, Ed, Smokey, Herb and Jim. Ed rode in rodeos and he was a good enough guitar player to tour as part of Bill Monroe's Bluegrass Boys. At one stage, Pete, Dean and Sonny had a similar bluegrass group, and Dean (as Dean Court) did write a song for Terry Noland.

When Sonny visited a friend who had moved to Lubbock, they went to the Gin Café which was run by Bob Montgomery's parents for the cotton workers. Bob returned from school and although there was a sandstorm, they went straight over to Buddy's house and started playing. Sonny did, however, think Buddy a little strange as he had dyed his hair blond and, as it was now growing out, it was two-coloured.

It is hard to imagine the poverty, and although these words from Sonny sound like a West Texas equivalent of *Four Yorkshiremen* or indeed Saddam Hussein's last days of freedom, they're the real thing. **Sonny Curtis (32)**: "I was born at the end of the Depression in a dugout in Texas, which is just a hole in the ground with a roof on it, and I was the fifth child and we all lived in that hole, about eight miles east of Meadow, Texas. We moved from that to a one-room shack which my dad built. My folks didn't have a name picked out for me. They just told the doctor that they would stop in at the court house and name me, and they never did. I was in New York City when I was 20 years old and I had to sign a contract. I needed my birth certificate and I sent to Austin for it. When it came back, it said, 'Unnamed baby Curtis'. I was told that I had to name myself and so I called myself 'Sonny' at a cost of $2.50."

Eventually, the family went from a tent to a shack and then his father had a farm and the family would work on it. **Sonny Curtis (33)**: "I never moved to Lubbock, but Lubbock was about 30 miles from Meadow and I moved to Slaton, my folks didn't move, which is about 10 miles from Lubbock and I finished schooling there. I hung out a lot with Buddy and Bob and their friends."

On Friday 19 February 1954, Buddy, Bob and Larry performed at a talent contest at Lubbock High School, and Bob had written "Flower Of My Heart", his first full composition, for the event. They won the contest and received a Westerner belt for their efforts. "Flower Of My Heart" was chosen as the official song for the Class Of 1954. **Bob Montgomery (34)**: "It was just a song that I wrote. I don't remember what the inspiration was. They had an original song contest at Lubbock High and it won the best song of the year, and that was when we were sophomores."

Sonny Curtis (35): "Buddy did not play in Chet Atkins style—he was more bluegrass—and when I first met him he was playing guitar and banjo."

And what was the Chet Atkins style? **Sonny Curtis (36)**: "The Chet Atkins style is where you employ the thumb to play the rhythm and then you play the melody with your fingers. You have both a rhythm and a melody going at the same time, so you can sound like two guitarists when you do it right. Buddy Holly liked Chet Atkins but he played more of a bluegrass style. He never played Chet's style."

In April 1954, 26 students represented Lubbock High School at a state meeting in Austin for the Vocational Industrial Club (VIC) of America. Bob Montgomery won the category for "Radio and TV Servicing", a category which implied that nobody had much ambition. Buddy sent a postcard home saying that he was enjoying swimming.

In May 1954, Buddy drew up a contract for the Rhythm Playboys (Buddy, Bob, Jack and David Bowen) to play a high school benefit in Brownfield, Texas for half of the net receipts.

When Buddy enrolled for final year at school in September 1954, he was elected vice present of the local VIC, while Bob captained the basketball team. One of the events that Buddy organised was a pillow-stuffing competition and as 68 people attended, you can appreciate that life was not very exciting in Lubbock.

Graham Morrison Turnbull was born in Nova Scotia and nicknamed Scotty. He represented Canada in the long jump at the British Empire Games in 1954, covering an impressive 26 feet 9 inches. He was awarded a scholarship post-grad at Texas Tech and he taught there as well with a young Mac Davis amongst the students. He met Hal Goodson from Muleshoe, Texas, a singer who could sound like Slim Whitman, and they had a group, Hal Goodson and the Raiders. They appear on the *Louisiana Hayride* and cut some singles. Scotty met Buddy Holly and he would allow Buddy to visit his apartment and play his Fender Stratocaster, even if he wasn't there.

Scotty and Buddy wrote several songs together. The titles were "Am I Ever Gonna Find It", "Not Too Late To Run", "Our House On The Hill" and "Lonely Little Lover Lost". When Scotty or that matter, Buddy, recorded in Clovis, none of the songs were used. The band moved to LA, managers ripped them off and Hal's wife, back in Lubbock, wanted a divorce. The Raiders remained in LA and became a backing group for Tommy Sands. Scotty met Buddy again when he was on *The Perry Como Show* with Sands. They started writing "The Memory Of You" for Sands, but didn't complete it.

In 1962, one of Buddy's songs with Scott Turner, "My Baby's Comin' Home", was recorded by Nilsson in 1962: it sounds like a Bobby Vee song. Another Holly song, a ballad, "I Know I'll Have The Blues Again", was recorded by Whitesidewalls, while Sonny Curtis put music to a Buddy Holly lyric, "Monetta", shortly before going on stage for a concert at BBC Radio Merseyside in 1990.

Although Lubbock was in the middle of nowhere, it was conveniently in the middle of nowhere. Touring shows, *en route* from Phoenix to Dallas, would find Lubbock a convenient stop. These would be white pop and country acts as there was not a sufficiently large black population to make it worthwhile for blues musicians. Many of the great country and bluegrass names spent their lives endlessly touring the Southern States, practically living on their tour buses, although sometimes the stars travelled separately in Cadil-

lacs. Bob Wills and his Texas Playboys were regulars in Lubbock. Buddy and Bob went to the shows and they were just as impressed by what was in the parking lot.

Bob Montgomery (37): "We thought that if you got a record contract, you were automatically rich. We had seen the country artists come through in their Cadillacs with Tennessee licence plates and we thought that all you had to do was get on record and you had it made."

I asked **Bob Montgomery (38)** if Buddy and Bob ever got to a gig and thought it was a terrible venue. "All the time. (Laughs) We played a lot of honky tonks, but it really didn't matter to us. Wherever we could find a place to play, we played. It got better after I got out of the picture as they played some roller rinks."

Peggy Sue Gerron (39): "There was a roller rink north of Lubbock where they played and they wanted to be a band and to record—it was Buddy's whole reason for existence. Elvis came around about then and made everyone aware of rock'n'roll."

In August 1954, Elvis Presley had started recording for Sun Records in Memphis. His first single, "That's All Right (Mama)"/ "Blue Moon Of Kentucky", is viewed as the most electrifying début of all time, but although it wasn't a big seller, it gave him a regional following with a younger audience than most of the country performers. Buddy was impressed and even more so, when he saw Elvis in a country package starring Billy Walker and Johnnie and Jack at the Cotton Club in Lubbock on 6 January 1955. The previous day, New Year's Day, Sonny had met Johnnie and Jack and had played on stage with them.

Sonny Curtis (40): "Elvis was wild, man. He was something else. I couldn't believe my eyes, there was so much magnetism there. We all freaked and fell immediately in love with Elvis. There were cotton bales around the stage and policemen were standing by them and it was just madness. The girls were trying to get to Elvis."

Jerry Naylor (41): "In 1955, I did a show with Elvis Presley somewhere in West Texas, it may have been Odessa, and there was Elvis, Johnny Horton and Carl Belew on the same show. Elvis had his first pink Cadillac, and the hairy-legged

West Texas boys were jealous of him. They put sugar in his gas tank and ruined it."

Buddy Knox (42): "I saw Elvis Presley in Amarillo, Texas on the Johnny Cash show and he was the most charismatic man I had ever seen. I didn't even stay for Johnny Cash and I love Johnny Cash. He was the best-looking guy I'd ever seen in my life and I went backstage with Jerry Allison. Elvis said, 'If you've got a band and some good songs, get yourself into a recording studio 'cause something's gonna happen.' That was a good piece of advice and I went to Clovis, New Mexico and got involved with Norman and Vi Petty. We cut 'Party Doll' and 'I'm Stickin' With You' there and sent them off to New York and to my surprise, I got a contract in New York."

Early in 1955, Buddy Holly and Bob Montgomery recorded some demos at the Nesman Recording Studios in Wichita Falls. They had Sonny Curtis playing fiddle, Larry Welborn on bass, and Don Guess on steel guitar. Mostly, they recorded Bob Montgomery's songs—"Gotta Get You Near Me Blues" (with Sonny dominant on fiddle) and four "heart" songs, "Flower Of My Heart" (written with Don Guess), "Door To My Heart", "I Gambled My Heart" (written with Buddy) and "Soft Place In My Heart".

Bob Montgomery (43): "We did some demos later on in Clovis, New Mexico, but first we used a little recording studio in Wichita Falls. We would do some construction work or whatever to earn some money and then we would use that money to go and record some demos."

All this driving did have its complications. Buddy collected several tickets for traffic violations, and a warrant for his arrest was issued when he failed to attend a summons in December 1954. Presumably, he paid the fine of $13 by return post.

On 4 February 1955, Buddy and Bob signed a publishing contract with Ridgeway Music and the publisher O.B. Woodward for the song, "I Just Don't Care". No advance was given and no one knows what happened to the song. In April 1955, two more songs were filed with Ridgeway Music in Nashville, "Flower Of My Heart" and "You And I Are Through", both written by Bob.

Elvis returned to top the bill at the Fair Park Coliseum on 13 February 1955 and because Dave

Stone was promoting the concert, he was able to add Buddy and Bob to the bill. Elvis played at the Cotton Club later in the evening. Apparently, Stone was able to secure Elvis for around $50: a year later Elvis would be taking the bank home with him. Elvis didn't tithe his salary: Colonel Parker took 50% and that was enough.

Jerry Naylor (44): "I met Buddy two or three times around 54/55 .We had a band called the Cavaliers at the same time he was working as Buddy and Bob and we were all doing country. Elvis did his first tour through Texas and was in Lubbock in January 55. We all saw him and the next day Buddy said that's what he wanted to do from then on."

As part of the VIC, schoolboys gathered work experience before they graduated. Buddy worked at the Glen Decorating Company in 1954 and at the Davidson Printing Works in 1955. He was a good worker but he was frequently late and was sacked from the printing works. His mother successfully had him reinstated as, otherwise, he might not have graduated.

In April 1955, Buddy's headmaster wrote to his parents to say that he was falling behind in geometry and recommended extra classes. Buddy's reaction: he traded his acoustic Les Paul guitar for a Fender Stratocaster, and life would never be the same again.

For this expensive purchase, Buddy had asked Larry to lend him $1,000 for a guitar, amplifier and stage clothes. Buddy said that he needed the best to develop, and Larry, something of a visionary, could appreciate his talent. Within two years, he was able to pay Larry back and the Strat is the instrument most associated with rock'n'roll and with Buddy Holly, in particular. Buddy bought it at Adair Music in Lubbock, where Sonny Curtis gave guitar lessons to budding Buddys. Buddy himself wasn't interested in lessons: he would figure it out himself. Joe B. Mauldin said it was the first instrument he had seen with a gear shift. Buddy used Black Diamond Strings, the subject of a song by another Texas musician, Guy Clark: "His fingers are bleedin' but he's keepin' good time, Playing Black Diamond Strings, he'll never quit tryin'."

Since 1892, graduating students from the white high schools had met as one and in 1955, there were 2,900 graduating (including Buddy Holly, scraping through with geometry, and Echo McGuire, an honours student). Echo's parents organised a graduation party for them, but it was ruined by a thunderstorm. Buddy often drove his family's Oldsmobile and he would tell friends that it was his graduation present: actually, his parents gave him a watch, but an alarm clock would have been more appropriate.

Echo McGuire went to two Christian colleges, one in Abilene and one in York, Nebraska, after graduation. She married a fellow student, Ron Griffith, on Valentine's Day, 1958. They made light of Echo's friendship with Buddy Holly, and Ron calls himself "the guy who beat Buddy Holly".

From time to time, Buddy and Bob and their associates played at the opening of a new store in Lubbock: Henry's Superette for example, for which they were paid $15. He opened the Furr Food Store and, clearly hitting the big time, Morris Fruit and Veg. The stores would advertise on air and KDAV would cover the opening.

Jerry Ivan Allison was born on a farm in Hill County, Texas on 31 August 1939, and his family settled in Lubbock in 1950. His father worked on the roads and his mother was a schoolteacher. She played the piano and although Jerry had lessons, he preferred the drums. He took lessons on drums and he played in the high school marching bands.

Jerry Allison (45): "I went to an American football game and I saw a guy going boom-boom with the bass drum and I thought it looked like fun. That was silly because the last thing you want to do in a band is carry the drums. I joined Buddy and we used to play for dances. We'd play for 45 minutes, take a 15 minute break and then play some more. We repeated a few tunes but we knew a lot of songs. We did Little Richard songs and instrumentals like 'Honky Tonk'. We once played for five hours at a dance and we started writing songs so that we would have more songs to play."

The first record that Jerry bought was Fats Domino's "Goin' To The River" (1953), which featured some very prominent drumming. Jerry went to Lubbock High School and he was stacking shelves in a grocery store when Cal Wayne asked him if he wanted to play in the Riverside Ranch Hands. This was a straight country band, performing the hits of Hank Williams and Hank Thompson.

Jerry Allison (46): "The first time I met Buddy was at the Cotton Club. Buddy, Bob and Sonny had gone to the Fair Park Coliseum to see Elvis and the acts would get an extra $25 to come out to Cotton Club to do a few numbers after the show, money in their hands. I was playing with Cal Wayne and the Riverside Ranch Hands while Elvis's show was going on. When they came in, Jim Ed Brown performed first and I thought it was Elvis as I didn't know what he looked like. He was okay, but then Elvis came out with 'Good Rockin' Tonight' and I went from the back of the Cotton Club to the front as I couldn't believe what I was hearing and seeing. We were talking afterwards and I said to him, 'How come you don't have a drummer?' He said, 'If we had a drummer, it'd come out like Bill Haley.' Next time Elvis came to Lubbock, he had D.J. Fontana with him, and of course he didn't sound like Bill Haley."

On 3 June 1955, Elvis Presley opened a Pontiac showroom in Lubbock for a $75 fee. Buddy and Bob were watching. They all played the Fair Park Coliseum, which drew an audience of 6,000. The bill included Ferlin Husky, whose "Gone" had topped the US country charts for 10 weeks and was also a pop hit. Because of this, it was Ferlin and not Elvis who had to escape from his fans through a window.

Sonny Curtis (47): "It was Buddy Holly and Bob Montgomery's group and I played fiddle. Larry Welborn played bass and Don Guess played steel guitar from time to time. We played country music, but when Elvis came along, Buddy fell in love with Elvis' style and we began to change. We had heard Elvis on those lovely Sun records, and he came to Lubbock when we were still in school, and we played on that show. The next day we became Elvis clones. I had a D-28 Martin and Buddy had a Fender Stratocaster. Buddy took my Martin and I took his Strat and he was like Elvis and I was like Scotty Moore. Don Guess played percussive bass like Bill Black, which filled in for the drums. Scotty Moore's style was like Chet Atkins but modified somewhat. I had Chet's style down as good as anybody in that area and so I could play Scotty's licks as soon as he left town."

The acoustic bass (or upright bass, double bass, string bass, bull fiddle) had been used for centuries but had originally been played as a bowed instrument. It was not a loud instrument and Duke Ellington had two bass players in his 1930s band so that it could be heard. A symphony orchestra might have half a dozen bass players. So it wasn't much use in noisy clubs. The instrument played a major role in rockabilly and the slapping of Bill Black's bass was a noted component of Elvis Presley's Sun records, and gave them a percussive sound as Presley at the time didn't have a drummer. It can be heard on "Move It On Over" (Hank Williams) and "Rock Around The Clock" (Bill Haley). Carl Perkins' brother, Clayton, made his own two-string bass. This is said of Carl Perkins in his authorised biography, *Go, Cat, Go!*: "He didn't want Clayton to play individual notes like he heard the bass players doing on the *Opry*, but to click the strings in time, to give him a sound like the one he heard when he tapped his foot on the rickety front porch of their shack when he practised the guitar alone."

In June 1955, Sonny Curtis booked his own session at the Nesman Recording Studio in Wichita Falls. He sang six songs and was backed up by Buddy Holly, Larry Welborn and Jerry Allison. There are four of his own songs—"Because You Love Me", "This Bottle", "Dallas Boogie", "One In A Million"—Don Guess' "Queen Of The Ballroom" and a mawkish country ballad, "I'll Miss My Heart". They are competent performances that could have secured a record contract. The quick section in "Because You Love Me" sounds like Sonny Curtis today.

Bob Montgomery (48): "That area of the world spawned a lot of talent because there wasn't a lot to do in Lubbock. Roy Orbison came from Odessa which is about 100 miles north-west of Lubbock and that's a pretty desolate area. There's definitely not a lot to do there. We didn't know Roy at the time but we heard people telling us how good he was. Later on, he did one of my songs, but I can't remember which." (Answer: "Two Of A Kind", which was also recorded by Sue Thompson.)

Soon Buddy Holly and Roy Orbison found their paths were crossing, and indeed, Roy's wife, Claudette, had gone to Lubbock High School.

Michael Gray (49): "Roy Orbison told me that they were rivals—he was the big rock'n'roll noise around Wink, and Holly was the same around Lubbock, and when they played in each other's territory they would meet but that Holly wasn't too friendly because of this professional rivalry they had as fellow Texans."

One of Buddy Holly's cousins had told him about a good station in Shreveport, *Stan's Record Rack*, which played rhythm and blues every night at 10.30pm. Although Shreveport was 1,000 miles from Lubbock, he and Sonny managed to pick it up but only on the car radio.

Sonny Curtis (50): "Buddy and I did try and write a little bit together but we never came up with anything. I used to go up and spend the night with him and we used to make it out to the car, turn on the radio and listen to *Stan's Record Rack* from Shreveport, Louisiana. That was a real good programme that played the black music of that period."

Pete Frame (51): "Lubbock makes Liverpool look like Paris, and so I don't think geography had a lot to do with Buddy's music—he just got bitten by the bug, as we all did. I can't imagine the local radio stations played R&B—he must have heard it on border radio or that station WLAC beaming out of Nashville. As Phil Walden once told me, 'On a clear night, that signal would go all the way to the moon.'"

In August 1955, some songs were recorded at KDAV with Buddy, Bob, Sonny and Don. They recorded two of Bob's own compositions, the sprightly "You And I Are Through" and "Memories" and one by Don Guess, "Queen Of The Ballroom". The fourth song, "Baby It's Love", has been given the strange credit of Bob Montgomery and Ella Holley, though it doesn't sound like a song you would write with your best friend's mother. As this track did not appear until after Buddy's death, it is possible that Norman Petty concocted this credit though what he was trying to achieve baffles me. To confuse matters even further, "Baby It's Love" was first recorded professionally by Johnny Angel in 1958 and the writer is credited as Jimmy Lee Fautherlee. It is possible that both these names refer to the same person.

I didn't get far when I quizzed **Bob Montgomery (52)** about this song but then it is 50 years ago, and it does sound like a thousand other country songs. "There are a lot more of my songs than Buddy's but that's just because I had more interest in writing than he did at the time. Quite frankly, I don't think the songs are that good, which is why I can't tell you much about them. We were just teenagers learning to write. Later on when I was in music publishing and trying to get songs cut, I never even thought of passing them over to other artists. The best things about the records are Buddy Holly's performances. I was doing the lead vocals but he was a great harmony singer. He had a lot of innate talent, much more than myself."

Harvey Andrews (53): "Buddy Holly was rooted in country music and every Holly fan has got that album of him and Bob Montgomery singing country songs. It's not very brilliant, in fact, it's hackneyed, but it shows where he was coming from, the white Southern roots in his music."

Kevin Montgomery (54): "I know my dad finds it painful to listen to those tracks, but they are young and they are pioneers in the rock'n'roll world. Sonny Curtis is a little out of tune on the fiddle and J.I. is out of rhythm, but it is coming together. They are learning to play together."

Sonny Curtis (55): "Elvis told us that the *Louisiana Hayride*, which came from Shreveport, was making him a star and he could get us on there. We went down there like he told us, but the Director of Programming said that Elvis didn't run the *Louisiana Hayride*, and he sent us back home. We were told that the show was hillbilly heaven and we couldn't just walk in and expect to be on the bill."

They had better luck with the *Big D Jamboree* from Dallas. The country musician, Sid King, was impressed when Buddy did a couple of songs with him at the Cotton Club. He told Buddy about the *Big D Jamboree* and promised to recommend him to the advertisers. Buddy turned up at Sid's house the next week and talked himself onto the programme. Next time Sid came to Lubbock he saw a sign, "Buddy Holly—Star of CBS Radio". Sid asked Don Law at Columbia Records to listen to Buddy's demos, but nothing happened there.

Sid King also told Buddy of a club in Wichita Falls: he wasn't going to fulfil an engagement as

he hadn't been paid for the last time. Buddy called the club and took the booking instead. Buddy didn't want to be conned, but he did want to play whenever and wherever he could.

In September 1955, to publicise the forthcoming South Plains Fair in Lubbock, several musicians including Buddy and Bob went on a bus trip to the neighbouring towns, and made several performances in a day.

On 14 October 1955, a fireball was seen in the Texas skies at 10 am. A little later in the day, another fireball was opening for Bill Haley and his Comets at the Fair Park Auditorium. It was Buddy with Bob and Larry and although they sang country music together, Buddy was incorporating a few rock'n'roll songs in the act.

The following day, Elvis was back for his fourth visit to Lubbock, again playing the Fair Park Auditorium on a marvellous package with Johnny Cash, Carl Perkins, Jimmy Newman and Wanda Jackson. Buddy knew Elvis by now and he drove him around Lubbock. They ended up at the Cotton Club. There is colour film of the day with Elvis looking like a Greek god and Johnny Cash wearing an elaborate white bow tie.

Jerry Allison (56): "No regular person looked or dressed like Elvis. It was beyond their reach and we looked like the boys next door. We realised that you didn't have to be different to make music. We were to have as many male fans as females."

Elvis was still working with Scotty Moore and Bill Black, but he had added a drummer he had met on the *Louisiana Hayride*, D.J. Fontana. The sound was like nothing that had been heard before in Lubbock. It was the start of rockabilly which was blues music blended with country by white performers.

Jerry Allison (57): "Buddy hadn't wanted drums because Elvis didn't have drums. Then one day Elvis came back to Lubbock with a drummer, and Buddy wanted a drummer then."

A full contingent involving two cars with Buddy, Bob, Larry, Sonny Curtis and Jerry Allison went to the Nesman studio in Wichita Falls, Texas. First they cut a demo of a rockabilly song, "Down The Line". This was not the Roy Orbison song, later recorded by Jerry Lee Lewis, but a new song by Buddy and Bob. It's a travelling song and the lyric suggests that there was plenty of speeding as drivers rushed from one town to another.

Bob Montgomery (58): "I was dating my first wife who lived in Albuquerque, New Mexico, and I wrote that on the way to Albuquerque—'The white lines flashing on the road below' and all that."

They made a good stab at Elvis Presley's recent single, "Baby Let's Play House", which was written by the blues musician, Arthur Gunter. Unlike many black musicians, Gunter did receive songwriting royalties—$6,500 in the first year—and on top of that, he won $50,000 in the Michigan State Lottery. Although they didn't record it, Buddy often sang Elvis Presley's "I Forgot To Remember To Forget" on stage.

The demo of "Down The Line" was probably intended for Elvis Presley. The collection of sheet music, *The Elvis Presley Album of Juke Box Favourites No.1,* included the song, which suggests that he had thought of recording it. Buddy also had a session at the Jim Beck Recording Studios in Dallas where he cut "Down The Line" again and "You And I Are Through", but these have yet to surface, if indeed they still exist.

Bob Montgomery (59): "Buddy had a unique sense of rhythm. He was doing his best to be an Elvis imitator but it became his own thing."

In September 1955, James Dean was killed in a foolhardy accident. His iconoclastic film, *Rebel Without A Cause,* opened in Lubbock in November. Buddy went to see it. His professional career was to start like Elvis Presley's but end like James Dean's. And how about this for an eerie Christmas gift: Echo gave a Buddy a book by the Fort Worth author, Wyatt Sawyer, *Must The Young Die Too?*

Buddy was full of hope and promise. This comment from **Snuff Garrett (60)** brings to mind Jacques Brel's barroom meetings in his descriptive song, "Les Bourgeois": "I knew Buddy Holly very well. We met in his home town of Lubbock when I was a disc jockey. Buddy was two years older than I was and we started hanging out together with another jock who was a kid of my age, Waylon Jennings. The three of us used to sit at night with a Tall Boy beer: they were a dollar each and we could afford two of them and we would make them last a long time. We would sit and talk about how we were going to make it in the music business. It turned out pretty good for all for us."

4

SHOCK OF THE NEW

"Son, you want to make a whole lot of money?
You should go into country music." (Roy Acuff)

On 28 October 1955, Buddy, Bob and Larry are opening at the Fair Park Auditorium in Lubbock for a *Grand Ole Opry* show with Marty Robbins, Porter Wagoner, Slim Whitman, Hank Locklin, Mitchell Torok and Autry Inman. After the show, Marty Robbins, who was riding high with his covers of "That's All Right (Mama)" and Chuck Berry's "Maybellene", jammed with Buddy at the Cotton Club.

Robbins' manager, Eddie Crandall, had now seen Buddy twice and was impressed, more by Buddy than by Buddy and Bob. He knew too that Presley's manager, Colonel Tom Parker, also liked Buddy, but wanted to concentrate on Presley alone. Early in December, Eddie Crandall wrote to Dave Stone at KDAV and said that, although he was busy, he would try and secure Buddy a record contract, but first he needed acetates of some original songs.

Losing no time, Buddy returned to the Nesman Recording Studios in Wichita Falls on 7 December 1955. This time Sonny Curtis was playing lead guitar, Don Guess bass and Jerry Allison drums. Some of the tracks ("Baby, Won't You Come Out Tonight", "I Guess I Was Just A Fool" and "Love Me"), sound as though they were recorded in the

house next door. It's partly because Buddy was hoping to achieve a reverb effect like Sun Records, but it's mainly because only copies of copies have made the market.

Two of the songs were written by Holly with Sue Parrish. She was raised in Lubbock but had married and moved to California. Her lyrics were lacking in originality, although "Don't Come Back Knockin'" does contain the memorable line, "Like a talent scout, you want some love that's new." The other song, the pleading "Love Me", is routine, but it suits the rockabilly feel very well.

"Don't Come Back Knockin'" is an excellent example of what Buddy Holly sounded like before any producer got to him. It is often said that Buddy was dissatisfied with what was done to his music in Nashville but this is identical to the performances recorded there. The track demonstrated his confidence—it starts with a classic "Well" and contains his instruction to the band, "Now, let's play it again, boys, let's go". If Buddy Holly had died at this point in his career, it would be regarded as a rockabilly classic. When they recorded this, they must have been confident that a recording contract was only a matter of time.

George Hamilton IV (61): "I have very warm memories of Buddy Holly. He was a gentleman but more important, he was a gentle man. I related to him because he was a quiet, thoughtful country boy and we hit it off well. Buddy Holly, Gene Vincent, Eddie Cochran and the Everly Brothers grew up on the same music as I did—Hank Williams, Ernest Tubb, Carl Smith, Little Jimmy Dickens—and we all listened to the *Opry*. We were different to Paul Anka, Frankie Avalon and Bobby Rydell, who were north-eastern boys and into Sinatra. We wanted to be *Opry* stars but we ended up on rock'n'roll shows, but country music was very popular then. Every time any of us left the dressing room or went out for a hot dog, we were in danger of losing our guitars. When we got back, Sam Cooke and Clyde McPhatter might be strumming them, playing a Hank Williams song and singing country. Chuck Berry liked country music too. I saw him listening to the Louvin Brothers on a portable recorder."

Phil Everly (62): "We were all country—Elvis Presley, Buddy Holly, Buddy Knox, Jimmy Bowen. We all enjoyed country music and we extended it just as Carl Smith had extended Jimmie Rodgers. It's hard for me to talk about our influences. We were kids and it's strange that people now analyse the historical aspects of what we did. If anything, we helped to popularise the sound of a guitar so that people no longer confused it with a banjo."

On 10 December 1955, Buddy went to the Fair Park Coliseum to see Fats Domino and Big Joe Turner, an indication that the younger element of Lubbock's largely white population wanted to see top R&B acts.

Paul McCartney (63): "The white rock'n'roll singers like Elvis Presley, Eddie Cochran, Jerry Lee Lewis and Buddy Holly were rooted in country. They got country and western—Grand Ole Opry and the like—from their own families and they merged it with black music, which was more naughty and frowned upon. Buddy Holly's dad had a tiling firm in Lubbock, Texas and Buddy and his brothers used to deliver the tiles. One day they stopped off at a little juke joint and a lot of black people were there. This little white kid with spectacles got up and at first his brother thought, 'Oh dear me', but they loved him 'cause he was really good."

Paul McCartney is not quite right as it was Larry's company but the story is true. Buddy did get up and perform Hank Ballard and the Midnighters' 1954 R&B hit, "Sexy Ways" with the band, a pants-down song, definitely not to be sung in polite company. (Hey, there are 200 churches in Lubbock.) He was well received, which stood him in good stead for the Apollo engagement later on.

In 1914, a firm of instrument manufacturers in the UK made a portable record player, which they called the Decca Dulcephone. They regarded it as the Mecca of perfection and with the "D" from their Dulcet trademark and the name of a holy city, they created the word "Decca". The player did well and they became the Decca Gramophone Co Ltd, being bought by a British stockbroker, Edward Lewis, in 1929. Within a few years, Decca Records was a front runner and when they bought the US label, Brunswick, they acquired Bing Crosby and Al Jolson. They gave contracts to Louis Armstrong, Billie Holiday, the Andrews Sisters and Judy Garland. They released the most successful single of all-time with Bing Crosby's "White Christmas": that is, until Elton John revisited "Candle In The Wind" for Princess Diana's funeral. Decca pioneered cast albums of 78rpm singles with Rodgers and Hammerstein musicals and, in 1954, they released "Rock Around The Clock" by Bill Haley and his Comets, which was made at the Pythian Temple Studio in New York.

From the late 1940s, Decca had a presence in Nashville, Tennessee and their executive, Paul Cohen, noted the talents of the studio owner and record producer, Owen Bradley. Bradley had been born in Tennessee in 1915 and he had worked as a pianist in Ted Weems' dance band. From 1940, he had been the musical director for WSM radio's live broadcasts in Nashville, which included the *Grand Ole Opry*. In 1947, he was hired by Cohen, to develop Decca's catalogue as Nashville was becoming the centre for country music. Owen and his guitarist brother, Harold (born in Nashville in 1926) recorded major country hits by Ernest Tubb and Kitty Wells. Unfortunately, their building had a demolition order, but Cohen told Bradley that he would guarantee a 100 sessions a year if he built a new studio with the best equipment.

Bradley chose an old army building on 16th Avenue South, and the greatest testimony to Bradley's success is that other studios and publishing companies developed around the site, which is now referred to as Music Row. Bradley had his studio in the basement but then he built a second studio in a Quonset hut next door. This was proved particularly effective for recording the echo-drenched rockabilly of the mid-50s.

Unlike New York where session musicians would be expected to read music and play the most complex pieces, the picture was very different in Nashville. Country music was simple and straightforward ("Three chords and the truth" to quote the songwriter, Harlan Howard) and so Bradley wanted musicians who would instinctively know what was wanted. He assembled a superb team including himself and Floyd Cramer on piano, his brother, Grady Martin and Hank Garland on guitars, Don Helms and Jimmy Day on steel, Bob Moore on bass, and Farris Coursey, Buddy Harman and Doug Kirkham on drums. Vocal backings came from the Anita Kerr Singers and the Jordanaires. To give its official title, the Bradley Film And Recording Studio was kept busy and although Bradley did not shoot any film of Buddy Holly, he made promotional films for another artist whose professional career was just beginning, Patsy Cline.

Paul Cohen thought that Buddy Holly had talent and signed him to Decca. Conveniently across the road from Bradley's studio was Cedarwood Music, owned by Jim Denny and Webb Pierce, and managed by Denny, who booked acts for the *Grand Ol' Opry*. He gave Buddy a songwriting contract and passed him a new song, "Midnight Shift", to record.

Jim Denny was described as "a short, fat bastard with artificial hair" on Gordon Terry's 1960 privately made parody of "Battle Of New Orleans", which questioned Cedarwood's business practices, and was no doubt sent to him anonymously. This track, which also features Johnny Cash, was eventually issued on the Gordon Terry compilation, *Lotta Lotta Women*. It is worth nothing the casual racism in the lyric, and there are many songs like this. Sometimes, Buddy Holly has been associated with a track, "Nigger Hatin' Me", but this had nothing to do with him. It was recorded

by Johnny Rebel, better known as Cliff Trahan. Trahan recorded several songs supporting the Ku Klux Klan, and as Kinky Friedman remarked, "Bigots have to be entertained too."

It took two days to drive from Lubbock to Nashville, a journey of some 900 miles. Jerry Allison and Larry Welborn couldn't make it as they were in school, and so Buddy went with Sonny Curtis, Don Guess and a Lubbock drummer, Charles Hill. They travelled in Mr Holley's Oldsmobile with Don's bass strapped onto the top.

On the journey to Nashville, Buddy realised that there might be a problem as none of them were in the Musicians' Union. The musicians arrived in Nashville on 26 January 1956 for a three hour session starting at 7pm. Bradley insisted that they must be members but they couldn't, for administrative reasons, join in Nashville. They spoke to the MU rep in Amarillo and all was well. Indeed, they immediately recouped their dues as each musician was entitled to the standard union fee for the evening's work. There was no need for Charles Hill to sign up as Bradley used his drummer, Doug Kirkham. He also determined that Buddy should not both sing and play, possibly because he couldn't get the separation he wanted, and he booked Grady Martin to play rhythm to Sonny's lead.

Sonny Curtis (64): "I couldn't wait to get out in front of Grady Martin, who played guitar for Red Foley and then played for Willie Nelson. He's a magnificent guitar player and I remember thinking, 'Boy, when I get out there, I'm gonna show him a thing or two.' How naive can you be—if I had to do that all over again, I'd be scared to death."

By now, Buddy was used to recording studios, albeit not ones used by major labels, so he wasn't intimidated and four songs were recorded in three hours. They started with the two songs written by Buddy and Sue Parrish, "Love Me" and "Don't Come Back Knockin'". "Love Me" is faster than the version at Wichita Falls and that lovable flexibility in Buddy's voice is developing. He lowers his voice for an Elvis like finale. Buddy opens "Don't Come Back Knockin'" with the "talent scout" verse coming first.

Hank Ballard and the Midnighters had an R&B hit with the innuendo-laden "Work With Me,

Annie", which led to the follow-up, "Annie Had A Baby". An Alabama singer/songwriter Luke McDaniel, who had recorded for King, wrote a third song, "Midnight Shift", in 1955 and made a demo for the music publisher under the name of Earl Lee. When he wrote it, he was travelling in a car with his friend, Jimmie Ainsworth, who was given a co-writing credit. The music publisher, Buddy Killen gave it to his friend, Jim Denny, who in turn passed it to Buddy Holly.

Sonny Curtis (65): "I remember the demo for 'Midnight Shift', which was just some good ol' boy with his guitar. We put some rock'n'roll into it, but sometime later, I kinda wanted to do it the old way and I remembered how it went." Sonny's slower-paced, country version is on his album, *No Stranger To The Rain* (1987).

Frankie Connor (66): "It's rather like the Beatles at Decca. The tapes have been given a bad press and almost written out of history, but they are actually pretty good. I love 'Midnight Shift', but when I first heard it as a child, I hadn't twigged that it was about a lady of the night."

Bob Dylan must have marvelled at Buddy Holly's vocal mannerisms on "Midnight Shift" as much of his style developed from it. Listen to the way Holly sings "car" and "far". As with Dylan, you sometimes think that Holly is making mistakes but in fact, what he is doing fits far better than what would be expected.

The fourth song was "Blue Days—Black Nights", written by Ben Hall, a Lubbock singer/songwriter. Ben had written "Blue Days—Black Nights", while he was married but living with his parents. It was snowing and he was looking out of the window, feeling sad and reflective. Buddy (guitar) and Sonny (fiddle) had backed Ben Hall on a session for Radio KSEL in Lubbock. They had put down two of Ben's songs, a mournful Hank Williams-styled ballad, "All From Loving You", and the up-tempo "Rose Of Monterey". Ben moved 100 miles to Big Spring, but when he returned to Lubbock for a visit, he was chatting on air on KDAV. Buddy heard him and got in touch: he was going to Nashville and had he any songs. Ben gave him "Blue Days—Black Nights". The song was recorded well with a very neat Chet Atkins-styled break from Sonny Curtis.

The accounts show that the session had cost $386, all of which would be deductible from Buddy's royalties. He had been given no advance royalties and, to save money, the group called in at his aunt's in East Texas for a meal on the way back to Lubbock.

On 8 February 1956, a day of immense snowdrifts in Lubbock, Buddy was sent a record contract by Decca, which misspelt his name as "Buddy Holly": couldn't they even get his name right? They wanted it back "immediately as it will hold up getting your record out" so he signed it, writing the name as typed. It was not countersigned by his parents, even though he was only 19. Decca asked for photographs (shouldn't they have been doing this?) and, a few weeks later, a biography. The time spent writing those autobiographical essays in school was not wasted. There were fierce winds that day so he stayed indoors to write it and signed his effort, "Buddy Holly".

As way of thanking Eddie Crandall, Buddy had sent him a decorated, leather billfold that he had made. Crandell was so impressed that he asked Buddy to quote a price for another 300, which Marty could give to TV presenters and DJs. However, it was evident Crandall was out of the loop. He said he was still hopeful of doing something with him, but at the moment he was tied up with promoting Marty's new record, a country music cover of Little Richard's "Long Tall Sally".

Buddy Holly's first Decca single was issued in the US on 16 April 1956. The A-side was "Blue Days—Black Nights" and the B-side, "Love Me". The industry paper, *Billboard*, said, "If the public will take more than one Presley or Perkins, as it well may, Holly stands a strong chance." The public had already taken more than one Presley or Perkins as both Elvis and Carl had made the charts, so who writes this nonsense? And, for what it's worth, Buddy wrote to Jim Denny to tell him that "Blue Days—Black Nights" was Number 6 in Lubbock: surely, that's not too good for the only show in town.

Peter Doggett (67): "After Elvis Presley, Buddy Holly is easily the most collectable artist of the rock'n'roll era and he's in the Top 10 of most collectable artists of all-time. If you are in America, you may be very lucky and pick up an original copy of his first single, 'Blue Days—Black Nights', but even the 45 rpm versions of his hit singles are hard to find in good condition."

Jerry Allison (68): "The postcards Buddy wrote to his family are fetching crazy prices in these auctions. It's kinda sad that his family isn't given the money. I don't have a lot of stuff myself but I do have a signed copy of the first single, 'Blue Days—Black Nights', and also a letter that the Beatles wrote to us in 1963, and all four of them signed it. I'm wondering what they'll give me for his bass player. I'll put Joe B. in the catalogue one day." Joe B. Mauldin added, "I come cheap. I might bring in a couple of pounds."

To prevent them being exploited and working for free, Hi Pockets Duncan had a management contract with the group, but once Buddy had a contract with Decca, he tore it up as he didn't want to hinder his success. This is honourable behaviour and quite different from the actions by many first managers of famous acts. By the time the single had come out, Duncan had moved to Amarillo and he arranged some bookings at the Clover Club. A later Cricket, Earl Sinks, jammed there with Buddy and they played golf together.

Buddy turned up one night at the Clover Club without a bass player and Rick Tucker from the Rhythm Teens sat in. Holly was impressed and invited him to play the next night at the Roller Rink in Lubbock. His father told him that he couldn't play with them anymore as he had to concentrate on school work.

In May 1956, Buddy with the Two Tones (that's Don Guess and Sonny Curtis in orange and blue shirts, aping the colour of a Cadillac) did a short tour on *Faron Young's Grand Ole Opry Tour* with Ray Price, Red Sovine, Carl Perkins and Tommy Collins. Buddy sang both sides of his single to open the show and was paid $10 a day for two shows a night. Faron Young was performing his recent US country Number 1 with its opening lines: "I want to live fast, love hard, die young, And leave a beautiful memory."

One night Buddy was appearing on stage without his glasses and he dropped a pick and had to go on his hands and knees to retrieve it. He felt embarrassed and saw an optometrist with a view to having contact lenses but he couldn't get used to them. He stuck with spectacles and decided to wear them on stage: they had a plastic and metal

frame which would be seen on the cover of *The Chirping Crickets* LP. (Now why didn't they call it *The Eyes Of Texas?*)

A London cockney, Tommy Hicks, was in the merchant navy. **Tommy Steele (69)**: "I saw Buddy Holly in Norfolk, Virginia in 1955 or 1956. The ship had gone in for some repairs and there was a show there that night at the local town hall called the *Grand Ole Opry Travelling Show*. I was a country guitar player, so I had to go and see that. All these great country acts were on, but there was also this feller in his glasses playing country music. He did a typical country 'You done me wrong' song and then he played another song and the rhythm changed. A lot of country music emphasises the second and fourth beat of the bar—there is a lot of that (demonstrates)—but he added fills that I'd never heard before, and it was Buddy Holly. I went away from there thinking that it was really great and then I went into New York and I heard 'Blue Suede Shoes' by Carl Perkins. I bought the sheet music and five days later, I was in London singing those type of songs. That's how it started for me."

Tommy Steele's vocal on his Top 10 hit, "Butterfingers", is not far from Buddy Holly. **Tommy Steele (70)**: "A lot of Holly's inflections are in 'Butterfingers', but all of us in those first months of rock and roll were learning from each other. We didn't have it in England until I arrived because we didn't have any country guitar players. Rock'n'roll is country music, and all the early rock'n'roll singers had been country singers."

On 4 May 1956, another young rockabilly singer, Gene Vincent, was making his way to Owen Bradley's studio. The session was produced by Ken Nelson for Capitol Records and they cut his first single, "Be-Bop-A-Lula". It was the first time that Vincent had been in a studio and it is, by any standards, an astonishing début. Many writers have said that Buddy was out of place in Nashville. I argue against that but even if he was, "Be-Bop-A-Lula" shows that great rock'n'roll could be made at Bradley's studio, admittedly not with Bradley and/or Cohen producing. When Buddy ran into Gene Vincent, Gene praised his single of "Blue Days—Black Nights".

Furthermore, in July 1956, the Johnny Burnette Trio had four consecutive days of sessions at Owen Bradley's studio for a Decca subsidiary, Coral. Buddy Harman, Grady Martin and Owen Bradley played on the sessions and they included such blistering rockabilly classics as "The Train Kept A-Rollin'", "Honey Hush" and "Lonesome Train (On A Lonesome Track)".

On Thursday 31 May 1956, a new western directed by John Ford and starring John Wayne, *The Searchers*, opened at the State Theatre on Texas Avenue in Lubbock. Buddy and Jerry Allison, who had just graduated, went to see it. During the film, John Wayne says "That'll be the day" when he disbelieves something. Cue for a song: cue also for the name of a Merseybeat group.

It is difficult to assess *The Searchers* in the light of today, though many film commentators call it a masterpiece. John Wayne kills a lot of Indians and is appalled that his niece may be brainwashed by them. Wayne was acting against type by playing a brooding anti-hero, which could have been setting the stage for Clint Eastwood. Maybe the character felt bad about what he was doing: who knows? It seems racist, but this was made in 1956 and my guess would be that the Lubbock people were applauding John Wayne every step of the way.

Peggy Sue Gerron (71): "Movies were always the big thing in Lubbock, and I know that Buddy and Jerry went back two or three times to see *The Searchers,* while writing 'That'll Be The Day'. It's a song that will always be around and I well remember Jerry calling me from New York to say it had got to Number 1 and sold a million and we were really thrilled."

Jerry Allison (72): "Buddy and I went to see *The Searchers* and for a couple of days afterwards, we were mocking the way John Wayne said, 'That'll be the day'. Then we wrote the song. The first time we recorded it was in Nashville for Decca Records. It was the summer of '56 and I had just gotten out of school. The producer said, 'That's the worst song I've ever heard in my life.' (Laughs) That hurt my feelings 'cause it was the first song I'd written! We also sent it to Roulette Records 'cause they had just signed Buddy Knox and Jimmy Bowen, but they turned it down."

Chas White (Dr Rock) (73): "I can relate to Buddy Holly's music and it is like a good wine as it gets better with age. Songs like 'Reminiscing'

have a great quality and simplicity about them and they are just marvellous. It's hard to believe that Owen Bradley thought that 'That'll Be The Day' was the worst song he'd ever heard, but maybe he'd just had a bad day."

Bob Montgomery (74): "Buddy didn't have that much interest in writing songs when I was with him. He didn't start writing a lot until he got his deal with Decca. Jerry Allison was very much a catalyst for Buddy's writing. He became very prolific in the short time that he was songwriting. He wrote all those great songs in 18 months."

The Searchers prompted another song. **Billy Swan (75)**: "'Do I have to draw you a picture' was written with Glen Clark who had seen the movie *The Searchers* in which John Wayne uttered the line and we thought it a neat title for a song."

On 17 June 1956, Lubbock's *Avalanche-Journal* started a series on the evils of rock'n'roll. When they showed the dancers at the out of town Bamboo Club when Holly was performing, they blacked out their eyes. These disreputable youngsters were dancing the "dirty bop". The newspaper said "The guitarist hoarsely shouted the unintelligible words of the song", the song being "Hound Dog". It said of the audience, "They are white teenagers from throughout the city, rich and poor, from good homes and bad." Mrs Holley wrote to defend the teenagers but her letter was not printed. It could have had a subliminal effect as two months later, the *Avalanche-Journal* wrote the more positive, "Buddy Holly Packs 'Em In".

Sonny Curtis (76): "You may have seen *Confidential* magazine. They would put people's pictures in there and they would put a black bar across their eyes. We played a club in Lubbock, Texas that was a bit questionable. It was a teenage club and they did the dirty bop. It was an extension of a dance called the bop and you can figure out the rest of it. The local newspaper took pictures of us playing there with the kids doing the dirty bop, and they put the picture in the paper with our eyes blacked out."

Maybe the controversy was too much as the Bamboo Club became the Glassarama. It was owned by Tommy Hancock (Thomas Clone Jerome Ward Newton Stevens Lukenbil Hancock Jr, to give him his full name), who also ran the Cotton Club. He had a special membership card for Unappreciated Musicians, which let them in for free. With this incentive, they could be relied upon to jam.

Jerry Allison (77): "Tommy Hancock played western swing in Lubbock with his group, the Roadside Playboys, and they played at the Glassarama. If you were a member of the Club for Unappreciated Musicians, you could get in free. Sonny Curtis was the Number 1 member, Buddy was Number 4 and I was Number 5."

One of Holly's favourite venues was Lawson's Roller Rink and he often played there, so much so that it has now been declared an historic building. Niki Sullivan, who comes into the story shortly, says that Buddy was always excellent at the Roller Rink.

The original Cotton Club had held 1,500 partygoers and even in a dry town like Lubbock there would be trouble as the booze was still there, but hidden. When the place burnt down, the owner gave Hancock the right to build a new Cotton Club outside the city and he used the old sign. Tommy often booked Bob Wills and his Texas Playboys. They played long versions of their best-known numbers without an intermission, and Tommy soon found out why. There was less fighting that way. Hancock had non-stop music whenever he could, alternating between live bands and records, and many Lubbock musicians cut their teeth in his house band.

Sleepy LaBeef (78): "Bill Haley was as much into western swing as rock'n'roll—'Rock Around The Clock' is like Bob Wills' boogie woogie, and it was Elvis who opened the door for many people who were ready to start performing like Bob Luman. He was doing country and he heard Elvis and added the beat. I started about three months after Elvis did and I started broadening my repertoire. Carl Perkins, Gene Vincent, Buddy Holly and Billy Lee Riley came along pretty soon. Right until Elvis came, Buddy was doing duets in the country vein like the Wilburn Brothers. Elvis turned him round and he made 'That'll Be The Day' and 'Peggy Sue'."

On 30 June 1956, Buddy was sent a royalty statement for his "Blue Days—Black Nights" single. He had sold 7,500 45s and 2,500 78s, making 10,000 in all. Somebody in the London head office of Decca Records thought it had

potential as it was given a UK release on their Brunswick subsidiary. Those sales sound promising, but Buddy was depressed that "Blue Days—Black Nights" was not a hit. His older friend, Scotty Turner, encouraged him to stick with it.

Buddy had gone through school with little sickness but the lack of success and a poor diet (too many pizzas, hamburgers and peanut butter sandwiches and a few cigarettes) affected his health, and for the rest of his life, he suffered from ulcers. He ignored medical advice to eat more sensibly and maybe, had he lived, he would have been another Elvis, though not in the way we would have hoped. He did, however, drink little as this had an immediate affect on his digestion. No Bud for Bud, then.

The second Nashville session with US Decca was arranged for Sunday 22 July 1956. This time Owen Bradley allowed Buddy to play his guitar and the other musicians were Sonny Curtis, Don Guess and Jerry Allison. Don Guess turned up without a double-bass, and Bradley said that if they didn't find one within half an hour, he was going water-skiing. They borrowed one from the *Grand Ole Opry* and all was well.

Buddy Holly's Nashville sessions have been unfairly criticised, not least by Buddy himself. They are three or four outstanding tracks and the best of all is the supercharged, rockabilly dance track, "Rock Around With Ollie Vee".

Sonny Curtis (79): "My dad's a farmer and we had a black man that helped us out called Willie Robertson. Willie's wife used to help my mam around the house sometimes—not on a fulltime basis 'cause we couldn't afford a maid, but just occasionally with the ironing or house-cleaning. Her name was Ollie Vee, but beyond that it's just a name. 'Rock Around With Ollie Vee' has nothing to do with her. I just used her name. I love Buddy's voice on that track—it's really nice."

Dave Williams (80): "I never tire of hearing 'Rock Around With Ollie Vee': there is so much energy in the guitar breaks and it is a great rockabilly number, really fast and with a good beat."

Tim Whitnall (81): "'Rock Around With Ollie Vee' is the moment in American music history where rockabilly was about to become rock'n'roll, and Buddy Holly nailed it absolutely. That record sounds awesome. I love the energy in his voice and the whole energy in the track. I remember Gary Busey and his band playing it live at the Roller Rink in *The Buddy Holly Story* and it sounds good by them too. It is a fabulous song and a brilliant record. You don't get much better country rockabilly than 'Blue Days—Black Nights' and 'Midnight Shift', so those Nashville sessions were by no means a write-off."

Ellis Amburn (82): "In 1956, Buddy Holly recorded a lot of songs in Nashville, not one of which sold but very few were released. He'd cut 'That'll be the Day' in Nashville for Owen Bradley but they wanted him 'country' and didn't know what to do with him. Had he not gone to Clovis and Norman Petty, who let him be himself, he might not have emerged at all."

Webb Pierce had told Buddy that you had to sing high if you wanted a hit. Terrible advice, but this is why Buddy sang his most commercial song to date, "That'll Be The Day", as high as he could. It was a mistake as he sounded uncomfortable and he was to record it much better later on. Still, Owen Bradley should have recognised its potential.

"I'm Changing All These Changes" is a good rockabilly song that Holly had written, but his voice sounded strained on Don Guess' ballad, "Girl On My Mind". There is a delightful reworking of a 1952 R&B hit from the Clovers, "Ting-A-Ling", which is close to the drum-and-guitar rapport that Holly and Allison developed with the Crickets. The song was written by the founder of Atlantic Records, Ahmet Ertegun, but he reversed his surname to Nugetre for composing credits. Five tracks had been recorded and the session costs were $546.

Ian Higham (83): "The Nashville recordings weren't generally released in the UK until after Buddy's death and certainly weren't well known until them. There are some great tracks there like 'Ting-A-Ling' and 'Girl On My Mind'."

In August 1956, Little Richard had appeared in Amarillo and been arrested for vagrancy, even though he had $2,700 on him. Quite possibly, the authorities found Richard so peculiar that they wanted to pin something on him. The next day he was to appear at the Cotton Club, supported by Buddy Holly, and Little Richard tells how Buddy took him to his house for a meal and

Mr Holley would not let him in. His performance at the Cotton Club caused a riot in the audience and the club had to shut early.

Jerry Allison (84): "The early Elvis records didn't have any drumming on them. I was listening to Little Richard's drummer, Earl Palmer. 'Lucille', 'Rip It Up' and 'Ready Teddy' are all great and he was playing rock'n'roll like I never heard it before. Fats Domino used Earl Palmer too. On the road, Little Richard was using Charles Connors, who also played good licks. We worked with Little Richard at the Brooklyn Paramount and the New York Paramount. We also saw him in Texas a time or two before we went on the road. He came through to the Cotton Club and we watched every move he and his band made, Charles Connors had a different way of playing the drums. He would lean over, rest his elbows on his knees and play. I became pretty good at stealing other people's licks."

Chas White (Dr Rock) (85): "Buddy Holly watched Little Richard as much as he could and he loved the beat in his songs. He idolised Little Richard and he recorded four of his songs— 'Ready Teddy', 'Slippin' And Slidin'', 'Send Me Some Lovin'' and 'Rip It Up'."

Buddy was feeling restless: Gene Vincent had a hit single and Elvis Presley's career was hitting the heights. Millions watched Elvis on *The Ed Sullivan Show*. Instead of wondering whether he could make it, Buddy was wondering when he could make it, and he thought Decca was to blame.

On 20 October 1956, Buddy appeared at a dance at the American Legion Hall in Lubbock with 350 attending. The *Evening Journal* carried a very favourable report. Holly said that he played guitar, banjo, mandolin and piano, and his hobbies were water-skiing and motorcycle riding. The rules for admittance at the Legion Hall dances included "neatness in boys dress and the banning of slacks, pedal pushers or blue jeans on girls attending the dances." No "dirty bop" in here. This could be the place where he could sing his more romantic songs like "Cindy Oh Cindy" and "Harbour Lights", the only British composition he sang publicly.

On 15 November 1956, Buddy has his third and final recording session for Decca Records in Nashville. Paul Cohen and Owen Bradley agreed that he should work with their musicians and apart from his travelling companion, Don Guess, on bass, Buddy was backed by Harold Bradley, Grady Martin, Floyd Cramer, Farris Coursey and, to show that they were no longer thinking of the country market, Dutch McMillin on saxophone.

They started at 9.30pm and recorded "Rock Around With Ollie Vee", reworking it in a Bill Haley-styled arrangement with a saxophone and a corny ending. Buddy called Jack Neal from the studio and asked if he could do his song, "Modern Don Juan": this was an inspired choice and a much better use of Dutch McMillin's saxophone. The third song was another one of Don Guess' ballads, "You Are My One Desire". This time the session cost $485.

Trevor Cajiao (86): "My favourite Holly track among the lesser-known ones is 'Modern Don Juan'. By 'lesser-known', I mean the ones that don't interest Joe Public. Just like Roy Orbison's Sun recordings don't appeal to the masses who know him for the big Monument hits, so it is with Buddy Holly's Decca sides in Nashville. They aren't as polished as his later recordings, but they appeal to me just as much. I love the feel of 'Modern Don Juan' with the saxophone of Dutch McMillin giving it a totally different feel to most of Holly's records. I love the way his vocals soar up and down. The whole record swings like a bucket of shit."

When "You Are My One Desire" was reissued as a single to capitalise on Holly's success, *Cash Box* said it was "An emotional love story chanted with great feeling. Kids'll flip over this one." They didn't.

Sonny Curtis (87): "Slim Whitman came through town and I knew Sammy Hodge who played guitar for Slim. Slim had another guitarist called Sugarfoot Collins who was ill, and Sammy got me the job of replacing him for a while. There's a very clear and simple explanation for me leaving Buddy's group and going on the road with Slim Whitman. Slim Whitman paid money, and that's something we weren't getting much of at the time."

The most impressive of all the rock'n'roll films, *The Girl Can't Help It*, starring Tom Ewell and Jayne Mansfield, was released in 1956. It had a witty script and a guest list to die for—Little Richard, Fats Domino, Eddie Cochran and Gene Vincent, for starters. Both Buddy and Jerry would see the film time and again.

Buddy's friend, Bobby Peeples had left school in Lubbock and worked for a local branch of the Sound And Photo Shop. He and his friend, Doug Walding, opened Venture Studios, which was little more than a few microphones and tape recorders in a garage on 19th Street. They knocked a hole in the wall and with microphones and piping, created a crude echo. Buddy sometimes used the studio for rehearsals, and around November and December 1956, the rehearsals were recorded.

One session was to nail down concert versions of Ferlin Husky's "Gone" and Ernest Tubb's "Have You Ever Been Lonely" as several attempts exist. It is good to hear how "Have You Ever Been Lonely" develops and how Holly moves away from Tubb's sombre, out-of-tune original. Buddy says "Mother" at the end of one take of "Have You Ever Been Lonely", so possibly his mum had looked in while she was out shopping. (It is possible that the songs were recorded at Holly's home.)

Buddy Holly's most uninhibited session has survived as he, Jerry Allison and an unknown bass player have enormous fun, spurring on each other to play as raucously as possible. The session starts with Chuck Berry's "Brown Eyed Handsome Man", which had been suggested by his brother, Larry. The song suits Holly perfectly but Holly omits the reference to the Venus De Milo, or in Chuck Berry's case, the Milo De Venus. He forgets some of the baseball verse, which is about Jackie Robinson or Willie Mays. Jerry is banging away on drums, an indication of what was to come. Buddy's love of Carl Perkins comes through with his song, "Blue Suede Shoes", and there is also Wynonie Harris' "Good Rockin' Tonight". There are two instrumentals, Bill Doggett's "Honky Tonk" and his own "Holly Hop". This was credited to his mother on release, but I think we can take it as Holly's composition.

Buddy is fantastically wild on Little Richard's "Rip It Up", again with Jerry Allison emulating his favourite drummer, Earl Palmer. Unfortunately, Jerry gets so carried away that the drums are distorted from then on. That apart, their version of Fats Domino's "Blue Monday" is excellent and I love the way that Buddy slurs the cunnilingus line, "Over the hill and way down underneath" in "Shake, Rattle And Roll". Jerry creates a solid Bo Diddley beat for the idiosyncratic "Bo Diddley", and Buddy has fun copying the voices that Clarence "Frogman" Henry created for "Ain't Got No Home". Buddy and Jerry sometimes did gigs on their own and you can tell that you wouldn't miss the rest of the band as this is glorious. A pity though that they never recorded two other rockers that they did in concert: Roy Orbison's Sun record, "Ooby Dooby", and the innuendo-packed blues song, "Keep Your Hands Off It (Birthday Cake)".

Jerry Allison (88): "I don't listen to the old records much but it's fun to think about those days because there weren't too musicians around Texas at the time and we were determined to have a band. Buddy Holly and I used to play a lot of four-hour dance jobs and it was fun 'cause he was my best friend. Every time it comes up, it's good memories, he was my favourite player and I was his favourite player. We learnt how to play together so I knew what he was going to play and he knew what I was going to play. It was always fun."

Bobby Peeples had the right idea with his little recording studio, but he did not go the right way about it. An audit from the head office of Sound And Photo revealed missing equipment and it was found in the studio. He maintained that he was testing it to give a better service to customers, but whatever the truth of the matter, he lost his job. He lost his premises through non-payment of rent. Many tapes from the Venture Studio have survived including several with another promising musician, Waylon Jennings.

Christmas Eve was a strange day to release a record but that's when Decca put out "Modern Don Juan" and "You Are My One Desire". Decca sent Buddy a letter a week later saying that it had generated $1,000 in royalties, so there were some strange buying habits back then, or are these just advance orders? The US trade paper, *Cash Box*, described "You Are My One Desire" as "An emotional love story charged with great feeling." They likened Holly's quavering vocal to Presley's on "Love Me Tender".

On Saturday 29 December 1956, 37 year old Vidal Rodriquez, who fancied himself as a modern Don Juan, grabbed six slips from a lingerie store, Franklin's, in Lubbock and the manageress, Mrs Sterling, went in pursuit. She asked a group of youths to help her and they were Buddy Holly, Jack Neal and four others. They cornered the suspect and held him down even though he threatened them with a knife. "We're all members of the American Legion Youth Centre and we believe in justice," Ken Austin told the *Avalanche-Journal*.

As the year turned into 1957, Buddy Holly felt that he had to get out of his Decca contract. Paul Cohen was feeling the same way. He thought Holly was a mistake and told his friends that "Buddy Holly is the biggest no talent I have ever worked with."

Harold Bradley told the journalist Jim Newcombe that the problem was that they didn't take Buddy seriously; "We thought we could make him rich and famous: he's a hillbilly and we know what to play. We didn't realise that he was trying to create a new sound. A couple of months before he died, he had a meal with my brother in New York and they laughed about it."

5

THE TEX-NEW MEX SOUND

"What petty follies they themselves commit"
(William Shakespeare)

Many of the great record producers were pioneers, people who were working independently of the major record companies. They did not have the security of corporate employment or large financial backing and they struggled with meagre resources to make records that would compete with the best: these spirited mavericks included Sam Phillips in Memphis, Lee Hazlewood in Phoenix, Bob Keane in Los Angeles, Huey P. Meaux in Houston, and Norman Petty in Clovis. Phil Spector comes into this category but with a few big hits, he soon had the financial backing to employ Los Angeles' best session musicians and made records which the major labels might have considered too profligate.

Norman Eugene Petty was born on 25 May 1927 during a sandstorm in Clovis, New Mexico. His parents were Sidney and Thelma Petty and they had three other children, Billy, Shirley and Edith. Norman started playing the piano when he was five, picking it up mostly by ear. As he grew older, he became interested in repairing radios and recording sound. When he was 12, his parents bought him a tape recorder on hire purchase. None of his neighbours had such hi-tech equipment, so he started recording weddings and

other social events for a small fee. Both country and middle-of-the-road music were popular in the area and so Norman played in a country band for rodeos and a more sophisticated unit for night clubs. A local radio station, KICA, was glad to see Norman around and he became adept with the technicalities of broadcasting.

Norman Petty was conscripted when he was 18 and he had a relatively easy and productive time as he recorded live events and arranged radio broadcasts for air force bands. He learnt to play the Hammond organ at the military chapel in Hampton, Virginia. Returning to civilian life, he worked at KICA as an announcer and engineer. He formed a three-piece, the Musical Tones, and played dances around Clovis. Mostly by correspondence, he acquired a degree in speech from the Eastern New Mexico University. He was polite, cordial and, in keeping with his degree, well spoken.

Violet Ann Brady had been born in Clovis on 17 September 1928. As a teenager, she was part of a vocal trio with her friends, Wanda Foster and Audrey Porter. Although she became an accomplished pianist, she never mastered the knack of singing and playing together and, in 1943, she asked Norman to accompany them on piano for a programme on KGNC in Amarillo. Vi studied piano and organ for two years at the University of Oklahoma.

Norman and Vi were married on 20 June 1948. Vi taught piano and Norman continued at KICA and also played organ during cinema intermissions. When his combo refused to work on New Year's Eve, he asked Vi to play piano and added a baseball player and country music fan, Jack Vaughn, on guitar. It was an odd mix: a classical guitarist, a jazz organist and a country guitarist, but the show was a success.

During 1949, the Pettys moved to Dallas, and Norman worked for a small recording studio, owned by Jim Beck. A booking agent asked him to form a trio for Southwest Tours Inc, so they reunited with Jack and added a good vocalist, Vi's cousin, Georgiana Veit. They worked continuously for a couple of years including a six month residency at the Menger Hotel in San Antonio.

Georgiana left at the end of 1951 to join the Johnny Muller Combo, and she sang professionally until 1958. Norman encouraged Vi to become the lead vocalist as well as playing keyboards. Norman recorded her keyboard parts in advance and she would sing live. This is an early example of backing tapes, albeit brought about by necessity. Norman realised that he might as well record other instruments, so the Norman Petty Trio could have a fuller sound.

In 1952, Norman bought some vacant premises at 1313 West 7th Street, Clovis, next door to his father's garage, while they lived at 1321. He was opening his own recording studio in the middle of nowhere, but he was primarily doing this to record his own trio. He always wanted good equipment and he bought two Ampex recorders, one portable, one fixed, and two high tech Telefunken microphones. He had filters to eliminate tape hiss. As he could not afford multi-tracking facilities, the idea was to start a tape he had recorded on one machine, play over the top of it, and then record the result on a second machine. This process could not be repeated too often as there would be some loss in quality.

Over the years, Norman was devising new ways of recording and adding equipment, including a trip to get what he wanted in Germany. For example, he had a tiny microphone that he would put inside the hole in a stand-up bass. It was an effective set-up and outside of the broadcasting studios in Clovis, there was nothing else in the area.

In 1953, the Norman Petty Trio toured the American midwest and whilst in the Hays Hotel ballroom in Jackson, Michigan, they recorded two popular stage numbers, Duke Ellington's "Mood Indigo" and Norman's own "Petty's Little Polka". When they were rejected by the major companies, Petty pressed 3,000 copies on their own label, Nor-Va-Jak: that is, Norman, Violet Ann and Jack. The catalogue number 1313 was simply the studio's street number. They sold copies on the road but they didn't want to distribute the record themselves as there could be difficulty in collecting money from the outlets. When RCA agreed to release their recordings, they had success with "Mood Indigo", making Number 14 on the national juke-box charts. Duke Ellington even invited Petty to join him on stage in New York for "Mood Indigo".

In 1955, Norma Jean Berry, who was nine days older than Vi, interviewed the Pettys for the *Clovis News Journal* and became a close friend and full-time employee. Indeed, Norman, Vi and Norma Jean ran the studios with little outside help. Unmarried, Norma Jean devoted her life to the studio, and as she ended up being buried in the same plot as the childless Pettys, there has been speculation about their private lives. It has been suggested that the butch Norma with her deep voice was simply Norman in drag. There is no foundation for this but there may have been a *ménage à trois*. However, Vi's consuming interests were her pets and her garden. Sometimes, she had as many as 10 cats around the studio.

The Bowman Brothers sometimes did backing vocals for Norman Petty, and when they heard him play part of a concerto that he had written, one of them said it sounded almost like paradise. Petty knew that he had the title for the piece, "Almost Paradise". Despite their competence, the Bowmans didn't work on any of Buddy Holly's records as rock'n'roll was against their religious convictions, and two of them became preachers.

The Norman Petty Trio played competent but cheesy music, ideal for cocktail lounges, and they did well in 1956 with "Almost Paradise", which was recorded at the Lyceum Theatre, Clovis. The pianist, Roger Williams, covered the tune and took it to Number 15 on the US charts and another version by Lou Stein made Number 31. Although Petty himself only reached Number 56, he had three entries in the US Hot 100 and it marked his first success as a songwriter. "Almost Paradise" did not receive much airplay in the UK but it was recorded by the trumpet player from Preston, Eddie Calvert. From time to time, the Norman Petty Trio added a drummer such as when they played Las Vegas in July 1956. Perhaps an indication of the audience is their album, *Corsage,* where all the tracks relate to flowers.

George Tomsco (89): "Vi Petty was a classically trained pianist and she is on our blues album, *Blue Fire*, and on 'Vaquero' too. Vi was busy all the time and I think really that she wanted to be a well-known singer. She made 'The First Kiss' with the Norman Petty Trio, but I don't think they released anything under her own name."

Norman soon realised that having a recording studio next door to his parents' garage was not a good idea as his father was repairing cars and trucks during the day and he could not afford decent soundproofing. He wanted to offer his services to Clovis residents but he could only record them in the evening or on location, perhaps at the Lyceum Theatre.

Whilst with RCA, the Norman Petty Trio had had to record in New York and St Louis. Norman hated the rigidity of the three hour, highly unionised sessions, and he determined a different approach. In his studio, he would charge by the song and the session would last as long as it took, the standard price being $60 for two songs. He might have changed his mind if a perfectionist like Paul Simon had been living in Clovis. Normally, the musicians paid for the sessions and owned the tapes, but Petty might give them an introduction to a record company. Sometimes, when he liked what he heard, Petty might not charge for the sessions but he would own the publishing of the songs and take a writing credit too. Roughly speaking, a songwriter would expect 50% of the publishing income from the record and the publisher would take the rest. With a writing credit, Petty would be keeping 75% and giving the songwriter 25%.

Holly's widow, Maria Elena, has no good words for Norman Petty and claims that he put his name to songs he didn't write. She claims that Norman Petty couldn't write anything. However, it is more complicated than that as Norman Petty was capable of writing melodies such as "Almost Paradise". He usually wrote music and later on in this book, Jerry Allison and Bob Montgomery give examples of his bad lyric writing: evidence that he could write lyrics, if not well.

Craig Baguley (90): "It is certainly not fair for Norman Petty to be singled out for vilification because it was a longtime and common industry practice going back to the turn of the twentieth century. Remember how Al Jolson's name appeared as co-writer on many songs? I'm sure the writers were happy to get a Jolson recording this way. Al Jolson would have said that he was the one making money for the writers. Similarly, Petty would be looking to increase his financial return on Buddy Holly, who would not have made headway without him. There are instances of this all over popular music. It is annoying for us not to know who really wrote a particular song, but while Norman Petty can be criticised, he shouldn't be vilified."

Justin Hayward (91) "Norman Petty's contribution to the 'sound' was just right, but even 10-year-olds like me sensed that Buddy would very quickly outgrow the influence and contribution of the people around him. I remember having an earnest conversation during a chemistry lesson about whether Petty deserved a writing credit when everybody knew it was 'all Buddy' really. As it turned out the instincts of my classmates and myself were right. Would Buddy have been doing that fatal tour if other people weren't arguing about their share of a part of him? I don't think so."

Norman Petty recorded dozens of Mexican artists, mostly singing Spanish ballads, and as Vi was able to both speak and read Spanish, she was an integral part of his set-up. Jimmy Self was the first American performer to record there and he used the dubbing facilities to double-track his vocal. Another early session was with Tommy Duncan from Bob Wills' Texas Playboys.

The son of a railwayman, Joe Sunny West was born in Lubbock County in 1937. The family moved back forth from Texas to New Mexico, ending up in Levelland, and Sunny was impressed when he saw Faron Young and Slim Whitman perform around 1955. He took his songs to Sam Phillips at Sun Records, who wasn't interested. He recorded for Norman Petty in August 1956, who changed the spelling of his name to **Sonny West (92)**. "We arranged for a session there in 1956 and Norman didn't have an echo chamber at the time. He had tried a theatre with some other artists and he said, 'We can do it there and it will be like a live recording.' We did that and he got a great concert hall sound. Norman was very good at getting the cleanest recording that he could. Our drummer played a cardboard box, a bass drum and cymbals. It was very easy to pick up on the mike and it doesn't drown everybody else. We did 'Rock-Ola Ruby', my first record, and 'Sweet Rockin' Baby' the same night. They were run-of-the-mill rockabilly songs, but it is the overall feeling that counts. You can still hear that today."

Sonny West (93) also found himself in one of Norman's deals. "We knew that you had to have a record to be anybody. You couldn't just go and play in a bowling alley or a teen dance and not have a record. You would not make enough money that way. We leased Norman's label to put it out: Norman had his artwork for his records through RCA in Chicago, and RCA did the pressing for his label. He said that I could pay him a little bit extra and use his label. That single came out on Nor-Va-Jak."

Norman Petty still kept in touch with Jim Beck's studio in Dallas and before he bought his own equipment for making acetates, he used them for transferring tapes to acetates. In March 1956, the Wink Westerners featuring Roy Orbison recorded a demo at Beck's studio. They sent it to Columbia Records, and although their A&R manager, Don Law, saw no merit in the group, he liked the song, "Ooby Dooby", and had it recorded by Sid King on 5 March 1956. "Ooby Dooby" had been written by Wade Moore and Dick Penner, fellow students with Orbison at North Texas State College in Denton.

Meanwhile, Jim Beck had told Orbison about the time facilities in Petty's studio. One of his band, the Teen Kings, James Morrow, was dating an accordionist and singer, Jeannie Oliver, and her father, Chester, an oil executive, agreed to finance a session. Roy Orbison came to Clovis on 4 March 1956. They recorded a new version of "Ooby Dooby", the first rock'n'roll song to be recorded in Clovis, and it's a good rockabilly performance, albeit lacking in echo, with good drumming from Billy Pat Ellis. Their second song, "Tryin' To Get To You", which had been recorded by the Eagles (1954) and Elvis Presley (1955), sounds like a night at the British Legion but Orbison's wide-ranging delivery is showing through. It is surprising that Petty with his acute musical ear hadn't picked up on Orbison's remarkable voice. The single was released on the Je-Wel label (Jeannie Oliver and another musician, Weldon Rogers), but it only sold locally. Within a couple of weeks, Sam Phillips of Sun Records had picked up on Roy Orbison and at the first session, he produced a new, more exciting version of "Ooby Dooby", full of slapback echo, which is the version that we know today. This was the first time that Norman Petty became aware of what was happening in Memphis and he was intrigued by Sam Phillips' echo and wanted to emulate it.

Many records in the mid-1950s were recorded with echo as it was thought that it made them more exciting and indeed, almost all of the new rockabilly records depended on some sort of echo effect. As there was a large, unused room above his parents' garage, Norman converted this into an echo chamber. He installed a speaker with microphones at different distances from it. The music from the studio came into the room via the speaker and was then picked up through the microphones and fed back to the control unit. Once Norman knew Buddy Holly, he was able to get this done on the cheap: the work was carried out by Larry Holley's company and Buddy's dad, Buddy and Bob Montgomery helped on the project. Norman noted that Bob Montgomery, who worked in a TV repair shop, had the same enthusiasm for the technicalities of recording as he did and later, he recruited him to modernise the studio. The elevation in Clovis was 3,500 feet and it was so cool at night that Norman Petty reckoned the echo chamber was at its best at 3am.

Tim Whitnall (94): "This type of invention is quite normal for the time. That amazing snare drum sound on 'Bridge Over Troubled Water' was obtained by putting Hal Blaine in a lift shaft. The studio was on the top floor and they put the drum at the bottom of the shaft and the sound travelled up. The original version of the 'Doctor Who' theme was done by running a 20 foot loop of tape down the corridor, and it was spinning between the tape recorders to get that sound. There's only one rule to making records: it works if it sounds right."

Mark Wirtz (95): "Certain studios were world-famous for their chambers—notably Capitol, CBS, RCA and EMI. Typically, not only the chambers, but also the monitors and microphones used were extremely expensive and space-hogging. Although those chambers were ideal for pristine classical recordings, they could be rock'n'roll poison. Anyway, big chambers were unaffordable for most smaller or independent studios, hence the stories of microphones in hallways, staircases, storage rooms and even toilets by resourceful producers, and these substitute chambers required absolute silence during recordings. Some studios simply relied on tape-repeat echoes, known as slapback, to create an ambience of distance and space, often to the point of obscuring the signal rather than merely enhancing it."

Ellis Amburn (96): "Norman Petty's studio looks like a gas station and used to be a grocery store. Buddy Holly helped out on building the echo chamber. It was a good job they were night birds as all day long they would have 18 wheelers roaring past full of cattle—it is the milk pail of the south-west. They worked all night to avoid the noise. Petty loved spontaneity so much, he would use a track he liked even if there was a cough or two on there."

When the Teen Kings were playing at West Texas College in Canyon, another musician, Jimmy Bowen told Roy Orbison of his wish to record. Orbison, in turn, told him about Norman Petty. Bowen and his friends had combined savings of $36 and Petty said it was $60 or nothing. Bowen contacted Orbison again who put him in touch with the oil man, Chester Oliver. He agreed to finance the recording.

Although Buddy Holly and the Crickets are regarded as the first modern beat group, Buddy Knox and the Rhythm Orchids were there first. They comprised Buddy Knox (singer, rhythm guitar), Donnie Lanier (lead guitar), Jimmy Bowen (double-bass) and Don Mills (drums). Unlike Buddy Holly, Knox had been named Buddy Wayne Knox, as a nod to his father's best friend. Knox was a good vocalist with a friendly, cheerful voice as befits a man who came from Happy, Texas, and what could have been better material than a song he and Bowen had written, "Party Doll". Don Mills couldn't go with them to Clovis as he was still at school, but Petty supplemented the musicians with Dave Alldred on percussion and Alex Rafael on bass, as he felt that Bowen was not competent enough. Petty, who wasn't sure how to cope with the volume of rock'n'roll, asked Alldred to bang a cardboard box, which worked very effectively. Petty was pleased with the sound but he thought the song a little risqué. Jimmy Bowen sang lead on a teenage ballad, "I'm Sticking With You".

"Party Doll" was issued on another label of Charlie Oliver's, Triple D, as it was thought that KDDD in Dumas, Texas would promote it. They did, and Roulette Records in New York was impressed enough to release it nationally. Both sides became US hits with Buddy Knox at Number 1 and Bowen's track, released on a separate single, at Number 14. This was a two-edged sword as Roulette was financed by the Mafia. Still, at the time, Charlie Oliver had made a tidy sum for his $60 investment, and Norman Petty was thinking....

Bob Montgomery (97): "I loved Buddy Knox's voice and I love the album that I later did with him. He had one of the most pleasant, listenable voices in the whole world."

Buddy Knox (98): "I really liked Norman Petty. He was a religious man and we even went to church with him—he wouldn't do anything until Sunday night when the services were over. He wouldn't allow us to smoke or drink in the studio, but, otherwise, we had a complete run of the place and his wife, Vi, was a sweetheart. He built that studio himself and he was an electrician and a genius with electronics. He flew to Germany to get a two-track system and that was the ultimate in recording then. We could sing along with ourselves and it seemed amazing. One thing though, we tended to record at eleven at night and go on 'til five in the morning, mainly because of Norman's echo chamber. That was on the top of his dad's garage next door. He had a speaker on one end of the roof and a microphone at the other end, and every time a truck passed by outside, it could be heard in the studio and we'd have to cut it again. Norm had a magic ear, he could spot things that you didn't know were there, but he realised he had missed something by allowing us to get signed up in New York. He made sure he hung onto Holly and the other guys."

The word of mouth continued when the Rhythm Orchids came to Lubbock in 1956, and Knox told Holly of Petty's studio. As Holly was under contract to Decca at the time, he cut some demo sessions to experiment with his sound, and Holly and possibly his musicians paid for them themselves. (That simple statement has been bound up with legal issues for many years: that is, who actually owns the tapes?) Buddy took with him Sonny Curtis, Don Guess and Jerry Allison, and they recorded six of his own songs and one other.

Norman was so impressed by Sonny Curtis' guitar playing that he wanted him to join his trio. Buddy said, "Man, don't do that, we're going to make it big ourselves." However, Sonny Curtis was soon to get an offer from Slim Whitman and go touring with him.

Sonny Curtis (99): "I did have a problem with Buddy over the lead guitar playing as we both wanted to do it. He was starting to play some lead and if I was just playing rhythm, I bristled. When I joined Slim Whitman, Buddy came into his own as a guitarist as he played lead all the time then."

Norman Petty uses his echo facilities for "Baby Won't You Come Out Tonight", which Buddy had already tried in Wichita Falls, and a strong rocker, "I'm Gonna Set My Foot Down". "Rock-A-Bye Rock" is not much of a song but it possesses the same shuffle rhythm as "That'll Be The Day" and there are other similar characteristics. It is as though Holly knew what he wanted to do but needed a stronger song to do it with. He recorded "I'm Changin' All Those Changes" with

Decca a few months later, and the slow country ballads, "I Guess I Was A Fool" and "Because I Love You", are okay, but only okay.

Weldon Myrick was born in Jayton, a little town 100 miles east of Lubbock. His brother, Tex, played the steel guitar and when he went into the air force, the eight-year-old Weldon tried to play it. He became proficient and spent his teenage years playing in various bands. He knew Ben Hall, who had moved to Lubbock and after graduating in 1956, he played on Ben's TV show. Later, he played with Bill Anderson's band and this let to working on the *Grand Ole Opry* for over 30 years.

Ben Hall gave Buddy a ballad, "It's Not My Fault", that he had written with another local musician, Weldon Myrick. It's a good song, but not as captivating as "Blue Days—Black Nights".

And there was no great trick to Norman Petty's production skills. Unlike many producers, he was a quiet, determined businessman. On his best records, it is like standing in front of the group and hearing them play live in your living room.

Mike Brocken (100): "There is nothing much in the studio in Clovis—a tape recorder, a microphone and acetate cutter, and they created a great sound in that room."

Norman Killon (101): "We went to Clovis and all the original equipment is there. All over the walls are records that he produced including his own trio. The guide sat me down in the chair behind the console and he said, 'Buddy sat here when he was listening to the playbacks' and then he played Buddy Holly over the system and it was like he was there. There was a flat behind the studio too, and the musicians would stay there. Clovis was much smaller than Lubbock, and this guide was so friendly that he even drove us to the cemetery where Norman Petty was buried."

Bruce Welch (102): "Norman Petty was a very innovative producer who left them to it a lot of the time. I know he ripped them off, but he still deserves a lot of credit."

Stuart Colman (103): "It is quite remarkable how the complexities of a recording are governed by the producer's personality. Consider the squirrely-bop of Sam Phillips at Sun Records, the whimsical works of Leiber and Stoller, the regimentation of Mitch Miller and the mercurial methods of Phil Spector. There, in a heart-beat, you have a bird's eye view of the moderators' makeup. Taking the theory a stage further, anyone who met and worked with Norman Petty would have been presented with a smartly turned out individual who spoke in clear and measured tones. I doubt if he wore a suit and tie in the studio but a neatly defined, well-arranged imagery is what arose from his recordings. Norman's high fidelity standards contrast perfectly with Buddy Holly's natural edginess. He had such good equipment that there was always a fair chance that something half decent was going to be captured on tape."

Huey P. Meaux (104): "I knew Norman Petty very well and I knew Buddy Holly some. Buddy Holly was an originator, a natural, someone who'll be here long after you and me are gone. The sound itself came from Norman Petty in a little studio no bigger than this room. They both liked acoustic things and you could do that in a small room. Norman Petty was very influential: the records that Buddy Holly did without Norman Petty you can tell a hundred miles apart. He got slushier and slushier when he went uptown, but I still like the original Buddy Holly things."

Early in 1957, Buddy returned to Norman Petty's studio to record two beaty rockers, Chuck Berry's "Brown Eyed Handsome Man" and Bo Diddley's "Bo Diddley". The partnership with Jerry Allison was coming to the fore. Buddy Holly repeated Chuck Berry's mistake by singing Milo De Venus instead of Venus De Milo.

Jerry Allison (105): "I've got nothing against the Fireballs but it irritates the heck out of me that those tracks were overdubbed after Buddy's death: 'Brown Eyed Handsome Man' especially, as it was a finished track."

Although it is reported that Buddy Holly had been unimpressed with the results of his Nash-ville sessions with Decca, I think he was more dis-appointed that only a couple of singles had been released and they hadn't had much promotion, and his contract expired in January 1957. On the other hand, Norman Petty had recorded a million seller, "Party Doll". Buddy Holly told Norman Petty, "If you can get Buddy Knox a hit, you can get me one."

As well as signing a contract with Norman Petty, those involved would also put their hands on the Bible.

6

RHYTHM METHOD

*"Was there ever anything more exciting than watching
rock'n'roll being born?"
(John Stewart, 2000)*
(To get the full effect of this quote, lower your voice to a deep whisper and say it slowly).

By the start of 1957, Buddy Holly was getting frustrated. He had been with Decca Records for a year, recorded an album's worth of tracks and yet only two singles ("Blue Days—Black Nights" and "Modern Don Juan") had been issued. Decca had not got behind the singles in either the country or the pop market, his contract was about to expire, and apart from gathering valuable experience, Buddy Holly was doing no better than he had been a year earlier.

Starting on 9 January 1957, Buddy Holly with Don Guess, Sonny Curtis and Jerry Allison went on a 15 day tour with Hank Thompson and his Brazos Valley Boys. It was a sturdy country package with Wanda Jackson, Mitchell Torok, Hank Locklin, Cowboy Copas, George Jones and Justin Tubb in support. Hank Thompson's band backed Wanda Jackson, and Buddy and his friends did the rest. Jerry realised how boring it was to drum for strict country acts: R&B was far more exciting. Still, he made $10 a day plus expenses and used the $140 from the tour to buy some Premier drums.

Hank Thompson did not consider Buddy Holly worth mentioning in his autobiography, *My Side Of Life* (completed after his death by Warren Kice in 2007) but he does state that the Cotton Club led the league in alcohol consumption and number of fights. I did interview Thompson on a UK tour and I kick my younger self for not asking him about Holly.

Kent Westbury, who wrote Ann-Margret's 1961 US hit, "I Just Don't Understand", caught the tour in Florida and recalls Buddy doing "Roll Over Beethoven", "Modern Don Juan" and one other. He says, "I liked him 'cause he could change chords faster than anybody I've ever seen."

Being part of a package show was frustrating as Buddy would only perform a couple of songs a night. His notebook gives a list of songs that he knew. He could have been the first Elvis tribute act as he could perform "Blue Suede Shoes", "Don't Be Cruel", "Hound Dog", "I Forgot To Remember To Forget", "I'll Never Let You Go (Little Darlin')", "I'm Left, You're Right, She's Gone", "Lawdy Miss Clawdy", "Money Honey", "That's All Right (Mama)" and "Tryin' To Get To You". He was well versed in Ray Charles ("I Got A Woman" and "Let The Good Times Roll" and planned to learn "Drown In My Own Tears" and "Ain't That Love"), Little Richard ("Tutti Frutti" and "Long Tall Sally" and planned to learn "All

Around The World" and "The Girl Can't Help It"), Chuck Berry ("Roll Over Beethoven" and planned to learn "Maybellene" and "Too Much Monkey Business"), Bill Haley ("Forty Cups Of Coffee" and "Razzle Dazzle" and planned to learn, a little late in the day, "Rock Around The Clock") and Roy Orbison ("Ooby Dooby" with plans to learn ""Rock House").

Buddy knew the Everly Brothers' "Hey Doll Baby", Sammy Kaye's 1950 hit, "Harbour Lights", the Robins' "Smokey Joe's Café", Hank Ballard and the Midnighters' "Annie Had A Baby", the Platters' "The Great Pretender" , Gene Vincent's "Be-Bop-A-Lula" and the standard "When Did You Leave Heaven", which had been written for the 1936 film, *Sing, Baby, Sing* and had been recorded by Big Bill Broonzy.

Buddy planned to learn Fats Domino's "Goin' Home", LaVern Baker's "Jim Dandy", Sonny James' "Young Love" and its B-side "You're The Reason I'm In Love", Marvin and Johnny's "Tick Tock", Edna McGriff's "Why Oh Why" and Charlie Gracie's "Butterfly". Buddy was working on new compositions—"I Feel Good", "Lost Dreams" and "Makin' Me A Used-To-Be". "Cindy Lou", which is on the list, was the original title for "Peggy Sue".

All was not well with Buddy's existing publishing contract with Cedarwood: Sue Parrish was getting little royalties from "Love Me", and, while Buddy was away, she wrote to Mrs Holley, asking if Buddy had only received $37 as well. She pointed out that the shops in her area did not stock "Love Me" and it took three weeks to order a copy. She sent Buddy a couple more lyrics, "Baby, Baby" and "Too Young", but nothing happened to them. In October 1957, she sent him two more, "That Don't Give You The Right" and "Lost As A Puppy", again without success.

Gary Dale Tollett was born in Amherst Texas on 13 December 1932, and his wife, Ramona, in Merced, California on 19 December 1936. They met while he was in the air force and were married in January 1955. On his discharge, Gary studied at Texas Tech and Ramona worked as a bank clerk. One of Gary's relations, June Clark, lived in Lubbock, with her husband, Nig. They had a spacious house and allowed Buddy and Gary to hold sessions there, where they developed a new arrangement for "That'll Be The Day". One day the tornado sirens went off and they all went to the shelter. There they received complaints about playing too loudly.

On 21 February 1957, Gary recorded two songs, the rockabilly "Go Boy Go", which had been recorded by Carl Smith, and the country hit, "Gone", at Radio KDAV with Buddy Holly on guitar and Jerry Allison on drums.

On 24 February 1957, two carloads of performers travelled to Clovis for a recording session: Buddy, Jerry, Larry Welborn, Niki Sullivan and Gary and Ramona Tollett. Buddy had a little, pointed Van Dyck beard and said he wouldn't shave it off until he had a hit, but it only lasted a few weeks.

Niki Sullivan had been born in South Gate, California on 23 June 1937, and his family moved to Lubbock when he was two. They returned to California in 1954 and Niki was on the *Rocket To Stardom* TV show singing "Baby Let's Play House" in September 1956. When he returned to Lubbock, he met Bobby Peeples and recorded "Piddle-De-Pat" at his makeshift studio. Ella Holley and his mother were good friends, but it wasn't until sometime later that they learnt that Buddy and Niki were third cousins. Both Buddy and Niki's families had turned up to see a show at a fair in Waco with Fats Domino and Chuck Berry but it had been badly publicised and the small audience got to know each other and discovered the link.

Buddy was completing the lyric for "I'm Lookin' For Someone To Love" as they drove to New Mexico. Larry suggested a saying of their uncle's about a drunk man. Buddy put the *non sequitur* into the song and it fit perfectly. The song has the quirkiness of Bob Dylan's *Basement Tapes*.

Harvey Andrews (106): "All the great songwriters that I personally admire—Lennon and McCartney, Paxton, Dylan, Paul Simon—were influenced by Holly. When rock'n'roll started, there was something about Holly that got them. They all liked Elvis and Little Richard but Holly is the one that they related to. He was the first singer-songwriter, but we didn't know it at the time. His lyrics are incredible: one verse of 'I'm Lookin' For Someone To Love' goes: 'Drunk man, street car, Foot slipped, there you are.'

Well, that's a book, a novel, a play and a film. Nine words, and it's lyric writing of the highest order."

Mark Lewisohn (107): "The Beatles loved Buddy's lyrics. Paul often talks about 'I'm Lookin' For Someone To Love'. As example of economy in terms of lyric writing, the 'Drunk man' verse is right up there."

At Clovis, Buddy Holly recorded "I'm Lookin' For Someone To Love" and his new version of "That'll Be The Day", which is not pitched as high as the Decca recording. There was Niki Sullivan (rhythm), Larry Welborn (bass) and Jerry Allison (drums) with Niki and the Tolletts providing the backing vocals. Buddy was pleased with the results but this was only a demo and, in a perfect world, he wanted to record "That'll Be The Day" with Ray Charles' girl singers, the Raelets.

Jerry Allison (108): "Buddy Holly sounded more mature on the second version of 'That'll Be The Day' and we were more familiar with the song as we had played it on gigs around Texas. We also had some friends singing background and there were no voices on the first one. Norman Petty used to say that he had found a diamond in the rough and refined us, but Buddy Holly knew what he wanted all the time."

The session ended at 2.30am on 25 February 1957 and they returned to Lubbock as some of them were working that day. They went back to Clovis on 1 March 1957, this time for a Gary Tollett session. They recorded "Go Boy Go" and "Gone" more professionally than at KDAV as well as the country favourites, "The Golden Rocket" (on which Gary tried to sound like Hank Snow) and, Ramona's favourite song, "I Overlooked An Orchid".

June Clark was Donnie Lanier's sister. His other sister, Teddy, lived in New York and knew the management at Roulette. She submitted the demos to the label. Morris Levy liked Buddy's songs and said he would take them for Buddy Knox. Buddy Holly wanted to have his own success with the tracks and declined the offer. Considering the Mob connections, it is surprising that Levy didn't ignore him and record the songs with Knox. Levy arranged for Gary Tollett to sign with the Gone label, run by another suspect character,

George Goldner. He cut a single, "Love Is Dynamite"/ "Pretty Baby" as Gary Dale.

Following standard practice, Buddy's contract with Decca prevented him from re-recording any songs from the 1956 sessions for five years. On 28 February 1957, Paul Cohen refused to waive this, not knowing that the conversation was being recorded covertly on Norman Petty's equipment. Buddy thought it was unfair if nothing further was being issued from the sessions. Cohen said, "We got money tied up in this thing and they may go ahead and release them. I don't know what they're liable to do. They'll play them over and may salvage them. You can't record them for any other company. You can record anything else you want to, any other new songs." Cohen did ask to hear any new material.

A little suspiciously, Cohen asked Buddy if he had already re-recorded any of the songs, but Buddy, lying, said no. Buddy wanted to speak to another executive, Milt Gabler, only to be told that there was no point as Gabler worked for Cohen: "He's only a vice president." Following this conversation, Buddy Holly took Norman Petty's advice and submitted "That'll Be The Day" under a group name rather than his own.

But what group name? Both Buddy and Jerry liked "Witchcraft" by the doo-wop group, the Spiders (a favourite of the Neville Brothers, as it happens) and they thought they would name themselves after insects. It would be a change from the doo-wop groups who often used bird names. They considered the Beetles, but Buddy thought that people might want to squash them, so Crickets it was. Crickets are noted for their singing, but the backing vocals on the Crickets' records was done by others.

After the failure at Roulette, Norman Petty submitted the demos to Mitch Miller at Columbia Records, but it was another rejection. When Norman was in New York, he played the tracks to Murray Deutch, who ran Southern Music. He recognised their potential and recommended the Crickets to Bob Thiele, who ran one of Decca's subsidiary labels, Coral.

Bob Thiele had been born in Brooklyn on 27 July 1922 and as a teenager, he played clarinet in his own jazz band. He formed his own mail order company, Signature Records, which did well. He had considerable success with Coleman Hawkins' spectacular "The Man I Love" (1943), a record he had difficulty producing as he had to hold down a conscientious cleaner. Bob Thiele could genuinely say "Play 'Misty' for me" as he published the song.

The main record labels (RCA, Decca and Columbia) wanted to eliminate the independents from muscling in on their territory. In 1949, Decca established Coral as a quasi-independent label, designed to compete with the rivals, often by covering their songs with superior artists. Bob Thiele joined them in 1952 and he developed Coral very successfully with the McGuire Sisters, Lawrence Welk and his Orchestra, and Teresa Brewer, who became his third wife in 1972. Thiele had recorded the Clara Ward Singers live at the Apollo, added jazz to Jack Kerouac's verse and changed jazz music with John Coltrane. This hip New Yorker was unlikely to be impressed by a hick producer from Clovis, New Mexico.

But he was. Thiele had produced some rockabilly sides, classic ones too, as he had worked with the Johnny Burnette Trio and recorded "Tear It Up" at the Pythian Temple in New York. He had commissioned their Nashville sessions in July 1956. Some tracks had been released on Coral but Decca's President had thought that rock'n'roll was tarnishing the label and wanted Thiele to release the tracks on another subsidiary, Brunswick, which had been associated with jazz and R&B but had been dormant for some time. Maybe it was economy but Thiele told Petty that there was no need to recut "That'll Be The Day". "But it's only a demo," said Petty. "No, that's it," said Thiele.

Jerry Allison (109): "We were only making demos and we thought that if we got a record contract, we would be remaking the record in New York. We had paid for the session and Norman did very little by way of production. I would say that Buddy and I really produced it, but of course Norman put out the microphones and ran the board. He was the engineer."

Jerry Naylor (110): "I love 'That'll Be The Day'. Some great records just have a famous hook and not much else, but this one has hooks and catchphrases going all the way through it. It is total magic."

Barry Holley (111): "Like most early fans, 'That'll be the Day' was my road to Damascus moment. It had everything—that ringing guitar sound, a bluesy swing, a strange intriguing lead vocal and a clarity which made it possible to hear and enjoy every element, even on a basic single speaker record player."

Frank Allen (112): "To be a star, you obviously need a desirable amount of talent, but the most important factor is individuality—and Buddy was distinctive and unmistakeable, both visually and aurally. While we were skiffling away, trying to find a fourth chord, Buddy was giving us the opening bars of 'That'll Be The Day' with unbelievable expertise and on an instrument that was the equivalent of a bullet-finned '59 Cadillac. He might have looked gangly and geekish with those glasses but that guitar made him unbelievably cool, and he knew how to play it. It was the revenge of the nerd. His records are almost without exception terrific. He got everything right."

It is possible that "That'll Be The Day" had been partly inspired by listening to blues guitarists.

Raphael Callaghan (113): "Lonnie Johnson played acoustic guitar and used a pick or a plectrum. Even on his 50s recordings for King where his guitar sound was amplified, I would guess it is still his acoustic guitar with a cheap pick-up rather than an electric instrument. He played fluid, clean lines in his solos with the strings ringing out clearly. That sums up Buddy on 'That'll Be The Day' too and his Fender Strat was much closer to an acoustic sound than the Telecaster or the Gibson Les Paul."

Is there any specific track that could have inspired "That'll Be The Day"? **Raphael Callaghan (114)**: "The rhythm guitar pattern on 'That'll Be The Day' duplicates the guitar shuffle rhythm pioneered by Johnny Temple on 'Lead Pencil Blues' in 1935, and lifted wholesale by Robert Johnson a year or two later for 'Sweet Home Chicago' and 'When You Got A Good Friend'. The style formed the backbone for many recordings by Jimmy Reed in the 50s and 60s. Put Lonnie Johnson and Jimmy Reed together and it is not hard to see how 'That'll Be The Day' ended up as it did."

Joe Benson Mauldin Jr was born in Lubbock on 8 July 1940, the son of Joe Benson and Winta Dean Mauldin. His parents moved to Dallas but they divorced when he was four, and he returned to Lubbock with his mother, where he went to Lubbock Junior High. He learnt a little piano, trumpet and steel guitar and his mother hoped he would be interested in classical music.

On 27 November 1953, Butch Jones, who was 14, and Joe B., then 13, were riding illegally on a motor scooter and taking records to play at a friend's house. They were driving alongside a car driven by Mauldin's friend, 14-year-old Mike Boydston, and they cut across him to turn left and crashed. The newspaper reported that Mauldin was "dangerously close to death" at Lubbock Memorial Hospital, something that newspapers don't say today, and he did recover. Boydston was driving with his dad's permission and although his father received a ticket for permitting an unlicensed driver to use his car, he was not penalised further.

Joe B. had seen Buddy and Bob, and his sister had had a request on their radio show. Joe B. saw Elvis on stage but was particularly impressed by Bill Black's double-bass. His friend, Terry Noland Church, had one in his house, and Joe B. said, "Show me how to play it." They formed a group, the Four Teens, with Larry Welborn (playing lead guitar) and Brownie Higgs. Joe B. had no ambitions of becoming professional and thought he might spend his life selling shoes.

Because Buddy was short of a bass player one evening, he asked Joe to play at the Elks Club in Carlsbad, New Mexico. It was a youth centre with a boxing arena and they removed the ropes for live performances. The booking on Saturday 2 March 1957 marked the first stage appearance of the Crickets and they were paid $65. Buddy realised that he, Jerry, Joe B. and Niki worked as a team and he invited Joe to become a Cricket that very night.

Joe B. was still with the Four Teens but the group was a democracy in which each member took turns to be the leader for a month. It was Joe's turn, so, with typical dry humour, he fired the others. Joe B. turned out to be solid and reliable, just right for the Crickets, and Norman Petty considered him window-dressing for the girls:

short and sexy! Joe B. was a happy guy and easy to get along with, whereas Petty had had trouble with Don Guess who had dared to smoke in his studio.

Don Guess, incidentally, was busy dating Wanda Jackson. He later gave up the business to sell insurance in Roswell. You can buy policies which pay out if you are abducted by aliens and Roswell is as good a place as any to start selling.

Gary Murphy (115): "Joe Mauldin was to make their sound distinctive and Bill Haley had the same effect with a double bass. Both Buddy Holly and Bill Haley knew it was more rhythmic than the electric bass and the players used to pull on the strings. They weren't miking up the bass drum then, and the bass added to the rhythmic sound of the bass drum."

Terry Noland Church had been born in Abilene but had moved to Lubbock when he was three. He went to the Tabernacle Baptist Church like Buddy. Terry had seen Buddy and Bob play, and he invited Larry Welborn to be part of the Four Teens. They went on the *Big D Jamboree* and cut "That Ain't Right" in Dallas. Once, the headmaster of Terry's school told him that his father was on the phone, but it was Buddy wanting to borrow his double-bass for a Nashville session. In 1957 and as Terry Noland, he made the solo record, "Hypnotised" with Norman Petty, and credited to Noland/ Petty. It wasn't a hit but it was given a doo-wop treatment by the Drifters on one of their B-sides. In May 1957, Terry had billing above the Crickets at the Village Theatre in Lubbock. He never fulfilled his potential but you'll never get far with titles like "There's A Fungus Among Us".

Because of their commitments, the Tolletts were not always available to record with the Crickets, and Norman Petty recommended the Picks. Billy Duane Pickering was born in East Texas on 5 April 1927 and he sang with his brother, John, in a family group from 1938 onwards. He knew Norman Petty in high school and working as a DJ at KLLL, he met Buddy when he came in to promote "Blue Days—Black Nights" and shortly afterwards, he moved to KICA in Clovis and also worked for Norman Petty. He was a good ol' boy who liked to drink and fight, but he got on well with the more refined Petty. His trio of session singers was called the Picks and featured Bill singing high, his brother John lead, and a friend, Bob Lapham baritone.

Ella Holley has suggested the title, "Maybe Baby" to Buddy, but it is not that unusual for parents to be involved in rock'n'roll songwriting. Freddy Cannon's "Tallahassee Lassie" was inspired by his mother, while Murray the K's mother suggested "Splish Splash" to Bobby Darin. Later on George Harrison's mum helped out with "Piggies", while Graham Gouldman's dad suggested the title and storyline for Herman's Hermits' hit, "No Milk Today".

Ellis Amburn (116): "Buddy's mother was always writing songs, but Buddy found her lyrics too sweet. She came up with "Maybe Baby" and he worked on it, turning it into what many consider his best song .She refused any credit as her fundamentalist Christian background made her look on rock'n'roll as the devil's music, although she made an exception for Buddy."

On 12 March 1957, the Crickets as a foursome returned to Clovis. "Maybe Baby" with its cha-cha beat and mumbling background vocals from the Picks wasn't right and even sounded weird when one of the vocalists rambled off in a silly voice. The whole effect is like a feeble version of the doo-wop group, the Diamonds. This song had immense potential but Holly knew it was back to the drawing board. The basic track for another Holly song, "Words Of Love", was put down, which was derivative of Mickey and Sylvia's "Love Is Strange". They had intended to cut it in a single take, but Niki had difficulty with his part, and Buddy realised it would be better to double-track something later. The third track, "Last Night", with the unlikely credit of Joe Mauldin and Norman Petty, was a sparse demo until the Picks' backing voices were added.

Joe Mauldin (117): "Buddy was very impressed by Mickey and Sylvia's 'Love Is Strange', and he worked out 'Words Of Love' from that. He knew what he wanted to do on the guitar before we recorded it. He told Norman that we were going to overdub it, and it worked perfectly."

The country star, Billy Walker was also recording that evening—he did "On My Mind Again" and "Viva La Matador" for Columbia Records—and Jerry Allison created some of the crowd noises for "Viva La Matador". Sometimes you

get an insight into someone without trying: some years back I was at Southport Theatre to interview Billy Walker, and he had been at Blackpool the night before. In both instances, one of the support acts was a 13-year-old local girl singing country. When I went in Billy's dressing room, he was lecturing her: "Okay, you did well last night, but you should not have sung another song. Only the star of the show sings encores." Insecure, me? When he said to me, "Have you come for the interview?", I was tempted to say, "No, I've come to talk to the little girl, oh, and by the way, is that a hairpiece?"

On 18 March 1957, Decca in New York assigned master numbers to "That'll Be The Day" and "I'm Lookin' For Someone To Love", intending to release the single on Brunswick. The next day the Crickets signed an agreement with Bob Thiele to purchase the masters. The contract did not mention Buddy Holly by name and was sent to Jerry Allison in Lubbock. Almost certainly, this was subterfuge by Norman Petty as Thiele might have been talking to Paul Cohen and discovered that Holly had already recorded the song for Decca.

On 20 March, Jimmy Bowen recorded "Last Night" in New York, but it lacked the personality of Buddy Holly's version. Bowen also wrote "I'm Keeping You" with Allison while they were on tour. It was recorded in Clovis in Feburary 1958 and when it was released the composing credit was Allison/ Petty.

An indication of Bob Thiele's confidence in the Crickets is that he wanted them to record one of his songs. Thiele often submitted songs to his artists under the pseudonym of Stanley Clayton so that his bosses would not find out. (Everybody, it seems, was in on the act!) He had been taken with Johnny Burnette's version of the Delmore Brothers' "Blues Stay Away From Me" and wrote the similar "Mailman, Bring Me No More Blues". It had already been cut by Herb Jeffries and he had another Coral artist, Don Cornell, lined up, but why not give it to the Crickets? The Crickets thought it was a decent song and Buddy, Jerry and Joe B. recorded it with Vi Petty on piano in Clovis on 8 April 1957. The result is a fine, white blues, well up to those recorded by Elvis Presley.

On the same day, Buddy had his first stab at overdubbing by adding another guitar part and vocal to "Words Of Love". For his harmony vocal, Holly was impersonating a female, and the finished result was magnificent, one of his greatest and most distinctive recordings. Bob Thiele agreed to release a single of "Words Of Love" and "Mailman, Bring Me No More Blues" (surprise, surprise) under Buddy's name on Coral. Buddy must have been feeling pleased with himself as he put a payment down on his first Cadillac.

While waiting for the releases of "That'll Be The Day" (Crickets) and "Words Of Love" (Holly), the Crickets kept busy with local bookings and sessions for Norman Petty.

On 28 April 1957, Jim Robinson cut "A Whole Lot Of Lovin'" and "It's A Wonderful Feeling", and Jack Huddle did "Starlight" and "Believe Me", with Buddy Holly playing lead on all four numbers.

Jim Robinson was from Littlefield. Jim's father was in the original Stamps Quartet and his cousin was the country singer, Johnny Horton. He was at the Clovis studio when the Crickets cut "That'll Be The Day", and both Huddle and Robinson recorded for one of Petty's labels, Petsey. He wrote with Jack Huddle, who was good with titles, one of them being "She Broke My Heart So I Broke Her Jaw".

"A Whole Lot Of Lovin'" is songwriting by numbers: it mimics Tommy Collins's "You Better Not Do That" and the song's much repeated phrase, "If you want to get along with me", comes from "Money Honey". Jerry Allison plays a cardboard box on "A Whole Lot Of Lovin'" and drums on "It's A Wonderful Feeling". "It's A Wonderful Feeling" may be a nothing of a song but the recording is enlivened by Vi Petty's piano which could have strayed from a classical recording session next door.

Jack Huddle presented a live TV show for children in Lubbock. He asked one child what his father did, and the kid replied that he was in Korea. Jack said, "And I guess you get to sleep with Mummy every night" and the child said, "Every night except Friday 'cause that's when Uncle John comes round to sleep with her."

"Starlight" is based on the nursery rhyme, "Starlight Starbright" and is a cheerful rockabilly number with an excellent guitar break from Buddy Holly; indeed, one of his best. "Believe Me" is cocktail lounge pop that Buddy suddenly shifts into rock'n'roll.

Hal Goodson was at Texas Tech in Lubbock and he formed Hal Goodson and the Raiders, who appeared on *Louisiana Hayride*. When they recorded four songs in Clovis on 2 May 1957, they asked Jerry Allison to sit in. "Later Baby" and "Who's Gonna Be The Next One, Honey" were released on Solo Records within three weeks, the first record to be issued featuring Jerry on drums. The other cuts were "Why" and "I Always Want To", the latter featuring Jerry Allison on cardboard box.

In June 1957, Fred Crawford recorded "By The Mission Wall" in Clovis. Buddy played lead guitar, George Atwood played bass, Jerry Allison played drums and the Bowman Brothers supplied the backing vocals. It's a typical western record but with a Crickets' backbeat. Later in the month, Jim Robinson recorded "A Man From Texas" at Clovis, again with Holly on guitar. The song, a marriage proposal, has a silly lyric based on the phrase, "You can always tell a man from Texas, But by golly, you can't tell him very much."

The Crickets' friend, Snuff Garrett, had an advance copy of "That'll Be The Day" and he played it on air before anyone else. The Brunswick single of "That'll Be The Day"/ "I'm Lookin' For Someone To Love", was released on 27 May 1957. Brunswick's full page ad in the industry paper, *Billboard*, is mostly taken up by the Lennon Sisters. The reviewer said, "Fine vocal by the group on a well-made side that should get play. Tune is a medium beat rockabilly. Performance is better than material."

On 29 May 1957, the Crickets were again in Clovis. Jerry Allison was banging that cardboard box on "Not Fade Away" and slapping his knees on "Everyday". Vi Petty played celeste on "Everyday". Instead of showing Buddy Holly as the writer, he was listed under his middle name "Hardin", and Norman Petty's name was added to both songs.

Jerry Allison (118): "We tried to get different sounds from the regular kit—we didn't have congas or any exotic percussion instruments. I had a basic set of Premier drums, one mounted tom-tom, a snare drum and a bass drum, one crash cymbal and one rise cymbal. I played the snare drum for the tom-tom sound on 'Peggy Sue' but a cardboard box sounded good on 'Not Fade Away', 'Baby I Don't Care' and a couple of other things. On 'Everyday', I patted my knees. Buddy was playing guitar and I was keeping the rhythm, so we recorded it like that. Never set a finger on the drums on that record, never moved. Being lazy, I guess."

Bruce Welch (119): "I love the percussion on 'Not Fade Away'. It was a dead sound but it was very unusual and Hank Marvin, Tony Meehan and I tried to work out what Jerry Allison was doing. It was only when I spoke to him that I found out that he had been banging a Jim Beam box. He might have consumed the contents first!"

Mike Brocken (120): "If anybody was hearing Buddy Holly's work for the first time and didn't know where he was from, they could make a pretty educated guess. It is very regional but its appeal is universal. The traditions that people like Buddy Holly are immersed in over the second half of the twentieth century are very important to them and they came out in their music, not just in their accents but in their styles: for example, The way he can play lead and rhythm at the same time is all to do with where he's from and the time he grew up in. The Crickets used drums with that really bassy dull thud. That cardboard box was a dull thud—you can also hear it on Buddy Knox's 'Party Doll'—and the lack of acoustic reverb makes an impact on you. You wonder at first how they got that sound and then you find it is a cardboard box, a very simple idea which is very effective."

Jerry Allison (121): "Buddy and I also wrote 'Not Fade Away' and again my name isn't on it. That verse about my love being bigger than a Cadillac is mine. The rhythm came from 'Hambone' and we'd heard that long before 'Bo Diddley'. We cut our version as a little three-piece and the Rolling Stones had a much fuller sound. They made a great record."

Bo Diddley (122): "I thought the Rolling Stones had ripped me off when I heard 'Not Fade Away' because the song was just like one of mine. I didn't find out until sometime later that it was a Buddy Holly song. He was the one responsible. I wish I'd heard his version while he was alive. I'd have told that dude something."

Sleepy LaBeef (123): "'Bo Diddley' was simply 'Hambone' with the old fiddle ending of shave-and-a-haircut-two-bits. You keep repeating that fast and you have the Bo Diddley beat. It was being performed long before Bo Diddley was born, but he kept that beat going and deserves the credit for that. A few of us—Buddy Holly with 'Not Fade Away', Johnny Otis with 'Willie And The Hand Jive' and myself with 'Ride On Josephine'—have cut that beat. Most people would call it a Bo Diddley beat but they don't know its origin."

Frank Allen (124): "Musically, Buddy and Jerry Allison were a wonderful partnership, but we mustn't overlook Joe B. on stand-up bass. He played simple figures which kept things solid and never got in the way of the song. His simplicity had something splendid about it."

The singer/ songwriter **John Stewart (125)** said in 2000: "Was there ever anything more exciting than watching rock'n'roll being born? I had a rock'n'roll band myself and I had the car radio on and I was driving fast with the top down. Everything looks brighter looking back, but it was a fun time and it did give birth to that extraordinary music. I loved the writers like Buddy Holly, Fats Domino, Boudleaux and Felice Bryant, and Jerry Leiber and Mike Stoller. It doesn't get any better than 'That'll Be The Day' or 'Peggy Sue'. (Sings) 'Everyday, it's a-getting closer, Goin' faster than a rollercoaster'—they're all classics, you know. The music had roots then. Rock'n'roll came from country and western and gospel and blues, but the roots of today's artists are acts like Tears For Fears. They don't have the connection to the past that we were lucky enough to have."

Bobby Vee (126): "Some people think that rock'n'roll songs are so simple that they are childish, but they capture the spirit of the day. Chuck Berry and Little Richard did it very well and I still am a huge Buddy Holly fan. In his young career, he captured the essence of rock'n'roll, which was, 'Don't think about it, just do it, let's rock.' Eddie Cochran did that with 'Summertime Blues' and 'C'mon Everybody' and also Gene Vincent in the early part of his career. That is the beauty of 50s rock'n'roll—all you have to do is listen to it. The generations that followed learnt a lot from what they did."

Bruce Welch (127): "Hank Marvin and I were friends from when we were 11 and we started writing when we were 16. Our influence was Buddy Holly as he was about the only pop star who wrote his own songs. Elvis didn't and Bill Haley didn't. Lonnie had his name on everything, but that's another story. We weren't writing instrumentals then and we wanted to write like Buddy Holly. He got lovely melodies out of simple chords and that appealed to me as I knew I wasn't a great player."

Phillip Goodhand-Tait (128): "I'd been a Buddy Holly fan at school. An older boy would bring in those Coral EPs and I loved them all. I spent hours taking down the lyrics, so instead of studying for GCEs I was analysing Buddy's lyrics. I knew all the songs and I found the attraction was in their simplicity: three or four chords but maybe one minor thrown in, as if he'd just discovered a new chord. Words were simple too, aimed directly (I thought) at my age group. 'What To Do', 'Maybe Baby', 'Well…All Right'. I saw celebration (when adolescent love was reciprocated) and I felt blues (when it wasn't). In the latter category was my favourite, 'Everyday'. I felt that although Buddy's delivery was upbeat, the words seemed to me to be about a love that was yet to be consummated, albeit 'getting closer'. That's why a straight backbeat wouldn't work, and so he had the continuous rhythm beating out, just someone slapping his thighs, and that wonderful celeste sounding like Christmas. There was a hint of sadness in the arrangement and when I got my opportunity to record it, I thought about Buddy's death. I felt 'Everyday' was a white man's blues, so that's the way I sang it. It has the simplest of lyrics and yet a simple lyric that says everything can be the hardest to write."

Dominic Pedler (129): "Amongst Buddy Holly's finest musical moments is the bridge to 'Everyday' which showcases his understanding of a classically derived, five-chord cycle which unfolds so irresistibly towards the song's musical and lyrical climax ('Do you ever long for true love from me?'). I don't know whether Holly had ever heard Marlene Dietrich's 'Falling In Love Again' but he manages a brilliant take on that concept

in that bridge, descending in inevitable fifths but creating a clever effect that ends on that hanging imperfect cadence rather than a settled resolution on the tonic note as in the vast majority of cycles of fifths: for example in 'Falling In Love Again', 'Can't help it' takes us to a feeling of closure."

Julian Lloyd Webber (130): "Andrew had been going to write something for me for some time and in the end we had a bet on the outcome of an Orient game. He was fed up with them and he bet me that they couldn't even get a draw in their last game, at home to Hull. I bet they would, and they did. He then had to write *Variations* for me. Very few people have picked up that the final variation was intended to sound like 'Peggy Sue' with Jerry Allison's drumming. You'll also find a Hank Marvin tribute amongst those *Variations*."

On being told the above, **Jerry Allison (131)** said: "You've really surprised me. That's really a compliment. I live in the sticks and it's only country music where I live. I've got a farm and I've got to feed the cows and bale hay and try to break even, so I haven't time to listen to anything else. I haven't bought any albums for a long time but I'll have to get that one."

The Canadian vocal group, the Diamonds, who had won a gold disc with "Little Darlin'", released a cover version of "Words Of Love", although it appeared in the shops and on the charts before Buddy's record came out. This was the first time that Buddy's name had appeared in the US Best Sellers, albeit as a writer and, was it an oversight, Petty hadn't put his name to the song. *Billboard* said of Holly's own version, "Soft low-toned dual-track vocal with sharp bright guitar backing on a Latin-type theme. Good clear sound. Side can do business." It didn't.

When Buddy's father was working for the Texas Roofing Company at Wichita Falls, Ella wrote to him. She was listening for radio plays, and when she saw the Diamonds singing "Words Of Love" on *The Vic Damone Show,* she was impressed. Although pleased to have something on the chart, Holly thought that the Diamonds had ruined the intimate nature of the song.

When Buddy did some tiling for Larry at a hospital, he told him that no one was recognising his ability. They returned home and Larry told him to call New York where he heard that "That'll Be The Day" was starting to sell.

Given the choice, Buddy Holly would have been recording in Clovis 24/7, and between May and June 1957, the Crickets had some productive sessions. The first session found the Crickets recording Little Richard's "Ready Teddy" (with Vi on piano) and Fats Domino's "Valley Of Tears" as well as a new Buddy and Jerry original, "Tell Me How", attributed to Hardin/ Allison/ Petty on release, and with Vi on piano and Norman on organ. It contains one of Holly's most playful vocals and *Billboard* was to describe it as "a rock-a-calypso". "Valley Of Tears" was to be issued as a single in Canada but not the US.

Trevor Cajiao (132): "Holly's 'Ready Teddy' is the most raucous thing he ever cut in a 'proper' studio: the so-called 'garage' recordings are a different thing all together—just kids having a blast for the sheer fun of it. It doesn't quite match the Little Richard original, but then what could?"

Peter Sarstedt (133): "One of my favourite Buddy Holly tracks is 'Ready Teddy' and it was one of the first songs I learned. It didn't matter that he wasn't good looking because his worthiness shone through!"

On 14 June 1957, Buddy Knox and the Rhythm Orchids played the Evelyn Theatre in Dumas, Texas. They were supported by the Crickets and by Gary and Ramona Tollett, who in turn were backed by the Crickets. Everybody did enormously well and Holly came off dripping with sweat as he had given so much. The following day they also played another show in the area, but Jerry had too much to drink before the performance, leading to the Crickets' most shambolic gig.

Generally, travelling did not bother the Crickets. If they were driving long into the night on straight roads, the driver would take No-Doz, which was sold over the counter at chemists. This was the truckdrivers' favourite.

With dust storms and temperatures over 100 degrees, the best place was to be in Norman Petty's studio at the end of June 1957. Especially as rock'n'roll history was being made.

Buddy's sister, Pat, now Patricia Weir, had given birth to a daughter, Cindy, on 22 May 1957. Taking the baby's name and Patricia's middle name, Lou, Buddy wrote "Cindy Lou". At first the Crickets were going to record "Cindy Lou" with a Latin beat. After some unsatisfactory attempts, Buddy asked Jerry to beef up his percussion by playing double paradiddles on the snare drum. In turn, Jerry asked that the song be renamed "Peggy Sue" for the girl he wanted to impress. This was no great difficulty as the song didn't tell the listener much about either Cindy Lou or Peggy Sue, for that matter.

Peggy Sue Gerron (134): "It is not unusual in the South to have two Christian names and I've been called Peggy Sue all my life. I went to school with Jerry—he was 9th Grade and I was 7th. We both played in the school band—me on alto sax and him on drums. By the time I followed him to high school—he and Buddy were good friends. I first met Buddy when he knocked me over carrying his guitar and amp into assembly. We later started double dating, me and Jerry, and Buddy and Maria. Buddy was a little older than us and was graduating the year I started high school."

Jerry Allison (135): "Peggy Sue was my first ex-wife. She was my high school sweetheart and we got married in 1958. We put "Peggy Sue" out under Buddy's name as Norman said we could put out two records at the same time by crediting one to the Crickets and the other to Buddy Holly. The idea was that the Crickets' records should have overdubbed, background voices and Buddy Holly's should feature the single voice. That lasted six months because we recorded 'Rave On' in New York and we had some guys come in and sing background vocals. Otherwise, there wasn't any difference. We played on all the records, apart from the string sessions in New York. We were there but they wouldn't let us play, which made me mad."

Peggy Sue Gerron (136): "Buddy had written a song called 'Cindy Lou'—it had a calypso beat and they were trying to record it at Norman Petty's studio. It wouldn't come together and he started to re-write it. Jerry asked him to put Peggy Sue on it and that's how it evolved. Norman Petty wrote the bridge and I don't know who thought of the tom-toms. Jerry sat out in the lobby and you can hear the drums rolling in and out of the echo chamber."

Jerry's drumming was so loud that it had leaked into other microphones, so Petty placed the drums in the reception area. From there, he ran the microphone wires through the echo chamber and got the in-and-out echo effect by manually raising and lowering the volume and amount of echo in time with the music. This gave the record a unique sound. But it wasn't all plain sailing: at one point, Buddy told Jerry, "If it's not right this time, I'm changing the title back to 'Cindy Lou'." His drumming is marvellous, propelling the song along in the same way that Al Jackson pushed Otis Redding to a remarkable performance with "Respect".

Jerry Allison (137): "I wasn't trying to be inventive when I did the paradiddles on the toms. I just wanted something that would fit the tune and make it sound good."

Jerry Allison acknowledges that his drumming on "Peggy Sue" was inspired by a Jaye P. Morgan B-side, "Dawn". Jerry used that as his template but he put more energy into it. It was the biggest drum sound in rock'n'roll history and although Buddy was singing about his best friend's girl, it's his best friend who wanted to be heard and to play the final sound as well.

Dominic Pedler (138): "Musos still talk of the 'Peggy Sue' chord—not a guitar shape, as such, but the distinctively dark, left-field harmony that lends such a knowing, evocative backdrop to the 'pretty, pretty, pretty' chant of that song's legendary bridge."

Gary Murphy (139): "On 'Peggy Sue', Buddy Holly's voice and guitar are usually quite dry, a clean sound, but the drums on 'Peggy Sue' are very reverberated. Sometimes Jerry Allison had reverb on the floor tom and then he doesn't have it on. Then he has it on another drum and then he doesn't have it on. It's brilliantly done."

Jerry Allison (140): "Norman Petty was an excellent engineer with a good studio and good equipment. I just played one drum on 'Peggy Sue' and Norman Petty switched it back and forth out of the echo chamber. He raised the volume and dropped it back. Even on CD, it still holds up."

Bobby Vee (141): "Anyone who has ever played rock'n'roll drums has been influenced by Jerry Allison. He is an incredible stylist and very innovative, and he still plays great. There were no rules

then so he could do what he liked, like slapping his knees on 'Everyday' or playing a cardboard box on 'Not Fade Away'. He has great wrists—he plays lead drums really."

Buddy had a problem playing "Peggy Sue" as he couldn't get his hand to the guitar switch for the break without missing a beat. Niki Sullivan knelt by Buddy and he switched the guitar for Buddy, something akin to Chris Barber's role on his million-selling "Petite Fleur". Buddy soon figured out to do it himself and so he could play "Peggy Sue" on *The Ed Sullivan Show*, for example.

Bruce Welch (142): "Buddy plays the bass pickup for most the song and then it's switched to the treble and then back again for verse. If you listen to the record on cans, you can hear Niki Sullivan turn the switch. It wouldn't have been any problem for Buddy to do it himself. He must have done it himself in concert: it would be that fraction of a second delay but you wouldn't notice it."

Neville Marten (143): "Buddy Holly was not a great guitarist in technical terms, but he was marvellous at evoking a feeling or excitement in his songs. The solo in 'Peggy Sue' is just brilliant chords: it shouted at you to buy a guitar."

Sonny Curtis (144): "On 'Peggy Sue', Buddy's playing is both hard and soft at the same time, which is just like his singing. He could sing real hard and then he could change his voice like he was talking to a baby in a pram. It's real colourful. On the instrumental for 'Peggy Sue', Niki Sullivan was standing in front of Buddy and he switched the toggle switch at the time the instrumental came and that's why the guitar jumps out at you. He switches it back when Buddy starts to sing again."

When you think about it, isn't "Pretty, pretty, pretty. pretty Peggy Sue" like talking to a baby in a pram? Originally, Buddy must have had "Pretty, pretty, pretty, pretty Cindy Lou" and the change of name fitted so easily and added alliteration.

Bruce Welch (145): "Buddy Holly didn't sound like anybody else and I loved that jerky, hiccupping style of his. He also played a Fender Strat and we had seen nothing like it before. The introduction to 'That'll Be the Day' always excites me and I loved his playing on 'Peggy Sue' and 'Oh Boy!' and 'Maybe Baby'."

Bert Weedon (146): "Buddy Holly was one of the first to use a Fender Stratocaster. Before that, guitars were hollow and this was the first solid body guitar. It had a particular sound all of its own and while Buddy Holly wasn't a brilliant player, he was certainly a good one and he could get a lot out of his instrument. Thousands of boys and girls started to play the guitar because of him."

Gary Murphy (147): "I liked the way he used bar chords. He wrote around three major chords really, and he would go to a minor occasionally when he wanted to change the mood. If you are a guitarist, you generally put down a major chord as a happy chord: if it was a D chord, you would play D major and it would sound happy, but a minor chord would make the music sound sad. Buddy Holly would change the mood of the song with the chords. He was one of the first to match the lyrics to the music. I loved his rhythm style of playing, he didn't really play lead guitar as such, he played a lot of rhythm with lead incorporated and so he was filling out the sound on his one guitar. When he was playing the lead solo in 'Peggy Sue', he was playing an A major to D, and there was no lead getting played, and it was the way he structured his rhythm playing with his right hand and he was an innovator of that. He made rhythm guitar sound so full but it was a lead solo. 'That'll Be The Day' was different because it was single notes as opposed to chords. The 'Peggy Sue' solo was all chords. He was an innovator of the guitar."

Tim Whitnall (148): "There are fantastic remasterings of Buddy Holly's work on the El Toro label and there are alternate takes of the classics as I've never heard them before. There's another version of 'Peggy Sue' and you can hear him playing down: most guitarists take a plectrum and play it down and then up. That's a 'chunka, chunka, chunka' sound but most of Buddy's playing is 'chunk, chunk, chunk'. Combine that with Jerry Allison's drumming which is going really fast, and you've got something really great. Of course, the master of 'Peggy Sue' is the best because the balance is so perfect. The way that they roll the reverb on the tom-toms and keep turning it on and off so that it sounds like you're in outer space is wonderful. I love Buddy Holly's voice: it is a really beautiful voice and there is very little of his hiccupping on that early take of 'Peggy Sue'. There's loads of it on the master version and I wonder if Petty heard it and thought, 'That's the hook, that's the trademark.' The whole treatment on the demo is much softer too."

Holly's vocal is as colourful as it is playful. The way he lowers his voice at the end is really inventive. The downstroke on his guitar playing comes from Bo Diddley and was also used by the Everly Brothers.

Justin Hayward (149) of the Moody Blues: "I met Maria Elena in the 70s: she came to a few of our gigs and I was always thrilled to be in her company. She told me that the most striking thing about his guitar-playing was the way he played the down strokes with his right hand—the sheer speed of his rhythm. You can see it on those few precious bits of film. His guitar always carried the groove and the feel of the songs, and it was through him that I came to realise what makes music truly swing."

Anton Barbeau (150): "Buddy Holly is one of my heroes. He was the first singer/songwriter and everything about him was great: a great guitar player, a great guy and great spectacles. He had a great image. Look at 'Peggy Sue'. He had discovered that all you had to do was go 'oh-ho-oh' with the right spirit and it would work: it said as much as you needed to say, but there's still a real depth of feeling in his work."

Being born in Holly Springs did give Charlie Feathers a start in the soundalike stakes, although he claimed, with little justification, that he was there first. **Charlie Feathers (151)** features the hiccup in overdrive: "I've been singing rockabilly most of my life. Buddy Holly would listen to me. He tried to get on Sun and then he went to Clovis, New Mexico and did 'Peggy Sue'. A lot of people say we sound alike. He used to listen to me do the hiccup, so who copied who?" Charlie, what about Elvis Presley's "Baby Lets Play House" (1955) and Gene Vincent's "Woman Love" (1956) and "Lotta Lovin'" (1957)?

Although they are great fun, Charlie Feathers' records have been too eccentric and erratic for mainstream acceptance. For example, he overdoes the stuttering, hiccupping delivery so that he sounds like Buddy Holly on speed. "Uh Huh

Honey" is an outlandish example from 1967, though the song is as light as Feathers. If Buddy Holly had recorded this, he would have been having fun: Feathers is deadly serious.

Then there is the lyric, which doesn't tell you very much about Peggy Sue. **Tim Rice (152)**: "Well, in 1957, few pop songs dug deep into emotional psychology and records were only two minutes long! However, the other aspects of the record, notably the different vocal timbres and gimmicks that Buddy adopted, that are almost comic at one point, were considered more important features to convey her character. Peggy Sue comes over as quirky and slightly unattainable, plus we discover that she is pretty. The singer is overwhelmed and reduced to showing off."

Paul Evans (153): "Maybe the rock'n'roll songs are less sophisticated than the later Brill Buildings ones, but rock'n'roll was always fun music to me, and 'Peggy Sue' was lots of fun. When I sang around New York with my rockabilly band, I would sing 'Peggy Sue', 'That'll Be The Day' and 'Oh Boy!' and the audiences would always sing along with me. That was one of the major reasons for Buddy's popularity."

Joe McGann (154): "I love the way that 'Peggy Sue' rolls: it is classic rock'n'roll. You can't stop your feet tapping when you hear it, an absolutely brilliant song. This is the essence of rock'n'roll, it was like the forerunner of punk, three chord tricks but delivered with maximum energy. People forget what a great singer he was and what great melodies he wrote. He was also a great balladeer. It is the energy of the white boy taking the black music and adding the element of western swing, BobWills stuff, and making this fantastic sound. Buddy Holly and Little Richard kicked rock'n'roll up the stairs and made it the big, big force that it was.

Andrew Doble (155): "You can't help tapping your feet, the table or a cardboard box when you hear them, the rhythm is fantastic. It was inspirational to people wanting to make their own music. If that bloke who wears glasses who doesn't look like a film star can do it, we can do it. He encouraged so many people. Maybe the songs are not as simple as they seem, but they have that wonderful simplicity."

Mike Brocken (156): "I think his lyrics are really good. Simplicity doesn't mean idiocy and you have to make sure that you don't confuse lyrics with poetry either. Buddy Holly is a very good lyric writer, he is a very spartan writer and he fully appreciates how a word works over a beat or a riff, so you get all of those great open vowel sounds from Buddy Holly over a particular chord progression which will blow you away. The use of words on rock'n'roll records is not examined in the right way: Holly's economical use of words is very interesting and the riffs are great."

Peter Carlin (157): "Buddy Holly was a huge influence on the songwriters who came after him. John and Paul for starters: they wrote songs because of him. He could make things sound simple and conversational even though there are some complex musical stuff and ideas going on inside there. That is the trick of any pop songwriter: making something simple that is not simple at all."

Robb Johnson (158): "As a kid, we got force-fed Andrew Marvell's *To His Coy Mistress* and we were all adamant that he couldn't have written such a brilliant poem unless he had a coy mistress and we refused to accept the English teacher going, 'No, it might just be an intellectual exercise.' Isn't art all about taking something that's real and then making it convincingly beyond the reality of the experience? That's what 'Peggy Sue' does and, when you do that, it's art."

In a feature on 'Top Teen Tunes' in *Washington Sunday Star*, Bob Thiele remarked, "The whole construction of 'Peggy Sue' is odd. It's a 76-bar song for one thing. The average tune is 32 bars. No one in his right mind would do it."

Gary Osborne (159): "'Peggy Sue' is the most basic and simple of love songs and when 'basic and simple' works, it REALLY works. The treatment is also beautifully stripped down. It sounds like three guys driving along the highway in a big old American car with the driver singing and his mate in the passenger's seat playing guitar while the drummer sits behind them, keeping time on the back of the driver's seat. A classic!"

Andy Wilkinson (160): "'Peggy Sue' works so well exactly because it doesn't tell us a thing about her, it shows us instead. So instead of being preached to, when the song's over we feel about

Peggy Sue the same way that the singer does. That's the best kind of writing."

Bob Stanley (161): "I love Buddy Holly and the Everly Brothers because they had such brilliant melodies. 'Peggy Sue' is an incredible production as it is so minimal, and it is a real art form to make a record that is so catchy and has such longevity and yet the lyrics barely exist. It's as though he is keeping her attractiveness a secret. If you keep an air of mystery in a song or a public persona, it is going to make things a lot more interesting."

As if one rock'n'roll classic wasn't enough: as well as recording "Peggy Sue" in Clovis, they cut "Listen To Me" and "Oh Boy!" on the same visit.

Sonny West worked for a Ford dealership in Levelland and he met Bill Tilghman at a garage. They formed a songwriting partnership and although both names are on "Oh Boy!", it was written by Sonny alone. Oh, there's a third name as well and yes, you've guessed it, Norman Petty. **Sonny West (162)**: "I knew I was going to have to start writing about something with a little more substance than 'Rock this' or 'Rock that' and so I came up with this little ditty using 'Oh Boy!' and I wrote the song myself and it was later on that Bill Tilghman got involved with writing with me and got his name on the song. Glen D. Hardin played the piano on my demo of 'Oh Boy!' that I made in Clovis. He was a little younger than me and a very good pianist, a natural musician. I knew if I had him I only had to have a couple of other instruments as that would fill it up. Norman made a few acetates of 'Oh Boy!'. I got about five and I sent off a couple to recording companies to see if I could get some action."

Sonny West (163) continued: "When I first wrote the song, I called it 'All My Love', which is the first three words. I was in a hurry to get it recorded and I wasn't thinking much about the title at the time. 'Oh Boy!' sounded a bit funny for a title but people said to me, 'Why don't you play "Oh Boy!"' so I changed it. 'That'll Be The Day' was starting to move for the Crickets, and Norman told me that Buddy had recorded my song and I had to come over and sign the contracts. I went to Clovis and his version made my hair stand up. It was much livelier than mine and it sounded great. Buddy was at the top of his

game. Buddy had found someone who could give him a really good sound. Buddy was happy, you can tell by listening to it."

And how come Norman got his name on there? **Sonny West (164)**: "Norman Petty gave me no choice. It was either that or not get it out. After I heard the way that Buddy's version sounded, there was no way that I could turn it down. Norman had the power and he did that to so many other guys. He took a half or a third of almost every song there plus the publishing. I wish things had been different but they're not and I can't change it."

Sonny West's record is directly addressed to the girl but Holly changes the words so that he is telling his friend about what's happening one moment and talking to his girl, the next. Buddy sings edgily and very fast on "Oh Boy!" and at the time, it was described as being like a kid who has been told he can stay up late. No, listen carefully. The song is about losing your virginity and Buddy can hardly contain his excitement. Dum-diddy-dum-dum, oh boy!

Tommy James (165): "'Oh Boy!' is the Buddy Holly record that I love the most. 'Oh Boy!' defines rock'n'roll and it jumps out of the grooves at you. I love party rock records: they usually start with drums and get everybody on the dance floor. 'Oh Boy!' was one of those records, the best actually."

John Firminger (166): "I guess my favourite Buddy Holly record is still 'Oh Boy!'. The song is ultra commercial and the combination of the arrangement and the sound really sparkles. Holly delivers his most exuberant performance ever. I love the scream as he goes into the guitar solo and the Picks' backing vocals are most effective."

Tim Riley (167): "Elvis Presley showed that accentuating your strangeness was a game that anybody could play, especially if you were the squarest looking guy in the class. Holly's success spoke for all the like-minded classmates who thrilled to Presley's songs and rebellion but found his sexual bravado out of reach."

They also recorded "Listen To Me" (this time Hardin/ Petty), a gorgeous song on which Holly double-tracked himself to sound like the Everly Brothers. Paul McCartney has said that it is his favourite Buddy Holly record.

Tony Jackson (168): "Buddy Holly was my main influence. When you're learning to play guitar and only know three chords, you generally end up playing Buddy Holly's stuff. Then you learn a minor chord, which is great, and you can do all his stuff! It wasn't that he had a limited technique, but he wrote very, very good melodies and he could get by with just four chords in his repertoire. 'Listen To Me' was one of my favourites and we recorded it in the Searchers. Mike Pender and I shared the lead vocals and I did the talking."

John Firminger (169): "I love 'Listen To Me', which is certainly a contrast from 'Oh Boy!' and recorded on the same day. Buddy demonstrates his creativity on guitar with a sound that virtually shimmers, enhanced by a very clever use of reverb and it is totally mesmerising. 'Listen To Me' also gives us the opportunity of hearing Buddy speak as he talks over the guitar solo. Fabulous!"

Bill Randle, a popular DJ at WERE in Cleveland, was playing "That'll Be The Day" and as a thank you and a promotional tool, the Crickets recorded a jingle In addition, the Crickets recorded jingles to thank Murray Deutch and Bob Thiele for their support. Those jingles, never intended for public airplay, ended with Buddy singing, "This was Norman's idea." "That'll Be The Day" was moving but not yet figuring on the national charts.

The following day they recorded another new song, then known as "Da Ching A Bop", but later as "I'm Gonna Love You Too". A critic likened Holly's singing to "sitting on a pneumatic drill." The songwriters were listed as Joe B. Mauldin, Niki Sullivan and Norman Petty. This took some time to record, partly because a cricket was trapped in the echo chamber while they were recording the song. You can hear the cricket at the end of the recording, after the Crickets.

Bobby Peeples sometimes came with the Crickets to Clovis. They would arrive about 7pm and leave around 3am. He liked hot rod racing and sometimes he and Buddy would go to the drag strip outside of Lubbock.

Several photographs of the Crickets were taken at Norman's studio, mostly by Vi or Norma Jean. They included the well-known, white T-shirt photographs. Now that success was imminent,

Norman took them to clothing stores in Lubbock and bought suits, shirts, shoes and ties. Buddy acquired a white linen suit.

On 4 July 1957, Lloyd Call recorded an instrumental track for "If I had Known" with Buddy on rhythm, Jerry drums, George bass and Vi piano. A second track, "Little Cowboy", was recorded. In June 1958, Homer Tankersley, working as Ken James (a curious reversal of the practice of choosing an outlandish stage name), and the Roses put their voices to "If I Had Known" and it was released. The Roses, who had backed Roy Orbison on some of his Sun sessions, consisted of Ray Rush, David Bigham and Robert Linville.

On 13 July 1957, the Picks were backing Ramona Locke, and Norman asked them if they could add backing vocals to "Oh Boy!" The arrangement took them less than an hour. Bill Pickering let out a rebel yell at the end of Buddy's guitar break, which was comparable to Dickie Harrell's shout in Gene Vincent's "Be-Bop-A- Lula". They overdubbed other tracks which appeared on *The Chirping Crickets* album.

The next day Norman Petty played the Crickets the new version of "Oh Boy!" and they all loved it. They backed Gary Tollett on another session for the Gone label. "Honey, Honey", written by Tollett, is typical rockabilly, influenced by Elvis Presley's "Too Much" and "All Shook Up", with Buddy rocking away on guitar. On the ballad, "Look To The Future", written by Niki Sullivan, Buddy plugged his Fender Strat into the amplifier for the Hammond organ for an unusual effect. Unfortunately, the record was turned down and Gary's career was effectively Gone.

On 15 July 1957 Carolyn Hester cut the folk tunes, "Scarlet Ribbons" and "Wreck Of The Old 97" with Buddy on acoustic and George Atwood on bass. Jerry Allison played brushes on a cardboard box for the sound of the train. Carolyn's dad, Gordon, created a train whistle on his harmonica.

Carolyn Hester (170): "I had gone to New York at 18 and my hero was Pete Seeger and I loved folk music so much. After two years, I spent the summer back home. My parents had moved from Austin to Lubbock and they found out about Norman Petty's studio in Clovis. My mother wrote him a note and said, 'Do you audition people?' He called her and said, 'Yes' and invited us over. It was in July, very hot, and we had to stop halfway at a little town called Muleshoe. You had to have a cold Dr Pepper and you reach down in this barrel of ice and grab a Dr Pepper. We got there and I sang for him and played guitar and he said, 'I don't know much about folk music, but do you think you have an album's worth?' I had about 10 songs and he told me to add a couple more and come the following weekend to record. He was confident because Buddy Holly was selling so well. I was on Coral which was part of the Decca family. I got to hang out with the Crickets and as I got a rhythmic feel from them, that's how I came to wed folk and rock."

George Atwood, who was born in Tuscaloosa, Alabama in 1920, liked jazz and played upright bass. His hip had been shattered during war service and he was one of the first recipients of an artificial hip. He played bass on many of Gene Krupa's records and worked with Benny Goodman and Harry James. After the war, he formed a band which played at the Cotton Club and was in the Lubbock Symphony Orchestra. In 1951, he had played the Surf Ballroom in Clear Lake with Gene Krupa. Buddy met George in December 1956 when George was working with Clyde Hankins, a singer/ guitarist who had shown Sonny Curtis some chords. Buddy once drove with George to Clovis and they wrote a song about the sun being like a big orange ball. It was never completed. As well as being a fine bass player, George worked at fairs as Go-Ee the Clown.

Carolyn Hester (171): "Buddy Holly was one of the few geniuses I actually knew—his love for music was overwhelming and we used to wonder, 'Is this guy ever going to relax?' He had a wonderful family and they were totally behind him."

On 20 July 1957, the Crickets recorded Little Richard's "Send Me Some Lovin'" and Chuck Willis' "It's Too Late" in Clovis. His voice soars on "It's Too Late", but the sudden change to echo is out of control. There is a much better use of echo on "Send Me Some Lovin'", and note Buddy's little cry at the end of the first verse. The backing vocals from the Picks are usually cooler than the Jordanaires, but they brought down "Send Me Some Lovin'" with some hackneyed harmonies.

Tim Whitnall (172): "Buddy was very experimental in the studio. I love 'It's Too Late' and the little trills in his voice show that he has been listening to Sam Cooke or Clyde McPhatter."

On the same day, Buddy played acoustic guitar on Norman Petty's instrumental, "Moondreams". Vi Petty's piano was surrounded by some swirling effects from Norman on organ, rather like a Joe Meek record. Some weeks later, the Picks added vocals.

On 26 July 1957, a pretty girl who performed on the *Big D Jamboree*, Sherry Davis recorded "Broken Promises" and "Humble Heart" at Clovis with Buddy Holly on lead guitar. The trouble is, if somebody can't say her r's, you shouldn't give them a song called "Broken Promises"—sorry, she wrote it so she had only herself to blame. The guitar break on "Broken Promises" doesn't sound like Holly at all, but "Humble Heart" is more in keeping.

On the same day, Buddy played guitar for Charlie Phillips, who recorded "Sugartime" and "One Faded Rose". "Sugartime" opens with an archetypal "Well". Buddy shares the instrumental break with Jimmy Blakely's steel guitar, while Norman's organ dominates "One Faded Rose". Buddy sang the chorus of "One Faded Rose" with Charlie, although you wouldn't know it was him.

Charlie had written "Sugartime" with Odis Echols. The original lyric, written while he was on his tractor, went: "Pussy in the morning, Pussy in the evening, Pussy at suppertime, Be my little pussy, And give me pussy all the time."

It reminds me of the story that "How Much Is That Doggie In The Window" was written after the songwriter saw prostitutes in shop windows.

When Bob Thiele came to visit Norman Petty, he heard "Sugartime" and took it back to New York. He gave it to the McGuire Sisters and they had a US hit record. In the UK, it was a hit for the McGuire Sisters (14), Alma Cogan (18) and Jim Dale (25).

Things were starting to happen for Buddy Holly. The Diamonds had sold half a million copies of his song, "Words Of Love", and "That'll Be The Day" had sales of 80,000 by the end of July. It had the makings of a big hit.

The Crickets agreed to a short tour with the promoter, Irving Feld, for $1,000 a week. Feld had assumed that they were the black doo-wop group, the Crickets, making a comeback and he had booked them on a black tour; indeed, the original Crickets' hit "Fine As Wine" was given on an early listing. They would play weeks in the Howard Theatre, Washington, the Royal Theatre, Baltimore and the Apollo, New York with Clyde McPhatter, the Cadillacs, Otis Rush, Edna McGriff, the Hearts, Oscar and Oscar, plus, for the dates at the Apollo, the G-Clefs, who did dance routines on hits like "Ka-Ding Dong". Norman Petty gave the Crickets written instructions for the tour, which even included "Take a small Bible with you and read it." As if. He added, "Be sure to send money back to Clovis for bank account." Naturally.

The tour started in Washington on 2 August 1957 and it was hard work as the acts had to play several times each day in a stage show between showings of a feature film. On the third day, Buddy Holly lost his voice but Niki took over without any problems. Unfortunately, Niki's new electric guitar was stolen two days later. Despite what has been written, there is no evidence that anyone threw anything specifically at the Crickets. Admittedly at the Royal, the audience would throw empty wine bottles onto the stage, but that could happen during any act, and one of the Hearts had to go to hospital for treatment. Buddy didn't care for Baltimore at all.

The Apollo Theatre had opened in 1919 as a variety theatre and it had become a key night spot for black entertainers. James Brown, who recorded the legendary *Live At The Apollo* (1962), did not make his debut there until September 1958, a year after the Crickets. There were 31 shows in the week: four shows a day at 12.30pm, 3.30pm, 6.30pm and 9.30pm and midnight shows on Wednesday, Saturday and Sunday. Because the shows started early and ended late, they stayed in a hotel across the road, although they had been advised not to stay in a black area. They had no problems at all.

This was not an audience that would be expecting a white act, but by then, the Crickets had worked out how to win them round. They started playing "Bo Diddley" before the curtains opened and got them that way. The Crickets were going to promote "That'll Be The Day" on Alan Freed's

TV show but it had been cancelled after the sponsors objected to Frankie Lymon dancing with a white girl. On 26 August 1957, the Crickets made their first national appearance for $300 on Dick Clark's *American Bandstand*.

Alan Freed had made a packet on his first Christmas show at the Brooklyn Paramount in 1956 and he had a formula for printing money. *The Alan Freed Holiday Show* was at the Paramount Theatre, Brooklyn, New York from August 30 to September 8. The bill included Little Richard, the Del Vikings, Mickey and Sylvia, the Moonglows, the Five Keys, Larry Williams, Jo Ann Campbell and the Cleftones with Alan Freed's Big Rock'n'Roll Orchestra. The Diamonds were doing "Little Darlin'" and "Zip Zip", but not "Words Of Love", and Little Richard as the headliner had five numbers. The contract specified 29 shows and the Crickets would be paid $1,000, no more than union scale. Jimmie Rodgers said that the audience screamed so much that it was impossible to sing ballads and he took a pair of Buddy's shoes home with him as he had forgotten them.

As with all rock'n'roll package shows, the Crickets were fortunate in being able to make their own music and even though there were great musicians like Sam "The Man" Taylor and King Curtis, the orchestral sound was not right for many performers. Holly was a very confident and relaxed performer. He might be nervous before a TV show but otherwise going out to perform was no trouble to him. Others might spend time tuning up but Holly was always ready and always in tune. He was a natural performer and very much himself on stage. He would do whatever he felt such as a Chuck Berry duckwalk.

Indeed, any "before show" rituals went by the board one day when Buddy looked in Little Richard's dressing room where Wee Dick and Larry Williams were having fun with the well- endowed Angel. Angel was proving that Richard was the hardest wanking man in show business. Buddy was invited to join in and, according to Richard, Buddy unzipped and he came and went just before the compère announced, "Buddy Holly and the Crickets". Did it happen or was it fantasy? I accept it: Buddy was a hot-blooded young man.

Chas White (Dr Rock) (173): "As Little Richard's biographer, I asked him a lot about Buddy Holly. He mentioned an incident in the Paramount Theatre in New York where Buddy got involved with Larry Williams and a girl called Angel in a naughty orgy. It was shock therapy to me because Buddy Holly had this bank clerk image, Mr Nice Guy with the glasses, and he didn't seem the sort who would be getting involved with wild women and wild orgies. My job as an author was to find out the facts and I checked it out with Angel and it turned out to be true. Buddy Holly's image as the nice, shy Texan with the glasses went out of the window—he was as wild as a coot. It's in line with Little Richard of course—he has always got off on watching other people—and there are lots of stories about Larry Williams' shenanigans."

And who would say no to Angel? **Chas White (Dr Rock) (174)**: "Exactly. Angel is very voluptuous and she does say, 'I am the woman Little Richard always wanted to be.' (Laughs) She's had an extraordinary life. She is well educated and she later married an English lord."

Whilst in New York, the Crickets had signed a contract with Irving Feld on behalf of GAC (General Artists Corporation) for a series of one nighters, *The Biggest Show Of Stars For 1957*. They would appear on 67 days out of 77 from 9 September 1957 to 24 November 1957. They would be paid $12,500 for the concert tour, mostly with two shows a night, and their ingenuousness is shown in Allison's letter home, but he is only just 18, "We signed contracts for about two hours today and for all I know, we may have joined the Foreign Legion." They were singing three songs in each show—always "That'll Be The Day", usually "Ready Teddy", and either "Peggy Sue" or "Oh Boy!".

Jerry Allison (175): "The 70 day tours were horrible and I wouldn't want to do them again."

George Hamilton IV (176): "They weren't the luxury touring buses that you get today. They were just coaches with standard seats and no bunks at all. Nearly everyone was backed by the house band and as far as I can recall, Buddy Holly was the only one who had his own group. We were backed by a black orchestra in satin suits and they had saxophones and trumpets. 'A Rose And A Baby Ruth' sounded very strange with brass instruments, and Buddy Holly very wisely had the Crickets with him."

Still adolescents, Jerry and Niki had had a fight in New York which resulted in Jerry getting a black eye. It happened just before a colour photo session on the roof of the Brooklyn Paramount and you can see Jerry's injury on the cover of *The Chirping Crickets* LP, released in the US in late November.

When Buddy spoke to Norman Petty on the phone, he learnt that Roy Orbison and his band were coming to Clovis and were short of a bass player. Buddy rang up a friend, a big red-faced singer called Rick Tucker and asked him to go over. Orbison recorded "An Empty Cup" and "A Cat Named Domino", a song sure to please Vi Petty. In return, Tucker put down "Patty Baby" and "Don't Do Me This Way", which feature Orbison. Some think that Buddy is on "Don't Do Me This Way", perhaps overdubbed later. Whether he is or not, the possible presence of Holly and Orbison is a damp squib.

There are many parallels between Buddy Holly and Roy Orbison, both of them being singer/ songwriters from Texas towns with highly individual voices. They were unlikely looking rock'n'roll stars: they both wore spectacles, often with big, black frames. Orbison in particular could never be considered a glamour boy. He had a fat face although he was not fat himself and in later years, it looked as though he wore a wig, but he didn't. Sorry, I'm going off into a Roy Orbison rant. Did I tell you that I once met his brother, Sam, and Sam looked exactly like him? Amazing!

The Crickets joined the package on 9 September 1957 in Norfolk, Virginia, and the astonishing bill featured Fats Domino and his band, Chuck Berry, the Everly Brothers, Frankie Lymon and the Teenagers, the Spaniels, Paul Anka, the Drifters, LaVern Baker and Clyde McPhatter. Some of them only performed for part of the tour and others—Buddy Knox and the Rhythm Orchids, the Diamonds, Eddie Cochran—were added later. There were over 130 people travelling from one city to the next, hence two coaches were needed. If they weren't sleeping on the bus, they would be in bad hotels with mediocre food.

"That'll Be The Day" was becoming a massive hit and it had been released in the UK. On 21

September 1957, the Crickets, Bob Thiele and Decca's national sales manager, Norm Wienstroer, appeared on the cover of *Cash Box*. They are pointing to 1 October 1957, the date when "That'll Be The Day" should pass a million sales.

Brunswick was an old label, going back to 1916, and its million-selling artists included Al Jolson, Bing Crosby, Fred Astaire and the Andrews Sisters. By the 1950s, the label was concentrating on jazz, and new releases had been discontinued in 1953. Brunswick was revived in April 1956 as a popular label and "That'll Be The Day" was the first big hit. The Crickets would be followed in a few months by Jackie Wilson. The huge hits by Bill Haley and his Comets were on US Decca but on Brunswick in the UK.

Decca now realised they'd had Buddy Holly on their books in 1956. It was in the company's interest to push the new product and establish him as a star, but Paul Cohen thought he had been deceived (which was true). In a ludicrous move that should have been vetoed, Decca released a single of the original version of "That'll Be The Day" with "Rock Around With Ollie Vee". It did not chart but *Cash Box* said it was a version by the composer as opposed to the Crickets' version. There were US covers of "That'll Be The Day" by the Ravens and Jeff Allen.

Ellis Amburn (177): "Paul Cohen hadn't appreciated what he had at Decca. How stars looked was as important back then as how they sounded, and that had been one of Paul Cohen's problems. Buddy Holly was not as good-looking as many of the country stars and Paul Cohen wanted a sex object like Elvis. As a result, he didn't recognise Buddy's musical talents."

On 23 September 1957, "That'll Be The Day" became the Number 1 record, displacing Jimmie Rodgers' "Honeycomb" but being itself replaced by the Everly Brothers' "Wake Up Little Suzie" the following week. When it was Number 1 in the US, it entered the UK charts and climbed to the top, replacing Paul Anka's "Diana" and staying there for three weeks.

Eric Bibb (178): "I prefer Bill Haley and the Comets to Buddy Holly and the Crickets, but I do like his records very much. His voice is so readily identifiable and I love the fact that they could do this stuff live in the studio and then go out and play it live. There are no elaborate studio tricks that they'd have to reproduce on stage. A good example of what you see is what you get."

Curiously, "That'll Be The Day" made Number 2 on the R&B charts—and "Peggy Sue", "Oh Boy!" and "Maybe Baby" were also Top 10 R&B singles. The charts are, however, lunatic: neither Buddy Holly nor the Crickets made the US country charts but cover versions by the Statler Brothers (1967), Kenny Vernon (1972), Linda Ronstadt (1976) and Pure Prairie League (1976) were listed. I don't believe these ridiculous charts: lots of country fans must have been buying Buddy's records.

Stuart Colman (179): "When the world and his dog began performing 'That'll Be The Day' live on stage, there were several things to consider if the interpretation was going to be done properly. The key of A was a priority, the distinctive intro needed to be in place and the emphasis on the final appearance of the phrase 'When you make me cry' was essential. The idea probably came from Jerry Allison whilst the Crickets were road-testing the song in front of a crowd. It acts as a second hook, adding that extra authority to the track at a point where the listener thinks he's heard it all."

Dave Williams (180): "My interest in Buddy Holly started in 1957 when I first heard 'That'll Be The Day' with those opening chords and that fantastic guitar break. I got a guitar that year and I've been a big Buddy Holly fan all my life. We had never seen a Fender Strat before but that helped to give the music its individuality."

Richard Thompson (181): "I had a big sister and she used to like Buddy Holly, so I used to hear his stuff, often through the bedroom wall. I thought he was absolutely great. 'That'll Be The Day' is probably my favourite and strangely enough, the electric guitar that I use is the same model as Holly's. I've always liked the very hard sound of that guitar. I thought, for example, that the Everly Brothers were absolutely fabulous but those Gibsons look very good but sound dreadful. (Laughs)"

Steve Gibbons (182): "I was turned on by Elvis first but Buddy and Jerry Lee quickly followed. I loved 'That'll Be The Day', which had such a simple and beautiful opening. I couldn't play a guitar then and I thought it was very clever. Elvis made his records with two experienced players, Scotty Moore and Bill Black, but Buddy's band was so young and so inventive."

Justin Hayward (183): "One Saturday night in the autumn of 1957, the 45 of Buddy Holly's 'That'll Be The Day' was being played over and over again at a church hall social that I sometimes attended in Swindon. After several plays the record would be turned over and we jigged and jerked around to "I'm Lookin' For Someone to Love", which was such a simple and true sentiment for all 50s teenagers. By the end of the evening I had committed every detail of both songs to memory, and as I walked home from the bus stop, I knew, in a mood of glorious euphoria, that my whole life was going to be different. For the next few years, my musical and emotional life revolved around Buddy Holly. He taught many of us how to play guitar properly too. Before Buddy we were stuck on a boring old open G skiffle riff."

If they wished (and they didn't) British record-buyers could buy an alternative "That'll Be The Day" by **Larry Page (184). "**I thought I was going to be like Ronnie Hilton or Perry Como because that was where the market was, but once rock'n'roll hit, I decided to drop the singing lessons and get out there and do something. I was signed by EMI and as I was working for them as a record packer, I was packing my own records. They found a song that I was told would never be released here called 'That'll Be The Day'. I recorded it with the Geoff Love Orchestra and the Rita Williams Singers, but it was a silly arrangement with no feel, and the minute we hit the market, the Crickets' record was released, which went straight to Number l. If you buy the original sheet music sheet, you'll find my face on it and not Buddy Holly's."

At the same time, US Coral released "Peggy Sue" and "Everyday" under Buddy Holly's name. *Cash Box* said, "'Peggy Sue' is a fast moving rockabilly item that could be a tremendous teenage favourite. It's got the lyrics and the melody the kids want in addition to a sensational galloping tempo guitar and drum backdrop that makes your feet jump." Mrs Holley wrote to Buddy and told him that she

and her husband had become important around Lubbock as a result of the hit.

Neil Foster (185): "When my friend, Charlie Richmond, and I joined the Victor Silvester Dance Studio, which was over the Odeon cinema in London Road, Liverpool, in order to take a ballroom dancing course, we were taught something called 'rhythm dancing'. This was a slow adaptation of a quickstep, which could be used in a crowded ballroom. The music for this was Buddy Holly's 'Everyday'."

John Tobler (186): "Elvis went in the army, which left the field wide open for Lonnie Donegan, the Everly Brothers, Cliff Richard—and Buddy Holly. While musically this quintet (Don *and* Phil) of stars all enjoyed their greatest success in the years preceding the arrival of the Beatles, the thing they had in common which particularly appealed to my generation was that you could play the B-sides of their singles without embarrassment (perhaps not 100%, but at least the vast majority of the time). With the inevitable limited budget of schooldays, maybe two or three singles each term—I was at a boarding school—was about all we could afford, so getting not only a hit, but also a flipside worth a spin, was what we wanted."

Meanwhile, the Crickets were on tour and they became very friendly with the Everly Brothers. Don and Phil realised that, even though the Crickets had seen Elvis early on, they didn't look right. They took them to Field's Men Shop in New York and said, "OK. You guys have looked funny enough for long enough, now buy these clothes." Out went the bright red jackets, baggy trousers and red shoes, and in came high-button Italian suits.

Jerry Allison (187): "Eddie Cochran, Don Lanier and myself made it our policy not to go to bed if there was anybody to stay up with. We had a lot of beers and a lot of good fun on that tour. Buddy wasn't as mad about staying up all night and drinking beer and shooting the breeze as we were, but he and Eddie liked each other a lot. Eddie was 18 years old, same as us, and we used to party after the show. A lot of people were in Eddie's room one night and the house detectives said that they would have to chase everybody out. Eddie told them, 'If Eddie Cochran was here, this wouldn't happen.'

Joe B. Mauldin (188): "Eddie Cochran was a real super guy and I got on with him real well. We toured quite a bit in the States and worked together at the New York Paramount. He left the bass playing to Guybo and he never asked to play my bass. Often there were jam sessions on the bus but I was left out of it as you couldn't get the bass on the bus: it was just singers and guitarists. Fats Domino had a bass player called Tubb and I liked him real well too."

Norman Petty was mortified when he saw a photograph in *Billboard* of the Crickets and Eddie Cochran, smoking and drinking Jack Daniel's. He called their hotel and told them, "You've blown it! You're all going to hell!" Oh, and get the Bible out.

Because of segregation, the Crickets, the Everly Brothers and Paul Anka did not perform from 23 to 27 September. The Crickets flew to Oklahoma City, where they were met by Norman Petty, who took them to the Tinker Air Force Base. In the Officers Club, they recorded "An Empty Cup" and "You've Got Love" (two Roy Orbison songs that Petty also had his name on), "Rock Me My Baby" (a Bo Diddley rhythm on a nursery rhyme, and Buddy sang the chorus, after some dubbing, with Bill Pickering), and the hit version of "Maybe Baby". "You've Got Love" was pitched as high as his Nashville recordings, suggesting that Buddy wasn't too uncomfortable in this register, and he has a rare vibrato effect on "Rock Me My Baby". "Maybe Baby", with its great ringing guitar intro, is the only track on which Niki played lead guitar along with Buddy. Roy Orbison said that it was his favourite Buddy Holly record.

Dale Hawkins (189): "I would hang out in New York with Buddy Holly and he played me 'Maybe Baby'. He was doing it slowly and I said, 'That's a great song but I would do it this way. Why not give it a Little Richard feel?' He liked that and they recorded it that way. It sounded like something out of Cosimo's studio and it had that New Orleans sound. After it was a hit, he said, 'Don't let anybody know that we were thinking of Little Richard. He'd only tell everybody he discovered us.' (Laughs)"

Jim Newcombe (190): "Geoff Taggart and I had written a few words to a song to be called 'Maybe Baby' and we were high as kites thinking we had been on the same wavelength as Buddy for even a couple of words."

Mr and Mrs Holley and Larry also met up with Buddy in Oklahoma City, and saw them on the package show on 29 September. A week later, the tour was in Corpus Christi and their hotel rooms were overrun with crickets. They had to run them out with brooms, but Jerry wouldn't kill any of them as that would have been bad luck.

On 11 October 1957, there was the first UK feature on the Crickets, written by Charles Govey for the *New Musical Express (NME)*. The Crickets were already thinking of their own musical publishing company and comment on the amount of talent in Texas: Govey wrote, "They'd certainly be happy if we in Britain began to associate Texas not just with cattle, oil and big buxom girls like Jayne Mansfield, but with the latest line in modern musical groups as well."

On 18 October 1957, the show had moved to the Auditorium in Sacramento, California. Peggy Sue was living there and Jerry Allison called her parents and asked if she could come to the show. Although the record had been out a month, this was the first time that she had heard "Peggy Sue". Buddy told her, "Aren't you glad your mother named you after my song?" Jerry Allison had a crew-cut and this can be seen, four days later, on KPTV's *Hightime* Show, where Buddy, Joe and Jerry mime to "That'll Be The Day" without instruments.

Peggy Sue Gerron (191): "I first heard 'Peggy Sue' when Buddy sang it on a stage show in Sacramento. I was embarrassed, sitting there wondering what they had done to me but am now thrilled to have been a part of it."

On 23 October 1957, Red Robinson interviewed Buddy backstage at the Georgia Auditorium, Vancouver. Buddy said that the group was formed in 1957. He is asked a leading question and confirms that rock'n'roll music is going out and he would prefer singing something quieter (What's wrong with "Everyday"?). Buddy preferred "Oh Boy!" to "That'll Be The Day", "but I'm no judge."

While in Seattle, Buddy Knox recorded "Swingin' Daddy" and "Whenever I'm Lonely", both written by Knox, and with Buddy Holly on lead guitar plus Joe B. on bass and Jerry on drums.

On 27 October 1957, Brunswick released "Oh Boy!" and "Not Fade Away". *Cash Box* said, "It's rare that a follow-up record is better than the artist's original hit. But that's the case with the new Crickets' release, 'Oh Boy!' It's an exciting rock'n'roll sequel to the boys' tremendous smash, 'That'll Be The Day', a tune that's still riding high on all charts." *Billboard* was equally enthusiastic: "Wild sounds and hollering build up a lot of excitement."

By the end of October, the show had moved to Canada where, naturally, Paul Anka did exceptionally well, and another local act, the Diamonds, joined them. The package performed before 9,000 fans at Edmonton Gardens and a reviewer described the audience as "noisy but orderly". On stage in his home city of Ottawa, Paul Anka received a gold disc for "Diana".

On 2 November 1957, Holly, Allison and Eddie Cochran had interviews with Freeman Hover for KCSR in Chadron, Nebraska. They were in Eddie Cochran's room at the Albany Hotel in Denver, Colorado. It was 2.30am and they had to be up at 6am for a plane. Freeman said that 'That'll Be The Day' was now a common expression and every time it was said, it was a plug for the record. Asked about the name for the group, Jerry Allison said, "We tried to come up with a name that hadn't been used before, and sure enough, it had been used before." Eddie Cochran was smoking a pipe during the interview. Buddy said that he would like to be in the rock'n'roll film that Eddie was making, but nothing happened.

Jerry Allison (192): "We never did any of the rock'n'roll films because Norman Petty was waiting for the big parts. We wanted to make some and we wanted to do *Go, Johnny, Go*, but Norman said, 'No, no, we will wait for a legit movie.' I don't think he liked rock'n'roll movies—sometimes, I don't think he liked rock'n'roll. (Laughs)"

There is another interview a few days later with Dale Lowery of KTOP from Topeka, Kansas. It is good that these interviews have survived but you long for somebody to ask a decent question. Marginally better is the telephone interview with *Melody Maker* from a hotel in Indianapolis. The headline said, "Without Elvis, we'd never have made it." A fuller version of the interview appeared in February 1958, and commenting on race, Buddy said, "We have the tradition of not going to school together, but we don't even think about it now. The people in our show are great."

On 4 November 1957, Buddy called Echo McGuire in Nebraska and told her he would be performing at the Civic Auditorium Music Hall in Omaha that evening. She received the call too late to attend. At Christmas, she told Buddy that she had found someone else.

On 6 November 1957, they performed at the Kiel Opera House in St Louis, Missouri. While scuffling backstage, Paul Anka knocked out one of the plugs, thus turning off the stage microphones. Buddy Holly was on stage and came off furious.

Johnny Moore (193) of the Drifters recalls a similar incident: "Paul Anka, being the practical joker he is, hid Buddy Holly's guitar just before they called out 'Buddy Holly' from the stage. Someone gave him a guitar to do his act and when he came off, he was in a rage; he was fit to kill Paul. Otherwise, he was a real nice guy—quiet, introverted, never spoke too much. He looked up to us because we'd had more hit records and he loved our music."

Another rock'n'roll singer, **Ben Hewitt (194)**, told a similar story: "I did several shows for Alan Freed when he was with WINS out of New York City and booking shows into the Brooklyn Paramount. I was there as a fill-in, part of 'and many others' at the bottom of the bill. You did the show, they ran the movie, you did the show, they ran the movie, you did the show, and they ran the movie. You could do five shows some days and I was singing the same songs. You can't change your act because the band has the charts, and so you do the same songs over and over again. One night J.P. Richardson, the Big Bopper, hid Ritchie Valens' guitar and Ritchie refused to go on. Ted Steel, the MC, was going, 'And now ladies and gentlemen, the hottest man on the West Coast, Del-Fi recording artist, Ritchie Valens.' Everybody was screaming and yelling and Ritchie was saying, 'Where's my guitar?' Ted Steel announced him again and still he didn't come on. The audience started booing and that's when Jape gave Ritchie his guitar."

Niki Sullivan was feeling isolated on the tour as he hated the Crickets' pranks and found the travelling tiring. He left the group at the end of the tour and received a $1,000 cash settlement. His song, "It's All Over", was inspired by his split from the Crickets. Now deceased, Niki Sullivan did occasional interviews and in particular, stated that Buddy Holly had a love child with a girl in Lubbock and paid for the upkeep. Peggy Sue Gerron's book makes it clear that Buddy was fond of this girl and helped when she was in trouble, but he was not the father. Sadly, this means that there is no one around with Buddy's genes.

Manny Greenfield became the Crickets' personal manager in a working agreement with Norman Petty. He earned his 5% commission for getting the Crickets on *The Ed Sullivan Show* on 1 December 1957 for a very acceptable $1,500. The director had built a set with the drums 10 foot high but they couldn't work as a unit if this were used. "It's television, it's how it looks," they were told. They did get the set changed, but the sound was mediocre, partly because they weren't ready for the rehearsal: Buddy was, but Jerry and Joe B. had been watching the judo act and were trying some judo of their own. They performed "That'll Be The Day" (far too fast) and "Peggy Sue", both with Niki not plugged in, and had a short interview with Sullivan. The Picks had been hoping that they would get to do *The Ed Sullivan Show* with the Crickets, but they weren't union members and Norman wasn't paying their dues.

Also on the bill were Sam Cooke, Bobby Helms, the Rays and Douglas Fairbanks: a hip show by Sullivan standards. Although Buddy was delighted to be on *The Ed Sullivan Show*, he rarely watched TV, being far too restless.

Marshall Crenshaw (195): "I loved Buddy Holly when I was a little boy as I'm old enough to have experienced his stuff first hand. I saw him on *The Ed Sullivan Show* when I was four years old and his music was so full of energy. All his songs are in major keys and so it's all, very joyful sounding stuff. There's a lot of *joie de vivre* in his music. Even though I was so young, it really grabbed me. I still love his stuff and I've never gotten tired of it.

I think a few of my songs are close to being Buddy Holly songs, and 'Cynical Girl' springs to mind."

"That'll Be The Day" was effectively the template for the rock'n'roll band: two guitars, bass and drums. However, the group was now down to a three piece with no real loss in quality. Buddy might have brought back Sonny Curtis but he was tied up in Nashville. **Sonny Curtis (196)**: "Leaving the band just before the hits started coming wasn't such a bad move as I might have ended up on that 'plane. Niki Sullivan replaced me in the Crickets. Niki left at the end of that tour—they didn't get along too well. It didn't make Buddy's job any harder as there was really only one guitarist in the band when Niki was there."

On 29 November, the Crickets won a *Cash Box* award for Most Promising Vocal Group of 1957. It goes to show how uninformed some awards are as Buddy was the only Cricket to have sung on the records. On 4 December, the Crickets returned to Lubbock. They had plugged Lubbock a lot—Buddy always said, "I'm from Lubbock, Texas"—and they had two million-selling records ("Peggy Sue" would make Number 3) and "Oh Boy!" was a new chart entry. No one was at the airport. Still, it was a culture shock for some people. The pastor, Ben Johnson had disapproved of rock'n'roll, but the money from the Crickets would modify his views.

Snuff Garrett (197): "Buddy was staying with me in Wichita Falls. He had just done *The Ed Sullivan Show* and he came to spend four or five days with me. We did my TV show and I had his album cover printed up on black and white pieces of paper for the kids to have signed as his show was closing. As the show was going off the air, he did that. I asked him to sign something for me, and he said, 'What would you want with my autograph?' I said, 'Well, you may get hit by a truck' and we both laughed. When they told me that Buddy was dead a few months later, that popped into my head."

By now, Holly's songs were getting further covers. Tina Robin recorded "Everyday" with the Neal Hefti Orchestra in New York, while Betty Madison sang "Tell Me How" with the Dick Jacobs Orchestra. Tom Edwards' "Goodnight Rock And Roll", released in December 1957, mentioned Buddy by name.

Trini Lopez (198): "I started playing clubs in Dallas when I was a kid and then I graduated to night clubs and I met Buddy Holly. He saw a show I did in Wichita Falls, Texas, a little town. Buddy liked me and asked me if I would like to meet his record producer and I said, 'Sure.' He told me to come to Clovis, New Mexico. I had five guys in the band. We got in my station wagon and I drove to Clovis, New Mexico to meet him. Unfortunately, everybody was very prejudiced against Latinos. The guys in my band were Anglo-American and not Latinos. The reason I did that was because I wanted to play rock'n'roll and Latinos were not known for playing that music. It backfired on me as the producer was prejudiced too. He didn't want me to sing and the band didn't want me to sing either. They wanted to do instrumentals. They didn't want to use my name—Trini Lopez and his Combo—even though it was my musicians, my uniforms, my equipment, my car, my everything. We were there a week and we recorded four instrumentals and I cried myself to sleep—and then we came to Texas and I dropped them off in their homes like a taxi driver and I said goodbye to the last guy in the band and said, 'I won't be seeing you anymore. I am going to start another band.' Then I started getting another group together."

On 17 December 1957, the Crickets recorded "Little Baby" in Clovis with C.W. Kendall of Trini Lopez's group, the Big Beats playing piano, the songwriting credit being split between Holly, Petty and Kendall. They also recorded "Look At Me" (Holly/ Allison/ Petty) and a song from *Jailhouse Rock*, Jerry Leiber and Mike Stoller's "Baby I Don't Care" with Jerry Allison back on the box.

Trevor Cajiao (199): "I'm not a big fan of Holly's version of 'Baby I Don't Care'. Elvis' original has a feeling of menace that isn't there on the Holly version. The guitar break is good, though."

Terry Wayne (200): "I love Buddy Holly's version of 'Baby I Don't Care'. I prefer it to Elvis' version as it is more guitar based. There is a terrific backing on that and Buddy plays a good solo. In fact, I put the song into my act."

Phillip Goodhand-Tait (201): "The early rock'n'roll records had big bands on them were difficult to figure out and were beyond our expertise, and of course a lot of jazz musicians played on them. When I got to hear Buddy Holly, I heard the guitar, bass and drums and I could work it out.

Tim Whitnall (202): "I like three pieces: the good ones have all got great stylists in there. Even the Police in their early days, it was reggae bass and Keith Moon-type drums and those incredible guitar figures that Andy Summers played. You can get a universal mind with a three piece band."

There are nine minutes of Buddy and Jerry working on Bo Diddley's "Mona". A lot of it is in short strummed sequences and there is not a complete take with a decent balance but this could have been a big one for Buddy. As they were driving to gigs, Buddy had often shown Jerry Allison guitar chords and some of his playing is on this session.

Buddy bought a $3,000 Chevrolet Impala as a Christmas present for his parents. Around 1999, a restored Chevvy was promoted at exhibitions as Holly's, but it was not the same vehicle. As a present to himself, he spent $300 on having his teeth capped and he had his curls slicked back by Jake Goss at the Shag'n'Shear Shop in Lubbock. Jerry Allison had now swapped his crew-cut for a kiss curl. However, the Crickets didn't spend Christmas in Lubbock.

The stage show, *Alan Freed's Holiday Of Stars*, was at the New York Paramount Theatre from five shows a day from 23 December 1957 through to 5 January 1958. The show included Fats Domino, Jerry Lee Lewis, the Everly Brothers, Buddy Holly and the Crickets (billed as separate acts), Danny and the Juniors, Paul Anka, Jo Ann Campbell, Terry Noland and Alan Freed's Rock'n'Roll Orchestra. The shows went fantastically well and thousands would queue in very cold weather for the seats. The show was to be staged in between the British film, *It's Great To Be Young*, starring John Mills, but the screenings were soon abandoned. Who wants a film about a headmaster wanting to disband the school orchestra when you can have Buddy Holly and the Crickets? And for $2.50 a ticket? *Alan Freed's Holiday Of Stars* grossed $32,000 on the first day and $300,000 overall, of which the Crickets received $4,200.

According to the trade paper, *Variety*: "A periodic madness descends alternately upon Broadway and Brooklyn during the holiday seasons.

Rock'n'roll still shows its strength for the very young. The juveniles all but create riots in and out of the house, and probably wouldn't stop at that but for the tremendous number of uniformed police." One reviewer complained about the screeching teenagers and how they spoilt his view and how he couldn't hear the music (not that he wanted to hear it anyway.) However, despite what *Variety* said, the crowds were not delinquent and were not ripping up seats, which had happened in the 1940s Swing era.

Just before the stage show opened, 22-year-old Jerry Lee Lewis had married his 13-year-old second cousin, Myra Gale Brown, the daughter of his bass player. It was his third marriage and the second time he had married bigamously. If the marriage (but not the bigamy, which was indefensible) had come to light that December in New York, would it have wrecked his career? I suspect not, because although New Yorkers were more sophisticated than their contemporaries down South, they accepted the fact that different laws applied in different States.

Fats Domino had seniority and his contract stated that he would close the show. Jerry Lee Lewis, who was only on his second hit, demanded that he should be closing and on the first day, he was so frenzied on stage that Domino did not want to follow him again.

Jerry Allison (203): "We had just finished a three month tour and only missed four states. We'd be getting on the bus and getting off at the next venue and getting on again. The best part was when we played the New York Paramount and we did better than anybody else on the bill. Every act was good but we got the most encores."

A 17-year-old girl sent Buddy a letter: "When I met you yesterday, I thought you were the most nicest (sic) person I met. I'm really proud of you for as much as you stood for from those maniacs in the audience. I know if I was in your place, I would not like it at all."

Paul Evans (204): "Al Byron, who wrote 'Roses Are Red' with me, looked like Buddy Holly. A couple of fans came up to him when he was eating at the Turf and asked for his autograph. Al said that he wasn't Buddy Holly. Their mother asked him for his autograph. He repeated that he wasn't Buddy Holly and he wouldn't sign Buddy's name.

She screamed at him and said that Buddy Holly's records were now banned from their house."

Whilst in New York, the Crickets usually stayed in the towering Hotel Edison on 47th Street, west of Broadway. Rather like the President Hotel in London, a lot of musicians stayed there and it became known as the Fingersnapper Hotel.

Buddy Holly had warned Terry Noland not to play Paul Anka any new songs "as he'll steal them". As it happened, Terry did play him "Puppy Love" and, in 1960, Paul Anka had a US Top 10 hit with an entirely different song he had written called "Puppy Love".

On 29 December 1957, the Crickets appeared on *The Arthur Murray Dance Party* in New York City and performed "Peggy Sue" for $2,000. The other guests were Sarah Vaughan, Bobby Helms, Farley Granger and Hedy Lamarr. The Crickets were introduced patronisingly by Kathryn Murray who said we should keep an open mind about rock'n'roll. Buddy is very dominant in the performance and it's like seeing a young Billy Bragg.

John Broven (205): "I can still recall bringing home in Polegate, Sussex the 78rpm of 'That'll Be The Day' on Vogue Coral in autumn 1957 with its wonderful title hook and ringing guitar. I'm holding it now: the legend reads 'The Crickets with Orchestral Accompaniment', with writer credits to 'Allison, Holly; Petty'. There was no orchestra, of course. I slipped the B-side onto the Garrard record player: 'I'm Lookin' For Someone To Love' was almost as good. Over the Christmas period, on a Coral 45 (no longer 'Vogue' but with tri centre!), confusingly came the mesmerising 'Peggy Sue' by Buddy Holly (no Crickets?) with the grow-on-you 'Everyday'. Equilibrium was restored when the Crickets weighed in again with the classic double-sider 'Oh, Boy!' and 'Not Fade Away'. There seemed to be no stopping Buddy Holly *and* the Crickets."

Keith Skues (206): "As a young teenager in the mid-1950s I identified with rock'n'roll music. I am very privileged to still be able to play that music via the BBC in the East of England. One of the first records I bought was Buddy's 'Peggy Sue' in December 1957. One of my favourite tracks is 'Everyday' which was the 'B' side of 'Peggy Sue'. It has a very simple melody but what sticks out in my mind, apart from Buddy's voice and his Fender Stratocaster, is the celeste which gave it a memorable sound. I remember my parents telling me that this hooligan, rock'n'roll music would never last. It did and there are dozens of books, films, stage shows and records to prove it."

On 30 December 1957, Mrs Louise Allison wrote to her son, Jerry: she had been listening to a radio programme which featured live cover versions of the hits. "I'm getting to where I sorta like the Crickets music. Surely irritates me the way *Your Hit Parade* butchers your songs. Wish they'd let you all do it for them. Their drums were putrid or it could have been their drummer." As it turned out Dick Jacobs was the long-running musical director of *Your Hit Parade* and he had Alan Copeland singing "Peggy Sue" every week for two months.

As the year crossed from 1957 to 1958, the Crickets went to the roof of the theatre and looked out over Times Square and out over the tall, tall buildings. They could see the celebrations and they realised just how far they had come.

7

HERE I GO, BREAKING ALL OF THE RULES

"Buddy Holly was impetuous. He was always saying, 'It's gotta happen now and I don't have time to waste.'"
(Maria Elena Holly, 2008)

In January 1958, the Crickets were on another GAC tour, *America's Greatest Teenage Recording Stars* this time, and many of the usual suspects—the Everly Brothers, Paul Anka and Jimmie Rodgers—were on hand. The Crickets' fee was $3,000 a week, and they were effectively getting a further raise as their money, after deductions, would be split between three members instead of four. Buddy was wearing his solid black frames and he would dance in the middle of "Peggy Sue". There was a photo session for Buddy in his new frames and he hated the picture where he is clicking his fingers. He was, incidentally, 5 foot 11 and 10 stone 5 pounds.

On 25 January 1958, the Crickets recorded "Rave On" and "That's My Desire" at the impressive Bell Sound Studios in New York, going through from 8pm to 2am. The listed A&R man and producer was Sonny Lester, but it is hard to believe that Norman Petty stayed quiet, especially as he was playing piano and collecting a scale fee of $44. The session musicians included the guitarist, Al Caiola, and the backing vocals came from the Jivetones, who were mostly over 40.

Buddy Holly had liked Sonny West's "Oh Boy!" and now he wanted to do his new song, "Rave On". The title came from a Carl Perkins' song about fighting in the dance hall, "Dixie Fried" with the lines: "Rave on, Trouble, I'm with you, Rave on, Cat, she cried. It's almost dawn and the cops have gone, So let's all get Dixie Fried."

Sonny West (207): "Bill Tilghman was toying around with the title and I thought it sounded a bit dorky the way he had it, he would write words, like poems, and it was a bit negative, 'Rave on, brother'. We tried to get it into a cohesive song and I went over to make a demo in Clovis in October 1957 and Norman heard a few bars of it, I was going to record it with an acoustic guitar, and he turned the recorder off and he said, 'That'll never work.' (Laughs) I did a lot of work on the lyrics and I changed it into a love song and made it more positive. It still was a little strange but it worked."

Sonny West's single came out on Atlantic, but failed to sell. **Sonny West (208)**: "I didn't know that Buddy was recording it in New York. He had gone there to do 'Oh Boy!' on *The Ed Sullivan Show*. He went to Bell Sound and Norman played the piano on that. It has a syncopated rhythm that is different from the way I did it. The way they did it sold the song and Buddy was not playing the guitar, he was only singing."

Geoff Goddard (209): "'Rave On' was a great record, full of power and very exciting and I'm not surprised that it still appeals to people today. His records still sound as fresh and exciting as when he made them. There's such a strong personality in his voice and even though it's good punchy rock music, there's a plaintive melancholy quality that I like."

Holly wanted to revive Frankie Laine's 1947 hit, "That's My Desire", but no one had been very encouraging. The clip-clop country setting would have even been too dated for the Nashville sessions, but nevertheless, it was a pleasant recording.

Meanwhile…over in the UK. **John Repsch (210):** "In January 1958, Joe Meek was involved in a séance with his friend, Jimmy Miller, and an Arab called Faud. Jimmy had his go and got a sensation of floating. His fingers went into Joe's knuckles and Joe let out a scream. The Arab had written, or been compelled to write, 'February 3, Buddy Holly dies'. Joe Meek said. 'We must warn him' but he hadn't been able to get through. February 3 passed without a sound, and Buddy Holly then gave some wonderful performances in England. Joe still had nightmares about the séance and they would end with a box of dirty clothes being stuffed into the boot of a car. The following year Buddy Holly died on February 3, and he died because he wanted his shirts cleaned. When the details of the tragedy emerged, Joe became convinced that Buddy's spirit was guiding his music and his life."

During rehearsals for *The Ed Sullivan Show* on 26 January 1958, Ed Sullivan thought "Oh Boy" was too raunchy. Buddy said that he'd do that song or nothing. The Crickets weren't around for a rehearsal and Ed Sullivan was furious. Their attitude may have gone against them as the sound was badly balanced with more of Jerry's drums than Buddy's guitar, and Jerry sounds like he's playing dustbin lids. (Now there's an idea.) However, Buddy had broken one of his strings and it might have been as a consequence of that. Still, they picked up a cheque for $2,000.

Ellis Amburn (211): "The first time on *The Ed Sullivan Show*, Ed and Buddy had had a nice conversation but the second time, he sang a song against Ed's wishes. Ed thought the lyric of 'Oh Boy!' was too suggestive and I think he sabotaged the song by telling his sound and lighting men to mess up the act. Buddy was furious and when he was asked later to go back on the show, he told him to shove it." I do find this hard to credit as surely Sullivan, in ratings mad America, would want the best show in all circumstances.

On Monday 27 January 1958, the Crickets flew to Honolulu, Hawaii, just before Hawaii became an American State. They arrived at 4.30pm and had to be on stage at the Civic Auditorium at 6.30pm. The bill included Paul Anka, Jerry Lee Lewis and 18-year-old Jodie Sands, who had had success with her single, "With All My Heart", and a reviewer said that Paul Anka "tried more than the others to do some refinements of modulation and crescendo."

The next morning Norman Petty took the famed colour photograph of Buddy plaintively looking out from his balcony at Kaiser Hotel. They toured Pearl Harbour with one of Petty's friends, Colonel Bill Leach. They left for a six day Australian tour, *The Big Show*, on a Pan-American Constellation plane. The plane developed engine trouble and was forced to land on the Canton Island terminal in the South Pacific. There were complaints from other passengers when Paul Anka and Jerry Lee Lewis had a pillow fight.

Lee Gordon was an American based in Australia. He had promoted Nat "King" Cole and several jazz stars in Australia, but after a couple of tours lost money, he switched to the new music, rock'n'roll. Naturally, it was difficult and expensive to arrange tours with the US stars. There had been a tour by Bill Haley and his Comets with the Platters in January 1957 and one with Little Richard, Gene Vincent and Eddie Cochran in October 1957. This tour had ended in disarray as Little Richard had thrown his rings off the Sydney Harbour Bridge and announced that he was becoming a church minister. Little Richard left the tour and after a few more performances, it was cancelled.

Jerry Lee Lewis was not happy with *The Big Show*, moaning that it was a waste of time and that he could be earning better money at home. He was incensed that the Crickets had top billing, but Holly who didn't care said, "Okay". There wasn't a national chart in Australia, but similar but separate charts for Melbourne and Sydney. "That'll Be The Day" had been Number 2 on both, but as "Diana" was currently Number 1, Lee Gordon wanted Paul Anka to close the shows. Buddy Holly told a reporter that he was lucky: some of the people who hadn't made it were just as talented as himself, hardly a thought that would have occurred to Jerry Lee Lewis.

The running order was a local act Johnny O'Keefe and his Dee-Jays, Jodie Sands, Jerry Lee Lewis, Buddy Holly and the Crickets, and Paul Anka, and the show was usually compèred by the road manager, Alan Hefferman. O'Keefe was having success with his EPs, *Whole Lotta Shakin'* and *Shakin' At The Stadium*. His most popular song was "Wild One", later known as "Real Wild Child".

On 31 January 1958, the first show at Newcastle Stadium had to be cancelled as the coach from Sydney was delayed and the touring party didn't arrive until 7.30pm. Over 2,500 saw the one show that they performed and it was well received, although it did not replicate the wild reception for Little Richard in 1957. According to a newspaper report, "One man who removed his shirt was ordered by the Stadium Manager to put it on again." Heavy stuff. During a backstage interview with Buddy Holly and Pat Barton, you can hear Jerry Lee Lewis on stage.

The Crickets performed "That'll Be The Day", "Oh Boy!", "Peggy Sue", "Everyday", "Rip It Up", "Ready Teddy" and "Long Tall Sally", and if an additional song was required, "Be-Bop-A-Lula". Judging from reports, Jerry Lee Lewis generally had the best reception, although it was Holly's night in Melbourne. There is a marvellous comment in one newspaper report that Jerry Lee Lewis was in the hotel lounge picking his toe nails: clearly doing his own thing as nobody else would want to do it with him.

Frank Ifield (212): "I recorded 'True Love Ways' as a dedication to Buddy Holly and it's the only time I ever attempted an impersonation on record. I love all his songs and that one in particular. I was very fortunate to be on the bill when he

played the Sydney Stadium in 1958. The whole guy was such an anti-image. Most rock'n'roll artists were trying to be flamboyant sex symbols but he was like a college kid, thin and bespectacled, and wearing your glasses on stage was unheard of in those days. He looked like he lacked confidence but the magic was in his sound. He showed that you didn't have to be glamorous to be noticed. He also was a very nice man to talk to."

Jerry Allison wrote home, "The first few shows went very badly for us but for the last three days we have been stealing the show as Norm would say." Jerry commented on how behind the Australians were in their dress sense. Pot, kettle and black spring to mind as only a few months earlier, Don and Phil Everly had been refining the Crickets' wardrobe.

On 3 February 1958, *The Big Show* played to 8,000 fans in two houses at the Cloudland Ballroom in Brisbane. Roger Covell, reviewing the show for *Courier-Mail,* said that the audience wanted "frenzied vocal showmanship over a steadily slugging rhythm and this is what they got for up to 29/6d a head. Holly was painfully ill at ease between numbers. He looked simply inexperienced." The tour party stayed at Broadbeech, a luxurious hotel on the Gold Coast, some 50 miles from Brisbane. Lennie Holmes, a radio presenter and entertainer, recorded Buddy and Jerry Lee having a jam session, but Jerry Lee demanded its deletion.

On 4 Feburary 1958, they moved to Melbourne. The *Herald* called Holly "the undoubted star of the show with his clever display of guitar techniques." The reviewer liked Jodie Sands' pleasant voice and easy stage manner and praised Johnny O'Keefe and his Dee Jays, saying they had improved since the Little Richard tour.

In Melbourne, Buddy appeared on radio with Stan "The Man" Rofe, who compèred the first show at the West Melbourne Stadium. Stan played Holly a local version of Jessie Hill's "Ooh Poo Pah Doo" and Holly, for once not being diplomatic, remarked that it was horrible. He was told it was by Johnny O'Keefe. Oops.

On 5 February 1958, the Crickets took part in a charity performance at the Nurses Memorial Centre in Melbourne. It was recorded for a radio broadcast on 3AW later in the month, but the broadcast has not been saved. The party returned home with the Crickets playing the Scofield Barracks in Honolulu for $500 on the way.

Also on 5 February 1958, Coral released a new Holly single, "Listen To Me" and "I'm Gonna Love You Too" in the US. *Cash Box* said, "The singer performs on multiple tracks as he chants a melodic country-flavoured rock'n'roll ballad set against a Latin rockin' tempo. Wonderful teenager romancer that could go all the way."

Not to be outdone, Brunswick released the Crickets' "Maybe Baby" and "Tell Me How" in the US. *Cash Box*, proving that it was written for the trade, said, "Both sides are powerful contenders for the charts and you can be sure the teenagers' reaction will be instantaneous."

Ian Higham (213): "I was 14 and had just got a paper round which for the first time gave me some money. I got 12/-d a week! I lived in a village on the outskirts of Southampton and I had to pedal six miles to Henry's Record Store, the nearest shop that sold rock'n'roll records. The first record I wanted was the EP, *The Sound Of The Crickets*, which cost me 12/6d. I still have it with the faded price pencilled on the rear of the sleeve. The EP combined the second and third singles and of course, most of the Crickets' releases had great B-sides. 'Tell Me How' is my all-time favourite Crickets track. I'm sure if it had been released as an A-side, the single would have done just as well. My next purchase was the *Listen To Me* EP and again it was a B-side that stood out for me, 'I'm Gonna Love You Too'. Technically, 'Listen To Me' and I'm Gonna Love You Too' are outstandingly advanced recordings for the time."

Buddy Knox was the first to take Buddy to Manny's 48th Street Musical Instruments store in New York and he was very impressed with their stock. In December 1957, he bought a Guild F-50 Navarre acoustic, which he used on "Well...All Right". This was recorded in Clovis on 12 February 1958, and Norman Petty put a microphone inside the guitar to create a very bright sound. The track featured Buddy with Joe B. on bass and Jerry on a solitary cymbal. Possibly, Norman intended to overdub some other instruments later, but he decided that it was fine as it was.

Sonny Curtis (214): "Buddy did 'Well...All Right' on acoustic guitar and it has always been one of my favourites—it has such a nice feel to it."

Joe B. Mauldin (215): "I loved Buddy's songs from the start and I thought he was great. I was fortunate enough to get in on two or three of the songs myself. We didn't do anything specific when we wrote 'Well...All Right'. It wasn't, 'Okay, you write the next verse.' We all threw in a line here and there and when I hear it now, it's hard for me to say who wrote what on that tune."

Dominic Pedler (216): "Quite apart from his use of full scale key changes, Holly always had an ear for the unexpected, often ambitiously hijacking chords from beyond the prevailing scale to create the subtle departure from cliché that typically defines songwriting brilliance. The opening line of 'Well...All Right' shunned traditional music theory and practice in favour of an early 'rock' cadence which, albeit with a bit more distortion, would dramatically come of age in the 1960s."

Jon Savage (217): "As a Beatle child—I was nine when 'Please Please Me' hit—I've always found classic rock'n'roll a bit hard to take. I realise this is my fault, but there's nothing I can do about it. The only exceptions are very early Elvis and almost all of Buddy Holly. There's something about Holly—the directness, the melodicism—that makes him still sound contemporary. Maybe it's his ability to get to the heart of the matter with subtlety rather than bombast. My favourite track of his—among many—is 'Well...All Right'. It's brutally simple but complex at the same time, with a fantastic acoustic guitar riff that has the power of a full band. Holly sounds at once tender, resigned, determined and furious. It's a generational statement before such things were consciously thought of, and could have been recorded yesterday."

The idea for "Well...All Right" had come out of touring with Little Richard, as Little Richard often yelled "Well...All Right". I asked **Dominic Pedler (218)** if Little Richard could have written the song. "Not that one. I don't hear Richard using this subtonic harmony (the bVII chord). The closest is merely in a stylistic passing context (that is, single-note riffs that use an individual subtonic note as a brief bluesy approach tone—and even then he only does that rarely as in 'All

Around The World'). I don't hear him using the relevant chord as structural harmony: he uses almost exclusively the I-IV-V chords, sometimes with a doo-wop relative minor thrown in."

Over the next couple of days, the Crickets recorded "Take Your Time", "Fool's Paradise" and "Think It Over". The Canadian singer and stooge for Jack Benny, Gisèle MacKenzie, had done well with "Never Go Away" in 1956, and its songwriter, Horace Linsley, also wrote "Fool's Paradise".

Tam White (219): "I do like some weird stuff but most of all, I like a simple melody with an endearing lyric: that is the whole secret of the game. 'Fool's Paradise' is a perfect example of that. It has a nice melody and it has a lyric that transcends time. Buddy Holly sang it in 1958 and I can sing it now. I was never an Elvis Presley fan: it was always Buddy Holly for me, and I've loved him ever since 'That'll Be The Day'."

Jerry Allison (220): "We wrote 'Take Your Time' in the back of the studio at Clovis, New Mexico and it's not one of my favourites and my name isn't on it. Norman Petty was writing with us and the line, 'Heartstrings will sing like a string of twine' is far too silly."

The lyrical message of "Take Your Time" is hardly typical of Holly's philosophy but it is a delightful cut with Norman Petty on organ and Jerry on cardboard box. The outtakes revealed that it was late at night and Buddy was getting tired. He was hitting bad notes and he stopped and said, "Boy, I can't just get on it, Norm, the page is blurred, can't even see the words." Norman Petty also recorded the song with Carolyn Hester.

Carolyn Hester (221): "I got to know Buddy pretty well and often saw him perform, and Jerry Allison played on my first album. I was once talking to Bob Dylan about 'Lonesome Tears' and 'Take Your Time' and saying how Buddy was really a roots musician. He fell about laughing but he told me he had been in a band doing Buddy Holly covers and he would have loved to have met him."

The key cut from the session was another Holly/Allison song (plus Petty), "Think It Over". Vi Petty played the piano ferociously and as a result, it became a classic rock'n'roll record.

Jerry Allison (222): "I had a ballad called 'Think It Over' and Buddy said it was a terrible

song. We changed it round and it worked as rock'n'roll."

Jerry Naylor (223): "When 'Think it Over' was being recorded, Vi Petty was out tending her vegetable patch and Norman asked her a couple of times to come in and lay down the piano break. She was busy with her own thing and eventually he really shouted at her to get on in. She came storming in, absolutely furious, sat down—still with mud on her hands and played that incredible over-dub in just one take. It really jumps out at you."

Jerry Allison took the lead vocal for Johnny O'Keefe's "Real Wild Child", while Bo Clark played drums. Buddy put both lead and rhythm guitar on the track and the Roses added backing vocals later. The song had also intrigued Jerry Lee Lewis and he recorded his version at Sun in April 1958. The first UK version was Jet Harris, backed by the Tremeloes, for an EP in 1962. It has also been recorded by Albert Lee.

Tim Whitnall (224): "I love 'Real Wild Child'. Everybody knows the Iggy Pop version and that is brilliant, but Jerry Allison sings the song in such a cool, laconic way. It's as though he couldn't be bothered."

Jerry's blubbering singing on "Oh You Beautiful Doll" had been learned from Sam Hirt, the trombonist for the Paul Williams Orchestra on *The Biggest Show Of Stars For 1957*. Water-filled wine glasses were played on "Oh You Beautiful Doll", which mimics the celesta on "Everyday". I don't care for the track myself, but I accept that it would appeal to fans of Freddie "Parrot-Face" Davies, if there are any.

Jerry Allison (225): "We did a tour in Australia and we met Johnny O'Keefe who was the Elvis Presley of Australia. He did 'Real Wild Child' which I thought was very funny. When I did it, I was trying to sing like Jimmy Cagney with Buddy playing the guitar licks. Bo Clark who played for the Roses was playing drums, not me. If Buddy saw me singing on stage now, I know he would make real fun of my vocals, which is what he did on 'Real Wild Child'."

The short, *Big Gold Record Stars Tour*, took place in Florida from 20 to 25 February 1958. It featured Bill Haley and his Comets (surprisingly, still topping the bill), the Everly Brothers, the Crickets, Jerry Lee Lewis and the Royal Teens (replacing a sick Jimmie Rodgers). The Everlys weren't happy with the band and used the Crickets instead. Jerry Lee Lewis had a long jacket trimmed with leopard skin and when his piano at Fort Lauderdale cracked up, he said, "I guess this piano's had it."

Bob Gaudio (226) of the Royal Teens: "I was 15 and the principal of my high school allowed me to leave high school to go on tour. It was a tough decision for my parents but they allowed me to go. I was touring with Buddy Holly, Jackie Wilson, Sam Cooke, the Everly Brothers, Paul Anka, Bo Diddley, LaVern Baker, Jimmy Reed and so it was amazing. I didn't get to know Buddy Holly very well, just hellos in passing, but he wasn't extroverted like Jackie Wilson, who was like that both on and off stage, one of the best performers I have ever seen. Sam Cooke was reserved and dignified but he knew how to capture an audience."

Joe B. Mauldin (227): "We only did one tour where we backed another group and that was in Florida with the Everly Brothers. The producers usually furnished a big band to back the other acts or they had their own groups with them."

Johnny Tillotson (228) lived in Florida. "That show was lots of fun: they all were very exciting with no frills. Buddy Holly walked on the stage, plugged into the amplifier, and he and the Crickets stole the show. What made them so good was that they had a number of hits in succession, either as 'Buddy Holly' or 'The Crickets', and so their set was very compact with hit after hit in a short time. They stole the show even though the Everly Brothers and Jerry Lee were phenomenal."

On 24 February 1958, Buddy did a radio interview with the DJ, Bob Chesney. Chesney captured snatches of the Crickets on stage doing "That'll Be The Day" and "Everyday" at the Dade County Auditorium, Florida. He caught Buddy Holly singing backstage to Jerry Lee Lewis's piano on Ray Charles' "Drown In My Own Tears" and "Hallelujah I Love Her So".

Now released in the UK, the cover photograph of *The Chirping Crickets* LP is of four boys and two guitars, but it said so much.

Bruce Welch (229): "We saw the cover of *The Chirping Crickets* and we really liked the look of the Strats on the cover. We had also seen a pho-tograph of Ricky Nelson with his guitarist. We couldn't see the top of his guitar but we thought it was a Fender Strat as well, although it turned out to be a Telecaster. There were some Board of Trade regulations at the time which meant that you couldn't buy American instruments, not even in Denmark Street, and we sent away for one. It was flamingo pink, gold-plated and maple coated. It looked like something out of the space age."

Terry Wayne (230): "I was knocked out when I saw the cover of *The Chirping Crickets* LP with those Fenders on the front. We'd never seen those in this country and you couldn't even buy them in the shops. You saw them and knew you wanted one."

Leo Sayer (231): "My older brother turned me on to music when I was a teenager. He had the Crickets first album and Dylan's and one by Jesse Fuller, whom I would play harp for years later."

John Tobler (232): "I can clearly remember my first sight of a copy of *The Chirping Crickets*, the breakthrough LP by that group, although it has never been clear to me why such a ludicrous title was chosen for what is one of the finest albums ever released. What first strikes me after playing *The Chirping Crickets* now is how immensely direct it is. The modern tendency for a half minute intro over which a disc jockey can speak doesn't exist here—the absolutely perfect 'That'll Be The Day' begins with an irresistible guitar riff which is a major reason for me writing about music rather than playing it. After many unsuccessful attempts to play that riff on my Framus cello guitar, it became clear that listening to music was a far less stressful way of enjoying music. The LP also included 'Oh Boy !', an exclamation of innocent teenage lust and perhaps an early example of bubblegum pop, which Mud proved with their revival in 1975. On the whole, I wasn't too keen on the backing vocals, as they tended to subtract from rather than enhance the sound. The *Buddy Holly* album was equally great."

Robb Johnson (233): "I don't normally like Stratocasters but he looks so good with a Stratocaster. He made it look so cool. How exciting it must have been for guys to be going somewhere that no one else had gone before. Everybody who has followed after, the terrain's been mapped; the three chords have been used. All the harmonies have been sung, we are trying to shuffle around those same three chords that Buddy Holly found and turned into absolute art. It must have been so exciting to be doing that."

Mark Kelly (234): "Buddy Holly didn't look cool and didn't dress cool. He wasn't like Elvis or Eddie Cochran. He looked like a nervous office clerk, fronting a band who were only booked for weddings. After the gig, he'd probably be the skinny weakling being bullied on the beach until he was rescued by a keen pupil of Charles Atlas. And that hiccup in his voice! It was how you'd imagine Norman Wisdom would sing. That was my view as a child. but, as the years went by, his songs stayed with me, I stopped caring about looks, (have you seen my wardrobe?) and now I reckon Buddy Holly was the best songwriter of his regrettably short time : simple, catchy melodies, quirky, varied arrangements, and lyrics which somehow, mysteriously, always seemed to work."

In March 1958, the British impresarios and brothers, Lew and Leslie Grade, wanted to present Buddy Holly and the Crickets on a UK tour. There were 25 concert venues including seven in London and usually in cinemas or municipal halls. A fee of $4,000 a week was agreed. After agency fees for Norman Petty, Manny Greenfield and GAC, Holly would get $1,500 a week and Jerry and Joe $750 each. Holly even told *Melody Maker* that they had two managers and an agent to support, a caustic quip if ever there was one.

Leslie Grade requested that the Crickets should perform for 25 minutes: he wrote, "You know how it is here. They expect the top of the bill to do a long act and if they did less than 25 minutes, the public would be very disappointed." Had the Crickets only been planning 15 minutes? Leslie Grade did offer the Crickets the use of the orchestra but they declined. Ironically, because of union restrictions, the orchestra had to sit on stage throughout their set.

The billing on the initial publicity listed Don Smith and his Orchestra, although this was changed to Ronnie Keene. Don Smith was an executive at the Musicians' Union and as the union usually disapproved of American artists coming to the UK on the grounds that it deprived British musicians of work, he felt it would be hypocritical to do this tour—thereby depriving British musi-

cians of work! Ronnie Keene's orchestra had been resident at the Royal Ballroom, Tottenham and he had conducted the score for Frankie Vaughan's film, *These Dangerous Years*. Keene had 12 musicians for the tour and a girl singer, Lynn Adams, and the repertoire included "In The Mood" and "One O'Clock Jump".

Johnnie Hamp (235): "Rock'n'roll tours were not like they are today. Des O'Connor was on the bill and other variety acts. I was a fan of Buddy Holly's and he was coming here and I booked the show into three of our Granada Theatres: the ones at East Ham, Woolwich and Walthamstow. They were 3,000 seaters and packed out, and he told me that he hadn't really worked big theatres before. In the States, he would be just one of six or seven big acts. Des O'Connor had been around a bit and he was a very good compère. On Sunday night, he couldn't tell jokes because of the regulations of the Lord Day's Observance Society. You couldn't laugh on Sunday! Des could introduce the acts, but he couldn't tell any jokes and he would whistle 'Swanee River'. He kept on doing it and the audience was hysterical. He always did a very good spot."

Carolyn Hester (236): "The boys told me that when they were in the UK, the fans found out which train they were travelling on and they had drawn a great big sign saying "Buddy Holly is Great". It stretched for yards and yards and they saw it from the train."

Stuart Colman (237): "The British take on rock'n'roll was unlike its counterpart in America. The differing cultures meant that whilst one society might accord a lengthy shelf-life to an artist with a hard-earned career, the other would forever be seeking out some new kid on the block. With the Draconian exchange rule applied by the Musicians' Union limiting the amount of American rock'n'rollers who could have work visas, British audiences rarely saw anything to compete with the Alan Freed and Dick Clark spectaculars that wowed the USA during the 1950s. The key names who did make the trip were lauded in a manner usually reserved for royalty. Buddy Holly's future as a timeless icon was assured, not by his death but by coming to Britain in 1958. He set the pattern for the archetypal rock'n'roller. It was an image that would be recast time and time again—from Hank Marvin to Elvis Costello— and I'm sure he would have been proud at what he had instigated."

The Crickets had been performing on rock'n'roll packages and a variety show was new to them. They topped the bill and they were supported by a middle of the road British singer, Gary Miller, who had had Top 20 hits with "The Yellow Rose Of Texas", "Robin Hood" and "Garden Of Eden". He would have attracted his own following: the Tanner Sisters (Frances and Stella) were a popular radio act, and the compère, Des O'Connor, had made a name for himself at Billy Butlin's holiday camps.

On 27 February 1958, the Crickets and the Pettys flew to London Airport (now Heathrow) and the next day was filled with publicity. They arrived late and had to be rushed to an ITV studio for Kent Walton's *Cool For Cats*, where they mimed to "I'm Gonna Love You Too". It was an unlikely choice as two new singles had been released, "Listen To Me" (Holly) and "Maybe Baby" (Crickets), and this was Holly's B-side. Better than the time *Cool For Cats* played "Not Fade Away" with bodybuilders flexing their muscles.

Chas Hodges (238): "I listened to my brother's records but I can remember wanting to buy one with my own money. I was in Edmonton market and I had enough money for one record only. I had to choose between Buddy Holly's 'Listen To Me' and Jerry Lee Lewis' 'Breathless'. I was a mad Jerry Lee fan even then but I chose 'Listen To Me'."

The Crickets were staying at the Cumberland Hotel in Marble Arch where your shoes would be shined overnight. Jerry and Joe B. were so enthralled that they waited for the shoeshine boy and gave him a £5 tip.

A publicity event was arranged at the Whiskey-A-Go-Go in Wardour Street, Soho. The Crickets were photographed dancing with young girls from the teenage love comic, *Valentine,* and posed for the national papers with two cricketers, Godfrey Evans and Denis Compton, both nearing the end of their careers. The combination of entertainment and sport for a news story was unusual in 1958. One of the dancing girls was Imogen Hassell, who later appeared in several comedy

and horror films. She was known as much for her cleavage as her acting and she was a main character in the National Theatre's play, *Cleo, Camping, Emmanuelle And Dick*. She died from an overdose in 1980.

Larry Page (239) had covered "That'll Be The Day" for the UK market: "The only good thing about the whole episode is that I got a chance to meet Buddy Holly when he came to England. He was with some cricketers and they were doing a promotion on the Crickets. He was a very, very nice guy and very shrewd and I was one of the first people to cover one of his songs. I was in Tower Records in LA a few years ago and someone came to me and asked me if I was 'Larry Page, The Teenage Rage'. It was unbelievable, right in the middle of Hollywood some American had got my version of 'That'll Be The Day'."

After shopping in Oxford Street, the Crickets performed their first UK shows at the Trocadero in the London suburb of Elephant and Castle on Saturday 1 March 1958. There were 1,500 at the first house and 3,000 at the second, which is roughly the way the whole tour (and indeed most pop tours) went. The top ticket price was 10/6d. Gary Miller had been entertaining troops in Cyprus and he arrived just in time to rehearse with the band.

Joe B. Mauldin (240): "We were the rock'n'roll act on a variety show, and I thought that was the deal over here, that people wanted to see a variety show rather than straight rock'n'roll. In America we had done the Alan Freed shows with 21 different acts, who were all rock'n'rollers. They'd say, 'And now the Crickets' and we'd do two tunes –and then it was 'And now Eddie Cochran' and he only got one song! It was quite different here 'cause we got to play for 30 minutes."

Des O'Connor (241): "I got £100 a week for being the compère and comic on the tour, which was big money then. We were touring with the Ronnie Keene Orchestra, which had a lot of brass, and then out came the Crickets, just three of them, and I couldn't work out how they were making ten times as much noise. It was so exciting and vibrant and I knew that something exciting was happening."

Although the Crickets were scheduled for 25 minutes, they only performed for 20, which was due to them hurrying the songs: "at feverish speed", according to a newspaper report. Buddy moved little and said less but he did announce, "Here's a sad little song with tender lyrics that really tell a story. The tune is likely to reduce you all to tears, not because of the sadness of the words, but on account of the pathetic way we sing it." The Crickets then performed "Rip It Up". It wasn't a bad joke but Buddy had pinched it from Elvis Presley on *The Ed Sullivan Show.* The Crickets were intrigued to see Teddy Boys with long hair, crepes and drapes in the audience as the fashion was unknown in America. At the other end of the social scale, they noted some lads wearing cravats.

While at the Trocadero, the Crickets met another sportsman, this time the South African boxing champion, Willie Toweel. He was training in Old Kent Road and his brother, Maurice, arranged for a backstage meeting. He told Buddy, "Boxing relies on rhythm and timing and that is why many boxers skip and train to rock music."

The Crickets continued their stay at the Cumberland Hotel, Marble Arch, and the following day, they appeared on the 100th edition of Val Parnell's ITV show, *Sunday Night At The London Palladium* with Bob Hope topping the bill. They had a rehearsal in the morning, did the early show at the Gaumont State Theatre, Kilburn and then rushed back for the second set. The day was so rushed that Buddy thought the TV show was called *Beat The Clock.* The compère was the portly actor, Robert Morley, who had stepped in for the regular host, Tommy Trinder, who had been suspended for a controversial joke.

Bruce Welch (242): "I'm not surprised that Robert Morley was like that. The presenters like Steve Race and Jack Payne looked down on the new music. They thought that it was crap and it wouldn't last. That's why 'Move It!' is such a great song. Ian Samwell, who wrote it, knew that the music would last, and so did we."

Neil Foster (243): "I remember watching Buddy's only appearance on *Sunday Night at the London Palladium* in 1958 and being intensely irritated by Robert Morley's pompous and unfunny introduction, in which he made fun of Buddy's name, that is, 'Is it Holly Buddy or is it Buddy Holly?' Comedians were usually the compères on

that show and no doubt Morley thought he could do comedy as well. He couldn't."

Mike Pender (244): "The sound was disappointing on the London Palladium show but later I did the Palladium with the Searchers and we had the same problem. They were more interested in how you looked than in how you sounded."

Alan Blakley (245): "There wasn't much live rock'n'roll in 1958 and we would be going to see dance bands play. There weren't bass guitars and you only saw a Fender Strat on photographs with Buddy Holly. We were all Buddy Holly barmy and I was very excited when Buddy Holly and the Crickets were going to do *Sunday Night At The London Palladium,* but they were only on for a few minutes so it was rather disappointing."

John Firminger (246): "Although the sound balance on *Sunday Night At The London Palladium* left something to be desired, it was just great to see him performing on stage after only hearing him on record. None of those TV appearances had been shown in the UK and he hadn't appeared in any rock'n'roll films."

Writing in *Disc,* the TV producer Jack Good (who was about to call his new programme, *Oh Boy!)* wrote, "Their appearance on *Sunday Night At The London Palladium* was a disaster comparable only with Napoleon's retreat from Moscow. They have one mike through which Buddy Holly despairingly bawls three numbers in quick succession to a horde of sedentary cold suet puddings, at an ever-increasing tempo (longing, no doubt, to be away from it all.) Then, without a word, they're off. And a reputation has died. What I want to know is, who gets the benefit? Why do it?"

Johnnie Hamp (247): "Buddy was moaning to me about the bad sound on *Sunday Night At The London Palladium.* They didn't carry enormous amplifiers then but we had very good sound systems at the Granada cinemas and theatres. He was terrific. The Palladium show had been live and everyone had been telling him that the television sound was naff: it may have been all right in the theatre."

There was an outcry when the Rolling Stones refused to appear on the roundabout at the end of their first appearance on *Sunday Night At The Palladium.* Well, the Crickets beat them to it, but in their case only because they had to return to Kilburn for the second house.

The Crickets did three songs on the Palladium—"That'll Be The Day", "Peggy Sue" and "Oh Boy!"- in a six minute set and Holly didn't speak. The Crickets included these songs in every performance as well as "Maybe Baby" and "Everyday". As well as their hits, the Crickets were performing "Keep-A Knockin'", "Rip It Up", "Great Balls Of Fire" and "Be-Bop A Lula" and closing with "Ready Teddy". At the Kilburn State, there was an unbilled final act as Norman Petty was fascinated by the theatre organ and started to play it.

The Crickets were chirping much more than at the Trocadero, and Holly was enjoying himself, grinning at his colleagues, running across the stage and almost doing the splits. The reviewer for *Hit Parade* said that their music was "fierce, blistering, exciting and authentic." The NME reviewer said, "The Crickets are the loudest, noisiest trio I've ever heard…Drummer Jerry Allison attacks his kit with murderous intent, but bassist Joe Mauldin remains relatively calm and looks rather miserable most of the time."

Brian Poole (248): "Buddy Holly and the Crickets were absolutely marvellous because they were the loudest thing we'd ever heard. It was a small band but they made such a crack when they came on and it was very, very exciting, and we had someone to look up to. We developed our style and we were doing Buddy Holly songs for the next five years. At one stage there was nothing in our act that wasn't a Buddy Holly song. We hadn't seen a Fender Stratocaster before—this was like a flat plank and now every guitar is like it. We were so much into Buddy Holly that I had the hair and the glasses exactly like him."

After the second show, the Crickets talked with Keith Goodwin of the NME and Allan Crawford of Southern Music. (Southern Music was based at 8 Denmark Street, a building now occupied by *The World Of Pianos*). Goodwin and Crawford talked with the Crickets about British cars and they went looking at showrooms at 2am.

Keith Goodwin (249): "Buddy Holly was a well brought-up college kid. There were only a couple of months between us but he used to call me 'Sir', which made me feel old and rather annoyed me. He was a very nice, easygoing lad. He did what he did simply because he felt that was the way it should be done. He wasn't out to change the world but he wasn't going to let the world change him. He would never relax. He wanted to see places and to get the feel of a town by walking around. He wasn't a star in his own eyes."

Buddy wanted an acoustic guitar for the tour bus, and **Des O'Connor (250)** took him to Denmark Street. "When we walked around Soho, he went into a music shop and tried about 17 guitars. They all sounded the same to me but he picked up a Gibson, said it had a good tone and bought it. He'd play it on the bus and he showed me how to play guitar. He taught me C, F and G but I wasn't meant to be a guitar player. When he left, he gave it to me. He said, 'You use this, Des, I've got too many of them anyway.' There are in-built memories with that guitar but as I'm still on C, F and G, I don't think he'd be too thrilled with his pupil."

On 3 March 1958, the touring package played the Gaumont in Southampton with many sailors in the audience, who had been given free tickets. A reviewer said that that "it was a little noisy but well appreciated. Buddy is 'real gone' once he gets going." After the engagement, they returned to London. Buddy couldn't sleep and he wrote to his parents at 4am. He told them that they were doing nine songs in each performance: "That seems like a lot but the people won't let us off the stage with the usual four or five numbers."

With very little sleep, Buddy got up at 8am for the tour bus to take them to the City Hall in Sheffield. This unusual venue sold platform seats for 3/6d and so Buddy had part of the audience sitting behind him, and was uncomfortable about this. And somewhere in the audience at Sheffield was a young Joe Cocker.

Dave Berry (251): "You would call Buddy Holly a geek now. The band wore white shirts and dinner jackets and they used a stand-up bass. I wasn't disappointed as I had gone to see them because of the songs, not because of the way they looked. They were quite easy to learn and we did a lot of Buddy Holly songs."

John Firminger (252): "The feelings towards Buddy's appearance in Sheffield were mixed.

Some say that he was fantastic, looking and sounding great, and others were disappointed by the somewhat formal look of Buddy onstage and there being only three Crickets instead of the four as seen on *The Chirping Crickets.*"

After the Globe in Stockton-on-Tees, they moved to Newcastle City Hall and they had added "I'm Lookin' For Someone To Love" to the repertoire. Before the show, Buddy told a reporter, "Audiences in the States just go wild: here, they are reserved." When he talked to a fan from Scotland, he asked, "Is Scotland as cold as England?" The weather got to him as had a cold when they went to Wolverhampton.

Steve Gibbons (253): "I was working at a plumber's mate at the time Buddy was in the area. I know I wanted to go but I couldn't afford it. Four of us were working on the same job and one of the others went to see Buddy and came back talking about what a wonderful guitarist he was. I was green with envy."

Going to Nottingham, the touring party ran into a snowstorm. Despite the extremes of weather in Lubbock, Buddy couldn't get used to the continual rain, sleet and snow. It was cold, wet and damp, not the type of bad weather they had in humid Lubbock. When he wrote to his sister Pat, he wondered if there ever was summer here.

Joe B. Mauldin (254): "All the hotels had a small heater on the wall that you had to put a sixpence in, and we were running out of sixpences. By the time we got some more, the room had gotten cold again, so we usually stayed downstairs by the fireplaces."

Des O'Connor (255): "We travelled together on the bus and I shared a room with Buddy a couple of times. I was the only one who could drag him out of bed. He was a devil to wake up and the only time he wasn't smiling was in the mornings. One day I woke him up by pulling his legs, and sounding like Deputy Dawg, he drawled, 'Don't do that, Des, I'm tall enough.'"

During the afternoon on 9 March, the Crickets saw the British war film, *The Bridge On The River Kwai,* starring Alec Guinness and William Holden. As the Tanner Sisters had a TV appearance in Birmingham, two Scotsmen with piano accordions were drafted in for the Bradford show and Norman Petty played the Wurlitzer as the audience left. Gary Miller was booed for a confident but lengthy performance of Rodgers and Hammerstein's "My Boy Bill" from *Carousel.* He closed his act with the audience shrieking "Get off!" As no comedians were allowed on stage on Sunday in Bradford (apart from Gary Miller, that is), Des O'Connor had to announce the acts without jokes, but he did pretend to play his guitar on stage with Jerry and Joe. After kicking his legs in the air and generally clowning about, he announced Buddy Holly. They had an unusual, but now commonplace, stage effect when they came on with ultra-violet lights picking out their white shirts. They performed a different set including "Money Honey" and Little Richard's "She's Got It" Buddy still had a cold but the tour was going well.

On Monday morning, 10 March 1958, the Crickets and Norman Petty visited the Austin factory at Longbridge, which had been arranged by Bob Kingston at Southern Music in London. They had an extensive tour of the factory, which prompted Norman to purchase an Austin Healey DeLuxe for £1,000 and have it shipped to Clovis. Joe B. fancied an Austin Healey, while Jerry told the press he wanted an MG, and Buddy a Jaguar or a Mercedes.

A jazz authority and biographer of J.B. Priestley, Peter Holdsworth, reviewed concerts for *Bradford Telegraph And Argus.* He wrote, "Unless they had previously read the lyrics or heard them sung by an articulate vocalist, I would have defied anyone in the audience to tell me what 70 per cent of the words were which issued from the lips of this foot-stamping, knee-falling musician. Where on earth is show business heading?"

On 11 March 1958, fans broke windows trying to get into Buddy's dressing room at the Gaumont, Worcester. Buddy met a girl called Pat, who clearly got the wrong message. She often wrote to him in Lubbock and although he did not respond, he kept her letters.

Then, after Croydon, they moved to East Ham, where Lonnie Donegan visited them backstage. When Lonnie turned professional, he left his job in Millets and according to Chris Barber, he left wearing several pairs of jacket and trousers. He was still wearing their clothes if the photos of Lonnie with the Crickets are anything to go by.

Lonnie Donegan (256): "I met Buddy Holly and the Crickets over a cup of tea when they played in Britain. He was the first person to bring a solid guitar into the country and because of the rulings with the Musicians' Union, it was very rare to see an American singer with his own band. I'd never seen a drummer like Jerry Allison before. He was all over his kit. It was great Texas drumming."

A performance on Jack Hylton's TV show, *See You In Soho*, was cancelled, perhaps because it broke the contract with the Grades as Hylton was a rival West End promoter. However, on 14 March, they filmed "Maybe Baby" for Jack Payne's BBC-TV show, *Off The Record*. Payne was a pain, an old-time bandleader who had no truck with the music of the day. The programme also featured Spike Milligan, George Melly and Ronnie Hilton and, according to *Radio Times*, "Buddy Holly and the Crickets were specifically telerecorded for this programme."

Norman Jopling (257): "I was only 14 and I wasn't going to concerts in '58, and the only time I saw Buddy Holly was on TV on Jack Payne's *Words & Music* when the Crickets performed 'Maybe Baby'. I collected his records when I was still at school: in fact when I sold my train layout to buy a little record player, my first LP was *The Chirping Crickets*."

On 14 March 1958, they played the Granada, Woolwich, and Mick Jagger was in the audience. **Bob Davis (258)**: "I was about 12 but my parents let me go with my sister Ann and her boyfriend. We went to the early show, which wasn't packed but pretty full. They took us by surprise by playing their new record, 'Maybe Baby', first. They had a great sound with plenty of volume and they were able to reproduce the sound of their records. I was to discover that a lot of live performances missed the mark, and they got a great reception. When we spilled out into Powis Street, there was a huge crowd milling around for the next performance. The town was buzzing, and that doesn't happen very often in Woolwich! I like to think that Mick Jagger had been at the same show as me as he was 14 and would have come from Dartford, so he would have gone to the early show so that he could get home and get to bed for grammar school in the morning."

Having been invited by Lonnie Donegan, the Crickets attended a midnight benefit for the blues singer, Big Bill Broonzy at the Dominion Theatre, featuring Donegan, Chris Barber and Ken Colyer. Joe B. was especially impressed as he had never seen Dixieland jazz played live before. Broonzy had collected many fans on his UK appearances but this benefit couldn't help his treatment as he died in August 1958.

From Ipswich, they moved to Doncaster. The Crickets' dinner consisted of pork chops and 10 Coca-Colas, so that's where the energy came from. Although they disliked the British weather, they enjoyed travelling in the UK as, unlike West Texas, there was always something to look at. There is footage of the group on tour in the UK with Joe Mauldin on the floor playing his double-bass. "He was the sex symbol of the group," says Jerry Allison.

When Norman Petty saw the *NME*, he must have been delighted. There were seven Nor-Va-Jak songs in the Top 30: two Crickets records (9, 28), Buddy Holly records (16, 19) and three versions of "Sugartime" (21, 22, 29). The following week was similar with Crickets (10, 15), Holly (16, 30) and "Sugartime" (26=, 26=, 28).

In 2005, **Alvin Stardust (259)** discovered that he still had his old acoustic guitar, covered in signatures. "It was a fluke. I was 12 when my mum bought me the guitar and it is over 50 years old now. She threw a lot of things away, thinking that I wasn't using them anymore. I would love to still have my first cowboy boots. I wore them on stage until they were falling apart and I loved them. She threw away loads of jackets. I had forgotten about my guitar, it was in the distant past, and then my mum died a couple of years ago, and I got all her stuff. We put a lot of it in the garage but last year I thought I had better go through it, and I found these two cases with my first ever 78s and 45s and there was 'Jailhouse Rock', the first record I bought. I had a Dansette record player and I would have loved to have that. Then I picked up this old guitar case which was blue with mould and I thought it would be going to the tip. Inside was this kid's guitar, a learn-to-play guitar but a proper one. The strings were rusty and I had put sequins all over it. I was 13 or 14 and I had gone on the bus to see Buddy Holly and the Crickets in

Doncaster and I took the guitar and I was trying to learn chords. I had never been to a music concert before and I walked in and somehow managed to get backstage. They were all so polite and quiet. They asked me how many chords I knew and I said, 'I know all three of them' and Buddy said, 'You can play all my songs then.' They made me get it out and we were singing 'Peggy Sue' together, and then Buddy signed it for me."

And what of the concert itself? **Alvin Stardust (260)**: "I had gone all that way and I didn't have a ticket. Buddy asked the road manager to find me a seat and they gave me a house seat right on the front row of the balcony, which was fantastic. I sat there with my guitar between my legs all night long and I wouldn't let go of it. Nobody knew that Buddy had signed it for me. He was so dynamic on stage, a powerhouse, even with the gentler songs. He had a real presence on stage and I got the same feeling when I first saw Billy Fury on stage. He was a real powerhouse too."

Alvin Stardust (261) still has that guitar, but for how long? "I took it with me everywhere I went and I always got it signed. In 1963, I did the Royal Albert Hall with the Beatles, I was still only 18, and they all signed it for me. The signatures are written in pencil and dug into the lacquer on the guitar. When I got it out, the first signature I saw was Buddy Holly's and I nearly died. I thought that the guitar must be worth several thousand quid and I had better do something about it. I took it to Rick Zigfield who runs a guitar shop and has a collectors' market on the internet. He told me that it was valuable. A specialist told me to get it insured for $500,000, and someone who owns a chain of casinos has offered me $1m. I saw that a guitar with Bryan Adams, Mick Jagger and Rod Stewart on went for £1.6m, so I know I've got something really valuable."

Because the show at St George's Hall, Blackburn had to be cancelled, it was moved to Ritz Theatre, Wigan. The good people of Wigan had to pay no more than 8/6d for the best seats. The Crickets stayed at the Grand Hotel, Wigan, and Buddy invited the receptionist, Barbara Bullough, to the concert. He dedicated "Everyday" and took her home in a taxi to Shevington. He wanted her to come on tour but she couldn't and heck, this was 1958.

John Rostron (262): "'I Wanna Say Hello' by Sir Hubert Pimm was the liveliest record I had heard until my Father bought Bill Haley and the Comets' 'Rock Around the Clock' for the 1955 New Years Eve party that they organised at his surgery. The whole world of music around me started to change with Elvis Presley hitting the scene with 'Heartbreak Hotel' and 'Hound Dog' and then Gene Vincent in June with 'Be-Bop-A-Lula'. Then in September 57 it struck, the opening riff of 'That'll Be The Day', the driving guitar, the hiccup in the voice and the lead singer of the Crickets did wear glasses. He was one of us. I was in the same year at King George V Grammar School in Southport as Malcolm Jones. He produced the box-set of Buddy Holly with Johnny Beecher. He became an early member of the Buddy Holly Fan Club and persuaded me to join and we talked about the Crickets at every opportunity. Buddy and the Crickets released a lot of singles in quick succession and it took up all my pocket money. I was 13 and the boys two years ahead of me organised to go to Wigan to see them on March 18 1958. My parents would not let me go but I loved their stories as to how good they were."

The next night the touring party was in Hull and a play to commemorate that, *Buddy Holly At The Regal,* has been staged in recent years. It is about a gangly fish processor who goes to the show and discovers Buddy looks ordinary, which changes his life. Yes, I know, it doesn't sound like much of a plot, and Buddy is depicted as rather mean-spirited in the play. There has also been a curious newspaper story about Geoff Lindley who had a Saturday job in Grimsby selling surgical appliances. According to him, Buddy Holly wandered into the store, wondering where guitar strings were. Geoff pointed him to an appropriate shop and Buddy gave him a signed copy of "Peggy Sue Got Married". Oh yes.

The touring party was back in the north-west the following day, 20 March 1958, for a concert at the Philharmonic Hall, Liverpool. Buddy met up with Barbara again, but this was the briefest of romances.

Mark Lewisohn (263): "The various members of the Beatles didn't see Buddy Holly when he came to Liverpool as it was also the opening night of the Morgue skiffle cellar in Oakhill Park and the Quarry Men were either playing that night or wanted to get in with the club. Considering what Holly fans they were, it's a bit of surprise that they did that, but also theatre tickets cost money."

The Philharmonic Hall staged classical concerts and speech days and as it was under council ownership, they were reluctant to book hit parade artists. On this occasion, the venue was hired by the music shop, Rushworth and Dreapers, who also booked the Paul Anka tour for the previous night. Like Holly, Anka was committed to performing 25 minutes on a variety showcase.

The reviewer for *Liverpool Echo* was an old-stager, George Harrison, who was soon to use his name as his meal ticket around the world. He reported that only 300 people were at the first concert, but, if it was only that many, I've met all of them. His numbers may be wrong but, just before Buddy Holly started to play, there was a loss of power in his amplifier. George Harrison wrote, "Harassed men dashed in from all directions, pushing electric plugs into plug-holes all over the place, but not a bleep came from the guitar. So the three Americans solemnly trooped off the stage and back to their dressing-room. The long gap was filled by a 'hot' band, but the fear was beginning to be mentioned that the top of the bill act would not go on. The road manager, Wally Stewart, who wore a bowler hat, unscrewed the bulb from a ceiling light and after running an extension lead to the guitar, it worked. However, Holly was not keen to go on after this delay and Stewart had to persuade him."

For once, it was provident that Ronnie Keene and his Orchestra were on stage. Miss J.A. Fox of Chester told the *NME*: "I feel I must say a word of praise for Ronnie Keene and the boys for doing an excellent job when Buddy Holly's amplifier broke down at Liverpool last week. Despite the shouts from the audience, who were too thick-headed to appreciate his unfortunate position, Ronnie Keene did his best to entertain the audience while the amplifier was mended. I sincerely hope that Buddy didn't take this display of bad manners to be typical of all British teenagers."

Again from the *Liverpool Echo*: "Significant perhaps of the growing tend in discrimination among audiences was the point that BOTH houses would not have half-filled the Empire Theatre." There does not seem to be much evidence for this lack of sales. There were even spectators in the tiered seats behind the stage. However, these were freebies handed out to American servicemen stationed at Burtonwood. **Gerry Standard (264)**: "I still have my ticket for the second performance at the Liverpool Philharmonic—seat D24, cost four shillings. While we were waiting outside, the first house came out and some of them were offering us double price for our tickets so they could go in again.

Jim Newcombe (265). "I went to as many rock'n'roll shows as I could. Before Buddy Holly, I had seen the Platters, Paul Anka and Charlie Gracie, all in Liverpool as back then not many families had cars and anyway, I was too young to drive. I was only 16 when I saw Buddy Holly in March. I went with Geoff Taggart to the second house and we were in the first rows of the circle. We were queuing outside as the first house was still in progress. We could hear the music through the walls but not clearly, and everyone was buzzing, talking about Buddy Holly and his songs. I am sure it was a full house. Des O'Connor had a few good jokes but as the show progressed, everybody wanted to see Buddy."

The second house had been so animated that Jerry Allison threw his drum sticks into the audience, and Buddy Holly played his guitar over his head. UK concertgoers had never seen a Fender Strat before, let alone one played that way and wannabe musicians like Mike Pender were blinded by the light.

Mike Pender (266): "I saw Buddy Holly at the Liverpool Philharmonic and from that night onwards, everything I learned, everything I played was based on Holly. Groups now have banks of amplifiers and speakers all over the place, and most times they still don't get the sound they want. Holly came on stage with just a double-bass, drums and one amplifier. He didn't have sex appeal and he wasn't that good-looking but he brought the house down. A lot of people have tried to imitate him over the years but nobody's ever got close. Bobby Vee did well with ballads but not the rock'n'roll stuff."

Tom Earley (267): "I saw Buddy Holly live at the Philharmonic. My friend's mother bought some tickets and my friend, Geoff Cannell, invited me along. This was the first time I had seen a Fender guitar and to see those three guys playing their hits was spectacular. I think that the bass was going through a stand-up mike on the floor, and there was just one small Fender amp on the stage for Buddy. Buddy Holly is still the king foe me and 'That'll Be The Day' sounds as fresh as ever."

Dave Williams (268): "I was in my last year at school and I went to the second house. Buddy had a long lead and he was in the choir stalls as they call them at the Phil, on his knees, on his back, everything, he really went to town. The audience participation pushed him on as he got a great audience reaction from Liverpool. Fantastic concert. I can't remember hearing much of Joe B though, it was mostly very loud guitar, loud by those standards. Jerry Allison was a loud drummer too. I was prepared to put up with the rest of the show as we knew Buddy was coming. Lots of people were bored sick and some of them were shouting for Buddy. Some of them may have come for Gary Miller but not very many. I was in the second row from the back in the stalls. Q22."

Gerry Standard (269): "Des O'Connor said, with a wave of the hand, 'Ladies and gentlemen, Buddy Holly and the Crickets.' The group ran on stage—Jerry to the drums, Joe to the double-bass and Buddy to the centre. He already had his guitar around his shoulder. They began with 'Oh Boy!' and Buddy said, 'It's great to be in Liverpool but who wants to hear me talking. Let's get on with the music.' They also did 'Ready Teddy', 'Rip It Up', 'Everyday', 'Not Fade Away' and 'That'll Be The Day'. They took three curtain calls and then did 'That'll Be The Day' again. It was a night I'll remember for the rest of my life."

Jim Newcombe (270): "When they were announced, the three of them walked on—Joe B. picking up the bass, Jerry getting on the drums and Buddy plugging in his Fender Strat and then it was 'Everyday' but faster than the record. Even though there were only three of them, it was a really strong sound. Every song was tough and Holly was a real rocker. He did 'Maybe Baby' and 'Peggy Sue'. He was dressed like the others in a grey suit and seemed very slim: he had loads of energy and danced around, one time doing a sort

of Chuck Berry duck walk across the stage over to Joe. He dropped on one knee and held his guitar high. There were surprises too as he announced 'Great Balls Of Fire' which suited his rip-roaring style, and 'Reddy Teddy' from his solo LP, which is the closest you get to his onstage style. When he said he had just seen the Everly Brothers do 'Be-Bop-A-Lula' on TV, I yelled out, "What about Gene?" His version was the faster Everlys' arrangement. He did 'Reddy Teddy' and 'Rip It Up' and I am pretty sure he closed with 'That'll Be The Day' and I don't remember an encore. His set wasn't long as the songs were short, especially the fast rockers. It was sheer pace and excitement with Buddy letting rip on guitar solos and Jerry belting those drums. At one stage people were dancing in the aisles and he said, 'If y'all don't quit dancing, I ain't gonna sing': no doubt he had been prompted by theatre staff to stop the dancing as I once saw them put the curtain down on Wee Willie Harris because he was dressed like a caveman and a Liverpool regulation said 'No costumes on a Sunday'. Geoff and I wanted to get an autograph or just shake Buddy's hand but when we got to the stage door there were so many people crowding around, and we had a bus to catch. We headed for the bus and naturally we talked about seeing him again."

Mike Pender (271): "I can remember going away from the theatre thinking that this is what I would like to do for a living. I was in my first job at Ray's Tugs, one of the Merseyside shipping companies. It was a magical night. It was music hall acts really, but Holly had his Fender Strat and there was just the three of them on the stage. It was still a big sound and loud and the audience was on its feet. It was fantastic!"

The tour moved to Walthamstow, where Buddy said, "'Be-Bop-A-Lula' will be performed the way the Everly Brothers perform it—up-tempo." Next stop was Salisbury. Buddy wrote home, "Everyone comments on how my jokes get bigger laughs than the comedian on the show. Who knows, we might change and be comedians instead of rock'n'roll stars."

Des O'Connor (272): "Someone published a letter that Buddy wrote home in which he said his jokes were going down better than mine, the little stinker! What he didn't say was that I was giving him the jokes. He had a real Southern drawl and I helped him to modify it so that the English would understand him. The audiences loved his accent, and jokes that I wouldn't get laughs with would be downright funny when he delivered them. One was, and I hope this won't offend anyone, 'Why can the Pakistanis beat the English at cricket and not at football? Because every time they get a corner, they open a shop.' Buddy said it, and no-one was offended."

Then it was Bristol and their only show outside England, in Cardiff. The former leader of the Labour party, Neil Kinnock saw the Welsh show. He was delighted to be just yards away from the group. The coach broke down and his party didn't give a damn as they had enjoyed the concert so much and being Welsh, they were singing all the way home.

On 25 March 1958, they were at Gaumont Theatre, Hammersmith, when Buddy's amplifier was again at fault. This time Norman Petty was on hand to repair it. He took some footage of the first show, which still exists. A blue plaque was unveiled at Gaumont Hammersmith by Bruce Welch in 2003.

This was the end of the tour and the Crickets were in a buoyant mood. The tour had been a great success, despite a few critics, and they were going home and they wouldn't be cold anymore. Between the two shows, Joe B. lit a large cigar and said he was going to fill the room with smoke and a scuffle broke out. During the scuffle, he accidentally knocked some caps off Buddy's teeth. Joe B, has a small scar on his forehead to this day. Marion Keene, Ronnie's wife, suggested that he spread some gum over his teeth and then do the show. Perhaps because he felt self-conscious, Holly gave a poor show. After the concert, they signed a programme for Keith Goodwin of the *NME* and Buddy told him that he was the best journalist they had met. Their final interview about the tour was very upbeat. They had loved meeting the fans and Buddy reckoned he had signed 100 autographs a day, and they enjoyed British politeness in which the fans would queue for autographs. In retrospect, they enjoyed being the sole rock'n'roll group on a variety show as they had got all the attention.

Jerry Allison (273): "We had a really good time here. It was cold and the beer was warm, which

was the wrong way round for us. The British audiences were more reserved during the songs but they really grooved afterwards. Even now we play places in England with big dance floors and wonder why no-one is dancing."

Johnny Watson, now the trombone player with the Glenn Miller orchestra, was given Jerry Allison's musical note cufflinks and tie-pin. The Crickets took an ad in the *NME* annual for 1959 to thank everybody for the great reception.

Buddy gave his acoustic guitar as a parting gift to Des O'Connor and everybody parted in good humour. The tour had been very successful. Once back in New York, Buddy had his teeth fixed and he bought another acoustic guitar, a Guild F-50, at Manny's. He gave the one he had used on "Well…All Right" to his brother Travis.

In New York, the Crickets met Sonny Curtis, who was cutting a single for Dot, prophetically titled "Wrong Again". He had had success as a songwriter as Webb Pierce's "Someday" had made Number 12 on US country chart in April 1957, but nothing since. Sonny played the *Phillip Morris Country Music show* with Carl Smith and Ronnie Self. He played fiddle to open, then rhythm guitar for Carl Smith and electric guitar for Ronnie Self. After being replaced by another musician, he stayed in Nashville for some months, hoping for other work but it was tough: "You try and get a meal for 25 cents," says Sonny.

Then it was back to package tours. The *Alan Freed Big Beat Tour* started at the Paramount Theatre in Brooklyn on 28 March 1958. It featured (among others!) the Crickets, Chuck Berry, Jerry Lee Lewis, Frankie Lymon, Danny and the Juniors, the Diamonds, Screamin' Jay Hawkins, Larry Williams, Dickie Doo and the Donts (Dickie Doo being Dave Allred from the Rhythm Orchids), the Shirelles and the Alan Freed Orchestra with Sam "The Man" Taylor. The Crickets were paid $5,000 a week. This time, Freed had dispensed with the feature films completely and these were complete two-and-a-half-hour shows with an interval. During their free time, the groups would play baseball or softball on a vacant lot.

A reviewer said that the show was loaded with amateurs and called it "a test of human endurance". Some acts were lost without an echo chamber but he noted Larry Williams with his modified striptease (albeit, copying Little Richard). The reviewer concluded, "Buddy Holly and the Crickets were standout clicks. Holly, a first rate guitarist and folk singer, knew all the wild rockabilly mannerisms and used them to get the kids out of their seats." As for Alan Freed, he was "serving mostly as a traffic cop to get the heavy pedestrian flow of combos on and off expeditiously."

A bit more than a traffic cop, actually. Before the first house, Jerry Lee Lewis had done his usual trick of demanding to close the show. Alan Freed told him that Chuck Berry had seniority and would top the bill. Okay, said, Jerry Lee, and went on just before Chuck Berry. During his closer, "Great Balls Of Fire", he poured lighter fuel on the piano, lit a match and walked off. As he passed Chuck Berry, he looked back at the flames and said, "Follow that, Nigger." It's surprising that Jerry Lee wasn't sacked for such outrageous behaviour, but he and Berry reached a compromise and took turns at closing the show.

Will Bratton (274): "Buddy Holly's music was different and new, but he wasn't dangerous. He was dressed like a nerd, like the boy that Dads want their daughters to marry: the sort of guy who's quirky now but will grow out of it when he matures. Buddy Holly was in no way a threatening male type at all, but his music can be taken as sexy, and I think there was a homoerotic element in his appeal. That is also true of the appeal of many of the British Invasion groups for American adolescent males. Jerry Lee Lewis, on the other hand, was more like the 300 pound gorilla: "How do we get this guy to leave our house and leave our daughter alone?' Of course, like Marlon Brando in *The Wild One*, that out-of-control characteristic had an appeal all of its own to an element of American society."

It was a strange tour with some unlikely gigs. My favourite was on 4 April 1958 at the Memorial Hall, Dayton, Ohio. You could buy your tickets from Loritt's Funeral Home. Buddy had at least one Strat stolen on the tour. There is a photograph of him on stage at Windsor, Ontario on 9 April with a borrowed Gibson. Buddy collected a complimentary Strat in Chicago on 7 July: whenever he had a Strat, he removed the tremolo arm.

In Milwaukee Buddy was given a song, "I Wish I Knew", which he said that he would like to record. At the theatre, the manager wanted him to go on first as the opening act was not ready. Buddy, clearly taking a lead from Jerry Lee Lewis, said, "I don't open shows, I close them."

A US single of "Rave On" and "Take Your Time" was released at the end of April 1958. *Billboard* said that "Rave On" was "a rockabilly item that he belts with hiccupy gusto. 'Take Your Time' is a less frantic effort, but it also has the money sound." *Cash Box* said that "Rave On" was "a potent rhythm rocker changed with gusto and with good hiccup vocalising the kids'll love."

Mike Heron (275): "As soon as you say 'Buddy Holly', there are so many associations for me. I used to go to the ice rink and I would hear his hits played distortedly over the speakers as I whirled round. The songs do transcend those memories though, and 'Rave On' is one of my favourites."

On *Music To Buy Time By*, a promotional album from NBC designed to sell advertising space, "Rave On" was described as "music to steal hubcaps by". Coral commented that "Holly is not the type of artist who deserves this kind of degrading treatment."

In May 1958, the age of Jerry Lee Lewis' young bride was revealed at the start of his British tour which led to the questions in the House, the cancellation of his appearances and effectively, the ruination of his career, though he was to make an impressive comeback. Nobody sprang to Jerry Lee's defence by saying it was a supreme act of defiance, or whatever. To make matters worse, Jerry Lee did wind up the audiences and the youths barracked him. The British press including the music papers were totally against him, possibly because this was an opportunity to lay into rock'n'roll.

On 1 May 1958, the ownership of the Lubbock radio station KLLL passed to Slim, Sky and Larry, the Corbin brothers. (Slim, by the time he got to Phoenix, was shot and killed by his girlfriend: there are some extraordinary endings in the Buddy Holly story.) Their DJs included Hi Pockets Duncan and Waylon Jennings and they were situated on the top floor of the 20 floor Plains Life Building, the tallest building between Fort Worth and Pacific coast. The coffee shop on the 19th floor was a popular meeting place for musicians.

Waylon Arnold Jennings had been born on 15 June 1937 in Littlefield, Texas. It was close to Levelland, but it was said the level in Littlefield was flatter than the level in Levelland. He was originally going to be called "Wayland", meaning "land by the highway", but there was a Wayland College for Baptist preachers and being staunch Church of Christ, his parents couldn't accept that and changed it to Waylon. He had been recommended to Radio KLLL by Gary Tollett who had been working there.

On 3 May 1958, Alan Freed promoted two shows at the Boston Arena with a total attendance of six thousand. The police had refused to lower the house lights and Alan Freed said on stage, "I guess the police in Boston don't want you kids to have a good time." Following an outbreak of violence, there were 15 offences including a stabbing, some beatings and several robberies. Alan Freed was blamed and this, just as much as payola, cost him his broadcasting job. The bookings for 6, 8 and 10 May were cancelled and indeed, his final promotions were at Brooklyn later in the year. The Mayor of Boston said, "If the kids of Boston are hungry for this music, they'll starve for it until they learn how to behave like citizens instead of hooligans. Boston will have no more rock'n'roll."

When Alan Freed's tour was over on 13 May 1958, the Crickets flew to Dallas. They visited a Harley-Davidson agency where the salesman thought they were kidding. They went across town to Ray Miller's Triumph Motorcycle shop and Buddy bought an Ariel Cyclone (which was quite a rare model), Jerry a Triumph Trophy and Joe a Triumph Thunderbird. Each cost over $1,000 and they paid cash from the monies Buddy held from the tour. However, they bought caps rather than helmets, rather an impractical way to save money in view of Joe B's previous accident. Before they rode to Lubbock, they went round to the first dealer to show him their purchases.

Tim Adams (276): "Neither Triumph nor Ariel was a particularly expensive or prestigious brand of motorcycle. The American brand of choice was, and remains, Harley-Davidson, but British brands were very popular with those who wanted something smaller and sportier, until the Japanese came along in the 60s and wiped out all the British firms on account of far superior technology and reliability. Ariel closed down in 1967, but Triumph stumbled on into the 70s and then went bust, before being revived to great effect by a wealthy businessman about 15 years ago."

After Buddy Holly's death, his father rode the bike. He sold it to a fan in Austin and then the Crickets bought it as birthday present for Waylon Jennings in 1979. It featured in an episode of *The Dukes Of Hazzard* when Waylon's travelling museum was hijacked.

Over the next few weeks, the Crickets spent some time in Clovis putting down new tracks. Buddy Holly met up with **Buddy Knox (277),** and the Crickets are on Knox's track, "All For You". "Everybody played on 'All For You'. All of my band was there, Buddy Holly and the Crickets, part of Trini Lopez's band and part of Sonny James' band. We all happened to be in Clovis, New Mexico and we ate Mexican food like crazy. I threw a song together, right off the cuff, called 'All For You' and they said, 'Let's record it.' Norman set the microphones and everybody started playing. I've never done the song in the United States or Canada but I have to play it when I come to England."

On 25 May 1958, which happened to be Petty's 31st birthday, the three Crickets recorded in Clovis, and Holly has added Tommy Allsup to the mix. He recorded a very effective guitar solo on "It's So Easy" and he is also featured on "Lonesome Tears". Joe Mauldin wasn't around the following day and so "Heartbeat" was recorded by Holly, Allison, Allsup and George Atwood (bass). A few days later, they cut "Love's Made A Fool Of You" and "Wishing". The records showed the growing maturity in Holly's work, and the last three songs were written with his old musical partner, Bob Montgomery.

How did **Bob Montgomery (278)** feel about his friend's success? Had he wanted to be a star himself? Was he jealous? "Lord, no. I did make a couple of recordings on my own so I suppose I wanted to be a star, but I soon realised that it wasn't what I was supposed to do. It's a tough life being a star. That lifestyle eats a lot of people alive."

Thomas Douglas Allsup was born, the twelfth child in a family of 13, in Owassa, Oklahoma on 24 November 1931, seven miles north of Tulsa. In the late 1940s, he bought an old bus and rode to school in it. He'd allow other kids to ride in it for 50 cents and he would take them to the dances on Saturday night. Very often, he was playing at the dances and so he brought his audience with him. He played in a western swing band and his guitar playing was influenced by Eldon Shamblin from Bob Wills and his Texas Playboys. He could play chords for every beat and he could "walk that bass line".

Tommy had been playing western swing ever since he left school and he went to Clovis to play on the Bowman Brothers' record, "Hey Punkin'". Both Norman Petty and the Crickets were impressed and Buddy Holly invited him to join one of their sessions. Tommy walked that bass line at the end of his solo on "It's So Easy" and Buddy loved what he had done. Tommy didn't know much about rock'n'roll as he had been playing western swing, and he maintains that he never had to change his style.

Tommy Allsup (279): "I first met Buddy in Clovis in '58 right after his UK tour. I was working sessions for Petty, and Buddy came in from Dallas on a motorcycle he had just bought. He heard my work and wanted an identifiable lick on 'It's So Easy'. The first take is the one you hear on the record. The riff just popped into my head as we played."

Dominic Pedler (280): "As far as the mechanics of his music are concerned, Buddy Holly was arguably the first rock 'n' roll pioneer to make a convincing crossover from traditional three-chord structures to harmonically sophisticated pop. Most Holly songs have subtle harmonic twists that distance themselves from the straight ahead, three-chord fare relied on relentlessly by, say, Chuck Berry, Little Richard and Jerry Lee Lewis. Even the simplest compositions like 'That'll Be The Day' and 'It's So Easy' enjoy watershed moments where a new chord deliberately cues that hanging end-of-bridge feeling that so reinforces the song's most poignant lyrical line: 'That some day, well, I'll be through' and 'Where you're concerned, my heart has learned', respectively."

Is that a Spanish guitar on "Heartbeat"? **Tommy Allsup (281)**: "It was a Fender Stratocaster I was playing, but Buddy asked me if I could play Spanish guitar. I thought, 'Well, I've played rumbas in our band in Oklahoma,' so I thought I could play that. I worked out an idea of what he wanted and then we cut it."

There is a Mexican influence on "Heartbeat". **Bob Montgomery (282)** "There were a lot of Latin influences where we came from. I don't like that line, "Why does a love kiss stay in my memory?" but that was Norman Petty's line. I thought it was a dipshit line, but what the hell, if it got the song recorded, you'd let it go."

Me: "And what about 'piddle de pat'? Couldn't you have put a better phrase in there?"

Bob: "What's wrong with that? That's the sound of the heartbeat."

Me: "Oh god, I've known the record for nearly 45 years and never realised that."

Bob: "There you go."

Holly double-tracked his vocals on the Bo Diddley-styled "Love's Made A Fool Of You" and "Wishing" as these songs were intended for the Everly Brothers. At the time, the Everlys were only recording Acuff-Rose songs for their singles, largely because (well, wholly because) their manager was Wesley Rose from Acuff-Rose. Talk about a conflict of interests: the Everly Brothers realised the problem, but the thorny Rose then cut them off from his writers. How these people come to run big businesses defeats me: well, no it doesn't—he was the son of the co-founder, Fred Rose.

Bob Montgomery (283): "The Crickets were on the road quite a bit, but we kept in touch whenever they came back to Lubbock. The Everly Brothers had asked him to write something for them and we had the Everlys in mind when we wrote "Wishing" and "Love's Made A Fool Of You". Wesley Rose wouldn't let them record the songs because he didn't have the publishing."

Joe B. Mauldin (284): "We were real close friends with Don and Phil and we backed them one time in Florida. Buddy wrote 'Love's Made A Fool Of You' for them but they told him that they couldn't improve on his demo."

As it happens, the Everly Brothers' next release, "Problems"/ "Love Of My Life, was a Top 10 single in both America and the UK, but those songs could have been equally successful. Fortunately, this was far more than a demo session, an indication that Holly was planning to use the songs at least for album tracks.

Tommy Allsup is playing jazz chords on "Wishing". **Tommy Allsup (285)**: "Kinda jazz licks, I really don't know what I played on that record. We only did one take and I said, 'Let's do another take', and Buddy said, 'I like what you're doing'. I didn't know what I was doing as I was just playing all over your words, but he liked it and we left it at that."

Why did Buddy use Tommy when he was a lead guitarist himself? **Tommy Allsup (286)**: "I never figured that out, but I figured that if you are going to play with Buddy Holly, you'd better play something good. Buddy was a good guitarist but he couldn't play that solo on 'It's So Easy', so that's called job security. He asked me to go on tour with the Crickets and that's how it started."

Barry Holley (287): "In 1957/8 Buddy's singles offered B sides that were refreshingly different without any loss in quality or creativity. In my view the only exceptions were 'Now We're One' and 'Take Your Time'. The final release with the Crickets in this period featured Tommy Allsup and the Roses; and the B side of 'It's So Easy', 'Lonesome Tears', has remained a firm favourite with me. The lyrics, like the best of Holly's compositions, are brief, clear and direct. They offer a simple structure for a breathtaking ensemble performance. It opens with four firecrackers from the guitar and drums. Then Buddy sings in synergy with the Roses to express his bitter distress at the loss of a love, and pleading and regret saturate the lyrics. The Crickets' frantic tempo underscores the restrained desperation of his delivery. Next, at the bridge comes a revelation as his voice soars upward to emphasise his devastation at her departure. Buddy knew how to rein in this emotional outburst in order to return to the more controlled tone of the final verse, again blending in a lower register with the understated singing of the Roses. Throughout the drumming is loose and powerful; Tommy's neat backup licks consisted of runs that Buddy could never have performed as he sang! The whole song is completed in less than a minute; then JI slams his kit to herald one of the most inspired guitar solos in the Holly canon. The simplicity of Tommy's phrasing is the framework for a rising crescendo of figures which complement the mixture of desperation and anger in the lyric. It achieves a peak that requires Buddy to resume his vocal at an even greater emotional pitch which he sustains to the end of the track. We are left exhausted by the power and aggression of the performance which concludes with two simple but effective chords. These provide a sense of completion and emphasise the collective achievement of the performers in this 105 second masterpiece."

John Tobler (288): ""When Bob Dylan and Carolyn Hester were first speaking, he asked her how she knew 'Lonesome Tears' and she said, truthfully, that Buddy had taught her the song. Dylan could hardly believe that he was talking to someone who knew Buddy Holly."

"Think It Over"/ "Fool's Paradise" was released as a single at the end of May, but more to the point, Buddy had been asked to report to the draft board for an Armed Forces medical on June 19, prior to being inducted. His poor eyesight and his ulcer kept him out of the service.

Joe B. Mauldin (289): "We were on our way to do a tour when Buddy got a letter to take his physical. He said, 'Don't worry about it. I'll stop in Amarillo. I'll go inside and then we'll head on down the road for the show.' Buddy took his physical and was considered 4F so he didn't have to go. With 4F, you are deferred for medical reasons and you never get called in. Buddy was real pleased about that." Woody Allen was similarly fortunate, leading to his great line, "In the event of war, I'm a hostage."

Ellis Amburn (290): "Buddy's diet was as bad as Elvis'. He loved his peanut butter sandwiches, okra fried in grease, and big thick steaks. He suffered from ulcers and his beer drinking exacerbated this."

Maria Elena may have met Buddy Holly earlier in the year. Nowadays she puts the date much later and tells it as a "love at first sight" story, but note this extract from *16* magazine in July 1959, which is written as a letter to Buddy: "The first time I saw you was early in January 1958 when I was working as a receptionist at the Southern Music Company. You were very shy and didn't say much." Norman Petty, Terry Noland and Carolyn Hester have all said that Buddy knew Maria Elena around this time. It takes an element away from the romance if this is true. The story we know is in keeping with the world of romantic songs being peddled in the Brill Building.

Maria Elena Santiago had been born outside San Juan, Puerto Rico, on 20 December 1932. Her father was a detective, but her mother, a nurse, died when she was seven. Because of her father's long working hours, she had to look after herself and her brother, Miguel. Her father remarried but when his second wife died, he sent Maria Elena to complete her education in America with her father's sister. Because of administrative confusion, her birthdate was recorded as 7 January 1933 and for convenience, she went along with it.

She then moved in with her mother's unmarried sister, Provi Garcia, who lived in Greenwich Village and was to run the Latin-American division at Southern Music. Maria Elena wanted to be a dancer in Broadway shows, but, by 1958, the chances for that were slim. She took a job working as a secretary for her aunt at Southern Music.

Maria Elena Holly (291): "I was a receptionist in the Brill Building as the one that they had quit and they needed a bilingual receptionist. My aunt was in charge of the Latin-American music department and at the same time I wanted to be in show business myself, on Broadway, so I was taking lessons for dancing and singing and drama, but when Buddy came along, that was gone. He said, 'It's either you or I, we cannot both do the same thing.' (Laughs) I said, 'Okay, since you've already started, I'll give up.'"

Surprisingly, **Maria Elena Holly (292)** was not used to dating: "I had never dated anybody at all, ever. I was 25 and I didn't have much time for dating as I was involved with so many things. My aunt was also very strict. She had told me when I went there that I was going to meet a lot of musicians, but I should not go out with them. She said that they were not responsible, but I saw Buddy coming through the door and it was like magic."

It was "Maria, Maria, I just met a girl named Maria" for Buddy, and something just as instant for Maria. **Maria Elena Holly (293)**: "Yes, but I was reserved and I didn't let him know. I said,

'Have this seat until Mr Deutch is ready to talk to you?' He said, 'Sure, I would like to sit here and talk to you.' He asked me about my accent and I said that it was Spanish and that I came from Puerto Rico. He said, 'I speak Spanish, senoriti.' I said, 'It is senorita.' I told him that he had an accent too, a Texas twang. He told Murray Deutch that he wanted to go out with me. He said, 'Her aunt is very strict and she doesn't like musicians.' Buddy exclaimed, 'She works here and she doesn't like musicians?' He said, 'That's why she doesn't like them, she knows what they're like.' (Laughs) Buddy said, 'Well, she'll like me if you'll put in a good word for me.' That is exactly what happened."

And a little help was on the way. **Maria Elena Holly (294)**: "Buddy asked Murray Deutch's secretary to take me to Howard Johnson's and not Jack Dempsey's for lunch. Buddy told her to go there as they were having lunch with his manager and the two Crickets. I said, 'We only have an hour and Howard Johnson's is always busy.' She said, 'We will get in, you'll see.' We went there and there was Buddy, Jerry and Joe and their manager. What a coincidence! I sat between Jerry and Buddy and we ordered sandwiches and when they brought the food, Buddy said, 'I'll take my sandwich and you take yours. Will you walk me with to Manny's so I can get some guitar strings?' We walked to Manny's and he asked me out that night. He told me that my aunt would be all right and that he had already made a reservation at P J Clarke's. My aunt was all right and she told me to be back by midnight."

So, **Maria Elena Holly (295)** went back to work: "I was finishing at 5.30pm and Buddy had told me, 'You have to be there by six as I am doing a jingle for a radio station, and they will pick us up.' It is difficult to get a cab in New York at that time but I said I would try. I had to go from 53rd to 42nd and it was 6.05pm when I got there, and I saw the limousine that was collecting Buddy. Buddy saw me, paid my cab driver and put me in the limo. We went from the radio station to P J's and we sat in a booth. He ordered Coke and I ordered water, and he said he would be right back. He came back with his hands behind his back. He produced a red rose and said, 'Will you marry me?' I said, 'Do you want to get married now or wait until after dinner?' He said, 'No, no, I'm serious.' I said, 'I wouldn't mind but you will have to ask my aunt first.' He said, 'I will do that tomorrow morning.'"

The next day was Saturday. **Maria Elena Holly (296):** "My aunt was in bed and the phone rang and it was the concierge saying that Buddy Holly was here to see her. I hadn't told her that he was coming as I never thought that he meant it. I let him in and my aunt was still in bed. She said, 'Can't he wait until Monday to see me at the office?' I was too scared to tell her what he was going to say. She told me to make some coffee and she got up and said, 'Buddy, what's so important that you have to come here on Saturday to see me?' He said, 'I want to marry Maria Elena.' My aunt said, 'Is he being funny, Maria Elena? I've told you what musicians are like.' Buddy said, 'Oh no, no, no, I am a nice person, and if you let me, I can call my mother.' He called his mother and she must have fainted on the other end as he kept saying, 'Mother, are you there?' My aunt was going to South America and she said that she wouldn't be able to do very much for a while. Buddy said, 'Don't worry about it, I'll take care of the wedding.' My aunt said, 'I know someone who can help her choose whatever she wants.' As my aunt was strict, I don't really know what won her round. Just Buddy, I guess."

Quite close to the Dakota building, the studio at the Pythian Temple in New York was a small auditorium in a large building owned by a Masonic organisation, the Knights of Pythius. It was noted for its excellent acoustics and many classical recordings were made there as well as Bill Haley's "Rock Around The Clock". Dick Jacobs, under the pseudonym of Henry Jerome, had arranged some rockabilly sides with the Johnny Burnette Rock'n'Roll Trio including "Tear It Up" (1956). Although this definitive rock'n'roll was produced by Bob Thiele, he didn't even mention Johnny Burnette in his autobiography, a telling indication of what he thought of the music.

In April 1958, Bobby Darin recorded "Early In The Morning" and "Now We're One" at the Pythian Studio. A super confident performer, he had had no hit records and was disillusioned with his label, Atlantic. In defiance of his contract, he recorded his new songs for Brunswick, using

the pseudonym, the Ding-Dongs, and the session was arranged and produced by Dick Jacobs. Atlantic soon found out what he had been doing. To avoid legal action, Norman Weinstroer was forced to give Atlantic the tracks, but he asked Buddy Holly to cover both sides for a Coral release. In June 1958, Buddy recorded the songs with most of the same musicians, including Sam "The Man" Taylor and four black girls from the Abyssinian Baptist Church, the Helen Way Singers. Their leader worked at the Post Office. Their vocals thrilled Holly as he wanted to record with a group like the Raelets. Buddy did something else important during the day: he bought an engagement ring for $550.

Norman Petty had been at the session but union restrictions forbade him from working as an engineer in New York. He was impressed at how Buddy adapted to the new surroundings and by his versatility. Both he and Buddy knew, he would sound great with strings and he marked this down for the future. He would have to find a suitable moment to tell Jerry and Joe B, but Buddy had to explore his potential.

Frankie Connor (297): "'Early In The Morning' is a great rock'n'roll track in a high register, and I love both versions. There's no evidence that Paul McCartney did this at the Cavern, but I'd like to bet he did as it would have been perfect for him. Buddy Holly had the edge on Bobby Darin as a rock'n'roller, but Darin's range was wider. I should think that they would have been friends and they both wanted to mature, Darin had a weak heart and knew what was around the corner, and Holly didn't."

Steve Gibbons (298): "I loved a lot of the B-sides like 'Fool's Paradise' and ;'Now We're One', and 'Brown Eyed Handsome Man' was just fantastic, a wonderful version of a great song. Even now, if I want a crowd-pleaser, I know I can't do better than 'Not Fade Away'—it's one of those songs that *always* works.

A rancher and part-time promoter, Harry Smythe, wanted the Crickets to appear at a party at his Buck Lake Ranch in Angola, Indiana and when they agreed, he arranged a series of consecutive dates in the area. The tour became known as the *Summer Dance Party* and it featured 10 musicians—the three Crickets and a support band formed and led by Tommy Allsup featuring Earl Sinks as a vocalist and including brass. Jerry Allison told Peggy Sue that the band really swung: he also told her that he had six blisters so he must have been working hard. By and large, they would be playing four hour dances and each band would perform two 45 minute sets. The Crickets included several songs that they did not normally perform—"Jailhouse Rock", "Roll Over Beethoven" and "Blueberry Hill".

They drove around in two vehicles: the Crickets in Buddy's powder blue Lincoln and the others with the instruments and equipment in a yellow De Soto station wagon. This had just been purchased by the Crickets for $4,000. Clearly, the Crickets were planning to do a lot more work and they felt that they worked very smoothly as a three piece. They were getting encores and if necessary, they could back other acts.

Tim Adams (299): "The 58 Cadillac and 58 Lincoln that Buddy bought were at the top end of the market, the luxury brands of the General Motors and Ford groups, respectively, so Buddy was splashing his cash about. Both cars were enormous, chrome-laden leviathans. It would have been unusual for anyone to support both brands at the same time—buyers would normally stick with one group's products. The De Soto station wagon was actually from the third main car manufacturer in the US, Chrysler. It was from the middle brand of Chrysler's five lines—below Imperial and Chrysler, above Dodge and Plymouth. It had been a very successful brand up to the mid 50s, but saw its market share plummet as Dodge and Plymouth moved up-market, with the result that De Soto was killed off in 1961. The 58 station wagon was huge with plenty of room for the musicians and their equipment."

Eddie Cochran's bass player had bought a new Fender electric bass and Joe B. thought he would have one himself. He played it on the *Summer Dance Party* tour, but it lacked distinction and returned to the upright bass. However, he did acknowledge that there was a problem as the bass could not be amplified properly for stage work. If they placed a microphone in front of it, it would also pick up the guitar and drums.

Joe B. Mauldin (300): "I bought an electric bass and I used it on one tour with Buddy in 1958 but it wasn't accepted as well as the stand-up bass. It seemed that everybody expected to see that when the Crickets came out, so I've hung in there with the stand-up. I do have an electric stand-up that I use in the States."

Although the electric bass was known, it didn't come into play until "Walk, Don't Run", the instrumental hit for the Ventures in 1960, and very soon the Precision electric bass was replacing the acoustic bass in rockabilly and rock'n'roll bands. A few years later, Paul McCartney came to the fore with his Hofner electric bass, which has a similar shape to the upright bass, but was much smaller. It was easier on the fingers: lots of would-be upright bass players had bloody fingers and then formed thick calluses. The portability of the electric instrument was also a factor, and indeed, Joe must be commended for carrying an instrument which was taller than he was.

On 3 July 1958 and on their way to Harry Smythe's party, the band pulled over at a truckstop in East St Louis and had some instruments stolen. What happened cannot have been explained properly to Smythe as he wrote to Holly's agent, GAC, complaining that the band had to borrow instruments. Buddy's stolen Stratocaster had been the free one he had been given a few months earlier. Manny's sent a replacement and it is this Strat he was playing on his final tour.

On 5 July 1958, only 16 days after it had been recorded, "Early In The Morning"/ "Now We're One" was released as a single in the US. Darin's version, now released as by the Rinky Dinks, sold better, but Buddy Holly's was a Top 20 hit in the UK.

In Waterloo, Iowa, on 8 July, they were supported by Eddie Randall and the Downbeats at the Electric Park, and Eddie also played with the Crickets, while Buddy watched from the wings. Buddy had broken his standard glasses and was wearing his dark ones, which he normally wore for driving. A photographer, Dick Cole, asked Buddy to take off his glasses, but he said no. He did tell one reporter, "I'm not trying to be a glamour boy. I'm trying to be a musician."

Maybe the broken glasses were just as well. At one gig, a lad complained about "that long necked bastard making eyes at my girl". He challenged

Buddy to a fight but he chickened out: Buddy Holly as King Leer.

They did some waterskiing in Waterloo when they rented a boat on the Cedar River. Joe Mauldin tried to walk across the water on floating logs. The logs rotated and he ended up in the river.

After further gigs in Decorah, Iowa, Duluth, Minnesota and Wausay, Wisconsin, the tour finished at the Crystal Rock Ballroom, Rhinelander, Wisconsin. The club owners also owned a holiday resort, and when Buddy swam to an island in the lake, the current was stronger than expected. He drifted off course and ended up on another property belonging, as it happened, to the family of the girl in the box office. Buddy was accident prone, but there were compensations. She wrapped him in a blanket and took him back.

A few weeks later, Buddy lost his wallet while waterskiing, begging the question as to why you take your wallet waterskiing. It was recovered when the lake was dredged years later. He was still carrying his membership card for Tommy Hancock's Club for Unappreciated Musicians.

Manny Greenfield had wanted to tour the Crickets as a main attraction during the summer but the Crickets wanted time off. Buddy was keen to get married and set up home, and he also bought a fishing licence for a trip to Mexico.

On 22 July 1958, Jerry Allison married Peggy Sue Gerron in Honey Grove, Texas. Buddy and Jerry had been talking about a double-wedding, but Peggy Sue was Catholic and Jerry Protestant and so the 18-year-olds eloped to circumvent family problems, something which rarely works. Holly himself may have been annoyed about this as when he got upset, he would get in his car and drive. This may be why he ended up with Snuff Garrett on KSYD radio in Wichita Falls.

On 4 August 1958, *Billboard* reviewed "Real Wild Child", which was released under Jerry Allison's middle name, Ivan: "Ivan's actual identity remains a secret but the performance has a strong southwestern flavour (Tex-Mex school of sound). An interesting novelty with a persistent rhythm." This might be the first time that the phrase "Tex-Mex" had been used. The record made the Hot 100 and at the end of August, Ivan even mimed to "Real Wild Child" at WCHS in Charleston,

West Virginia. Norman Petty told Joe B. that his turn was next.

Buddy Holly and the Crickets' singles were no longer automatic hits in the US, although one way or another, they had been on the US Hot 100 for a year. In the UK, they had had six hit records in nine months. The new release, "Early In The Morning", was about to join them. The *NME* said, "For 'Early In The Morning', the banjos join in, and Buddy takes over where Sophie Tucker left off, which is a mighty unusual role for Mr Holly." Er, can't hear any banjos on "Early In The Morning". In the NME chart for 27 August 1958, "Rave On" was Number 10, "Think It Over" 15 and "Early In The Morning" 19.

"Rave On" was a much bigger single in the UK than in the US: maybe the tide was turning for Buddy Holly. **Sonny West (301)**: "'Rave On' was a hit in Britain. He seemed to be more popular there than here. There was so much competition from the young heart-throbs here."

Just before he came to England, Buddy Holly had purchased some land in Lubbock. The property, known as Bobalet Heights, would have six rooms and four bathrooms and would cost $55,000. The multi-function building would be his Lubbock base, his parents' home and a recording studio. He was keen to open a studio in Lubbock, but he also wanted to work in New York in order to learn more about how they operated. He discussed the project with his father who would be working on it.

Buddy also wanted to form his own record label. At first it was going to be called Taupe, after the colour of his Cadillac, but he changed it to Prism. Both Buddy Holly and Ray Rush invested $3,500 apiece as joint owners, and Norman Petty would be in charge of sales and treasurer (an indication that Buddy wasn't that unhappy about Norman's accounting at the time). Buddy bought some equipment as the company's first purchase and Prism would pay for their first session at Clovis.

On 15 August 1958, Buddy and Maria Elena were married at the Holley's current home on 1606 39th Street, something which could not happen in the UK. Very few people were there: Ella and Lawrence, Larry, Travis and Patricia and their spouses, Jerry and Peggy Sue, and Joe Mauldin. Buddy gave the minister, Ben Johnson, a cheque for $1,000, and Jerry put Buddy's latest single on the player: "Now We're One".

Maria Elena Holly (302): "We didn't talk about religion. He was a Baptist because his family was staunch Baptist and went to church all the time. That was not an issue with either my aunt or, apparently, his folks. We got married in Lubbock and I had to fly there by myself. It was a shock to see somewhere that was so flat. He picked me up at the airport and I stayed with his parents."

Buddy was still wearing dark glasses in his wedding pictures, which suggests that his standard frames had not been repaired. Buddy and Maria, Jerry and Peggy Sue drove to El Paso in the station wagon and then moved to Acapulco for a double honeymoon. They later transferred to El Cano, which was on the beach. There is a photograph of all four of them having dinner in Mexico City.

Maria Elena Holly (303): "We had our honeymoon with Jerry Allison who had married Peggy Sue in June. Jerry suggested that we all went to Acapulco. I said I didn't mind, but Buddy said, 'I do mind because I do not like Peggy Sue.' He would be uncomfortable but I said that it would just be a short break. Peggy Sue had been upset as they had not had a honeymoon so that is why Jerry took the opportunity." Even though Buddy was singing "I love you, Peggy Sue" every night on tour, Maria Elena suggests that Buddy did not like her at all.

Norman Petty didn't care for Maria Elena but that might have been self-preservation. As Maria Elena was working for Norman Petty's agent, she might expose some truths about publishing contracts to Buddy. Indeed, she did feel that Petty had not done enough for Buddy and that she could do a better job herself of managing and promoting him. She felt that Petty didn't believe in advertising or spending on promotion and this is why "Heartbeat" and "It's So Easy" hadn't sold. She said that Norman wouldn't even pay for a photographer and preferred to do the job himself or ask his secretary.

On 17 August 1958, a feature in *Lubbock Avalanche-Journal* stated that Lubbock was the capital of rockabilly music. The Crickets, Sonny Curtis, Terry Noland, Niki Sullivan, Jerry Clement and the Jokers were mentioned, and Niki Sullivan's

"It's All Over" had been a local hit. According to the paper, more people are buying records as prices are not going up, and some of the new buyers are, wait for it, "older people".

George Tomsco (304): "I was in college at New Mexico Tech which is in Socorro, New Mexico and a friend heard an acetate that we had cut in my parents' living room with the band director who had a record cutting machine. I was listening to it in my dorm and this feller said, 'Who's that?' I said it was the Fireballs, my little band in Raton. He told me that it sounded good and he came from Clovis, New Mexico. He told me that I should go to Norman Petty's studio in Clovis, where Buddy Holly and the Crickets recorded. I had no idea that they recorded there. I fixed up a time to see him and we cut a record, and that was the start of it."

On 31 August 1958, the Fireballs with their guitarist, George Tomsco were recording in Clovis and during a break in the session, Buddy arrived and played "Malaguena" on his guitar. The following day Buddy recorded a couple of jingles for KLLL using "Peggy Sue" and "Everyday". **George Tomsco (305):** "We set up for our first recording session and Norman wanted to record at night as there was less noise from trucks going by. Before we got started, he told us to get a bite to eat as we were going to work late. We went to the local drive-in and had some burgers and when we came back, there was a Cadillac with Texas licence plates in front of the studio. We wondered who it was and there was this guy with funny-looking glasses playing my guitar with his foot on my amplifier. I was very protective of my new guitar and my new amplifier, and I stormed into the control room and said to Norman Petty, 'Who's playing my guitar with his foot on my amp?' Norman looked through the double-pane window into the studio and said, 'Buddy Holly', and I made a tremendously quick attitude adjustment. Norman asked Buddy to come in and meet me and we shook hands. He said, 'What y'all doing, gonna cut a record?' We said, 'Yeah' and then Buddy got in his car and left. I never saw him again and five months later, he had the plane crash "

On 6 September 1958, Jerry Engler, who had cut "Sputnik" for Brunswick in 1957 and had opened some Alan Freed shows, recorded "What

A'You Gonna Do" and the organ-dominated "I Sent You Roses" at Clovis with Holly, Atwood and Bo Clark. Buddy Holly played guitar on "I Sent You Roses" and put the bells on the other one.

It would have been excellent if Buddy had got together with Sonny West in Clovis and seen if he could top his songs, "Oh Boy"!" and "Rave On", but **Sonny West (306)** had had enough of Norman Petty. "I'd recorded 'The Hula Hoop Song' with Norman and I told him that I would not give him writer's credit on the song as he had nothing to do with it. He already had the contract typed out and he ripped it up and threw it down on the table and got real upset. That's the last time I recorded there. I kept a tape of the song but I did nothing with the song and things did not work out too well financially. I had to get other jobs and just play at night. I moved to Odessa for a while and then in the first part of 1959, I moved to the western side of New Mexico and my brother and his wife were living there and he got me a day job and I did some playing at night, but I didn't do any more recording for about three years. I got married in 1962 and I had a young family and I had to do other things as my royalties were not all that great during that time as the music world had pretty well forgotten Buddy Holly. I worked on servicing jukeboxes for about 10 years. I did some writing but I didn't like the country night club stuff, it bored me to tears."

Whilst on tour, Buddy Holly had befriended the New York sax player, King Curtis, who also did sessions for Bob Thiele including the McGuire Sisters. Buddy loved his work with the Coasters and invited him to Clovis, primarily to accompany him on a new song, "Reminiscing". He met him at Amarillo Airport and drove him to the studio.

Norman Petty liked the compositions of Bob Venable and Eddie Reeves for the Nighthawks, but he wanted better ones. When they returned with "When Sin Stops", Buddy liked it so much that he wanted to record it. They said no, they wanted to do it themselves. Once it was released (and didn't hit), Buddy said, "Okay, I can do the song now" and he marked it down for Waylon

Jennings, who would be the first artist on his Prism label.

The songs chosen were "When Sin Stops" and Harry Choates' Cajun waltz, "Jole Blon". The B-side therefore featured a country performer (Waylon Jennings), an R&B saxophonist (King Curtis) and a rock'n'roller (Buddy Holly) doing a Cajun classic with strange lyrics and a rockabilly beat. The instrumental track for "When Sin Stops" was recorded first and it sounds better without the vocals as it is an excellent King Curtis instrumental

Buddy's own recording, and his final session in Clovis, was excellent. "Reminiscing" is a sad song, but as so often with Holly, he doesn't sound too cut up about it, and his vocal acrobatics include a great "bayee-ayee-bee", semi-yodelling and much more. Writing out the lyric phonetically would be a lot different from the actual words. "Come Back Baby" was written by a young Fred Neil. Norman Petty had met him at the Brill Building and brought the song back to Clovis.

In 1959, Norman Petty recorded Buddy Knox in Clovis on a Bobby Darin song, "I Ain't Sharin' Sharon" It is disappointing and indicates that Buddy Holly knew more about recording saxophones than Norman Petty.

Maria Elena had been in Lubbock while Buddy was in Clovis, but on 12 September they drove to California and back for a few days' holiday with some promotional work for "It's So Easy" thrown in. Buddy visited a top promotions company in Hollywood: they dealt with the McGuire Sisters and were possibly a recommendation from Bob Thiele. He was probably sussing out what he needed to do with Prism Records. Buddy went to Ray Charles' house in California but he was on tour: Buddy left a number but Ray never called.

Then, Buddy and Maria drove from Clovis to New York, again holidaying along the way and arriving in the city on 28 September. He bought a yellow leather coat with a fur collar for $90, and he was wearing that coat at the time of his death.

While their wives were out shopping, Don Everly and Buddy Holly went to Manny's. In September 1958, Buddy bought an acoustic Gibson J-200 acoustic, soon to be used for the *Apartment Tapes*. He bought a Magnatone Custom 280 Stereo-Vibrato Amplifier, which had two 12 inch speakers. It is now owned by the country song-writer, Paul Kennerley. When Buddy learnt that the salesman was getting married, he gave him a cheque for $15.

On 30 September 1958, Lou Giordano recorded at the Beltone studio for the second Prism single, produced by Buddy Holly and Phil Everly. The songs were Holly's "Stay Close To Me" and Everlys' "Doncha Know", with both producers playing guitar. Giordano sounded like Paul Anka on "Doncha Know", and Buddy, Phil and Joey Villa enjoyed adding falsetto harmonies. No demo has been found for Holly's own recording of "Stay Close To Me", but there must have been one. The single, which was released a week before Buddy died, sold 5,000 copies. When Mike Berry covered this song, he changed the melody, giving it a "Love Is Strange" feel and ending with a quote from "Words Of Love".

On 2 October 1958, Buddy appeared on his own for the TV show, *Alan Freed's Dance Party* and mimed to "It's So Easy". During an interview with Freed, they talk light-heartedly about flying. Freed says that they call Joe B. "Buyus" as he is always saying, "Buy us a Coke."

The Biggest Show Of Stars For '58—Fall Edition involved 14 shows a week and the Crickets, who had Tommy Allsup and the Roses with them, were being paid $10,000 for 16 days. For the first time, Holly was using backing vocalists on stage. The bill included Dion and the Belmonts, Jimmy Clanton, Frankie Avalon, Clyde McPhatter, Bobby Darin, Jack Scott, the Coasters, Bobby Freeman, the Olympics, the Elegants, Little Anthony and the Imperials and an orchestra led by the great jazz saxophonist, Sil Austin with Harold Cromer as MC. Duane Eddy joined the party after a couple of days.

Duane Eddy (307): "I worked the last big bus tour that Buddy Holly did and it was my first big one. We worked five weeks together and we used to talk everyday. We tried each other's guitars and he was a good player. He played a Fender but that's just a matter of taste."

A few moments from the tour…When Buddy met Frankie Avalon, he said, "I've only got one of your records, 'De De Dinah' but it's de de darned good.'"…When they crossed into Canada, Maria Elena said that she was not a US citizen

and as they were delayed, Buddy was annoyed with her…Joe B. was back to playing stand-up bass…In Indianapolis, Buddy told the audience that Robert Linville of the Roses was Pat Boone's cousin and used that as an excuse to make a quick getaway…The DJ in Scranton, Pennsylvania said that Buddy looked like Dave Brubeck…Joe B. was fined for speeding, but Holly got out of speeding tickets by signing autographs.

Jerry Allison had a new three-headed cricket cartoon drawn by his brother, James, on his drumhead. (James incidentally also shot the home movie footage in which Buddy and Jerry have a mock knife fight like Marlon Brando in *The Wild One*.) Jerry was including "Real Wild Child" in the act, going up front and playing guitar while Tommy played drums.

Not many wives or girlfriends travelled with the performers and Maria Elena thought it was a good idea to keep their marriage quiet, and on the road she would say that she was Buddy's secretary. She told him to pick up the money *before* he performed as otherwise he might not get paid, and she gave the advice to other performers too.

Buddy Holly had had a couple of singles which hadn't made the charts, and some Decca executives might have been nursing doubts about him. Fortunately, both Bob Thiele and Dick Jacobs recognised his potential and agreed to finance an orchestral session at the Pythian studio in New York. This took place on 21 October 1958 with Dick Jacobs writing the arrangements and producing the session and Jack Hansen acting as the orchestral contractor, that is, securing the right musicians for the date. As well as the regular instruments, there were eight violins, two violas, a cello and a harp. But there was no place for Jerry or Joe B.

The three and a half hour session was to record four songs: "True Love Ways", "Raining In My Heart", "Moondreams" and possibly "Stay Close To Me", although that is speculation. During the afternoon, Buddy Holly asked Dick Jacobs if that fourth song could be replaced by a new song he'd been given by Paul Anka, "It Doesn't Matter Anymore". Jacobs could see its potential and that Holly might give a better performance as Anka was coming to the session. Jacobs could write three arrangements in a day, so he was used to pressure. However, he only had time to write an arrangement using pizzicato strings in unison, a sound pioneered by Tchaikovsky.

The songs were to be recorded in both mono and stereo and they started with the wonderful ballad, "True Love Ways", effectively Buddy Holly's "Yesterday". It's intriguing to wonder what inspired this song, but it is not far away from Marlene Dietrich's "Falling In Love Again".

Norman Petty shared the songwriting credit for "True Love Ways". He maintained that Buddy had come over to Clovis with his parents, who were going to see an aunt in Portales. Buddy had the melody, which had been inspired by a gospel record, "I'll Be Alright" by the Angelic Gospel Singers, and by the time they returned the following day, he had finished the lyric, and Vi sang it to Buddy. It hadn't been thought right for him then as they hadn't thought of a string session.

This, admittedly, is Norman Petty's version of events: we haven't got Buddy's, or have we? The opening notes of "True Love Ways" are identical to "I'll Be Alright", which then veers off onto a melody similar to "We Shall Overcome". I played "I'll Be Alright" to the musicologist, **Dominic Pedler (308)**: "That's fascinating—clearly, it was the source for 'True Love Ways', although Holly did a good job of making it his own. There are some similarities in the structure, melodic pitches and melodic rhythms. The pick-up melody is almost identical ('I'll be alright'/ 'Just you know why'); with both tunes displaying a run of 1-3-6-5 in terms of the major scale notes—1 being the tonic ('do' in terms of do re mi): here a Bb in the key of Bb. Thereafter, the main similarity is the deliberate quarter notes of the lyrics emphasising the same pattern in a repeated two-bar motif bar of 4/4—rest, 2, 3,4, 1, rest, rest, rest (repeat). But the actual pitches do now differ as early as the second phrase : where the gospel song works its way back down 6-5-4-3, while 'True Love Ways' does also descend but only after jumping up to the octave—8-7-6-5 ('Why you and I'). While potential influences abound, a plagiarism lawyer would argue succesfully that the similarities are more apparent than real, with the common motifs rarely overlapping—with, additionally, the more gospel chord changes (rather than the 'True Love Ways' sweet doo-wop pop cycle) confirm-

ing some important differences in underlying harmony. And, of course, there is nothing in the Gospel song resembling that magnificent middle of 'True Love Ways'."

Maria Elena regards "True Love Ways" as very personal and she would not think so if she believed that Norman Petty, whom she detested, had written the words. It is reasonable therefore to assume that they are Buddy's words and, if anything, Norman Petty wrote the music for the bridge.

The saxophone on the session was played by Abraham "Boomie" Richman, who had played with swing bands like Cootie Williams and Tommy Dorsey. Perhaps because Holly was not used to performing songs like this and indeed, not using his trademarks, his vocal has a delightful lightness of touch and airiness about it.

Bruce Welch (309): "Buddy comes in so perfectly with that A at the start of 'True Love Ways'. What we don't hear is that there was a note on the piano first. He is given an A and then he sings, 'Just you know why.'"

Maria Elena Holly (310): "He wrote 'True Love Ways' when we got married. He told me that he had a song started for me. He said it was going to be our song. It's a very difficult song to sing as it goes up and down."

Tony Joe White (311): "When people hear me, they go Louisiana or Mississippi. When I first heard Buddy Holly playing and singing, I thought he was a California boy. Later on, I found he was from the same place as Waylon. He was great as he could write songs that made people jump up and down and he also could do those quiet little masterpieces like 'True Love Ways'."

Steve Gibbons (312): "True Love Ways' is the most perfect song you can hear. It has the most perfect chord sequence and a beautifully played sax solo. I love the way that Buddy's voice drops down too. I can't fault that record in any way."

Simon Warner (313): "I can't remember when I first heard 'True Love Ways' but it would have been the early 60s and maybe at a fairground when I was on holiday. It had an instant, sentimental appeal, even to young ears. It reminded me of Acker Bilk's 'Stranger On The Shore' with the same emotional lure, the same sense of longing, and the same ring of nostalgia. Listening to it again, it brings to mind Kurt Weill's 'September Song' and it has a lilting, happy/ sad quality that often marks the very best popular music. When listening to Holly now, there is that powerful hint of sadness, the feeling of loss because his career was so tragically cut short."

Dominic Pedler (314): "'September Song' could well have been an influence and there are some important similarities: notably in the melodic rhythm (the long held notes and pauses); and also with the opening bridge chord—a highly novel subdominant minor (IVm) that in both cases briefly aborts the expected modulation. Whenever I play 'True Love Ways' on my acoustic guitar, I always wonder where Holly was inspired to do that. Perhaps 'September Song' is the answer!"

Bobby Vee (315): "I have thought for years that Buddy Holly made some of the best records from that period. The records that he and Norman Petty made were light years ahead of the competition. If you listen to 'True Love Ways' on CD, it's as though you are in the studio, it's wonderful. Buddy Holly recorded so few songs during his short career and I've never heard one that I didn't like. He sang from the heart and he had a wonderful voice, very stylised. He also was a great songwriter and he spoke to the youth of the world at that time."

Then Buddy Holly and the orchestra nailed "It Doesn't Matter Anymore" in one take, and Paul Anka was ecstatic. Anka was only just 17 and it was a remarkable composition for one so young.

Martin Simpson (316): "I thought 'It Doesn't Matter Anymore' was a real good song that said a great deal about relationships and the way things go wrong. 'Learning The Game' is another great song."

Andrew Doble (317): "My feelings about Buddy Holly have always been mixed as his records in general have always been wonderfully catchy and work extremely well melodically. I have never been convinced lyrically as to me, lyrics did, and still do, matter very much, even simple lyrics. I was more into the Brill Building material or the early Elvis songs. When Buddy recorded 'It Doesn't Matter Anymore', it hit me harder than any of his own songs. It was a better

written song and it touched me lyrically in a way that Holly's own songs didn't."

Dominic Pedler (318): "Whether it was his own or other people's material, Buddy Holly made a point of recording songs with a wide variety of novel harmony, such as Paul Anka's 'It Doesn't Matter Anymore', whose shifts between major (verse) and minor (bridge) tonalities would become another quintessential Beatles ploy."

"Raining In My Heart" was written by Boudleaux and Felice Bryant, who wrote several of the Everly Brothers' biggest hits including "Bye Bye Love" and "All I Have To Do Is Dream". Buddy was buoyed by his performance on the lovelorn "Raining In My Heart"? He had told his brother, Larry, that it was his best-ever vocal.

Robert Wyatt (319): "I have always loved Buddy Holly. He was such an unlikely rock'n'roll star as he didn't look the part, but what a lovely singer. I associate Buddy Holly with my teens. I was going into cafés and playing jukeboxes and looking at girls across the tables. It was a magic place and time. I loved his songwriting although 'Raining In My Heart', which I recorded, is written by the Bryants. Bits of his magic have stayed with me so thank you, Buddy Holly."

Phil Everly (320): "I love Buddy Holly's music and I like 'That'll Be The Day' and 'Everyday' best. Boudleaux Bryant wrote 'Raining In My Heart' for us and Buddy was in the room when we first heard it. We passed it over to him and he recorded it."

Bill Dees (321): "Buddy Holly had so much feeling and emotion in his voice, that 'Peggy Sue, oh, oh, oh', for example. I was very influenced by Buddy Holly and I know that when I first started writing with Roy Orbison, I did a little hiccup like 'Raining In My Heart' and Roy knew where I had got it from. Roy wasn't the sort of singer who went round praising other people but I know he recognised his talent."

The fourth and final song, Norman Petty's string-laden "Moondreams" involved no rock'n'roll instruments. Petty didn't extend the courtesy by adding Holly's name to a song that he hadn't written. In all probability, Norman Petty was impressed with an album by the romantic balladeer, Dick Haymes, called *Moondreams*, which was released by Capitol in 1957. The album of standards didn't include a song called "Moon-dreams", but Petty could appreciate that it was a good title and wrote one accordingly.

Snuff Garrett (322): "Buddy's last session was with strings and he called my house in Wichita Falls, and we listened to them over and over on the phone. I love (Sings) "Strange things take place in my moondreams". God, I love that song, which Norman wrote."

Dick Jacobs saw this as an important session, demonstrating that Holly was at home in any studio environment, whether working out songs with a small group in the middle of night at Clovis or recording four songs with an orchestra in three hours in New York.

A couple of weeks after this session, Bobby Darin underwent an even bigger transformation for Atlantic as he recorded an album of standards, *That's All*. Whilst Darin could have performed all four of Holly's songs with confidence, Holly would have struggled on "Mack The Knife" and "Beyond The Sea". On the other hand, Holly was a far more convincing rock'n'roll performer.

The final appearance of Buddy, Jerry and Joe B. was on *Dick Clark's American Bandstand* on 28 October 1958, when they mimed to "It's So Easy". Although it was not on the charts, the single was a decent seller in Lubbock.

Maybe the positive results from the string session had given Holly extra confidence, I don't know, but almost as soon as it was over, he was making changes. As Norman Petty remarked, he'd been "a busy little boy".

First of all, he decided to split with Norman Petty. He told Petty that it was over and that he wanted all the back payments owing to him. He wrote to the songwriting organisation (effectively the union), BMI, about having the credits corrected and, in particular, he had written "Peggy Sue" and not Jerry Allison and Norman Petty. He wrote to Decca asking for a copy of all agreements involving himself.

Carolyn Hester (323): "Maybe money was the reason that he and Petty fell out. Norman was averse to Buddy getting married. He didn't want his superstar to have a life-changing moment—more a case of 'Let's go in the studio and make another hit.' Buddy was very mature for his age and Petty couldn't handle it. Strangely, they left

him out of the movie, *The Buddy Holly Story,* and I don't think that works."

Petty's power of attorney was cancelled and both Buddy and his attorney repeatedly asked for receipt books and tax returns. According to one letter, "Mr Holly is about to engage in certain business enterprises in which he will need any available funds." Petty's replies give the impression that he was being helpful while doing the opposite. Indeed, Petty instructed Coral that all payments were to be made to him as that is what the contract stated. "I will then make payment to the individual parties." Who trusted who?

Petty said that the record royalties had the top 40% taken and set aside in equal amounts for our churches: Petty had 10% of remainder. After that, Holly had 77½% after those deductions, Allison 12½% and Mauldin 10%. This is blatantly wrong. If the earnings were $10,000, then on Petty's basis, the church would receive $4,000, Petty himself $600, Holly $4,185, Allison $675 and Mauldin $540. A tithe is 10% and so the correct figures, based on the percentage splits, should be Petty $900, Holly $6,277, Allison $1,013 and Mauldin $810. Petty would be paying out $5,400 to the musicians instead of $8,100, and we don't have to guess where the $2,700 was going. Norman, it seemed, was paying the musicians with Petty cash.

There were grievances from the agent, Manny Greenfield and it could have been that his legal action had legitimately tied up the funds. He felt that he was entitled to 5% of all the group's earnings, not just the concerts which he had arranged. The matter would not be settled until 1960.

On stage performances, Petty said that his records only showed what was deposited, which was less than half of that actually earned. Holly collected the money and Petty didn't know what he gave the others. As the Crickets' manager, this is atrocious and showed a dereliction of duty, if true. Petty was working up to saying that Holly was profligate and there was nothing left.

Norman Petty was devastated when Buddy Holly stopped recording in Clovis. When asked about Presley, he stated that "Buddy was much the better artist." If he really believed that, then why didn't he get the finances right? He must have figured that Buddy would be too busy to notice.

Quite possibly, he had persuaded the Crickets to stay because he felt it might act as a lever to get Buddy back to Clovis.

Maria Elena Holly (324): "Buddy didn't have any money because his manager didn't want to let the money go. I guess he was too proud to take money from my aunt."

Secondly, Buddy Holly split with the Crickets as they wanted to remain in Lubbock while he settled in New York. They had considered going to New York, but Norman, and probably Peggy Sue, had talked them out of it. They were younger than Buddy—19 and 17, respectively—so it would be a bigger move for them, and besides, it was easier to ride your motorbike in Lubbock.

Joe B. Mauldin (325): "Buddy had wanted to be active in New York even before he was married and then he married a girl from New York. J.I. had married Peggy Sue and we decided to stay in the area where we had been for so long and we had an amicable split. Buddy told us to use the name 'The Crickets' because he wasn't going to use it. He said, 'If any of us gets uncomfortable and feels it isn't going to work, all it takes is a phone call to get back together.'"

Peggy Sue Gerron (326): "It's hard to have camaraderie in a band all the time and when two new people, me and Maria, came in, it altered the moods and everyday scheduling. The split made me very sad as Buddy was my hero. He accomplished things we didn't think possible and I admire that greatly."

Jerry Allison (327): "I am sure in my own mind that Buddy wasn't fed up with us. He was fed up with Norman Petty as Norman had power of attorney. Norman kept telling us, 'When the money comes in, we'll divide it up.' Until the records came out, we didn't know who would get the credits on the songs, so Buddy got fed up. We had been luckier than some though as some groups didn't even own their names." An example being the Drifters, whose personnel was according to the manager's whim.

Sonny Curtis (328): "I joined the Crickets just before Buddy's death. Buddy had moved to New York and wanted to work from there. Joe Mauldin and J.I. wanted to stay in Texas. It was a friendly split and most of the books have it wrong.

J.I. called and asked if I wanted to join the Crickets. I was at a loose end so that's what I did."

Within a few weeks, Jerry and Joe B. were recording with a new lead vocalist, Sonny Curtis, but although the songs were good—the western "Red Headed Stranger" and the chirpy "Talk About My Baby"—they were too country for the band. They came out as a solo single by Sonny Curtis, and then they added Earl Sinks to make a quartet. Their first recordings, "Someone, Someone", and "Love's Made A Fool Of You, were excellent. Holly had already cut "Love's Made A Fool Of You" at Clovis, so this looked like deliberate provocation from Norman Petty. How did he know that Holly wouldn't want this song for himself?

On 15 December 1958, Petty produced a second Ivan session for Jerry Allison with "Frankie Frankenstein", written by Jim Robinson, and "That'll Be Alright", another Johnny O'Keefe song. This time it really was Ivan the Terrible. Apart from these recordings, there was not much happening for the Crickets and both Jerry Allison and Sonny Curtis made appearances as part of the Norman Petty Trio.

On 24 November 1958 and with no ill feelings, Ray Rush's partnership in Prism was absolved with the repayment of his contribution, but Buddy was determined to go ahead with a new recording complex in Lubbock.

Buddy and Maria Elena had moved into a flat in Greenwich Village, 4-H 11 Fifth Avenue. The ground floor was a bank and the rest were apartments. They had new furniture including a dining table and chairs from Buddy's parents and Buddy had a new, watch, worth over $1,000. Buddy liked Greenwich Village. If you were awake at two in the morning, you could go to a coffee house and hear some entertainment, perhaps jazz and poetry and folk songs

On his final trip to Lubbock, he had purchased an Ampex recorder from Norman Petty and this would enable him to make good quality home recordings. It was the tape recorder on which he had recorded "Peggy Sue" and the one that Norman had taken to the airport base for "Maybe Baby".

Ellis Amburn (329): "The newly weds were living by Washington Square and loved Greenwich Village. Buddy had written most of his hits in Clovis but he had an equally productive spell in their apartment. Norman Petty was still holding on to his money and he would write using his guitar and often visiting the aunt's apartment to use her piano .The plan was to use all the songs on an album as soon as he got off the tour."

It was a bad New York Winter and Buddy worked on new songs, now known as the *Apartment Tapes*. A follow-up to "Peggy Sue" had been his father's idea and so he recorded his own answer song, "Peggy Sue Got Married". He told his parents, "Please don't mention it to anyone. I want it to be a complete surprise." The secrecy in the song's lyric was Holly's comment on the fact that pop stars were not supposed to get married.

The line, "You recall the girl that's been in nearly every song", is intriguing. Almost certainly, it is a nod to Bobby Darin who had had his first hit single with "Splish Splash". The lyric said, "There was Lollipop with Peggy Sue, Good Golly Miss Molly was even there too."

And then in his follow-up hit, "Queen Of The Hop", he said, "You can talk about Julie and your Peggy Sue, You can keep your Miss Molly and your Mary Lou."

Probably unknown to Holly, a New York group, the Regents had written "Barbara Ann", which mentioned Peggy Sue, but they weren't to record it for three years. Similarly, Ritchie Valens' "Ooh! My Head" referred to Peggy Sue but had yet to be released.

Another inspiration was the song that Jimmy Lee Fautheree recorded as Johnny Angel in 1958 called "Teenage Wedding", which has the opening line, "Peggy Sue's got married". Buddy Holly is even mentioned in the lyric. To add to the confusion, the B-side is a version of Buddy and Bob's "Baby, It's Love".

But "nearly every song"? What was Buddy saying with that phrase: was he admitting that most of his songs were really about her and therefore he was secretly in love with her, or was it merely loose writing? Peggy Sue's biography suggests that Buddy's marriage was unhappy and he wanted to marry Peggy Sue, whose own marriage to Jerry Allison was stormy.

Bruce Welch (330): "I love those apartment tapes. They are such perfect songs and I love

doing 'Peggy Sue Got Married' in my *Shadowmania* shows."

Peggy Sue Gerron (331): "'Peggy Sue Got Married' was on a tape in his apartment and we first heard it after the funeral. It was a great surprise and I loved it. He had written to his mother about it and made her promise not to spoil the surprise. Jerry says Peggy Sue rhymes with everything and that's why she turns up in so many songs."

Billy Bragg (332): "After Chuck Berry's initial burst of songs, there had been a bit of relapse but Buddy Holly cut through that with his vision of what songs could be. 'True Love Ways' is incredible—just a two and a half minute song—but it is the work of a visionary. I'd love to have written 'Peggy Sue Got Married' as I am very fond of that song, and I also love 'Raining In My Heart', although I know he didn't write it."

Gary Osborne (333): "My favourite Buddy Holly song of all is 'Peggy Sue Got Married' which I adore with a vengeance. It's full of wit and inventiveness and the way he takes the character and moves her on is clever, classy, cute and cool. After the naive simplicity of 'Peggy Sue', it's like he's suddenly raised the bar a notch or two. The greatest lyrics are always the most conversational and what could be more conversational than 'I don't know if it's true, I'll just leave that up to you, If you don't believe me, I'll understand' or again, 'You recall the girl that's been in nearly every song. This is what I heard (of course the story could be wrong).' I love the way he confides in you; it's as though he's buttonholed you in a pub for a bit of gossip. If this is the direction his songwriting was heading, then his death was an even bigger loss than most people think. It's a marvellous tune, too. It was finished after his death and the producer, the musicians, the backing singers and the lead guitarist rose spectacularly to the occasion."

What do "That's What They Say", "What To Do", "That Makes It Tough", "Crying, Waiting, Hoping" and "Learning The Game" have in common? Answer: they are all songs of love lost. Isn't it odd that Buddy Holly, recently married and setting up home for the first time, should choose to write about love going wrong and the marriage of his best friend?

Maria Elena Holly (334): "He was writing them in the apartment. I was in the kitchen clanking the plates and in one of the recordings, you can hear him say, 'Sssh, I'm recording.' He was using both the electric guitar and the acoustic. He was going from one to the other and testing different sounds for the songs. My aunt didn't live far away from us. We lived on 8th street and my aunt lived on 10th. She had a piano and we used to go there and he played that. Those *Apartment Tapes* are really wonderful songs: they were going to be on the next album."

Tim Whitnall (335): "My favourite song is 'Learning The Game' but not the one with the band and the strings on it: the one he sings with a big old Gibson and it is fantastic. I once included the melody as background music in a Shakespeare play and so it could have been written in any age at any time."

Harvey Andrews (336): "One record label said, 'Give us a hit single, Harv.' I don't write hit singles, so, with their money, I went in the studios for four hours and did a pastiche of all Holly's various techniques on 'Learning The Game'. There's everything in there, even the hiccup. It only sold 500 copies but the Northern Ireland Buddy Holly Appreciation Society voted it their favourite cover version of a Buddy Holly song, which is rather nice."

Mike Brocken (337): "Songs like 'What To Do' are real music and by saying they're down to earth seems to run them down a little bit. Buddy Holly has a very interesting take on life and how it can be expressed in song. It is also typical of the southern states. They don't use elevated language when they don't have to and that's clear from the great country songs. They won't use anything overly expressive if they know a basic idea will work well."

Billy Butler (338): "There is magic in the *Apartment Tapes*, especially 'Learning The Game', but there is so much loneliness in those songs that you wonder what state of mind Buddy was in. Just listen to 'What To Do' and 'That's What They Say' which both ask, 'Where do I go from here?' Around 1990, Billy Swan was in a group called Black Tie and they made a tremendous album, *When The Night Falls*. They did a terrific version of 'Learning The Game' with some great harmonies: it could have been done completely acappella. Dave Mason of Traffic put 'Crying Waiting Hoping' and 'Peggy Sue Got Married' together and did them with a calypso beat that was very good."

The Apartment Tapes are full of sadness: five songs of love going wrong. Can we read anything into this? **Tim Whitnall (339):** "Don't think so. He would have been influenced by the other hits from that time: there are lots of songs of heartbreak and heartache and, of course, country music is full of it. When I worked in Nashville, I took some songs to a publisher who said, 'They're great, but let me play you something' and he played me a song about a young boy who had watched his father beat his mother from behind a sofa. It was mind-blowing and he said, 'That was written three years ago and we're looking for something now that will be as powerful as that in three years' time.' Did the composer write that song from personal experience or did he draw on something he had read? A lot of writers are inspired by books, and good writers keep their ears and eyes open."

Jimmie Dale Gilmore (340): "I got married when I was very young and had a daughter when I was 19. The breakup of that marriage was when I wrote 'Treat Me Like A Saturday Night'. Music comes out of heartbreak a lot of times, and that happened with me. When you're happy and having a good time, you aren't sitting around playing the guitar. You're out doing things and when you're sad that's when you're on your own with your guitar. That is not 100% true but it is a little bit true."

Dick Jacobs had thoughts of pairing Buddy Holly with Count Basie and his Orchestra, and it is possible that "That Makes It Tough" would have been suitable, and it could have worked with Ray Charles as well. The song incorporated some chords that Buddy had been shown by Tommy Allsup. Dick Jacobs did put Count Basie and his Orchestra with Jackie Wilson in 1963 for the dynamic "Baby Workout".

Buddy hadn't rushed into a new management deal. Ideally, he would have liked his brother, Larry, who was someone he could completely trust and would do a good job, but Larry preferred to stay in Lubbock with his family.

Buddy was thinking about whom he could write for and produce. He wanted to work with Ray Charles in some way, perhaps doing duets with him, and he wanted to produce Paul Anka. He told Terry Noland he had some songs for him and he would like to have them arranged by Jessie Stone and recorded at the Pythian studio in March 1959. He planned to record Jack Neal. The rockabilly performer, Ray Campi, had also been in touch as he had heard that Buddy was looking for songs. He contacted Guild about making a blond, light, semi-hollow body, electric guitar to be marketed as the Buddy Holly model.

Jerry Allison (341): "I think Buddy Holly would have loved 'What'd I Say' by Ray Charles because he was a big Ray Charles fan. It's a pity that he didn't get to hear that, and he would have loved the Beatles and the Stones and the whole English Invasion. He would have kept coming up with stuff because he was coming up with something new all the time. He wanted to do a gospel album with Ray Charles using his arrangers if he could."

Tommy Allsup (342): "I didn't hear about him wanting to make a record with Ray Charles but he did want to make a Christmas album with Neal Hefti, who was a big arranger and orchestra leader in those days. He was going to call *Deck The Halls With Hefti Holly*. (Laughs)" Holly almost certainly knew Hefti as he arranged and conducted for several Coral acts including the McGuire Sisters.

He had also noted **Bob Montgomery**'s (343) aptitude: "There is no telling what Buddy would have done. I know he was trying to get more involved in the business end and he would have liked a little record label of his own. One of the last times we were together, he wanted me to come to New York. He was going to start a publishing company and he wanted me to run it .I didn't want to go to New York and at that time I couldn't even spell publishing, much less be a publisher." Maria Elena's experience would also be invaluable for this publishing venture.

Alan Freed's Christmas Rock'n'Roll Spectacular opened at Lowe's State Theatre in New York for two weeks with Johnnie Ray, Jackie Wilson, Chuck Berry, Bo Diddley, Eddie Cochran, Dion and the Belmonts, Frankie Avalon, Jimmy Clanton, the Moonglows, the Flamingos and King Curtis. Johnnie Ray was the wrong generation and sound for the teenage audience and he was replaced by the Everly Brothers after a few days. Asked for views on rock'n'roll, Johnnie Ray said, "I can take it or leave it", the answer he might well have given if also asked about his sexuality.

Punk before its time, **Dion (344)** and the Belmonts took their name from Belmont Avenue in the Bronx. "There were no stage monitors to hear yourself. We had no legal protection. We were just a bunch of street singers regarded by society as degenerate infidels, one small step away from the jail or the gutter. It was a creative time, rock and roll didn't exist and we were making it up as it went along. It was very cool to be travelling with the likes of Buddy Holly, Gene Vincent, Eddie Cochran and Sam Cooke."

Now that Buddy was living in New York and wanted some quick money, why didn't he do the spectacular? Why didn't he replace Johnnie Ray? Surely it was preferable to the *Winter Dance Party*. I don't know: maybe he just felt his private life came first and he had made arrangements to take Maria Elena to Lubbock for Christmas. It might be that he was never offered the dates at all.

Buddy and Maria Elena spent Christmas with the Holleys at 1606 39th Street in Lubbock. There are home movies of Buddy at Christmas. As usual, he is dressed meticulously and is watching presents being opened. He gave a donation of $800 to the Baptist Church, and another to a muscular dystrophy charity. This suggests that he wasn't as short of cash as everybody thinks and it wasn't the Dickensian scenario that many authors have painted.

On 27 December 1958, Buddy was hanging around KLLL, and somebody bet him that he couldn't write a song in 30 minutes. He came up with "You're The One". It was recorded at the station with Buddy singing and playing, plus Waylon Jennings and Ray Slim Corbin handclapping. When the track was eventually released, they obtained 25% each for handclapping, though they are out of time! There are also two fragments of Waylon on his songs, "More And More" (not the country standard) and "When You Are Lonely", but these are more likely to be Waylon on both voice and guitar as Buddy wouldn't know the songs.

Neil Foster (345): "One of my favourite tracks is 'You're The One' because it is a very good example of what Buddy Holly could do with so little. There's some sparse guitar accompaniment and some simple, almost hackneyed lyrics, and yet once heard, it's unforgettable."

At KLLL, Buddy also met Larry Welborn who was promoting a Four Teens record. He told Larry that he had the *Winter Dance Party* coming up and he could play bass if he wished. Larry preferred to stay with the Four Teens. He chanced upon Hi Pockets Duncan and he told Maria Elena, "If it wasn't for him, I wouldn't have you."

Buddy told George Atwood of his plans to build a recording studio and he would be a good PR man with his many contacts. As he wanted Snuff Garrett with him as well, he seemed to be sounding out everyone he knew, and offering them potential jobs, either in Lubbock or New York.

Snuff Garrett (346): "Buddy wanted to start his own record company in New York and the label was to be called Taupe Records, which was the colour of his Cadillac. Waylon and I were supposed to go to New York and work for Buddy in the record company, but he died before any of that could happen. He knew that my leanings were towards being a record producer and being in the record business. I wanted to find songs for people and that is what I ended up doing for the whole of my working lifetime."

On 30 December 1958, Buddy and Ray Rush drove to Odessa and met Tommy Allsup who was performing at the Silver Saddle Club, backing the country pianist, Moon Mullican. Buddy asked Tommy to join the *Winter Dance Party* and they discussed a drummer.

Carl Bunch had been born in Big Spring, Texas on 24 November 1939 and raised in Odessa. He loved Al Jolson and his youthful ambition was to be a Broadway show dancer. Then he got cancer in his leg and was in hospital and recovering for a year. He had played with Roy Orbison for a short while, and Buddy saw him at Clovis when he was drumming for the Poor Boys, who featured Ronnie Smith. Possibly, Buddy was impressed because Jerry Allison had given Carl a bit of advice, "Kick that bass drum hard." Buddy asked Tommy to get him.

Tommy Allsup (347): "On New Years Eve, I was playing a club in Odessa with Moon Mullican and he came and asked me to tour with him. Moon's drummer was late that night and Buddy stood in for him—he was a good drummer. He'd hired me on guitar, Waylon Jennings on bass and Carl Bunch on drums and we were going out as the New Crickets."

On 31 December 1958, Buddy and Maria Elena flew back to New York. As the year ended, Buddy Holly had left Lubbock for the last time.

8

BROKEN WINGS

"Unravelling the subtle, complex chain of events leading to aviation deaths is proving more elusive than ever."
(Wall Street Journal, 1999)

On 5 January 1959, Coral released a new Buddy Holly single, "It Doesn't Matter Anymore"/ "Raining In My Heart" in the US. *Cash Box* said that "Buddy Holly has a pair of winners back to back that could join hands to give him his biggest money-maker since 'Peggy Sue'." The trade magazine was effectively saying, "OK, his last few singles have been left on your shelves, but don't write him off yet."

Ron Sexsmith (348): "My mum had a great collection of 45s and I used to put them on when I was about five. I loved 'It Doesn't Matter Anymore' as I liked the way he'd go from a low voice to that hiccup. The music is at odds with the theme of the song as the guy is trying to get over his broken heart by saying that the person doesn't matter anymore, but maybe he's really saying that it matters a lot. I like that contradiction although, of course, I didn't understand the depth of the song when I was that young."

The Christmas Number 1 was a novelty single, "The Chipmunk Song" from David Seville and the Chipmunks. Seville had used speeded-up voices to create Alvin, Simon and Theodore, named after the top executives of Liberty Records: Alvin Bennett, Simon Waronker and Theodore

Keep. Holly was intrigued by these records and he wanted to resolve what Seville was doing. It might be no more than playing a tape at twice the normal speed, and he decided to work it through with one of his favourite songs, Little Richard's "Slippin' And Slidin'", which was the US B-side of "Long Tall Sally". He recorded a voice and guitar version at 7½ inches a second with a deliberately slow vocal that makes it hard to decipher the lyrics. Indeed, the most effective section is where Buddy is singing some wordless vocals over his guitar accompaniment. He must have played it back at 15 inches a second and realised that he hadn't quite got it (you have, for example, to play the instrumental backing at standard speed), but had he realised that his slowed-down version at standard speed was both charming and eerie? At times, he sounded like someone who was breathing his last. Quite unknowingly, Buddy Holly had created a unique sound—and we don't know what he would have done with this discovery had he lived.

Buddy also recorded a faster version of "Slippin' And Slidin'", which opens with the chords of the Everly Brothers' "Bird Dog". There has been talk of a piano version of "Slippin' And Slidin'", but I've never heard it.

Chloë Alexander (349): "Starting as an eagle-eyed eight-year old in 1964, it was when I bothered to read the credits for 'Words Of Love' on *Beatles For Sale* that I became familiar with Buddy's string of pure pop hits, charting the ups and downs of teenage love. The highly-produced arrangements with upbeat lyrics and soaring strings somehow masked a real earthiness and craft. Discovering Holly properly years later in the wake of my ongoing quest for the musical origins of my favourite bands, along with Elvis Costello's blatant image grab, I could see how his influence was enormous. The 'Slippin' And Slidin'' B side came my way on the compilation, *John Lennon's Jukebox* in 2004. I was immediately struck by its languid and intimate tone. It is much, much slower than the Little Richard version, and it has that homespun quality of a demo recording being made on the quiet. Buddy displays his trademark gurgling and yodelling but only softly and experimentally. The recording has a natural earnestness which must have been so attractive to wannabe songwriters in Britain in the early 1960s, sounding like it was recorded itself in an upstairs suburban bedroom. Holly could well be perched on the edge of a well-made bed, singing and strumming his guitar to impress his teenage pals coming round for tea, much as John would have done to Paul or George. His slow and deliberate delivery makes the lyric far more suggestive and subversive than Little Richard's version, which is on the same collection. That in itself is fascinating as Little Richard is a far naughtier artist than Buddy ever was. As ever with Buddy Holly, listening to any of his tracks only serves to make me wonder—what would have happened if that plane had made it through the snowstorm?"

Otherwise, the January part of the *Apartment Tapes* is less substantial than the songs recorded in December. There is "Love Is Strange" itself, Bo Diddley's "Dearest" (sometimes called "Ummm Oh Yeah"), the Robins' "Smokey Joe's Café" (a 1955 single written by Jerry Leiber and Mike Stoller, with Buddy's voice rising and falling), one of his mother's favourite songs, "Wait Till The Sun Shines, Nellie" (written in 1905 and with Buddy on electric guitar), a snatch of Ray Charles'

"Drown In My Own Tears", and an instrumental, which has become known as "Buddy's Guitar", but is probably Ray Charles' "Leave My Woman Alone". Some short conversations with Maria Elena and their cleaner (again, how come they were short of money if they had a cleaner?) have been preserved.

Paul Kennerley (350): "During the 80s, I was having a run of luck with my songs, so I started to collect a few things. I wanted something of Buddy Holly's and I got in touch with somebody in Lubbock, who ran the Buddy Holly society, and told him that I wasn't after a pair of socks, I wanted something musical. He told me that a member of the family had his Magnatone amplifier and they were thinking of selling it. It took a long time to get it. I was seriously pursuing this thing and I kept offering them a bit more money and as it turns out, my wife went behind my back and bought it for me. It is the amplifier that was in his apartment at the time of his death. After his death, they issued those home recordings that he did, like 'Learning The Game' and 'Slippin' And Slidin'', and when he used an electric guitar, that was the amplifier he used. I was very proud to have it but I felt a bit guilty that it was here in my house and nobody could see it so I have loaned it to the Rock And Roll Hall Of Fame in Cleveland."

On 7 January 1959, it was Maria Elena's 26th birthday and Buddy drank some champagne to celebrate. His ulcer played up and he was sick the following day.

Buddy never met the top executives at US Decca, but he had lunch with Dick Jacobs and his manager, Marty Solkin. Buddy gave Dick a tape of the new songs he had recorded in December. They would discuss the arrangements on his return.

Buddy was still hoping to resolve things with Norman Petty although when he wrote to him, very politely, on 8 January, he undoubtedly had his lawyer over his shoulder. He signed it, "Thanking you in advance, I remain, Buddy Holly."

Norman Petty told Coral that the Crickets' records would no longer feature Buddy Holly, but he was informed that the records must feature Holly if they were to use the name. Petty responded that it had always been Buddy Holly

118

EVERYDAY

and the Crickets, which wasn't true, and so Holly had never been a Cricket, also not true. He continued, "Mr Holly is definitely not at liberty to use the name in any artistic presentation without their express written consent." As a result of this stand-off, there were court orders on Coral Records, Southern Music and the Clovis National Bank not to dispense any funds until the matter was settled.

At the time, Norman Petty wasn't aware that Buddy was about to tour as Buddy Holly and the New Crickets, but he was angry when he found out. In a radio promo for the tour, Buddy referred to just "the Crickets" and my guess would be that he did it deliberately to rile Petty.

Petty did not bother with lawyers and he recorded a confrontational call with Coral's lawyer George Schiffer on 27 January 1959. Petty tried to sound as reasonable as possible and he said of the tour dates, "Buddy decided that he should receive the monies personally. Buddy gambled quite a bit and all the boys did as far as that goes, and I had no way whatsoever of keeping up with the money they received." An identical ploy was used by Don Arden to the Small Faces' parents in 1966.

Ellis Amburn (351): "Norman Petty handled Buddy's affairs very badly, freezing his money and forcing him into some terrible moves. The *Winter Dance Party* was a third rate tour which he wouldn't have done had he had control of his finances."

Buddy had been preparing for the *Winter Dance Party*. He had assembled his band over the Christmas period in Lubbock, which seems late in the day for a group that would also be backing other artists. The New Crickets featured Tommy Allsup (electric guitar), Waylon Jennings (electric bass) and Carl Bunch (drums). Waylon was no bass player but Tommy told him to play four strings. He wouldn't be able to play chords but he could get by. Waylon was still unsure about the tour: it was in bad weather, he was playing unknown parts and he was leaving his pregnant wife, Maxine, and two children in Littlefield.

Carl's mother drove Carl, Tommy and Waylon to the airport at Amarillo and they flew to New York. The same flight had crashed into a river only a few days earlier. The musicians arrived in

New York on 20 January to prepare for the *Winter Dance Party* and they rehearsed in Buddy's apartment with Maria Elena cooking for them.

Maria Elena Holly (352): "I wanted to go with Buddy, but I was pregnant and had morning sickness. Buddy wanted to make some money as he felt bad that my aunt was taking care of us. He wanted to open a recording studio and I wanted that too as I would be helping him there. He wanted to have a publishing company and a record company, and he wanted to do it all. He had been to England and he wanted to take me there. He even thought of opening a studio in London. He said, 'You'll see how much talent there is in England.' I think he would have established studios in London, New York and Lubbock."

Tommy Allsup (353): "The story went that Maria was pregnant at the time but I'd stayed a couple of nights in their apartment and nothing was said and in two weeks on tour, Buddy never mentioned it."

There might be a good reason for this. Buddy's marriage was still private and maybe he didn't want anything to slip out before he made an announcement. The fewer people that knew about Maria Elena's pregnancy the better.

The four musicians—Buddy, Tommy, Waylon and Carl—went to Chicago by train on 22 January. It was windy and snowing and the hapless Carl, who was carrying a drum, fell out of the train at the station and into some slush. In Chicago, they met the other performers who would be on the tour—Ritchie Valens, the Big Bopper, Dion and the Belmonts and Frankie Sardo. The money would be $2,500 for Buddy Holly (including his musicians, who would get extra for backing the other acts) and $1,000 each for Valens and the Bopper.

Jiles Perry (Jape) Richardson, the Big Bopper, was born in Sabine Pass, Texas on 24 October 1930. He became a popular DJ on KTRM in Beaumont, Texas, one of the first radio stations in Texas to mix black and white records, and, at 17 stone, he was a larger than life character in both appearance and presentation. In May 1957, he did the Japeathon in which he went for the world record for non-stop broadcasting. The record of 122 hours had been set by an El Paso DJ, and the Bopper beat it by eight minutes, playing Elvis

Presley's "All Shook Up" to win. His final record was Dinah Shore's version of "Cattle Call", which would make anyone give up. The undertaking wasn't as easy as it sounded as the Bopper had to be given oxygen. Towards the end, he was getting hallucinations and thinking he was dead. He told his friends that dying wasn't all that bad. His feat has long been surpassed, and you'd have to go for four weeks non-stop to come up trumps today.

Big Bopper Jr (354): "Dad had many talents and the Big Bopper thing was something he created for radio. He did it for a sponsor who wanted to appeal to a younger audience. He came up with this wild cat with black dialect and he was also on a major label, Mercury, as a country artist. His world record was typical of him. He'd been the Number 1 disc-jockey in Beaumont, Texas, but he'd had to do his military service. When he got out, he wanted everyone to know he was back and within six weeks, he'd talked the station owner into the Japeathon and he did that radio programme in the lobby of a theatre in Beaumont for 122 hours 8 minutes. He played 1,800 records. *The Guinness Book Of Records* didn't recognise his achievement as he hadn't followed the guidelines but my dad was sure he had broken the record. He did it for five days straight, right in the lobby, and everybody could come by anytime of day or night and see him spinning those records."

On his composition, "Chantilly Lace", the Big Bopper sounded like a comic Fats Domino. He made a promotional film and he somewhat prophetically told *Disc* that "Records will be filmed!" When the record became a hit, he asked for leave of absence to promote it on the *Winter Dance Party.*

Big Bopper Jr (355): "'Purple People Eater' and 'Witch Doctor' were two songs that were doing well, and Dad thought if I do 'Purple People Eater Meets The Witch Doctor', that has got to be a smash hit. He went to the studio and recorded that and on the flipside, he did 'You Know What I Like', which became 'Chantilly Lace', and this was the first record he had done in character as the Big Bopper. He sent it to Mercury Records and they said, 'Thanks but no thanks. We will keep you as 'J P Richardson'. 'Well, they released it on a local label in Houston and it sold 8,000 copies within a couple of weeks,

and Mercury invited him back and signed him as the Big Bopper."

On 'Purple People Eater Meets The Witch Doctor', the Big Bopper was also experimenting with speeded-up voices, so this was the flavour of the month. Jape's real love was New Orleans jazz, and he had a French Cajun wife, Adrianne (Teetsie) and a daughter Debby, age 5. Teetsie was eight months pregnant at the time of his death, which means that Buddy, the Bopper and Waylon Jennings had left pregnant wives behind to do the tour. Unlike Buddy, the Bopper was constantly talking about his forthcoming child.

Big Bopper Jr. (356): "My father was a completely different person to the Big Bopper: it was a character he played. The Big Bopper was not my dad. There is a song, 'Someone Watching Over You', that my father wrote and that is more like my father than the character of the Big Bopper. The Big Bopper was a vehicle for my father to take care of his family. He created it for radio and took it into music. I think my father would have given up performing and would have bought a radio station as that was his first love."

Coming from a Mexican family, Ritchie Valens was born in Pacoima, Los Angeles on 31 May 1941 and he was discovered by Bob Keane of Del-Fi Records in 1958. He recorded his first session in July 1958. His own song, the electrifying "Come On Let's Go", was as good a début single as you can find but it only made Number 42 on the US chart, and it had to compete with a US cover from Guy Mitchell. A British cover from Tommy Steele, totally drenched in echo by Joe Meek, made the UK Top 10. The song was a US hit for the McCoys in 1966 and an international one for Los Lobos in 1987.

Valens' plaintive song for his girlfriend, Donna, was written after an argument, but they were back together by the time of its release. "Donna" was coupled with "La Bamba" for a fantastic double-sided single. Ritchie Valens loved this Mexican wedding song and Bob Keane encouraged him to cut a rock'n'roll version.

Flaco Jiminez (357): "'La Bamba' is just slang. To dance La Bamba is to go ahead and enjoy yourself, a bit like Chubby Checker saying, 'Come on, baby, let's do the Twist.'"

"Donna" made Number 2 in the US and "La Bamba", Number 22, although "La Bamba" is now seen as more significant. After all, you could say folk-rock starts here. Los Lobos took the song to the top of the UK charts and it has been recorded by Neil Diamond, Trini Lopez, the Ventures and Shirley Bassey. The Crickets gave us an English lyric—"I saw La Bamba at the beach now, She liked the surf beneath her feet"—but somehow I prefer "Yo no soy marinero".

Chris Montez (358): "I was just a young guy and he'd released 'Donna' and I went to see him. The place was crowded with about 500 there, but I could see the stage very well. Ritchie was about to go on stage and I found he was standing to my right. I did a double-take and I was thrilled to meet him. He smiled and was real gracious and then they called him up and he did his set. I vowed that if I ever made it big, I would treat people the way that Ritchie Valens treated me."

On 10 December 1958, a performance at his high school was recorded, but the album, *Live At Pacioma Jr High*, includes studio tracks with dubbed applause. The only existing footage of Ritchie Valens is his performance of "Ooh! My Head" in the rock'n'roll film, *Go, Johnny, Go!* Looking at his heavy set features, it is hard to believe he was only 17: he would pass for 30 anywhere. Including demos, there are 33 different songs that Ritchie Valens recorded in his short career including "That's My Little Suzie", "Hurry Up" (written by Sharon Sheeley) and "In A Turkish Town".

Chris Montez (359): "The Everly Brothers and Eddie Cochran were very good but there were no Latinos doing rock'n'roll. Then Ritchie Valens opened the door for us and said, 'Come on, let's go.' Because Ritchie was Latin, I really tuned into him and wanted to be like him. Elvis Presley may have been the King of Rock'n'Roll, but Ritchie Valens was the King on our block. He had broken through the barrier of the recording industry. He was Mexican and he was successful."

Dion DiMucci had been born in the Bronx on 18 July 1939 and I'm sure he looked cool from the word go. This guy looked like a star, and knew it. **Dion (360)**: "The teachers at school thought I didn't know what to do and there was no such thing as teenagers then, let alone teenage music.

From 13 to 19 years old, you were supposed to not talk and then you became an adult and could listen to adult music. Then we had rock'n'roll which was at its best an expression of individual freedom. Music opened my whole world."

But unlike Lubbock, children were more rebellious in the Bronx. Songwriter **Ernie Maresca (361)**: "I got a tattoo when I was 17 and my father was very strict. I wore long-sleeved pyjamas and it was a 90 degree temperature in New York. We were having breakfast and my dad said, 'What are you wearing pyjamas for?' and when he saw the tattoo, he went crazy. Everybody's got tattoos now, but when I wrote 'The Wanderer', you only had a tattoo if you were in the navy."

Dion was complemented by Carlo Mastrangleo (baritone), Angelo D'Aleo (first tenor) and Fred Milano (second tenor). **Dion (362)**: "When I got a contract with Laurie Records they put me with the Timberlanes and it sounded real lame, real square. I said, 'Let me go back to my neighbourhood and round up some guys who can sing.' I went back and gathered up the best of the street corner singers and we recorded 'I Wonder Why',"

There were a lot of Italian singers back then. Was this because they had sung in church? **Ernie Maresca (363)**: "Well, I didn't sing in church and Dion didn't sing in church. I look at this way: the comics were Jewish and the Italians were singers. Not that we are all Frank Sinatras and Perry Comos."

Dion and the Belmonts started recording in 1957, and they had their first hit in 1958 with "I Wonder Why", which made Number 22 in the US. Like the Crickets, they had been a white act on the Apollo and they had done well. It was followed by "No One Knows" (Number 19) and their new release was "Don't Pity Me".

Ernie Maresca (364): "'No One Knows' was written about the girls in the neighbourhood. I lived on Garden Street and it went, 'In Garden Street where I come from, All the girls are a bunch of bums.'

I did a demo and they put it on in the pool room and Dion flipped over it. The lyric got changed to 'No one knows what I go through'."

Born on 16 September 1936, Frankie Sardo was another Italian-American from New York City. He played piano and bongos and his brother Johnny wrote songs. At first, they were a comedy team but they went into music. Frankie had served in Korea and now he had a solo single with a catchy dance record that was breaking out, "Fake Out", on ABC-Paramount. In line with "Peggy Sue", "Donna" and the Bopper's "It's The Truth, Ruth", his new single was "Oh Linda". The first purchase for a would-be songwriter was a book of girls' names.

The *Winter Dance Party* was a three week tour in extremely cold weather and there were often several hundred miles between dates. An essential requirement, you would think, would be a well-equipped bus with bunk beds and good heating. No way. The buses came from Trailways in Chicago and were requisitioned school buses that were not made for extreme conditions. I write "buses" because they kept breaking down and had to be replaced.

On 23 January 1959, the first show of the *Winter Dance Party* tour took place at George Devine's ballroom in Milwaukee, Wisconsin. Buddy Holly was opening his part of the show with "Gotta Travel On", a Top 10 hit for Billy Grammer, with Tommy and Waylon harmonising. Buddy always started with this but he didn't keep to a set list and responded to requests and what he felt was right at that moment. At each venue, 10 copies of Buddy's new single, "It Doesn't Matter Anymore", were given away.

The next show was at the Eagles Ballroom, Kenosha, Wisconsin and Debbie Dean, the wife of the TV presenter and master of ceremonies, Jim Lounsbury, was added to the bill. There are photographs of Ritchie Valens doing a duck walk and the Big Bopper carrying Frankie Sardo around, so despite bad weather and appalling travelling conditions, they had high spirits. Before one of the shows, the Big Bopper introduced himself and the other singers to a waitress and she said, "Yeah, and I'm Lucille Ball." The Bopper went back to the restaurant with a signed poster.

On the bus and backstage, the tour members would play poker and craps, but Buddy wouldn't allow the young Carl Bunch to gamble. He would say, "I'm not paying you enough." They had a silly game called Skunk in which they would entice the victim into saying something stupid. Carl

would be picked on by the Belmonts, but Ritchie Valens told him to take no notice.

Fred Milano of the Belmonts had a replica gun and, from time to time, he would point it at the driver and go "Bang! You're dead!", not something that the driver, who was as cold as the rest of them and negotiating treacherous roads, appreciated. But Buddy had a real one, acquired from Tommy Allsup. **Dion (365)**: "Buddy Holly carried a gun. This is the 50s and if you carried a gun in my neighbourhood, you were a gangster, but Buddy was from Lubbock, Texas. Everybody had guns in Lubbock, Texas, they mounted them on the back of their trucks, but I didn't know this. He had a shoulder holster. He said, 'Nobody's gonna steal my money.'"

This is true, just about. Buddy Holly had a German pistol, often known as a Saturday night special, which he had been given by Tommy Allsup. He'd had problems with outsiders in the past and he was often carrying large sums of money. He carried it in the false bottom of his bathroom bag.

From time to time, the musicians started writing songs together, but they were generally too cold to be bothered. Whatever they did has been lost. Buddy, Waylon and the Bopper did write "Move Over Blues", but all we know is that title. The Bopper's notebook survived the crash with the lyrics to a new song, "If I Ever Lost You".

On 25 January 1959, the tour came to the Kato Ballroom in Mankato, Minnesota, and on the following day, Eau Claire in Wisconsin. Next came the Fiesta Ballroom, Montevideo, Minnesota and the Promenade Ballroom, St Paul, Minnesota. On 29 January 1959, the *Winter Dance Party* was at the Capitol Theatre in Davenport, Iowa. On 30 January 1959, they had an unscheduled stop at the Gaul Motor Company, Tipton for repairs. Then they were on their way to Laramar Ballroom, Fort Dodge, Iowa.

On 31 January 1959, they were at the National Guard Armoury, Duluth, Minnesota. Lew Latto was the MC and tickets were $2. 2,000 teenagers attended the dance and among them was Bob Dylan.

Tommy Allsup (366): "You could tell that Buddy missed Maria Elena. After the show, Waylon, the Bopper and me would usually go for a beer but Buddy didn't come. He didn't drink at all on that tour."

Dion (367): "It was a rough winter, sub-zero degrees and we didn't have those beautiful, luxury, touring buses that we have today. It was a school bus and we slept in the luggage racks and it kept breaking down. We got very close with each other, so close that Buddy and I would cover ourselves up with a blanket and I would tell him about characters in the Bronx, people like Frankie Yunk-Yunk and Joe Beebee-Eyes and he would laugh, man, and tell me stories about Lubbock, Texas."

Dave Williams (368): "People never believe us when we tell them about the cold in that part of the world. We have been to Clear Lake in the February when it was been 50 and 70 degrees below. They have had to leave the cars at the Surf Ballroom ticking over all night with the keys in as otherwise, they wouldn't start again. If you walked a hundred yards you wouldn't be able to breathe. Buddy himself wasn't really used to snow and it must have been horrendous." Buddy's British tour must have seemed like heaven by comparison and he did talk to Tommy about returning.

The tour was scheduled to end on13 February 1959 and the promoter, Irving Feld for GAC announced a new tour from 20 February with Buddy Holly, the Crests, Ritchie Valens and Linda Lurine. (In terms of rhyming slang, Linda Lurine sounds as unfortunate as Paul Anka.) The first date would be in Washington DC. The weather would be better and evidently, Holly was holding nothing against Irving Feld or GAC despite the appalling conditions. In addition, Lee Gordon and Alan Hefferman were in Hawaii to work out a package with Buddy Holly, Ritchie Valens and the Big Bopper in Australia.

On 1 February 1959, the temperature was 30 degrees below and after midnight, the heater on the bus failed. The Belmonts lit newspapers in the aisles to keep warm. They didn't realise until Tommy Allsup told them that they might suffocate or even worse, the bus might explode. They opened windows to clear the smoke and there was a blizzard outside. For his 2000 CD, *Déja Nu*, Dion wrote "Hug My Radiator", a phrase he used on the tour and a tune similar to Chuck Berry's "Promised Land". The album also contained his reflections on Buddy, "Every Day (That I'm With You)". One mile north of Pine Lake on Highway 51, the engine froze and they were stranded. After some delay, the sheriff sent cars to pick up the passengers. The bus was taken to the Iron County Garage in Hurley, Wisconsin.

The snow was very deep and Carl Bunch stepped into it. When he tried to get warm, he put on further pairs of socks and stuck his feet back in the same shoes. This cut off the circulation, and his feet froze. He was taken to Grand View Hospital in Ironwood, Michigan with frostbite. This has been overstated by some writers: Bunch had frostbite, not gangrene, and just needed to thaw out. If they'd only had Sir Ranulph Fiennes leading the tour party: he'd have said, "Right, chaps", organised everything properly, and everyone would still be alive.

Tommy Allsup (369): "We'd had four or five buses—the company kept sending out old clunkers which were always breaking down and this one died on us. The guys were lighting paper in the aisles to keep warm. Carl's feet turned brown with frostbite and it was half an hour before a car came along. Carl was taken to hospital and the local sheriff came out with a posse and picked the rest of us up. We carried on to Green Bay and borrowed a drummer for the night."

Ellis Amburn (370): "Buddy knew how uncomfortable touring was, especially in the coldest winter ever but he could not get out of it. They nearly froze to death in Wisconsin when the bus broke down. Their drummer got frostbite and had to be left in hospital in Michigan. Though he wanted to come home, Buddy was a professional—he was the headliner and could not leave. He played back-up for some of the acts and always put on a great show despite the conditions."

In Hurley, they ate at the Club Carnival restaurant, but the black driver had to eat at the garage. The matinee at the Cinderella Ballroom in Appleton was cancelled and they were to travel directly to Green Bay, Wisconsin. They left at 11.30am and they performed at Riverside Ballroom in Green Bay. A friend of Buddy's from 12 July 1958, Bob Oestreich of the Runabouts was brought in to play drums for Buddy. Ritchie Valens played for Dion and the Belmonts, while Carlo of the Belmonts played for Frankie Sardo.

Buddy offered Bob a job for the rest of the tour, but Bob, wise man, declined. The next venue was the following day, 2 February 1959, at the Surf Ballroom, Clear Lake, Iowa. Clear Lake was half-way between Minneapolis and Des Moines.

Monday 2 February 1959

8.00am

Roger Arthur Peterson was born, the son of a pilot, in Alta, Iowa on 24 May, 1937. He gradu-ated in 1954 and he became a commercial pilot for Dwyer's Flying Service in Mason City, Iowa, which had been the setting for the musical, *The Music Man*. He was a handsome lad and he had married DeAnn Letz on 14 September 1958. She worked for the accounts department of the radio station, KGLO. He had flown for over 700 hours, 128 of them in Beech Bonanzas. In March 1958, he had failed an instrument test. On 6 January 1959, a flight instructor gave him a three hour lesson in instrument flying. He had told the flight instructor that very day that he planned more training for the following week. At 8am, he showed up at Dwyer's Flying Service for his day's work. No flights were scheduled for the day and so he did some welding.

9.00am

The *Winter Dance Party* tour bus—their sixth—set off from Green Lake, Wisconsin, with all the performers on board. It was a 350 mile journey to Clear Lake, Iowa.

2.00pm

The tour bus pulled in at a service station near the Mississippi River to repair a faulty heater.

2.15pm

The Big Bopper, who had influenza, bought a new sleeping bag. He hated the hours that he had to stay on the bus as he was a big man who found the seats uncomfortable.

Buddy Holly phoned his lawyer in New York and learnt that Norman Petty was still refusing to release his earnings.

2.30pm

The Big Bopper got back on the coach with his sleeping bag. "Man, I'm gonna be warm tonight," he told other passengers.
Buddy Holly followed him on to the coach. "He was mad," said Waylon Jennings, "the maddest I'd ever seen him."

3.30pm

The coach was back on the road. The musicians were tired and dirty: it was very cold and they were homesick and they hated the uncomfort-able seats and bucket toilets. Because of ice on the roads, the coach often couldn't go faster than 25mph. This leg of the tour could have been better planned: if, for example, they had played the Surf Ballroom on 31 January and gone to Moorhead on 3 February.

4.30pm

A promotional appearance at a record store in Mason City had to be cancelled as the coach hadn't arrived.

5.15pm

Roger Peterson went home for the day.

6.00pm

The coach arrived at the Surf Ballroom, Clear Lake. The ballroom, which was part of a chain, opened in 1934 and had a décor of palm trees and clouds. It suffered a fire in 1947 but reopened in 1948. The nearby lake was frozen solid during the winter, but it was a draw in the summer.

Carroll Anderson had managed the Surf Ball-room since 1950 and he was now 38. He had paid $850 for the *Winter Dance Party*. He was selling tickets for $1.25, and as Anderson wanted to quash reports that rock'n'roll was about juve-nile delinquency, adults would be admitted for 10 cents—an indication, incidentally, that no sane adult would want to hear rock'n'roll. The adults would be parents checking on their children.

6.15pm

Buddy Holly, Ritchie Valens and the Big Bopper ate at the nearby Witke's Restaurant, joined by Carroll Anderson, his wife Lucille, their eight-year-old son and the MC, Bob Hale, the DJ from KRIB in Mason City, who was doing the job for $25. Everybody else was at the soundcheck.

6.25pm

There was talk of a snowstorm and GAC had been asked if they would cancel the following night's show and let them stay in Clear Lake. The answer, don't you just know it, was no.

Because they were often only in hotels for a few hours at a time, they had no time to get their laundry done and they must have smelt bad as there were no deodorants to speak of back then.

On stage and often off, the Big Bopper wore his leopard-skin coat, which had never been cleaned. Similarly, Ritchie Valens wore the same black jeans suit with silver studs every night. Buddy Holly always wanted to look well groomed and so this was particularly tough on him.

Tommy Allsup (371): "We only carried three shirts each and we'd had no laundry for a couple of weeks and the shirts could have stood up on their own."

6.30pm

Another bus had been secured to take them to the next destination, but Buddy Holly told Carroll Anderson that he'd like to charter a plane to take him, Tommy and Waylon to the next booking, which was at the Armoury, Moorhead, Minnesota, some 500 miles away. That way they could have a decent rest and get their laundry done. The bus trip would take 10 hours (if they were lucky): the plane only three (if they were lucky).

Tommy Allsup (372): "We were freezing our butts off and it was the tour from hell. Buddy had tried to charter a plane the night before. We were in Green Bay but they weren't flying that night, so next day he said, 'Maybe we can get one out of Clear Lake.' We'd had five buses in 12 days and the heaters wouldn't work on any of them. We had played Duluth, Minnesota, man, and the bus just froze, we were going up a little gradient. It just kept going slower and slower and just stopped. Lights went out. We played Green Bay and we had the drummer from the house band but the night we played Clear Lake, Buddy played drums for Ritchie, and Ritchie was playing drums for Buddy. That was something you would never normally see."

7.00pm

Carroll Anderson called Jerry Dwyer, the owner of Dwyer's Flying Services in nearby Mason City, and was told that a flight would cost $108. The pilot, Roger Peterson, would call them back.

Tommy Allsup (373): "We coughed $36 apiece for that flight. I can't remember how I felt about flying in that weather, but we were told that Roger Peterson was a very good pilot."

7.15pm

Peterson, who was star-struck by the thought of transporting Buddy Holly, called back and con-firmed that he could fly them to Fargo Airport, North Dakota, which was close to Moorhead. The plane was scheduled to leave at 12.30am.

Dion (374): "I was supposed to be on that plane as the more people we could get on it, the less the fare would be. When I found out that it was going to cost $36, I bowed out of it. Coming out of New York City, my parents were paying $36 rent a month and my head hadn't expanded to where I could spend a month's rent on a short plane journey, so $36 saved my life, by the grace of God."

7.30pm

Peterson realised that he was too tired to undertake the seven-hour round flight in poor conditions and asked another pilot, Dwayne Mansfield to take over. "No thanks," joked Mansfield, "I'm a Lawrence Welk fan."

Doors opened at the Surf Ballroom and 1,200 teenagers attended the *Winter Dance Party* for $1.25. The total attendance was 1,500 and Anderson made a profit. The backstage riders were for beers, Coca-Colas, 7-Ups and clean towels.

8.10pm

Bob Hale introduced the opening act, Frankie Sardo. Although the show is billed as a dance, the crowds gathered in front of the stage.

8.35pm

The Big Bopper began a lively performance, full of jokes and novelty numbers, but he was feeling bad and was covered in sweat. During his set, he went off stage, but he returned with his telephone prop and wowed the crowd with a "Helllooo Baby!", which led into "Chantilly Lace".

9.05pm

17 year old Ritchie Valens scored with his current single, "Donna"/ "La Bamba", as well as his earlier success, "Come On, Let's Go".

9.10pm

Buddy Holly called Maria Elena in New York. He told her that morale was low and he was going ahead of the others to make arrangements for the following night. He didn't explain what this meant and Maria Elena didn't know that he was going to fly.

Maria Elena Holly (375): "He didn't tell me because he knew that I wouldn't like that. The tour was only going to be two weeks but it was the Tour of Hell. Everybody got sick, it was bad weather and very cold and he would call me every night before going to the next venue. He called me in Clear Lake but he never told me about the plane. He told me that they were going to get a new bus. The buses were horrible as they were always breaking down and had no heat. That was Buddy, always taking over, but he didn't tell me that he that he was going in a 'plane."

9.40pm

Interval at the Surf Ballroom during which fans line up for autographs. Although he has yet to appear, Buddy signed copies of "It Doesn't Matter Anymore".

10.00pm

The original Crickets, Jerry and Joe B, returned to Lubbock and called Maria Elena. They told her that they, too, were breaking with Norman Petty and wanted to get back with Buddy. Maria Elena told them to contact the Surf Ballroom and speak to him when he got off stage.

10.10pm

Dion and the Belmonts performed their current doo-wop success, "I Wonder Why". Buddy Holly was playing drums, his face hidden by the cymbals.

10.15pm

Ritchie Valens phoned home. He had had some arguments with his brother Bob but he agreed to meet him in New York after the tour, and around the time he would be presented with his gold disc for "Donna".

10.20pm

The Big Bopper asked Waylon Jennings if he could take his place on the plane. Despite drinking whiskey, his cold was no better, and in exchange for his seat, he offered Waylon his new sleeping-bag. Waylon said, "If it's all right with Buddy, it's all right with me." (Presumably Holly might not want to be close to someone with 'flu.)

Big Bopper Jr (376): "My father didn't ring my mother that night, so he can't have thought it was that big a deal. Buddy had chartered the flight and was tired of riding on that bus. It kept breaking down and he thought that he would get to the next town and get some rest. My father was feeling ill, and Waylon said, 'It's fine with me if it

is all right with Buddy.' I have the receipt for $36 which was Dad's third of the flight."

10.25pm

Not to be outdone, Ritchie Valens asked Tommy Allsup if he could take his place on the plane. "No way," says Allsup.

10.40pm

Dion introduced his new drummer, Buddy Holly. Dion and the Belmonts left the stage and Buddy, Tommy and Waylon opened with "Gotta Travel On".

10.45pm

Buddy Holly with Waylon on harmony sang "Salty Dog Blues". Fred Milano loved hearing them do "It's So Easy" as he loved the way that Buddy sang "fall" with his Texas drawl. Buddy included "Bo Diddley" in his set.

11.20pm

The rest of the performers joined Holly on stage for the final songs of the evening, "La Bamba" and "Brown-Eyed Handsome Man", the final songs of Buddy's life. Since the start of their first hit, "That'll Be The Day", Buddy Holly had performed in 200 venues in 18 months. He had been on stage over 500 times.

11.30pm

Waylon Jennings went to the Ballroom's snack bar for hot dogs.

The Big Bopper asked Buddy if he could take Waylon's place. "I hope your ol' bus freezes up again," joked Holly as Waylon returned. "Well, I hope your ol' plane crashes," Waylon chuckled back. It was the last words that Waylon ever said to Buddy and it haunted him for evermore.

11.45pm

Carroll Anderson probably gave Buddy the fee for the show. (This is another of the mysteries as only $200 was found in the wreckage. There is an interview recorded by a fan in 1998 in which Anderson says he gave Buddy $300 to tide him over and this was taken from Buddy's body at the crash site and returned to Anderson.)

11.50pm

The Crickets phoned the Surf Ballroom but Buddy Holly could not be located. Instead, they called the next venue and left a message for Holly to call them. (This seems astonishingly late to be making calls, but these are musicians, after all.)

Jerry Allison (377): "Buddy had told Waylon that he wanted to be back with us and do a tour of England. This got back to us and that's why we wanted to speak to him. It was fine with us."

Tuesday 3 February 1959

Midnight

While Carroll Anderson was loading Holly, Allsup and the Big Bopper's baggage into the station wagon to take them to the airport. Holly asked Allsup to check that they had everything.

12.05am

Ritchie Valens, who was still signing autographs, saw Allsup and again pleaded for a seat on the plane. Reluctantly, Allsup tossed a 50 cent piece. Ritchie Valens called "Heads" and won. He exclaimed, "Gee, that's the first time I've won anything in my life."

Tommy Allsup (378): "Several times during the night, Ritchie asked me if he could fly in my place. There are stories that he was scared to fly but he wasn't. He was only 17 years old and he was raring to go. I'd already got my dirty shirts off the bus and put them in the station wagon. Buddy said, 'Tommy, go back in and make sure we have got everything loaded.' He'd never said anything like that before but I went back in and Ritchie was still signing autographs in the doorway going into the ballroom. He said again, C'mon, guy, are you going to let me fly?' For some reason, I pulled out a 50 cent piece and flipped it and said, 'Call it.' He said, 'Heads', so he got to fly."

12.10am

Allsup asked Holly to collect a registered letter with a cheque for a tax refund from his mother from the post office in Moorhead.

Tommy Allsup (379): "When I went back to the car to tell Buddy that Ritchie was going, I said that I had got a letter waiting for me at the post office from my mother and I asked him to pick it up. He said, 'Give me some ID', so I pulled out my wallet and I was fishing for my driver's licence in the cold. Buddy said, 'Just give me your wallet.' He took the whole wallet and stuck it inside his pocket. The next morning they found five IDs and only four bodies."

12.15am

Exit the tour bus and also Anderson's party left for the airport. Anderson had his wife and son with him. It was snowing lightly.

12.20am

Over the telephone, Jerry Dwyer and Roger Peterson had been checking weather reports. All were acceptable, recording visibility of 10 miles or more. Peterson was not given crucial information by Air Traffic Control: he might have to fly by instruments, and he has failed the examination for that.

It is possible that Roger Peterson was nursing doubts about taking off, but the singers were desperate to get away. Why didn't they stay overnight and fly in the morning?

12.30am

The flight was due to leave Mason City, but Anderson has only just arrived. The snow was now falling more heavily and there were 35mph gusts.

12.45pm

Holly told Dwyer that he had been taking flying lessons. He told Anderson that he would return to Clear Lake in the spring for another engagement and go water-skiing. Carroll Anderson wished them goodbye and said, "I wish you only the best."

Harvey Andrews, a singer-songwriter from Birmingham, England, has written tributes to his heroes (Tony Hancock, Harry Chapin, Phil Ochs). In 1988, it was Buddy Holly's turn in "Please Don't Get On The Plane": "I know that you're tired, And you hired it to go on ahead of the gang, But please don't get on the plane, Take your time, Like the words of the song you just sang."

Harvey Andrews (380): "It took me sometime to find a way to write a song about Buddy Holly. I wanted to write something oblique and come into it at an angle, to find some different way of saying something. It took over twenty years, I suppose, and it came to me after I watched the *Arena* special on Buddy Holly. I went to bed and I was dreaming that I was there in the snow and frantically waving at this plane and nobody saw me. I woke up in a sweat—I was 15 in my dream but I was 44 when I woke up—the lyric was in my head and I wrote it down there and then at four in the morning. It's frightening—it's like the song was fed in. It's as though somebody else had written it for me."

12.50am

The passengers board the Beechcraft Bonanza. It had been built in 1947 and had had several owners before Jerry Dwyer bought it in October 1958. The pilot and Buddy Holly were up front, and Ritchie and the Bopper at the back.

12.55am

The plane took off. It levelled off south of the airfield, then headed north-west to Fargo, North Dakota.

1.00am

Peterson was forced to depend upon instruments. Most likely, he misread the Sperry gyroscope as it was different to the one he had trained on. He probably believed that the plane was climbing when it was descending. Dwyer, who was watching, thought he saw the plane descend but considered it an optical illusion.

Undoubtedly, their last moments were spent in terror. The plane crashed at 170mph on farmland owned by Albert and Delbert Juel. The right wing hit the ground first and was ripped off. The plane bounced 50 feet and skidded another 500 feet before crashing into a fence. Peterson's body remained in the plane, but it had to be cut loose with torches, while the fuselage had split open and the other bodies had been thrown out. The Big Bopper's body had been thrown across the fence and was in an adjoining cornfield. The bodies of the three entertainers were mangled and all had died instantaneously.

The conspiracy theory has Buddy Holly, with the added persuasion of his handgun, taking over the controls from an incompetent pilot. Wholly implausible, especially as Buddy had had less than two hours' flying experience. When the gun was handed to the authorities some time later, one bullet had been fired. Why? It turned out that the farmer had fired a shot to check it was still working.

Waylon Jennings, of all people, has fuelled this controversy by saying, "There's a good chance that Buddy was flying that plane. A good chance." I think it was Waylon who was flying that day.

Ellis Amburn (381): "Implausible but not impossible. Buddy had some flying time and might have considered taking over when he saw how incompetent Roger Peterson was, that he couldn't fly at night or read instruments and might have been panicking."

1.15am

Attempts were made to contact the plane by radio, but there was no answer.

1.30am

Jerry Dwyer checked with Mason City airport, and later with Fargo, but nothing had been heard.

5.00am

An alert was issued for the missing aircraft.

6.00am

A radio ham picked up the alert and informed a local radio station. The possibility of a crash was mentioned, but no names were given.

8.45am

Jerry Dwyer took his own 'plane on the same course as Roger Peterson.

9.00am

Dwyer spotted the wreckage, eight miles northwest of his landing strip. He used his radio to call the police.

9.30am

The promoter at the Armoury, Moorheard, Rod Lucier, saw how bad the weather was and thought it would be best to cancel the concert. "No," said the agency, "a contract is a contract, and the touring party is on its way."

10.00am

The police—Sheriff Jerry Allen and Deputy Sheriff Bill McGill—arrived at the scene and viewed the carnage. Carroll Anderson identified the bodies, pending official identification.

Jerry Dwyer told a friend of his, the TV reporter, Bob Booe, about the crash. Associated Press were informed and the information was put on the wires. There has been much criticism of issuing that bulletin so early but Booe has said, "These are prominent guys. You don't sit on their names while they notify the next of kin because this is a very significant story." Oh yes, you do.

10.30am

The police found Tommy Allsup's wallet and asked Anderson if that could be Buddy Holly's real name. Then it was thought that there might be five bodies.

11.00am

Larry Corbin at KLLL read out the wire report from Associated Press and believed that the families had been notified. After the funeral, he went to the Holleys' home and apologised. The station had to fight to keep its licence after this *faux pas* although it wasn't their fault.

As it happened, Mr and Mrs Holley had not heard the bulletin, but Mrs Sullivan, Niki's mother, had. She rang the Holleys immediately and as they didn't know, she didn't tell them. She told Niki to get round there immediately. He arrived at the same time as their pastor, Ben Johnson.

11.15am

The coroner arrived at the scene and other patrol cars and the press were arriving. The bodies of the victims were frozen.

Travis Holley, working on a tiling job, had a coffee break. The waitress said, "Shouldn't you go home as your brother's been killed?" He thought Larry must have had an accident and dashed to his house. He then went to his parents' house. Meanwhile, Larry had gone to tell Travis and when there was no one there, he too went to his parents' house.

Jerry and Peggy Sue Allison were at the Allisons' home in Lubbock with Sonny Curtis on the living-room couch.

Sonny Curtis (382): "We had driven from Clovis to Lubbock and I had spent the night with Jerry Allison. A lady from across the street came over to the house with the sad news and I was the one who had to wake him up and tell him."

Joe B. Mauldin (383): "When my sister called me up and told me that Buddy had been killed, I didn't believe it. I thought it was a publicity stunt that had gone wrong."

11.30am

Maria Elena, who had morning sickness, switched on the radio and heard the news. Her aunt and Holly's protégé, Lou Giordano, comforted her.

Tommy Donaldson, a DJ at KFXM in San Bernadino, California, had to deal with broken-hearted teenagers. Later in the day, while driving home, he thought of writing a tribute song, "Three Stars". A few weeks earlier, Tom Hull had been in the station with Ginny Wright and a record called "Are You Mine". Hull worked for American Music and he had told him that American Music was always looking for good, new songs. He completed "Three Stars" and decided to take it to American Music in the morning.

The Brill Building songwriter, **Paul Evans (384)**, had taken a break. "There were two restaurants where the writers hung out. One was Dempsey's, which was for the older writers, and the other was the Turf, where the younger crew was, and we had great fun there. A lot of us were having brunch in the Turf one morning and somebody told us about the plane crash which had killed Buddy Holly, Ritchie Valens and the Big Bopper. The place just emptied, emptied just like that, and I knew where they all going. They were going back to their cubicles to write songs. That seemed a little too current for me, but New York was always a current town."

Noon

The tour bus reached Moorhead—on time. Tommy Allsup went into the lobby of Hotel Comstock while the others were sleeping. He was going to register and the desk clerk told him what had happened.

Narvel Felts (385): "Though I never met Buddy Holly, the night he died is etched in my memory along with the deaths of President Kennedy and Elvis Presley. I remember exactly where I was and what I was doing. My band, the Rockets, and I opened for what would be a four week stand at the Brass Rail in London, Ontario, Canada on Monday night, 2nd February 1959. We stayed at the Embassy Hotel. On the next day, we heard Dave 'Dean' Hagopian on CKSL Radio tell the tragic news that Buddy Holly, the Big Bopper and Ritchie Valens as well as the pilot had been killed when their small plane crashed shortly after take off from the Mason City, Iowa airport. Buddy's current hit, 'It Doesn't Matter Anymore', was being played a lot on the radio at that time. Although he was a star for less than two years, his legacy lives on."

12.05pm

Allsup got back on the bus and said, "Boys, they didn't make it." They all went to their respective rooms and called home.

Dion (386): "We were top of the world one day and the rug was pulled out from under us. At the age of 19, I was baffled, I wondered why I was here and where I was going and what the meaning of life was."

12.10pm

Tommy Allsup (387): "As soon as we checked in the hotel, I called my mother and asked her if she had been watching TV and she said no. But while I was talking to her, her neighbour was trying to get through. She had heard on a Tulsa radio station that I could be one of the bodies. After we'd spoken, this lady called again and told my mom and she said, 'No, I just talked to Tommy on the phone and he's all right.'"

12.30pm

Buddy Knox (388): "I had done some dates on a tour in Canada and then I went to see some friends in Regina, Saskatchewan. I started heading back home. I was living in Nashville at the time and I drove into a snowstorm. It was snowing so hard that I couldn't drive so I holed up in a gas station and kept my car engine and heater running 'cause it was so cold. I went to sleep and the next day I was driving along in the afternoon when I heard on the radio about three singers getting killed. I pulled over and checked my map and at the time they crashed, I was about 30 miles away. They had been crazy to fly in that weather. It had been impossible to drive in it, so imagine what it was like 4,000 feet up. Once they hit that storm, they should have told the kid to land. I'd have said, 'If we're going to miss a date, we miss a date.'"

1.00pm

Nobody wanted to continue with the show, but the promoters talked them into a tribute concert. Tommy called the Holley family in Lubbock who told him to go ahead. An announcement cancelling the show had already been made and now the date was reinstated. There would just be one performance that night.

Rod Lucier announced auditions for local replacements. 15-year-old **Bobby Vee (389)**, who had come home from school for lunch, heard the announcement and decided to audition: "I used to go to all the shows that came through my home area, which is Fargo in North Dakota. I had tickets in the front row for the Buddy Holly show and I was a big fan. I was a sophomore in high school in the tenth grade. I came home for lunch and my brother told me of the tragedy as the radio station had been making announcements. The local radio was promoting the show and they decided to go ahead with the remainder of the show which included Dion and the Belmonts, Frankie Sardo and the New Crickets. They wanted local entertainers to fill out the evening and one of the guys in our band rang the station and volunteered our services."

2.00pm

Snuff Garrett at KSYD in Wichita Falls hosted a tribute programme. He talked to Norman Petty, Jerry Allison and Joe B. Mauldin by telephone. Norman Petty said, "We often wonder why things like this happen, but there is always bound to be a reason somewhere." Asked what was in the can, he said he had some tracks in Clovis as well as two in New York.

3.00pm

Bob and Carol Montgomery were driving back to Lubbock after visiting his parents. He had told Carol that they must drive carefully as he had a feeling that something bad was going to happen. The car radio was broken and they heard the news at a gas station in Lubbock.

Bob Montgomery (390):"I had driven down to a little town close to Lampasas, where my folks had a farm. I visited with them and I was coming back to Clovis, New Mexico which is where I was living. I was working for Norman Petty as an engineer at his studio. I stopped off in Lubbock and I called Echo McGuire and she said, 'Isn't it awful?' And I said, 'What?' as I hadn't had the radio on. She was the one who told me about the plane crash."

6.00pm

In past weeks, Phil Spector had told his girlfriend Donna Kass that he had written "Donna" for her. When she watched the news and saw Ritchie's girlfriend, she realised that Phil had lied. (Spector's 1958 track for the Teddy Bears, "Don't You Worry My Little Pet" was influenced by Holly.)

8.00pm

There are 1,700 at the Armoury, Moorheard and the MC is Charlie Boone at KFGO. Frankie Sardo started the show with a tribute to all three performers by performing their hits.

8.20pm

Bobby Vee and his group, the Shadows, did well as a replacement in front of 1,700 fans. Bing Bingston is impressed and asked to manage him. **Bobby Vee (391):** "As we were only a garage band, we didn't have a name. I told them that we were the Shadows with a question mark, and that was our first job in front of a large audience. There was a tradition that the show must go on but both the performers and the audience were in shock. I was too young to rationalise it."

10.30pm

Tommy and Waylon were certainly in shock when they closed the show, looking washed out and with sunken cheeks. Tommy had tears streaming down his face, but somehow Waylon managed to sing Buddy's hits and did them well.

Tommy Allsup (392): "Me and Waylon were in a blue haze for four days; we weren't drunk or anything, but we couldn't figure out what had happened. We had to do the shows but I don't remember much about them. I remember us getting out there playing the first night and the house was packed and everybody in the audience was crying. Waylon and me have talked about it and we don't remember what we played. The tour had to go on and we didn't get to the funeral. Mr Holley ordered a closed casket and said that Buddy would have wanted the tour to continue."

11.00pm

After the show, the management at the Armoury wanted to reduce the fee because the main performers weren't there. "Real nice people," commented Waylon Jennings.

Back in the UK, the evening papers were on the streets. **Jim Newcombe (393):** "I remember hearing the news at home. I worked a few minutes walk from home and I was already there when my father came home and he told me some rock'n'roll singers had died and he gave me the paper to look at, I couldn't believe it and for the next day or so I kept hoping it was all a mistake and Buddy had survived."

Wednesday 4 February 1959

The *Lubbock Morning-Avalanche* ran the crash as its main story, calling it "a mishap". Jerry Dwyer insisted that his plane was in good condition. Some press reports treated Ritchie Valens and the Big Bopper as bigger artists as they had current hits. The *Daily Mirror* had with the Big Bopper and his outstretched arms across the top of front page. This was the most significant report in the UK: the broadsheets only mentioned the crash in passing, if at all. It wasn't in *The Times*.

In New York, a 13-year-old Don McLean delivered the morning papers. He knew that Holly had died but until then, he didn't know about his "widowed bride" and something touched him deep inside.

Phillip Goodhand-Tait (394): "I was a schoolboy delivering newspapers on the Bushy Hill housing estate, Guildford and that's when I read of the crash that killed Buddy Holly, the Big Bopper and Richie Valens. It was front page news and I stood outside a council house devastated until the householder came outside and shouted at me. He wanted his newspaper before he went to work."

John Broven (395): "Around this time our generation was devastated by the Manchester United Munich air disaster. There was an equal feeling of desolation when news of the Holly plane crash came through. I remember it well: I was standing on Polegate railway station on a clear, cold February morning, waiting for the train to take us on the daily trip to Bexhill Grammar School. Buddy had died young but he had certainly made his mark (along with the Big Bopper and Ritchie Valens), and the music has lived on—and how.'"

John Rostron (396): "Tragedy struck on February 3rd 1959 as I was woken up by my mother at 7.30am to be told that my grandfather had died. The next morning, the *Daily Mirror* carried the story that Buddy Holly had died along with the Big Bopper and Richie Valens, but where, I wondered, were the other Crickets as we had not heard of a split."

At the Liverpool College of Art, John Lennon was unusually quiet. He had lost his mother, a huge influence on his early music, the previous July, and now he had lost one of his heroes.

Tony Macaulay (397): "Most people in the late 50s were into Elvis Presley, but Buddy Holly was the nerd's hero. He wasn't very sexual and he wasn't particularly good looking and his voice wasn't very strong but he had great warmth and he invented the two guitars, bass and drums line-up as we understand it now. I think he got more spotty, pre-pubescent boys writing songs and playing the guitar than anybody else, and I was one of them. His death had such an impact on young boys, more so I think than if Elvis Presley had died."

Tommy Donaldson took his song, "Three Stars" to American Music and they arranged to have Eddie Cochran record it that very evening. Cochran kept breaking down during the recitation. Cochran wanted it released as a single for charity but Liberty's accountants blocked such an innovative release. The track wasn't issued until it appeared in the UK in 1966. It's mawkish, but Cochran's husky, tearful delivery (compiled from eight takes) makes it work. Cochran became fearful of flying, having premonitions of his own death. He agreed to appear in the UK because, once he'd arrived, he would be travelling by road and rail. Eddie Cochran died in a car-crash in England in April 1960.

Because of the delay, Tommy Donaldson cut his own version as Tommy Dee, backed by Carol Kay and the Teen-airs. It made the US Top 20. A cover version, also American, by Ruby Wright and Dick Pike was a hit in the UK.

Maria Elena and her aunt arrived in Lubbock at 5pm on 4 February 1959.

Larry and his brother-in-law, J.E. Weir, went to Mason City to identify Buddy's body and bring it back home. Weir identified the body to spare Larry's emotions. The chartered plane bringing Buddy Holly's body to Lubbock was grounded in Des Moines. It flew to Lubbock on 5 February.

Irving Feld said that the tour must go on. Jimmy Clanton, Frankie Avalon and Debbie Dean joined the troupe. Jimmy Clanton, who was in Charlotte, North Carolina on tour with Bo Diddley and Duane Eddy, was sent to the *Winter Dance Party*. When he got on the bus, he found that many of the victims' possessions were still around.

Clanton did a couple of Buddy's songs each night as a tribute and even played his guitar: he later performed "Rockabilly Days", which was about filling in for Buddy. Ronnie Smith from Odessa, whom Carl had played with, joined as well and he did some Elvis songs. Flying through a storm, Carl Bunch rejoined the touring party in Sioux City, Iowa, and was met at the airport by Clanton and Ronnie Smith.

Tommy Allsup (398): "Carl came back and every night, Waylon got better and better. He said, 'Oh, it's just sympathy,' but I said, 'No, man, they are digging you. You are going to be a star.' He said, 'Naw.'"

When Tommy, Waylon, Ronnie and Carl signed autographs, they added "Crickets". Artists came and went on the show, with Fabian replacing Frankie Avalon after a few days, and Bill Parsons ("All American Boy") coming on board.

On 5 February 1959, a memorial service for Roger Peterson was held at the Redeemer Lutheran Church in Ventura, Iowa and he was buried at the Buena Vista Memorial Cemetery, Storm Lake.

On 6 February 1959, the Big Bopper was buried in the Forest Lawn Memorial Park in Los Angeles with most of the staff of KTRM in attendance.

On 7 February 1959, Buddy Holly's funeral took place at the Tabernacle Baptist Church, Lubbock with the service conducted by Ben Johnson and over 1,000 people in attendance. It was the biggest funeral ever seen in Lubbock. The pallbearers were Bob Montgomery, Niki Sullivan, Jerry Allison, Joe B. Mauldin, Sonny Curtis and Phil Everly. Although Maria Elena was in Lubbock, she did not feel up to attending the service. A large photograph of Buddy was placed on the coffin, and a telegram of condolence from Elvis and the Colonel was read out.

Bill Pickering from the Picks sang "Beyond The Sunset" and Buddy's favourite gospel record, "I'll Be Alright" by the Angelic Gospel Singers, was played. At the time, very few of the congregation would have heard "True Love Ways" and wouldn't connect the two songs: so, unknowingly, at Holly's funeral, it was effectively confirmed that the link between the two songs was not coincidental.

The same day, Ritchie Valens was buried in San Fernando. Losing no time, Norman Petty applied for the patent for the name of the Crickets so that it would be owned by Jerry Allison and Joe B. Mauldin.

On 9 February 1959, *Billboard* announced that Coral was rush-releasing *The Buddy Holly Story*. The follow-up single for the Big Bopper is changed to the comforting "Someone Watching Over You", and Del-Fi dropped plans for a Ritchie Valens album to be released on 14 February, *Valens-Time Day*. Ritchie Valens' single, "Donna", was issued in the UK after his death but a cover version by Marty Wilde was the major hit.

On 13 February 1959, "It Doesn't Matter Anymore" was released in the UK. This is the first instance in the UK of a record becoming a hit after the artist's death. After Holly, it has happened with Eddie Cochran, Jim Reeves, Otis Redding, Elvis Presley, Freddie Mercury (Queen) and Kurt Cobain (Nirvana). In addition, the compilation, *The Buddy Holly Story*, was a huge success in both Britain and America, remaining on the US charts for over three years. It was helped by a cover photograph from Hal Buksbaum, which was a large portrait of Buddy in his black-framed glasses.

There is also the irony of the title of his final single. Nothing unique about prescient titles, though, as there are plenty of them: "I'll Never Get Out Of This World Alive" (Hank Williams), "What Am I Living For" and "Hang Up My Rock'n'Roll Shoes" (both Chuck Willis, who died from cancer and probably knew what was happening), "Three Steps To Heaven" (Eddie Cochran), "When I'm Gone" (Phil Ochs), "Goodbye" (Gene Ammons) and "Way Down" (Elvis Presley). "I Won't Forget You" was in the charts for Jim Reeves when he died, and in "Voodoo Chile", Jimi Hendrix says, "And I want to say one last thing". Spooky ol' world, isn't it.

Ronnie Smith came to the *Winter Dance Party* with drugs he had bought in Mexico, and Waylon was regularly taking them. The final dates for the *Winter Dance Party* were cancelled, and the New Crickets had to take the train from Chicago to New York. Waylon was so hyped up that he couldn't sit down and was pacing the floor. According to Tommy Allsup, Waylon walked all the way! When they reached New York, GAC

refused to pay them, saying that they had given the money to Maria Elena.

Paul Anka had been in Italy and he did not know of the crash until he got to London a couple of days later. On 13 February, he told the *NME* that they had played 150 shows together and he added, not too diplomatically but then he was still young, "I feel especially unhappy for Buddy's widow Maria who, to the best of my knowledge, is expecting a baby. Buddy's marriage was a very happy one, even though the ceremony itself was kept quiet, presumably because Maria is Puerto Rican, which could have aroused a certain amount of controversy and perhaps scorn in America." This comment confirms the pregnancy and I think that Buddy simply preferred to keep it a secret among his working associates until it was further advanced. After all, at the time of his death, his marriage hadn't even been in the press.

Unfortunately, **Maria Elena Holly (399)** lost their baby. "It was the shock. I was in bed, and one of the young men that he was recording, Lou Giordano, called me and I told him that I was still in bed. I was not feeling good in the mornings. He said, 'Don't put on the TV and just wait 'til I get there.' My aunt had also heard the news and she was on her way over. Of course, I got up and put the television on and they were talking about the crash. When my aunt came in, I was running around like a demented person and that is when I lost the child." Maria started to cry and I said, "I can see you're reliving it as we talk "Yes." If Maria Elena had not lost the baby, their son or daughter would have been 21 when John Lennon was murdered in December 1980.

Within a day of the crash, the coroner, Dr Ralph Smiley, conducted the medical investigation including an autopsy of Roger Peterson. The report by the Civil Aeronautics Bound was concluded on 16 February but not published until 23 September 1959. These are the conclusions:

"At night, with an overcast sky, snow falling, no definite horizon, and a proposed flight over a sparsely settled area with an absence of ground lights, a requirement for control of the aircraft solely by reference to flight instruments can be predicted with virtual certainty.

"The Board concludes that pilot Peterson, when a short distance from the airport, was confronted with this situation. Because of fluctuation of the instruments caused by gusty winds he would have been forced to concentrate and rely greatly on the attitude gyro, an instrument with which he was not completely familiar. The pitch display of this instrument is the reverse of the instrument he was accustomed to; therefore, he could have become confused and thought that he was making a climbing turn when in reality he was making a descending turn. The fact that the aircraft struck the ground in a steep turn but with the nose lowered only slightly, indicates that some control was being effected at the time. The weather briefing supplied to the pilot was seriously inadequate in that it failed to even mention adverse flying conditions which should have been highlighted.

"The Board determines that the probable cause of this accident was the pilot's unwise decision to embark on a flight which would necessitate flying solely by instruments when he was not properly certificated or qualified to do so. Contributing factors were serious deficiencies in the weather briefing, and the pilot's unfamiliarity with the instrument which determines the attitude of the aircraft."

Each family received $25,000 insurance from Jerry Dwyer's indemnity policy for the crash. An insurance company would have grounds for not meeting a claim if it appeared that due care had not being taken, but they did not pursue this.

Jerry Dwyer refused all interview requests to talk about the crash, which is hardly surprising.

Buddy Holly had died intestate and so Maria Elena received the first $5,000 of the net estate, with the remainder of $50,000 being shared with his parents. Three guitars went to the Holley family with Maria Elena keeping the Gibson J-200. Buddy Holly's claim against Norman Petty was settled in April 1959 for $40,000 and he was acknowledged as the composer of "Peggy Sue".

During the 1970s, the Buddy Holly biographer, John Goldrosen, was speaking to Sheriff Jerry Allen about the crash, and Allen discovered that Tommy Allsup's wallet was in the files at Mason City. Goldrosen told Allsup, who applied for its return. When he got it back in 1980, he was working on an album for Don McLean, which included his UK Number 1 cover of Roy Orbison's "Crying", and he showed them his find. The wallet is now part of a touring exhibition with the Hard Rock Café.

Many of Buddy Holly's possessions had been given either to the family or to Maria Elena. She had the watch which she had given him for the *Winter Dance Party* and the family had the pistol. At one stage, she traded the watch for the pistol as she would feel more secure in New York with it. If that was the case, why didn't she get a new gun? Why use a gun that had been in an air crash and could well have developed faults? There's strange behaviour in Holly world, to be sure.

9

BUDDY HOLLY LIVES

*"Who has not, for sake of his good reputation,
sacrificed himself once?" (Nietzsche)*

A young American star, who wore glasses, was at the forefront of musical change and died in a plane crash, became a legend. The year was 1944 and the musician was Glenn Miller. And who wouldn't mind a life so short if it was so fulfilling?

In January 1953, 20,000 people filed past Hank Williams' body as it lay in an embroidered Nudie suit (a star to the last) at the Montgomery Municipal Auditorium. There was a growing demand for his records—album tracks became successful singles and demos were overdubbed. Hank Williams recorded 170 songs and yet there are 200 tribute records. Hank Williams became the Phantom of the *Opry*. His son, Hank Williams Jr, has remarked, "I'm sick of hearing people tell me how much they loved my daddy. They hated him in Nashville."

So, there were precedents for having a very successful career after death. We don't know for certain but "It Doesn't Matter Anymore" was a very commercial record that would probably have been a hit despite the publicity surrounding Buddy Holly's death. There was, however, speculation that some people bought this record, not because they wanted to enjoy it but because Buddy Holly

had died. This impression of these ghoulish things has persisted whenever a major rock figure has died, notably John Lennon and Freddie Mercury. I can't imagine my mother-in-law buying "Imagine" in any other circumstances.

"It Doesn't Matter Anymore" went to Number 13 in the US and was on the charts for three months: not a staggering success but his biggest single since "Oh Boy!": "Raining In My Heart" was also listed, but got no higher than Number 88. In both Britain and Australia, the single was Number 1 and it sold over 400,000 in the UK.

The choice for the follow-up single to "It Doesn't Matter Anymore" was a no-brainer: it had to be "True Love Ways". With all the morbid publicity and being such a great song, it would surely have been a posthumous Number 1. Inexplicably, Coral held onto this track for a year by which time, some odd choices had been made.

In the UK, "It Doesn't Matter Anymore" was followed, totally ridiculously, by "Midnight Shift". I know one was on Coral and one on Brunswick but they were both in the Decca group and there would have been joint production meetings to approve its release. Although this is a wonderful performance, it was too far removed from what was making the UK charts at the time and could only hope for novelty sales.

There had been correspondence at US Decca to determine just what they held on Buddy Holly. Dick Jacobs had "True Love Ways" and "Moondreams" ready for release and he held the tapes of the six new songs that Buddy had given him before the *Winter Dance Party*. Norman Petty said that he had four masters, including "Reminiscing". If they were combined, there was enough for a new Buddy Holly album.

Part of the problem was the falling out between Buddy Holly and Norman Petty before his death, which had led to Petty being cut off from both the record and publishing companies. The most sensible solution, to give *The Apartment Tapes* to Norman Petty to complete and master, possibly with the Crickets, was not practicable. What's more, Norman Petty could have done that in Clovis without any union hassles. It was a different matter in New York: overdubbing was forbidden and Dick Jacobs had to plead a special case to the Musicians' Union.

When this was cleared, Dick Jacobs allocated the work to Jack Hansen. Hansen had worked on Holly's recordings in New York, so it was not an insensitive choice. Dick Jacobs asked him to prepare "Peggy Sue Got Married" and "Crying, Waiting, Hoping", for a single as a simple voice and guitar demo would not sell. Hansen added piano, drums and bass and then the Ray Charles Singers, who supplied the accompaniment on *The Perry Como Show*. Jacobs and Hansen were concerned that they would lose the quality of the original tape with overdubbing, but the arrangements did the most harm. They were unimaginative but the quality of the songs shone through. However, the single flopped in the US but the single did make the UK Top 20.

In January 1960, Hansen and the same musicians worked on "That's What They Say", "What To Do", "Learning The Game" and "That Makes It Tough" in a similar fashion. The six apartment songs formed half of the new album, *The Buddy Holly Story, Volume II,* and both "Learning The Game" and "What To Do" made the UK Top 40. Maria Elena wrote the sleeve note, or did she, as she said, "I feel justified in assuming many of the songs were sung directly to me." If they were,

then their marriage was in a bad shape. In May 1960, "True Love Ways" was finally released as a single, but without any fanfare: it made the UK Top 30 and flopped in the States.

Donovan (400): "My songwriting really comes from reading poetry and listening to Buddy Holly and then Woody Guthrie. The songs of the Everly Brothers were also very interesting but Buddy Holly wrote many of his own songs and I used to buy every single eagerly. He wrote simple songs, and it is not easy to write simple songs. Buddy came from Texas and I can imagine that part of his inspiration came from listening to Mexican music on the radio as there was a great romantic feeling in that music and in his songs. I love 'Maybe Baby', 'Not Fade Away' and 'That'll Be The Day' of course, but I would pick 'Learning The Game' as my favourite, which is perfect."

Although Norman Petty was still in dispute with Coral, he was collecting tapes of Buddy Holly from various sources: from Buddy's family and friends; from Bob Montgomery; and from Hi Pockets Duncan. By 1962, he had gained quality control over Holly's catalogue and he set about preparing new tracks for release.

Throughout the 1960s, Norman Petty overdubbed Holly's home and studio recordings, but because he felt betrayed, he did not use Holly's musicians—Jerry Allison, Joe B. Mauldin, Sonny Curtis or Bob Montgomery. Is it too late now to find out what Jerry and Joe B. would have done with *The Apartment Tapes*?

Ellis Amburn (401): "Jerry Allison was furious that they were not asked to work on those tapes, but it was the Crickets' own fault. They had abandoned Buddy before the *Winter Dance Party* because Norman Petty said he could make them all stars and that Buddy would be nothing without them. This was absurd and they had fallen out of the picture."

Instead, Norman Petty employed the Fireballs with their excellent lead guitarist, George Tomsco. Petty had his own agenda in doing this as the Fireballs, sometimes with vocalist Jimmy Gilmer, were making hit records in their own right and this was additional publicity. They had instrumental hits with "Torquay" (1959),"Bulldog" (1960, with Bob Montgomery on rhythm guitar) and "Quite A Party!" (1961). **George Tomsco (402)**: "We were helping Norman out at a theatre that he was turning into a recording studio and sound stage. We were taking seats apart and cleaning up the building and doing all kinds of manual labour. I went across the street to get a bite to eat and when I came back, Eric Budd had his drums on stage and was playing this crazy beat. I said, "Oh man, that's really great, just keep playing that." I grabbed my guitar and plugged it in and I was just fishing for a guitar line that would go with it. That led to 'Quite A Party!'"

After the instrumental hits, the Fireballs had two major hits with Jimmy Gilmer—"Sugar Shack" (US Number 1 in 1963) and "Daisy Petal Pickin'" (1964)—as well as a Top 10 single with the Tom Paxton song, "Bottle Of Wine" (1968), all produced by Norman Petty. George Tomsco has no complaints about Norman Petty's song-writing and arrangements: Norman's name is on "Vaquero" because he co-wrote it. Norman Petty also produced the String-A-Longs, who had an international hit with his instrumental composition, "Wheels" in 1961. However, "Wheels" is now associated with male strippers hiding their naughty bits with balloons, and the Fireballs are best remembered for their work with Buddy Holly.

George Tomsco (403): "Norman Petty told me that he had been authorised to complete these tapes of Buddy's and he wanted the Fireballs for the project. I said, 'Why don't you use the Crickets?' and he said that they weren't available. I said, 'Okay' and we did it. I've got a list of 32 tracks that I worked on but it's so long ago that it's hard to remember what I did. Some were demos and some were complete recordings that just needed a bit more adding to them. I had to match Buddy's guitar on 'Brown-Eyed Handsome Man' and that meant playing at full steam and doing it at the intensity with which he was playing. It was spooky working with a singer who had died and who had had his hits in that studio. We were just enhancing the tapes really, but I love the way 'Slippin' And Slidin' and his instrumental, 'Holly Hop', turned out. His vocal on 'Slippin' And Slidin'' is great—it is like somebody chewing something and then spitting it out. We had fun with 'Bo Diddley' too."

The Fireballs, who were proud to have the assignment, captured the quirkiness of "Slippin' And Slidin'" and "Dearest" very well, but the deep-voiced vocal on "Smokey Joe's Café" was preposterous. They are to be congratulated for turning the fragment of "Wait Till The Sun Shines, Nellie" into a full track: a similar effort had been made by Little Richard's producer on the 57 seconds of "Keep A-Knockin'" after Richard went into the ministry.

Norman Petty took care with his overdubbing, but he took criticism for it. He told *Goldmine*, "It is natural I should feel that any additions I made to Buddy's tapes were valid ones based on ideas I developed when I had the opportunity to work with the exceptional talent of Buddy Holly. I think I have a pretty good idea of what he liked and what he did not like."

The Jack Hansen arrangements for the apartment songs were much of a muchness, and the Fireballs, under Petty's guidance, showed more inventiveness and they weren't dragged down by the Ray Charles Singers. However, I still prefer to hear the voice and guitar originals without additional accompaniment. **George Tomsco (404):** "Well, I can see the argument for saying that the tapes should be left as they are. I understand the concept of keeping it simple, but Norman wanted to enhance them. Some Buddy Holly fans really like what we did, and we have certainly had more positive comments than the Jack Hansen dub-ins. We got the job and I think we did it well. We all knew the music from the West Texas area, but we followed a lot of Norman's ideas as he was calling the shots. You are hearing his production and his direction and it's all his input, just using the Fireballs to get what he wanted."

Liverpool impresario and long-time Holly fan, **David Crosby (405):** "'That's What They Say' was a wistful and melodic song that was recorded as a demo, with Buddy accompanying himself on guitar. A simple backing track of strings and vocals was added by Jack Hansen, and this complemented the minor key simple melody of the song. As well as being part of the new album, *The Buddy Holly Story, Volume 2,* 'That's What They Say' was issued as a single, as the B-side of another simple, but wonderful, apartment demo. 'What To Do'. Released in January 1961, the single had little impact on the charts. In 1963, Norman Petty created a new version with accompaniment from the Fireballs. I found the sound a little thin and unsuited to the song. There is a third version with the vocal group, the Picks, backing Buddy, but I would recommend everybody to the one with Jack Hansen's accompaniment."

Mike Jones (406): "The first impact on Buddy Holly on me was two of his posthumous hits 'Brown Eyed Handsome Man' and 'Bo Diddley'. I thought they were great records. A friend's father had the *Reminiscing* album—at a time when albums were comparatively rare and unusual items in most homes. There was something about the gravity of the portrait on the sleeve that convinced me that he was a major force, then as I heard his songs performed by the Rolling Stones and the Beatles, I realised that he was."

In 1964, Norman Petty added the Fireballs to some of the earliest recordings for an album called *Holly In The Hills*: what hills? Buddy and Bob's recordings from 1954/5 already featured three or four musicians, and there are simply too many musicians for rockabilly. "Queen Of The Ballroom" is a clunky mess with an irritating organ and military-styled drumming, but "Gotta Get You Near Me Blues" works fine and is first rate.

Bob Montgomery (407): "Oh, all the tracks were better in their unedited form, but Norman wanted to use the Fireballs. The original tracks were just Buddy and me on guitars with Sonny Curtis on fiddle on a couple. I admit that we weren't the most accomplished musicians, but I prefer them as they were."

Marshall Crenshaw (408): "One of my real favourites is 'Down The Line', but it is impossible to make out what the lyrics are."

Coming onto the 1956 recordings, the Fireballs do a good job on "Baby Won't You Come Out Tonight". They also do creditable work on the original March 1957 version of "Maybe Baby", which had been marred by silly background vocals, but presumably they could have been lost anyway.

By far, the most successful overdubs are with "Brown-Eyed Handsome Man" and "Bo Diddley", which had featured Buddy Holly, Jerry Allison and a bass player. The Fireballs fill out the sound very well and despite the pressure on

chart places during the Merseybeat era, Buddy made Number 3 with "Brown-Eyed Handsome Man" and Number 4 with "Bo Diddley". However, they failed to make the US Hot 100. The Fireballs do well with "Blue Monday", but even though Norman Petty reduced the distortion, it was still there. There's a feel of the Champs about "Shake, Rattle And Roll" and it was a good idea to speed up "Holly Hop".

Studying the files of the BBC's Popular Music Policy Committee for another project (the box set, *This Record Is Not To Be Broadcast*), I was surprised to find that Buddy Holly's "Brown Eyed Handsome Man" was placed on the banned list in 1963. Chuck Berry's song had been around for some time, but it was only then that the Committee realised that the lyric referred to a commercial airline, TWA, which was tantamount to advertising. I am sure I heard the single on the BBC and it is likely that it was edited for broadcasting.

Making up for lost time, Coral released so many singles in the UK that he could have been a current artist. Holly had chart entries with "Reminiscing" (Number 17, 1962), "Wishing" (Number 10, 1963) and "Love's Made A Fool Of You" (Number 39, 1964).

It is not too late for new Holly compositions to come to light. There is a ballad registered with Nor-Va-Jak, "I Know I'll Have The Blues Again", written by John Mackey and Buddy Holly. Mackey listed his share as 90%, but what did Holly do? In 1982, Whitesidewalls recorded this song. In 1991, Sonny recorded a solo concert for BBC Radio Merseyside and before the concert, he put music to a lyric of Buddy Holly's "Monetta", the first Holly/ Curtis composition, which he then performed.

In April 1963, the NME ran a feature by Alan Smith that said, "The Top 10 success of Buddy Holly's new single, 'Brown-Eyed Handsome Man' has brought with it a shocking tasteless rumour that Buddy Holly is still alive, but disfigured. The story is that Buddy preferred to be thought dead because he wanted people to remember him as he was." Another rumour was that a Holly clone was making new recordings and releasing them under his name. *Record Mirror*, was always running stories about new Buddy Holly recordings.

Norman Jopling (409): "When I started writing for *Record Mirror*, I was 17 and I wrote about Holly at every possible opportunity, every release, every newly-discovered tape, every rumour, and we got so much positive feedback from our readers that I was encouraged to do so. One of our freelances, Graeme Andrews, was even keener than me, and he got some great exclusives from America, but I did get a 'Thank-you' card from Buddy's parents."

For the first time, **Norman Jopling (410)** is prepared to confess to a hoax in the 6 July 1963 edition of *Record Mirror*. "I saved the lead letter spot in that issue for a particular piece of mischief-making titled *Holly? Is It A Hoax?—Two Readers Ask*. In light of Buddy Holly's recent extraordinary posthumous success, two readers—one from Norway—wrote in on a similar theme, with what must be one of pop's first conspiracy theories"

The letters read:

"With the reappearance of another 'Buddy Holly' disc in the charts isn't it about time someone found out if it really is Buddy singing, or just another copyist. If Tommy Roe, Mike Berry, Earl Sinks and many more can sound just like Buddy, surely it is possible for these 'Buddy Holly' recordings of late to be by an impostor. The last two releases 'Bo Diddley' and 'Brown Eyed Handsome Man' do not sound to me as if they were made pre-1959. We are told that the backings have been added, but the actual voice is so clear that it seems impossible to get this sound on an ordinary tape recorder, and after the tape has lain around for over four years! Now comes the news that another Holly tape has been found and, of course, these will be released and sell like hot cakes, but would someone please explain how a tape that has been lying around for four years has only just been found? Don't get me wrong. I'm a Holly fan and saw him when he came over, but are today's record buying fans sure it is their idol, or are we being taken for one of the biggest rides in modern record history?"—Jim Costello, 40 Stainton Road, Enfield, Middlesex."

"It was very interesting to read your discography on Buddy Holly some weeks ago. But it's also interesting to find that except for 'Baby I Don't Care', a hit in July '61, all Buddy's singles from 'Peggy Sue Got Married' in September '59 to 'Reminisc-ing' in October '62 have been flops. In the last few months there has been much written about Holly and it has been written that Norman Petty back in the U.S. has plenty of recording material left of Buddy's—enough to have records released for many years to come. But isn't it strange that these tapes haven't been issued as records many years ago when Buddy's releases all flopped in a row? Is the reason that US Brunswick needed a guy who sang so like Buddy that with some technical arrangements, it was impossible to hear the difference? I find it very strange that Mr Petty has such a great number of released tapes. Mr Norman Jopling said 'A perfect tape had just been found by some U.S. DJs of Buddy singing 20 R&B standards.' Seems like Buddy has gone around and recorded whenever he had a spare minute. Tapes are found by his mother, by Petty, or just by some DJs! Although I'm a keen Holly fan, I for one find this very strange."—Peter Knutzen, Terrasseveien-14, Stabekk, Oslo, Norway

Norman Jopling (411): "Everyone who knows Buddy Holly's records knows what a brilliant record producer Norman Petty was. But at the time of Holly's death, unknown to the press and public, Holly was escaping from Petty's control. Tracks like 'Rave On', 'Early In The Morning', 'It Doesn't Matter Anymore' and 'True Love Ways' had already shown that Holly could make great records without Petty. Nevertheless, four years after Buddy's death, Petty was now working with the Holley family and in charge of sprucing up Buddy's unissued tapes…and making a fine job of it too. The recent hits 'Reminiscing', 'Brown-Eyed Handsome Man', 'Bo Diddley' and the forthcoming 'Wishing' were testament to that. It was understandable the Holley family would want to work with Petty—he was local, they knew him well, they trusted him. And when, in mid-'59, US Decca themselves had attempted to spruce up Holly's demos for his final songs ('Peggy Sue Got Married', 'Learning The Game', 'That Makes It Tough'), they'd botched the job. Predictably Petty rose magnificently to the dangled bait of our two lead letters. His reply was in the following week's issue: he'd sent it by telegram as air mail would not have been quick enough."

"It is most surprising to think how difficult it is for some people to accept the truth of any situation. Make something complicated…tell small stories…then it is easy to sell…but it is very difficult indeed to think that some of your readers still doubt the authentic voice of Buddy Holly. True, there have been many who have tried to sound like Buddy, but sound alone is not enough, regardless of what your readers might think. The term 'feel' must be brought forward—that is exactly what could not be copied—since Buddy Holly did have his own feel and true record friends can spot the copies and the 'real thing'. Your readers have not been fully informed concerning the background of 'all those tapes' you are now hearing about. The tapes have not just been found as some trade papers would have you believe—they have been around all the time. We knew about them, so did the record companies. Legal difficulties, not necessarily the problems of yours truly but of all concerned, prevent the public from knowing the full story behind the tapes. You can rest assured that a record company with the reputation of Decca would not be part of 'a hoax' at any cost. They could not care less for the money involved at this point. As stated before, Decca has known of these tapes for some time. The press has known of them. It makes this reader very angry to be blamed for vague stories about the tapes. It is my obligation and trust to dress up to the best of my ability all tapes concerning Buddy Holly. In fact, we do not hold but a very few useable tapes and these will not be released until they are up to the standards we know were possible with the ability of Buddy Holly. We did not arrange any of the release dates of 'the flops' or any other releases there. The very early tapes did not go through us but were sent directly from Decca here to your country. You and your readers should rest assured that much has been written among all parties concerned with these tapes and all can be authenticated. However, this seems pointless at this stage. The simple truth, all the tapes that have been released are Buddy Holly. Few remain, to be released only when completed. As a matter of fact, Decca Records here and in England have had the recording of 'Wishing' by Buddy Holly since the first of the year. It is a great record in my opinion and you will be able to hear it when the greater powers that be decide to release it. It was my rare pleasure to be the record-ing engineer, the musician, a co-writer of many songs, the manager and a friend associated with Buddy Holly. Best, Norman Petty"

Norman Jopling (412): "A week later a letter arrived from Buddy's parents. Petty had chided us for printing the two letters, but Mr and Mrs Holley were more realistic: 'Naturally we do not consider you or your staff of reporters responsible for the opinions expressed by your readers…' The Holleys went on to write a long, gentle letter about their son and his music and the tapes. They concluded with a message to Record Mirror's readers: 'Please tell them that when they are listening to Buddy's songs they may rest assured that they really are hearing Buddy and not another. We could not and would not betray the trust and love they have shown to his memory and to us also.'"

For all their concerns, Buddy Holly's legacy has not been conserved as well as it should have been because of disgreements between the record company, Buddy's family, Maria Elena and the Pettys. It proved difficult to get all parties on board at the same time and it was very frustrating for everyone involved, not to mention the fans.

In 1957, the Picks had overdubbed backing vocals on nine tracks on the LP, *The Chirping Crickets*. In 1984, they took another 21 Buddy Holly tracks and added backing vocals without much regard to the differences in studio conditions. According to the publicity, the tracks "offer a unique chance to hear what might have been had not fate tragically intervened", but fate has nothing to do with it. Holly didn't want the Picks on "Reminiscing" or "Everyday" so why add their voices now? Their audacity defied logic and just who had allowed them to work with the master tapes in this way?

The results are dire as the backing vocals are now in the foreground and it is no wonder that MCA turned the results down. At best, they don't spoil the originals ("That Makes It Tough", "Because I Love You") but mostly, it's pathetic. Bill Pickering adds a rebel yell to "Rock-A-Bye Rock". They add lyrics to "Words Of Love", while "Well..All Right" is a sub-Jordanaires morass. The Picks have leased these tracks to a several small labels, who often issue them without crediting the Picks. My own copy, *Buddy Holly And The Picks—The Original*

Voices Of The Crickets, was released in the UK by Magnum Force in 1993, but I wouldn't recommend any of their work. And nor, apparently does anyone else as you can pick up collections on Amazon for a penny. When Bill Pickering died in 1985, "True Love Ways" was played at his funeral: I shudder to think which version.

But it gets worse. The 3CD set, *Buddy Holly—The Ultimate Collection*, was released by Union Square in 2008 with 45 tracks that were all attributed to "Buddy Holly and the Crickets" or "Buddy Holly and the Picks". The sleeve notes by Neil Kellas are both deceitful and disgraceful. For "Quando, Quando, Quando", he writes, "Another example of Buddy Holly's restlessly eclectic approach is witnessed with his choice to record this standard more usually associated with easy listening crooners than tough outfits like the Crickets. Co-written by Pat Boone, this Latin-influenced number revealed a more unusual side to Holly's work." Quite a remarkable side, in fact, as the song was written three years after Buddy died, and although Pat Boone made the US charts with it, he did not write it. Buddy, apparently, pays homage to Elvis Presley with "Good Luck Charm" and to himself with "Forever 22". The song refers to the Beatles and Neil Kellas writes, "Holly liked to indulge his catholic taste from time to time and demonstrated his versatility on songs like this." Even more imaginative is Buddy Holly's version of "You've Lost That Lovin' Feelin'". Just how thick does this label think we are?

All manner of Buddy Holly compilations have made the charts and he has had several Top 10 albums including appearances on rock'n'roll compilations. Buddy topped the UK charts with the TV-advertised *20 Golden Greats* in 1978, but the album did not have a picture of Buddy Holly on the cover. Instead, there was a brick wall with graffiti, which read, "Buddy Holly lives". The record company had done some test marketing and discovered that the kids didn't like the way that that Buddy Holly looked. A few months later, Elvis Costello, so there you go.

The six album box set, *The Complete Buddy Holly* (1979), was a very good anthology with full liner notes and an impressive book of cuttings and commentary from John Beecher and Mal-

colm Jones. Norman Petty worked on some stereo versions for the album and the *Apartment Tapes* without overdubs were heard for the first time.

After this, it looked as if things were working well on the Holly front. An MCA executive wanted to release Holly's early demos for Cedarwood. When Norman Petty heard the album, *For The First Time Anywhere* (1983), he was appalled by the poor quality of "Bo Diddley" and searched his own archives for the master. In so doing, he found material he had overlooked. He became ill and died and the executive borrowed the tapes from Vi Petty to make digital transfers. On return, the tapes looked different but the executive maintained that they had been treated to avoid oxide loss. The originals were found at his home and he was dismissed. This created even more tension between the warring factions over Buddy Holly's catalogue.

In 1995, there was an unexpected fourth version of "Peggy Sue Got Married" where the Hollies, including Allan Clarke and Graham Nash, added their accompaniment. This works surprisingly well, although the guitar break is more 1970s than 1950s.

Bobby Elliott (413): "Graham Nash called us and told us that Decca Records in Nashville were putting together a tribute album to Buddy and we ended up being the only non-American act on there. Graham was given a tape of Buddy singing 'Peggy Sue Got Married' with just an acoustic guitar. He said, 'If we isolate Buddy's voice, we could do "Peggy Sue Got Married" with Buddy Holly.' Ray Stiles is a whiz-kid and he managed to separate them and we went into Abbey Road and recorded it."

Graham Nash (414): "The most exciting thing that we did as the Hollies was to sing with Buddy Holly. There was a very popular movie called *Peggy Sue Got Married* and one of the producers, Paul Gurian, had been given a demo of 'Peggy Sue Got Married' by Buddy's family, which was recorded on a tape recorder in his apartment in New York. It was fabulous and it was just Buddy on an acoustic guitar and he asked me what I wanted to do with it. I said, 'In a perfect world, I would get Phil Collins on drums, Paul on bass, George on guitar, and we would overdub on the track.' I could never work it out because everyone's schedule was much too tight. Then I thought, 'Well, the Hollies could do this, we were named after Buddy, after all, so I called Tony and Allan and Bobby and they thought it was a great idea.' I sent the track over and they put it into some Pro-Tools software and isolated his voice from his guitar and slowed it down and rearranged it slightly and then we overdubbed drums, bass and harmonies. And that was a thrill, to sing with Buddy Holly."

In the CD age, there has been the chart-topping compilation, *Words Of Love* (1993), but collectors have been crying, waiting and hoping for some creative compilations. Holly is the only major rock'n'roller not to benefit from an officially released CD box set, full of outtakes and curios. Ideally, there should be a *Greatest Hits* package for the Asda/ Tesco shoppers, a four CD set for the collectors, and an ultimate collectors set with absolutely everything they can find and licence on it, all being taken from the master tapes. This hasn't happened because of the disagreements between the current owners, Universal, and Maria Elena.

Maria Elena Holly (415): "I have been in litigation with MCA and Universal for years but I will never give up. We know from that telephone conversation with Paul Cohen that Buddy's original contract was suspect, and his one with Brunswick was as well. Norman Petty—I call him 'The Evil Man'—had signed the contracts and he had no reason to sign for Buddy Holly. Buddy couldn't remember signing anything. Even in litigation, they wouldn't let me see the contract and then they said that someone had got into the office and ripped the signature out, a fan, and I said, 'In your office? You know, that that isn't possible.'"

There have been bootleg sets like the 4CD set, *What You Been A-Missin'* (1995) and more recently, the 10CD, *The Complete Buddy Holly*. Time may make the decision for them as, with supreme irony, everything Buddy Holly has recorded will be out of copyright by the end of 2009 unless the law is changed beforehand.

At the time of writing (August 2008), all recordings prior to 1958 are in the public domain, but, encouraged by French rock star Johnny Hallyday, the French president Nicolas Sarkozy has pledged to push legislation through the European Parliament to extend the copyright period. There may be opposition to this, but if the legislation is carried, it has to be ratified by the member countries.

This is a difficult issue with good arguments on both sides, but as far as Buddy Holly is concerned, the bickering between the differing parties has shown that they do not have the fan's interests at heart, and also much could be done to introduce Holly to new audiences. I hope that the Holly catalogue does become free from copyright as I am sure some reissue labels will devise packages with flair and real merit.

Having written these rather critical paragraphs about the current ownership of Buddy Holly's music, some progress has been made with the release of two CD packages to mark the 50th anniversary of Buddy Holly's death. The 3CD set, *Memorial Collection*, is currently one of the UK's top selling albums and the 2CD, *Down The Line—Rarities* is also doing well. The sound is as good as it gets and many of the tracks are without the accompaniment added after his death.

10

GRAVE ON

"There's a man on my radio,
He died young so he can't grow old."
("Buddy's Waiting On The Flatland Road",
Terry Clarke, Bucks Music, 1990)

Although tribute records have been made on all manner of subjects and events, the general public has usually been suspicious. What are the motives of the performers? Is a particular record to pay tribute to a deceased star, or is it to use the dead star as a platform for their own careers (not, of course, that anyone would ever admit to that)?

Tribute songs are nothing new—there were some for the sinking of the Titanic and others for the deaths of Rudolph Valentino and Hank Williams—but the speed at which the tributes to the rock'n'roll stars were issued was remarkable, the first on the market being Hershel Almond's "The Great Tragedy" and Bernie Barnes' "Gold Records In The Snow". The rockabilly artist, Ray Campi, was produced by Norman Petty for "The Man I Met" (Campi's personal recollection of the Bopper...) and "Ballad Of Donna And Peggy Sue" (a tribute to Valens and Holly). Donna Ludwig, however, was capable of recording her own tribute to Ritchie, "Lost Without You"/ "Now That You're Gone", but she subsequently claimed that she had been talked into it by her father.

The BBC nursed some doubts about the Ruby Wright single, "Three Stars", when it was released by Parlophone. Should the record be banned? On

4 June 1959, the Assistant Head of Gramophone Programmes sought clarification from the Assistant Director, Sound Broadcasting: "This is a song about three stars, all of whom were killed in a recent plane crash in America. It has been passed in sheet music form by the Dance Music Policy Committee with the Head of Religious Broadcasting's approval, but both sheet music and record may not be played without reference to the Assistant Head, Light Entertainment (Sound) and the Assistant Head, Gramophone Programmes." In other words, it's not quite banned, but almost there.

The note continued, "In general, the record has met with a bad press and the general opinion of disc jockeys is that it is a nauseating piece of material. Our only query is this, possibly next week we may be confronted with this song appearing in the Top Twenty and once again, do we ignore this or must we keep faith in the *Pick Of The Pops* programme and play it? There is little doubt that it will hardly appear at all in any other record programmes."

The response came the following day: "I entirely share your dislike for this record and agree its use should be severely restricted. On the other hand, if it gets into the Top Twenty, I think we should play fair and include it in *Pick Of The Pops*."

From ghastly to ghostly now as the British record producer Joe Meek was besotted by the occult and by Buddy Holly, so he held a séance to obtain Buddy's approval for "Tribute To Buddy Holly", written by his foremost writer, Geoff Goddard, in 1961. If Holly had been available, he might have improved on it as "The snow was snowing" is a brain-dead opening line. Joe Meek's echo is used for ethereal effects. The producer, Joe Meek, shot himself on the anniversary of Holly's death in 1967 and the events could be related.

John Repsch (416): "Whilst they were making 'Tribute to Buddy Holly', Joe Meek and Geoff Goddard held a séance hoping to contact Buddy's ghost. Supposedly, he came through and forecast a Number 1 for John Leyton's 'Johnny Remember Me' and when asked about Mike Berry's chances said, 'See you in the charts'."

Geoff Goddard (417): "I didn't write the tribute with the idea of commercial gain. It was just something I felt like doing. It came out naturally and Joe Meek liked it very much. He played it to Mike Berry and one thing led to another. Joe Meek was very interested in the occult and he held a few seancés to try and contact Buddy Holly. They were just card and tumbler affairs, which is a bit way off mid-stream spiritualism."

Mike Berry (418): "Joe Meek said he had been in touch with Buddy Holly and that it was okay to release the tribute. I didn't believe a word of it, but I liked the idea of a tribute to Buddy Holly. The song could have had a better lyric. When I re-recorded it, I changed it from 'The snow was snowing' to 'The snow was falling', which it does. I was wary of being accused of cashing in on Buddy Holly, but Joe got the Buddy Holly Appreciation Society to give the record its seal of approval."

It has often been said, even by Mike Berry, that "Tribute To Buddy Holly" was banned by the BBC: not true, I have seen the paperwork and can confirm that "Tribute To Buddy Holly" was passed for broadcasting. It may not have been played very often but that would be because individual producers did not care for it.

"Buddy's Song" by Bobby Vee (1963) is an upbeat tribute to Holly's music, cheerfully weaving ten of his titles into the lyric and taking its melody from "Peggy Sue Got Married". "Buddy's Song", which has also been covered by Fleetwood Mac, was put together by Buddy's mother, Ella, with Waylon Jennings.

Waylon Jennings himself has paid tribute to Buddy with "The Stage" (1963), "Old Friend" (1976) and "A Long Time Ago" (1978), not to mention touring and recording with the Crickets and cutting several of Buddy's songs including "It's So Easy" and "It Doesn't Matter Anymore". "Old Friend" describes how the media misrepresented Holly, and is better than the slushy "The Stage" with "The angels stand in silence as Buddy sings." So much for outlaw country.

Waylon Jennings has at different times recorded most of Buddy Holly's set from the *Winter Dance Party*. He recorded "Well…All Right", "It's So Easy", "Maybe Baby" and "Peggy Sue" in a 1978 medley with the Crickets. He has also cut "Rave On", "Brown-Eyed Handsome Man", "It Doesn't Matter Anymore" and a stunning, slow version of "Learning The Game" with Mark Knopfler. Waylon has said, "More than anything, Buddy taught me about attitude and never to compromise on my music."

Snuff Garrett (419): When I was about 40 or so, my secretary said, 'There's Waylon Jennings on the phone' and he said, 'What are you doing?'. I said, 'I'm talking to you in my office. I'm at the corner of Sunset and Vine, tenth floor on that big building on the corner.' He said, 'I'm coming by to pick you up. Can I do that?' I said, 'I'm walking down the stairs now.' He came up in a great big tour bus, but it was just him and the driver. He handed me a Lone Star beer and we cried and laughed about all our times with Buddy and revisited our young lives for a couple of hours, and then he dropped me back at the office. We'd had a wonderful afternoon."

Waylon's ultimate tribute was in naming his son, Buddy, who was born on 21 March 1960. In 1985, Lee Jackson wrote and recorded his tribute, "I Named My Little Girl Holly" and it has been covered by both Mike Berry and Buddy Knox. Lee Jackson has also released his instrumental track with a narration from Peggy Sue.

Buddy Knox (420): "Lee Jackson is a songwriter from Lubbock and he asked me if I'd like to do 'I Named My Little Girl Holly" I changed the melody to fit my style and I cut it in Lubbock in a studio right next to the Buddy Holly statue. The Maines Brothers were on it and we were all tickled pink. Somebody then did it in Europe and spoiled our release schedule but the song was a lovely tribute to him." (That somebody was Mike Berry.)

Don McLean's "American Pie" (1971) begs the question; why was an American folkie lamenting the death of rock'n'roll? Don McLean became the spokesman for a generation by describing 3rd February 1959 as the day the music died. In order to retain its mystery, McLean has never discussed the song at length. This is fortunate for the many university students who have written theses on the subject.

Mark Kelly (421):"Buddy Holly has never been alive in my memory as his death came when I was too young to have heard him. As the first major rock'n'roll star to die, I guess all the questions of ethics and taste were first explored, and so firmly settled in favour of endless, shameless exploitation and tackiness in the case of Elvis Presley. Buddy was the first artist to have more hits posthumously than when he was alive. I remember my brother coming home with an album of previously unreleased material; I wondered whether Buddy would have wanted it to be released? Some sounded as though they were recorded in the bathroom, possibly while he was having a bath. Then there were the tribute records, some perhaps sincere, others not. And they kept on coming.... 'I Feel Like Buddy Holly' did at least let you know what it felt like to be in a sickening crash! But the worst was 'American Pie' in which Don McLean whined on and on about the day the music died. This was taken as a reference to Buddy Holly's plane crash, although Don McLean has always refused to explain the lyrics—probably for the simple reason that they are nonsense. Next on the McLean hit list was Vincent Van Gogh, who would have cut off his other ear rather than endure the pseudo-poetic balladry of 'Vincent'. It is a supreme irony that Buddy Holly's nosedive to death may have been partly responsible for launching such garbage into the charts."

There is worse. How about the Righteous Brothers' tribute, "Rock And Roll Heaven", admittedly a US Number 3 from 1974, so somebody liked it: "If you believe in forever, Then life is just a one night stand, If there's a rock and roll heaven, You know, they've got a hell of a band."

Was it Buddy hell though as this outlandish lyric mentions Bobby Darin, Jimi Hendrix, Janis Joplin, JimMorrison, Otis Redding and even Jim Croce, but not Buddy Holly.

Songwriting Tip No. 59—Never put "rock and roll" in the title of your song; it's bound to be dreadful. Consider the evidence: "Rock And Roll Heaven" (Righteous Brothers), "Rock'n'Roll" (Status Quo), "Rock'n'Roll Lady" (Showaddywaddy), "Rock'n'Roll Damnation" (and several other titles from AC/DC), "Rock'n'Roll Mercanaries" (admittedly, one man's Meat Loaf is another man's poison), "Rock'n'Roll Gypsy" (Saxon), "Rock'n'Roll High School" (Ramones), "Rock'n'Roll Is King" (ELO), "I've Got A Rock'n'Roll Heart" (Eric Clapton), "Rock And Roll Never Forgets" (Bob Seger). "Rock And Roll Love Letter" (Bay City Rollers), "Rock And Roll Waltz" (Kay Starr) and "Rock And Roll Could Never Hip Hop Like This" (Handsome Boy Modelling School). There are exceptions—"Rock And Roll Is Here To Stay" (Danny and the Juniors), "Rock And Roll Girls" (John Fogerty) and "Rock And Roll Doctor" (Little Feat)—but not many. And who would want to write "Rock And Roll (Part 3)"? On the other hand, you can put "rock" or "roll" acceptably into a song—"Rock Around The Clock" and "Roll Over Beethoven" are okay, and heck, I even like "Rock On" by David Essex.

Sonny Curtis wrote "The Real Buddy Holly Story" after seeing the film, *The Buddy Holly Story*, in 1979. The following year, a Lubbock boy, Mac Davis, mentioned Holly in both "Hooked On Music" and "Texas In My Rear-View Mirror

Larry Holley has recorded tributes to his brother from time to time: on "Buddy Holly And The Crickets", a track on *Holly's House*, a family album issued in 1980, he sings, "Buddy Holly and the Crickets, You know I bought those tickets, Just to hear that rockabilly beat."

Bit mean really: why didn't his brother get freebies? Maybe for the same reason that Tommy and Waylon were expected to purchase their own tickets on the plane. The album featured another brother, Travis, and Larry's children, Sherry and Randy. Sherry released her own album, *Looking Through Buddy's Eyes* in 1992. They are intriguing curios, but don't expect Buddy's talent. Larry also produced Tinker Carlin's song about Texas dance halls, "Lookin' For The Hi-D-Ho".

The Picks' tribute, "Buddy Holly Not Fade Away" (1982) is as dire as the backing vocals they added to his tracks after his death. Sample lyric: "And the soul that he is and the soul that he was, Never laid down 'neath the sod, Mama raised him in the church, And Buddy Holly is at home with God".

Why does Alvin Stardust feel like Buddy Holly on "I Feel Like Buddy Holly" (1984)? Does he feel like he's gone down in a 'plane crash or does he feel upbeat and happy like so many of Holly's hits? Neither actually—Alvin feels like Buddy Holly "Cause it's raining in my heart." All a bit tenuous—and if we're being pedantic, Paul McCartney doesn't sing, "I wish it was yesterday". Songwriter **Mike Batt (422)**: "Well, I may misquote the words, but I don't misquote the thought. It's a very personal song and everything on the record is true. It was a rainy Sunday morning, the planes were coming over and I wrote the song."

Alvin Stardust (423): "One of the questions in some market research by my old record company was, 'What do you think about Alvin Stardust doing a ballad?', and it was a 98% response of 'No way. It won't work.' When we recorded 'I Feel Like Buddy Holly', my new label Chrysalis said, 'Oh, we like that. It's a single.' and I knew I mustn't tell them about the research. It might have blown the deal."

It is easier to see what Buddy has to do with Weezer's Top 20 hit, "Buddy Holly" from 1995. The singer is being pestered because he looks like a geek: "Woo-ee-oo, I look just like Buddy Holly,, Oh, oh, and you're Mary Tyler Moore, I don't care what they say about us anyway, I don't care about that."

The mysterious rhinestone cowboy, David Allan Coe, did his own "Three Stars" in "A Country Boy (Who Rolled The Rock Away" (1986), only his three were Hank Williams, Buddy Holly and Elvis Presley. Coe missed the opportunity to add a fourth verse about Jesus being a coun-

try boy who rolled the rock away. Gene Vincent refers to Buddy in his 1968 history lesson, "Story Of The Rockers", but then he could hardly leave him out, and the Rubettes recorded "My Buddy Holly Days".

In 1990, Terry Clarke, a contemporary country performer from Reading, England, was recording in the Fire Station Studio in San Marcos, Texas. **Terry Clarke (424)**: "We'd recorded all the songs we had planned to do but there was still some tape left on the reel. I looked west out of the window at a brilliant Texas morning and thought of Buddy Holly." Later in the same year, Clarke wrote "Lubbock Calling", a tribute to Holly after seeing Joe Ely playing live. It includes a snatch of "Oh Boy!" and as the lyrics state, "The ghosts have got it right, Buddy Holly's singing to Joe Ely tonight."

"Three Stars" and, indeed, none of the other tribute songs pay attention to the pilot, but he is the subject of Andy Wilkinson's "Leave It In The Hands Of Fate" (1992), which scores a double whammy as a curio as Sonny Curtis is playing guitar.

In 1996, Steve Gibbons wrote and performed the Tex-Mex tribute, "Hey Buddy" on his album, *Stained Glass*. The song says, "There's something about the way you play that makes you sound divine." **Steve Gibbons (425)**: "I do like tributes. I love 'Tribute To Buddy Holly'. It has a great atmosphere and Mike Berry's vocal is sublime—he's someone who never gets enough credit. I'd wanted to write a tribute to Sun studios for some years and I had a beginning but not a middle or an end. I realised that I was trying to put too much in and wrote it as a tribute to Elvis which is on the *From Birmingham To Memphis* LP. That seemed to work okay, so I decided that Buddy Holly should have a whole song to himself. I wrote 'Hey Buddy' but not as one of the morbid death songs. I wanted to say what he had given to the youth of the world."

Rather than tributes, I prefer it when Buddy Holly is mentioned *en passant* during some song as it shows how he has been accepted into the public culture or, possibly, how easy it is to rhyme something with "Holly". He is one of Ian Dury's reasons to be cheerful and he is included in Terry Jacks' version of "Rock'n'Roll (I Gave You The

Best Years Of My Life)", replacing a reference to Chuck Berry in the original. (Yet another "rock and roll" song—you get my drift?) Billy Joel includes him in his history of the 20th Century, "We Didn't Start The Fire", and he is also mentioned in Tom Paxton's satirical "Jesus Christ, SRO", Phil Everly's "New Old Song" and on the soundtrack of the *Rocky Horror Picture Show*.

Some Buddyholics collect tributes and would, I know, like a complete list of all the Holly-related ones. Well, get a life: most of the tributes have little merit and add nothing to our understanding of Buddy Holly. It is also impossible to create a complete, or near complete, collection. Working for local radio, I have had several tributes passed to me and I would guess that this is duplicated through Britain and America. One of the best I've been sent is "On The Toss Of A Coin" by David Slater, who wrote and recorded his demo after attending a songwriting course in Crete, which included Tommy Allsup as a tutor.

It's a brave man who does a tribute with humour so how about Stanley Accrington's "Tribute To Buddy" (1991)? This stalwart of British folk clubs sang: "He taught me how to be modest, With a talent oh so big, But most of all he taught me, Don't catch a plane home after a gig."

11

LISTEN TO ME

"Buddy Holly is in everybody.
That's not bad for a guy from Lubbock, right?"
(Keith Richards)

Soundalikes

1959 was the year that Xerox introduced the first commercial copier. How apt. **Tommy Steele (426)**: "Buddy Holly had the sort of voice that every coffee-bar singer tried to imitate."

There are lots of artists who have been influenced by Buddy Holly. Although a commendable actor with devastatingly good looks, Adam Faith was a lightweight pop singer who has said of his own CD reissues, "Who buys this crap?" His first hit, "What Do You Want" (1959), topped the UK charts and lent heavily on "It Doesn't Matter Anymore" in terms of Faith's performance and John Barry's pizzicato strings. When Faith received a silver disc, he thought of splitting it in three—one part for himself, one for songwriter Johnny Worth and one for John Barry. It should have been four as Buddy deserved a portion. John Barry arranged another Top 10 hit, "Be Mine", for Lance Fortune in 1960, which, rather like the diminishing Russian dolls, sounds like a tribute to Adam Faith.

Johnny Worth (427): "I can remember standing on the Hungerford Bridge and working out an arrangement for 'What Do You Want', and this was before Buddy Holly. I loved the way Tchaikovsky had used pizzicato strings and I thought, 'That's what I'll use if I ever make a record. I'll have a classical sound and it won't be rock'n'roll.' Johnny Kidd tried it as a rock'n'roll number but I wasn't going to have it done that way. By the time Adam Faith was going to record it, 'It Doesn't Matter Anymore' had been No 1 and I said to Adam, 'Let's do a Holly on it because there's nothing more successful at the moment, especially with his distinctive pronunciation of "baby". We'll stick that in.' I noticed that Adam's top teeth rested on his bottom lip which made 'what' and 'want' come out as 'vot' and 'vont', so the end result was "Vot do you vont if you don't vont money, Vish you vonted my love, bay-beh." There was a record store in the East End who refused to stock the record on the grounds that it was anti-Semitic, which of course it wasn't."

Jim Newcombe (428), who wrote songs with Geoff Taggart: "We wrote a few songs in the Holly style and gave one to Adam Faith, it was called 'I Know You Do'. Adam talked to us in

Manchester and told us to give it to the leader of his band, the Roulettes, who was the bass player John Rogers. 'If he likes it, I'll like it,' he said. A couple of weeks later, the bandleader was killed in a crash, and about two years later the tape came back: maybe someone had found it in his effects."

There is some justification in citing Bobby Vee as a Holly copycat. **Snuff Garrett (429)**: "I had my first hit record at Liberty with Johnny Burnette and then I signed Bobby Vee. Somebody sent me a record from a little label in Minnesota and I thought he really sounded like Buddy Holly. I thought I could do something with him and pick up where Buddy left off. Bud wanted to record with strings and I was continuing with that." For all that, Bobby Vee does not often sound like Holly, an exception being "Someday (When I'm Gone From You)", which he recorded with the Crickets in 1962.

Tommy Roe brazenly copied Holly's hiccuping vocal and Jerry Allison's torrid drumming on "Sheila", who was a close cousin to "Peggy Sue" and, ironically, considering Buddy's problems in Nashville, it was cut there. At the time, the single did better than "Peggy Sue", becoming a transatlantic Number l in 1962. **Tommy Roe (430)**: "I wrote 'Sheila' when I was 14 and it was a local hit on Judd Records, which was a label out of Memphis that Sam Phillips' brother started. When I got out of high school, I met Felton Jarvis who wanted to re-record 'Sheila' and we did it in Nashville. It was Felton's idea to have that drumming as he thought it a good gimmick to get airplay. Buddy Harman did the drumming, Bob Moore was on bass and Jerry Reed and Wayne Moss played guitars. That's a very good band. I play acoustic guitar on most of my things but you can't hear me on that: Felton took me out of the picture as he had such great players. When I came here to tour, the headlines were 'The Ghost Of Holly Returns'."

Several little-known Texas artists were collected for the CD, *Buddy Holly Days*, which claimed to contain "30 Rare Buddy Holly Soundalikes". The tracks by the likes of Sonny Curtis, Ronnie Smith, Earl Sinks and Ray Ruff have their appeal but not many sound like Buddy and many of them are feeble. Well worthy of a mention is Leen Teens' "So Shy" from 1959. I'm not sure what they are really singing but it sounds like "She's a cute little

bugger, she is." In the UK, Mike Berry and the Outlaws and Buddy Britten and the Regents have got far closer to Holly's sound. Britten's "Long Gone Baby" is a Terry Noland song, produced by Norman Petty.

Mike Berry (431) started by performing Holly's songs: "I was weaned on Buddy Holly. I was mad on his songs and I found that I could sing like him, still can. In the early days, we didn't know enough chords to do the songs properly so we just sang the tune across the wrong chord. The audiences didn't seem to mind."

Michael Bourne was renamed Mike Berry by producer Joe Meek as a nod to Buddy Holly. After "Tribute To Buddy Holly" (1961), he had a Top 10 hit with "Don't You Think It's Time" (1963), written by Meek with **Geoff Goddard (432)**. "Joe Meek would say to me, 'Play "Maybe Baby" and that'll get us in the mood to come up with something.' That's why 'Don't You Think It's Time' has such a Holly feel."

Like Mike Berry, Brian Poole and the Tremeloes began by playing Buddy Holly's repertoire, and Brian made a spectacle of himself by having the same thick-framed glasses. They found their own style by the time they were signed to Decca in 1962, and when Norman Petty, came to London, he played piano and co-produced three of their singles, "Someone, Someone", "The Three Bells" and "After Awhile". When Petty returned to Clovis, he sent an individual thank you letter to each member of the band.

Brian Poole (433): "We went into Decca to record 'Someone, Someone' and our manager brought Norman Petty over to play on the session. Norman had written the song and we didn't know he was coming. We never got to meet Buddy Holly but Norman Petty was the next best thing, and that was one of our biggest-selling singles."

Despite its originality, "I Fought The Law", which was written by Sonny Curtis for the Crickets, still has "Buddy Holly" stamped all over it. In 1966, a band from El Paso, the Bobby Fuller Four, had a US Top 10 hit with the song. I was going to write "a garage band from El Paso", but Fuller's parents allowed him and his brother, Randy, to convert the living room into a recording studio. They recorded there and with Norman Petty in Clovis, but their hit records were made with Ritchie Valens' producer, Bob Keane, in Los Angeles.

Bob Keane (434): "I knew that the Buddy Holly influence in Bobby Fuller's songs would make him a star someday, but I was a stickler for getting the right sound. I had sent him back to El Paso to smooth out his act. I could tell that there was something there and he was a good writer. He came back with a great sound. In my opinion, the Bobby Fuller Four had the makings of the next Beatles. Bobby had his own sound but he wasn't able to develop it before he was killed."

It may be that Bobby Fuller was dating the girlfriend of someone connected with the Mob, nobody really knows, but while he was enjoying his second hit, a prophetic revival of "Love's Made A Fool Of You", he was taken into the desert outside Los Angeles where he was beaten up and petrol poured down his throat. The coroner deemed it suicide, which is scarcely credible. Bobby Fuller died, aged 22 on 18 July 1965, having lived 119 days more than Buddy Holly.

Sonny Curtis (435): "I thought Bobby Fuller's version of 'I Fought The Law' was real good. He embellished our arrangement and had a hit with it, but I really like the Clash's version. That's alive and kicking. It's great. The song isn't about me having trouble with the law, that's something we didn't do in those days. It's just a song."

Oddly enough, Bobby Fuller's version of "I Fought The Law" is more subversive than the Clash's. Bobby double-tracked his vocals and he first sang, "I missed my baby and good fuck" and then sang the correct lyric, "I missed my baby and good fun", over the top. Play the record and it's apparent.

Paul Raven became Gary Glitter; Shane Fenton mutated into Alvin Stardust, so what might Jess Conrad have done? Jess updated Holly's sound on "Save It For A Rainy Day" (1977), a cheerful record produced by Dave Dee. He couldn't capture Buddy Holly's nuances but it's easy to imagine Buddy Holly performing the song. With a new name and a new image, Jess Conrad might have had a hit.

In 1979, Keith Sykes, a folk/ country performer associated with John Prine and Jerry Jeff Walker, cut a blistering piece of rock'n'roll, "Makin' It Before They Got Married", sounding as close to

Buddy Holly as he could. The theme would have been too controversial for the 50s but it sounds like Holly for the 70s. Think of Buddy Holly in Africa, and you have "Malamba D'Amour", which was recorded by Orchestre Super Mazembe in 1982.

Joe Ely has recorded "Midnight Shift" and "Rock Me My Baby" (a nice Tex-Mex touch with the accordion) and he switched from country music to neo-rockabilly when he toured with the Clash, and the *Musta Notta Gotta Lotta* album is from that period, 1981 to be precise. The hard-driving title song is very much like a latter-day Holly. Other Holly-styled tracks are "Cool Rockin' Loretta" and "Wishin' For You".

Despite his love for recording cover versions, Elvis Costello has yet to record any Buddy Holly compositions. Nevertheless, Holly's influence is all over his work (and face!) and it's easy to imagine Holly doing a killer version of "Oliver's Army". Buddy's influence was particularly strong when two Hollyphiles—McCartney and Costello—combined their talents for "Veronica" (1989). Similarly, one of Richard Thompson's wittiest songs, "Valerie", owes a lot to Holly.

Marshall Crenshaw played Buddy Holly in the Ritchie Valens biopic, *La Bamba*, and a glance at his stance on the back cover of his 1989 CD, *Good Evening*, makes you think of Buddy Holly. "Whatever Way The Wind Blows" with James Burton on lead guitar owes a lot of Holly and so do "Yvonne" and "I'm Sorry (But So Is Brenda Lee)".

The opening cut on the first solo album from the former leader of the Wagoneers, Monte Warden, "Don't Know A Thing" (1993), is a dead ringer for Buddy Holly. The whole of *Monte Warden* could have been written and recorded by Buddy Holly, and "Just To Hear Your Voice" would have been the perfect follow-up to "True Love Ways". To quote one title, "It's Amazing", but the second album, *Here I Am*, sounds more like Bobby Vee.

Doug and Ricky Lee Phelps of the Kentucky Headhunters parody the Crickets on "Four Leaf Clover" (1993), complete with Buddy Holly hiccups and Albert Lee's lead guitar. The title track of the album, *Let Go*, also recalls Buddy Holly. Dwight Yoakam is too stone country to copy

Buddy exactly, but the song and performance on "Gone (That'll Be Me)" (1995) has Holly written through it, right down to Jim Christie's "Peggy Sue"-slanted drumming.

Gerry Devine and the Hi-Beams are a New York quartet, whose debut album, *Fire Lane* (1994), had strong overtones of the Searchers, Gram Parsons and Buddy Holly. The songs may be derivative but the album is very entertaining. The cheerful opening song, "Anybody Else" would suit Holly; and if Buddy had moved into country-rock (or even invented it!), "Excuses, Excuses" would have been fine.

Stephen Bruton spent many years in Kris Kristofferson's band and developed into a New Country artist. The cheerful song, "The Face Of Love" (1993) featured solid Holly-styled playing and vocals. When I told him that it sounded like a 1990s Buddy Holly recording, he said that I couldn't have given a bigger compliment. **Stephen Bruton (436)**: "Rockabilly was the music that inspired me to play guitar, especially a song by Mac Curtis called 'Grandaddy's Rockin'. I do 'The Face Of Love' like a straight Texas shuffle, and I think that Buddy Holly would have liked the song. His songwriting was almost country and yet at the same time, it is the roots of rock'n'roll. His songs are fantastic and he is one of the major sources for popular music."

Influencing The 60s

The tame teen idols of the early 60s (Frankie Avalon, Jimmy Clanton, Fabian and to some extent, Ricky Nelson, Bobby Vee and even Elvis himself) had diluted the potent, heady brew of rock'n'roll. It was the British Invasion which reclaimed it, but added its own components.

First though Cliff Richard and the Shadows played the Lubbock Coliseum in February 1960. They were part of *The Biggest Show Of 1960* with Frankie Avalon, Bobby Rydell and Clyde McPhatter.

Bruce Welch (437) of the Shadows: "It was a big stadium that we were playing in Lubbock. We went out in maroon suits and blue ties and

Hank had the Fender Strat and the black specs. Hank is tall and slim and he looked so much like Buddy that the audience went quiet. I think his brother, Larry, and his dad were in the audience that night."

The Liverpool-dominated beat boom of the early 1960s was, and still is, the most exciting thing that ever happened to British popular music. Its reverberations are heard today as each new successful British band is hailed as the latest Beatles and each new songwriter as the new Lennon or McCartney. But, in the early stages at least, the Liverpool music was decidedly second-hand. Every group, including the Beatles, covered American rock'n'roll, R&B and sometimes country songs. Much of this repertoire was recorded by the Liverpool bands, which means we can identify the performers who influenced them the most.

Prior to 1967, there are over 350 cover versions recorded by the Liverpool bands and the most covered artists are Chuck Berry (20 cover versions on 14 songs), Little Richard (18 cover versions on 12 songs) and the Drifters (13 cover versions on 11 songs). The rating for Buddy Holly is lower than I expected—only 9 covers on 8 songs—but there are good reasons for this.

Five of those eight Buddy Holly covers have Beatle associations: "That'll Be The Day" (The Quarry Men at Percy Phillips' studio, 1958), "Reminiscing" (*Live At The Star-Club, Hamburg, 1962*), "Crying Waiting Hoping" (*The Beatles Live At The BBC*), "Words Of Love" (*Beatles For Sale*) and a busked "Mailman Bring Me No More Blues" during the *Let It Be* sessions. Around the same time as the Quarry Men, the Firecrests (which featured Lance Fortune and Dave Williams of the Jaywalkers) from Birkenhead High School made a private recording of "That'll Be The Day".

The Cavern DJ, **Bob Wooler (438)**, talking to me in 2000, said: "Brian Matthew played 'That'll Be The Day' on *Sounds Of The Sixties* the other day, and I could see how that song influenced both John Lennon and Paul McCartney. Both of them liked its structure. The original rock'n'rollers like Buddy Holly and Bobby Darin were influenced by the people who preceded them and although their songs were regarded as radical, they still retained a Tin Pan Alley feel."

Philip Norman (439): "John and Paul used to do a pastiche of Buddy Holly, but then everybody used to imitate Buddy, that was the whole point. Buddy's voice almost invited you to imitate him and if you did that, you could see how the songs were put together. The fact that he was writing his own material was crucial to the development of both the Beatles, the Rolling Stones and a lot of other groups."

Gillian Gaar (440): "There was simplicity about Buddy Holly's songs: they weren't difficult to learn so that was how the Beatles knew so many. It was one step beyond skiffle. With Buddy Holly, it was much more about the song than the production and the records are very spare. At first, John and Paul were more about the song too, though it changed later."

To complete the Merseybeat covers, the Searchers performed "Listen To Me" (*Sugar And Spice*), while the Swinging Blue Jeans did "You've Got Love" and Denny Seyton and the Sabres contributed "I'm Gonna Love You Too". There are also covers of three songs recorded by the Crickets after Buddy Holly's death—"Don't Cha (sic) Know" (Searchers), "Don't Ever Change" (Beatles) and "When You Ask About Love" (Billy J. Kramer).

On the Beatles' original demo of "How Do You Do It", John Lennon sounds like Holly at the end of the two middle eights, the only inspired moments on the recording. You can also hear a Holly influence in Gerry and the Pacemakers' "How Do You Do It", the Big Three's "By The Way" and Billy J. Kramer's "I'll Be On My Way". The reference to "The sun is up, the sky is blue" in "Dear Prudence" is surely a nod to "Raining In My Heart".

Dominic Pedler (441): "The intuitive appreciation of musical and lyrical semantics would intensify as Lennon and McCartney's songwriting structures matured and they began incorporating the Holly trademark of an ambitious key change within the middle eight. In this regard, his catalogue represented essential listening for the Beatles in their formative years. Indeed, it is no surprise that the origins of several distinctive Beatles chord progressions and songwriting manoeuvres can be traced to some of their favourite Holly songs—many of which they covered in the early days. Paul McCartney would nominate the middle eight of 'From Me To You' as 'a pivotal moment', noting how the music 'went to a surprising place': 'I've got arms that want to hold you'. Specifically, he was referring to the novelty of a key change whose chord progression he would have heard identically on 'Raining In My Heart' ('Oh, misery…'). While the latter was admittedly a Felice and Boudleaux Bryant composition, Buddy would write an inspired variation on the same theme in the memorably meandering middle eight of 'True Love Ways' ('Throughout the days…'). With its verse also featuring an unusual take on the predictable doo-wop turnarounds of the era, here was one song that would not have been out of place in the portfolio of a sophisticated Brill Building songwriting team."

Maria Elena Holly (442): "It is obvious that the Beatles were influenced by Buddy Holly, especially John Lennon. I am sure that Buddy would have been good friends with John. They would have cooperated with each other."

Going into the 1970s, John Lennon sang "Peggy Sue" on his *Rock'n'Roll* album and Paul McCartney produced Denny Laine's tribute album, *Holly Days*, which includes an instrumental workout of "I'm Lookin' For Someone To Love" and the single of "It's So Easy". The Denny Laine album is distinctive enough in its own right and yet doesn't lose track of the quality of the songs. Laine and McCartney's Tex-Mex sound is more pronounced than on Holly's own recordings and is close to reggae on "Fool's Paradise".

Denny Laine (443): "I was into everything that was going on with the rock'n'roll stars, but I was an especially big fan of Buddy Holly. The Strat was the first solid body guitar to come out: it had a clean sound and it was really a rhythm guitar, a good rhythm to accompany yourself as a singer. I loved nearly all of Buddy Holly's stuff, and there's only a few tracks that I'm not wild about. I love 'It's So Easy' 'Raining In My Heart' and 'It Doesn't Matter Anymore'. I prefer the ones that have full productions rather than the 'Peggy Sue' side of it."

Paul McCartney bought Buddy Holly's catalogue as an investment but Buddy was a major influence on his work. Would Paul have written "Yesterday" if Buddy hadn't come up with "True Love Ways"? "Eat At Home" (1971) isn't one of Paul's best songs, but it does demonstrate how Buddy Holly meets "Day Tripper".

Despite his love for Holly, McCartney hasn't often performed his songs on stage: even "Brown-Eyed Handsome Man" on *Run Devil Run* is a Holly cover rather than a Holly song. Still, Holly's influence is all-embracing as the Beatles even took their name as a tribute to the Crickets.

Hans Olof Gottfridsson (444): "To me, Buddy Holly and the Crickets is the prototype for the Beatles not only by name, but also by spirit. The Crickets were the first pop group in the world and Buddy himself was a brilliant singer and songwriter as well as an influential guitarist. Although his career was very brief his harmonies and strong melodies created a genuine pop sound later to be copied by so many. He mixed the best of black rhythm and blues and white country into red hot music. Holly also led the way by not only writing his own songs but also showing an interest in the whole music making process from arranging to producing the right sound in the studio, something later to be standard among leading pop groups. In my book Buddy and his band are the first Mersey Beaters and Lubbock, Texas is just across the Mersey…"

Mike Brocken (445): "Look at those early Beatles' performances when they didn't have a drummer and when they said, 'The rhythm's in the guitars.' They weren't pulling a fast one. The rhythm was in those guitars and it was in Buddy Holly's guitar too, so there is a link to Holly there."

John Jorgenson (446): "I loved the acoustic guitars on the Everly Brothers' records: Don, probably more than Phil, came up with some really good parts, and Chet Atkins knew how to record them. Buddy Holly sometimes used the combination of electric and acoustic guitars, and Eddie Cochran took it further, using the acoustic guitar for great percussive sounds. That combination set the pattern for most bands in the 1960s—you get it with the Shadows—Bruce Welch's acoustic rhythm and Hank Marvin's electric lead, which are both great. Later on, you get John Lennon's full-bodied Gibson J160E, an acoustic guitar with an electric pickup, which was plugged into a Vox amp for a unusual sound. If you listen to 'I Feel Fine' again, you'll hear that it sounds like the

electric piano that Ray Charles played on 'What'd I Say'. The riff and the drum part are also very similar to 'What'd I Say'."

So can we explain the discrepancy between Buddy Holly's obvious link on the Liverpool groups and the number of his songs they covered? **Mark Lewisohn (447)** believes it's because the available recordings of Liverpool groups don't really begin until 1962. "If there were more recordings from the 1958 to 1961 period, I am sure you would hear a lot more Buddy Holly. For example, the Beatles, in their various embryo forms, performed many other Holly covers—'Everyday', 'Midnight Shift', 'It's So Easy', 'Maybe Baby' and 'Raining In My Heart', and doubtless many others that we don't know about. Buddy's stamp was certainly all over the earliest Lennon and McCartney songs. 'Thinking Of Linking' is definitely Holly's style and so is 'I'll Be On My Way' and 'Hello Little Girl'. There's an unreleased rehearsal recording from 1960 of John's first composition, 'Hello Little Girl', and it sounds like it's straight out of Lubbock; by the time it got to the studio though, in 1962, it had been re-arranged. We also know from what they said in interviews that 'Love Me Do' started out very much in the Holly vein too, though unfortunately, no such recording exists. Buddy Holly was an absolutely enormous influence on the Beatles. Without him showing the way that you can be so interesting with three chords, I don't think they would have got that message. It was that seeming simplicity that inspired them to have a go."

Paul Kennerley (448): "I am 60 now. I was very young when I first heard Elvis Presley and Lonnie Donegan and so everything went along in order for me. A youngster today would not be sure as to who came before whom. Buddy Holly made the music a lot more accessible for me. Elvis was in such a different class, nobody could be like Elvis at all—the way he looked, the way he sang—but you could identify with Buddy Holly when you were a schoolboy and so it was easier to attain the fantasy to become like him. I can remember hearing 'Peggy Sue' for the first time and it had a huge effect upon me and my life. Even today, he is still as fresh as tomorrow. You put on those records and it is like they have been sitting in the fridge. They are terribly easy for youngsters to play and sing, they are so lively and simple and hummable, which is always a good thing."

Bryan Dodson (449): "I loved Little Richard and Fats Domino, but they had special New Orleans drumming, which is not easy even if you know how to play. I loved hearing Jerry Allison with Buddy Holly and I would be copying that before I even had a drum set. I remember being at a family wedding and the band asked me to look after their instruments while they took a break. There I was, 14 years old, and looking at my first real live drum set. Everything stopped when I started playing, and there was applause when I went for a crash cymbal at the end. I could see the band returning and I thought, 'Oh dear', but my uncle said, 'Look, if he's done any damage, we will pay for it.' There was a band in Waterloo called the Black Velvets and when their drummer joined the circus, I was asked to take over and I could use his kit. This is the early 60s and it was great as they did lots of Buddy Holly covers. I was playing Jerry Allison's parts to the best of my ability but it would have taken a while before I was any good."

Phillip Goodhand-Tait (450): "I already had a group at school, three guitars and me singing at the piano, no drums, but we were useless. It wasn't just that the guitarists didn't know any chords, but it wasn't until I heard Buddy Holly that I could work out the instrumentation on rock records. Elvis and the other Americans who made the charts and came before Buddy made records with lots of session guys and complicated instrumentation. From his recordings, it was easy to hear guitar, bass and drums with occasional piano combined with simple vocal harmonies. He was inspirational. I believe that was Buddy's major contribution to the British Beat group boom that was to come."

The music publishers in New York worked in the Brill Building, a major source of songs in the pre-rock'n'roll era. Some of the older writers adapted to the changing circumstances and also a team of new, young writers including Carole King and Neil Sedaka was assembled across the road by Al Nevins and Don Kirshner for Aldon Music. The teenage subject-matter was new (as were teenage stars themselves) but the songs themselves were written conventionally, that is,

verse/ chorus, verse/ chorus, middle eight, verse/ chorus. As before, sometimes it would be a verse with a title line and sometimes there would be no middle eight, but very few rock'n'roll songs do not have a conventional construction. Chuck Berry's "Let It Rock" has three verses and no chorus and the title doesn't appear, but I suspect that this was a work in progress that somehow got released. Buddy Holly's curious and intimate "Umm Oh Yeah", originally done by Mickey and Sylvia, meanders around its bizarre title line and the title is unusually placed in "Love's Made A Fool Of You". There is no obvious structure to Bo Diddley's "Say Man" and "Mona", which suggests that Bo may be more of a songwriting pioneer than he's given credit for. However, you don't have the radical re-working with song construction until the Beatles and their acolytes.

In terms of lyrics, the most radical reworkings of the popular songs came with Bob Dylan. Although Dylan owed much to folk artists of the previous decades, notably Woody Guthrie and Leadbelly, there is much similarity between Bob Dylan and Buddy Holly. Both had unique, instantly recognisable voices; both broke the rules; and both were ambitious, knowing what they wanted from their music. They could have done great duets on "I Don't Believe You" and "Midnight Shift", but the most Hollylike of Dylan's performances is "Odd And Ends", which was recorded as part of *The Basement Tapes* in 1967, but not issued until 1975. "You go your way and I'll go mine" from "It Doesn't Matter Anymore" is echoed in Bob Dylan's "Most Likely You Go Your Way And I'll Go Mine", a song on the album, *Blonde On Blonde* (1966).

Michael Gray (451), author of the definitive book on Dylan's music, *Song And Dance Man*: "Dylan was very proud at having seen Buddy Holly on his last tour, and he'd been in the front row. No musician who had an interest in rock'n'roll could avoid being influenced by Buddy Holly. He was the first person who knew what he was doing—he did the arrangements, he did the writing, he formed a group, he wasn't just a singer being moulded by a manager and having somebody else's orchestra behind him. He had rather a strange voice and he sounded like nobody else. Nik Cohn's book, *Awopbopaloobop Alopbambboom*, says that Holly was without talent and stood as the typical acne-kid that everybody liked precisely for that reason. It's also rubbish to say that Bob Dylan can't sing, but I hear it all the time, but they can't sing like Picasso can't paint. They broke rules, they knew what they were doing and they took no notice of anybody else. They were very ambitious and they had absolutely unique sounds. Holly's first attempts at recording were complete failures and he was sent back to Lubbock, Texas, which is one of the most god-forsaken spots in the universe, but he refused to become the small town hick. He knew he could make great records and he did it, and there's an interesting comparison with Dylan there. There are several pieces by Dylan where you can hear a very strong Buddy Holly influence: 'Maybe Someday' on *Knocked Out Loaded* is very Hollyish."

Remember the TV ads for Remington which were fronted by the owner Victor Kiam, saying, "I liked the shaver so much, I bought the company." In that sense, Paul McCartney has to be the ultimate Buddy Holly fan. **Mark Lewisohn (452)**: "Paul McCartney had been taking business advice since 1969 from his father-in-law, Lee Eastman, and he had made his money from being a song publisher. In a sense, the publishers can make more money than the writers. His advice to Paul was to buy songs. Do you really want to invest in oil companies, why not invest in what you love which is music? Norman Petty was selling Nor Va Jak for $3m. The thought that he could own Buddy Holly's songs of all catalogues was very tempting. He didn't acquire the world rights, but he secured the American rights. Over here, the songs are with Southern Music in perpetuity. Paul felt he had been ripped off by music publishers and he has made sure that any living writers who wrote songs that he owns would be dealt with fairly and properly."

Sonny West (453): "My songs picked up a lot in the 70s after Paul McCartney bought the Buddy Holly catalogue. He promoted the songs a lot more and probably took care of the books a lot better. That was the best thing that happened to me. It helped me out an awful lot and it has allowed me to do a few more things that I wanted to do."

Mark Lewisohn (454): "Paul McCartney owns thousands of songs, but he doesn't have the catalogue that he really wanted, the Beatles' catalogue, I am pretty certain now that he never will. It is out of his reach: even Paul McCartney couldn't afford to buy the catalogue now."

Cover versions—It's So Easy, Or Is It?

The Diamonds' "Words Of Love" was the first of many successful covers of Buddy Holly's songs. It has been a very mixed bag and the best ones tend to be the ones that try something different. Bobby Vee, Don McLean and Mike Berry have recorded many songs from his catalogue. There have been tribute albums from the Crickets (and individual members), Tommy Allsup (*The Buddy Holly Songbook,* 1964), Bobby Vee (*I Remember Buddy Holly,* 1963 and *Down The Line,* 1999), Jimmy Gilmer (*Buddy's Buddy,* 1964, although he never met him), Skeeter Davis (*Skeeter Davis Sings Buddy Holly,* 1967). Denny Laine (*Holly Days,* 1977), the Hollies (*The Hollies Sing Buddy Holly,* 1980) and Connie Francis (*I Remember Buddy Holly,* 2000). There are various artists compilations (*Buddy's Buddys,* 1992 and *Buddy—Different Views,* 1999), but there is only one of newly recorded material (*notfadeaway,* 1996).

When Buddy did "Slippin' And Slidin'", he planned to speed up his vocals so that he would sound like the Chipmunks. Skeeter Davis manages it without technical trickery and her versions of "Early In The Morning" and "Maybe Baby" are hideous.

Bobby Elliott (455) of the Hollies: "Just before 'Long Cool Woman In A Black Dress', Allan Clarke would do a throwaway version of 'Peggy Sue'. It always went down well and Tony Hicks suggested that we did an album of all Buddy Holly material. We produced it ourselves and we were pleased with the end product. But true Buddy Holly supporters didn't like the way we rearranged the songs."

Stuart Colman (456) produced the Connie Francis tribute album, on which she was supported by the Jordanaires: "Connie knew Buddy Holly well and that's why the album is called *I Remember Buddy Holly*. Larry Knecthel played the keyboards and wrote the arrangements, but boy, I had to work hard. She would say, 'I have sung this twice, that's enough' and I would use my tried and tested gee-up line, 'We're not here to make a great record. We're here to make a stunning record.' She would dress up for the studio and I always saw her beautifully dressed and with great make-up. She said that a photographer or another artist might look in and she didn't want to be caught in sneakers and jeans. She was really sweet. Whilst we were cutting the tracks, someone told her it was my birthday and she arranged for a huge cake to be delivered to the studio."

The most intriguing track on Connie's album is "Peggy Sue", which is a feller's song unless k.d. lang chooses to perform it. Sonny Curtis, who played guitar on the session, added new lyrics and gave the song a storyline, "I really love that boy but now he's crazy 'bout Peggy Sue." Connie even adds, "I'm gonna give that girl a smack right in the mouth", which might sum up Jerry Allison's feelings.

Bobby Vee has made a second career out of recording Buddy Holly songs and he has appeared on many shows with the Crickets. He has never had a hit single with a Holly song, but he has frequently dipped into the songbook. Bobby Vee has 32 songs in common with Buddy Holly and he also recorded "Buddy's Song" and "Whatever Happened To Peggy Sue", which he wrote with Tim Rice. **Bobby Vee (457)** spoke to me in 2002: "Tim Rice was in Minneapolis for the opening of *Aida* and he invited us along. We had lunch and we were talking about rock'n'roll and he said, 'Whatever happened to Peggy Sue?', and I chuckled and said, 'That sounds like a song title.' Five months later, he sent me a wonderful lyric, 'Whatever Happened to Peggy Sue?' and he asked me to put music to it. We jumped at that and I've put it out as a single for my UK tour. I have a UK barcode so I am now in the British record business."

Buddy's friends, the Everly Brothers, have also recorded his songs and recorded a drum-heavy version of "That'll Be The Day" (Number 30, 1965), with James Burton on guitar, as well as "Oh Boy!" (1967) and "Not Fade Away" (1973). They had a hit with a song that Buddy had also recorded—"Love Is Strange". Bob Montgomery produced an excellent version of "Wishing", which was written for them, by his son, Kevin, and Mary Chapin Carpenter.

The Rolling Stones' third single and first Top 10 hit was with "Not Fade Away" in 1964. **Gene Pitney (458)**: "I was on my way home from Paris and I stopped in London for the day. Andrew Loog Oldham called me at the hotel and said, 'You've got to help me.' The Rolling Stones had had a hit and Decca was screaming for a follow-up. Andrew had got them into a studio but he said, 'It's one of those days where they hate each other and I can't get them to record anything.' We had some brandy with us as a duty free thing, so we took that with us and went over to the studio and told everybody that it was my birthday, and it was a custom that everybody should have a glass of cognac with me. It broke the ice. Phil Spector stopped by, he was in a big black Rolls, and the credits on the album say that Phil Spector played maracas but he didn't: he was playing an empty cognac bottle with an American half-dollar, just holding it with one hand and clinking it with the other. I played piano on the session and they came off with a very big hit in 'Not Fade Away'."

"Not Fade Away" was the first Stones' record on which Mick Jagger sounded like Mick Jagger and it emphasised the Bo Diddley beat more than Holly's original. The Stones returned to the song in 1995 for a semi-acoustic version on their *Stripped* CD.

Andy Wilkinson (459): "I love Buddy's songs, they are full of melody and rhythm and are tightly written and still fresh after half a century. There have been a lot of great rock covers of Buddy's stuff. The Rolling Stones' cover of 'Not Fade Away' on their album, *Stripped*, is incredible. The best version I have ever heard."

"Not Fade Away" was recorded with additional lyrics by Stephen Stills in 1978 and also by the Grateful Dead, who have performed 10 minute versions of this tune and used it for audience singalongs. It appears on their 1996 live album, *Dozin' At The Knick*, and I marvel how a group with two drummers could be so lacklustre: still, the version of Chuck Berry's "Around And Around" on the same CD is even more tedious, so Buddy was lucky.

Bob Dylan was doing "Not Fade Away" on tour during 1999/ 2000 and, totally out of character, doing a rock star's dance while he performed. Bruce Springsteen and the E Street Band have used the song as a highly energetic closer. You could spend all day on *youtube* watching Patti Smith, Tanya Tucker, Rush, the Byrds, Status Quo and many more belting out "Not Fade Away". The most unlikely cover has to be from Bo Diddley, unlikely because he claimed that Holly had nicked his rhythm in the first place. Sheryl Crow's "Not Fade Away" has been used to sell Revlon, while Persil Automatic has been promoted by "Everyday".

On that same tour, Bob Dylan performed "That'll Be The Day" with Paul Simon and maybe this prompted Simon's Buddy Holly chording in "Old". The first verse is about Buddy Holly hearing "Peggy Sue" when he was 12 years old.

There is a slow treatment of "Learning The Game" which works very well by Linda Ronstadt's pianist, Andrew Gold. Ronstadt has done much to popularise Buddy Holly and US hits with "That'll Be The Day" (Number 11, 1976) and "It's So Easy" (Number 5, 1977). She sings "It Doesn't Matter Anymore" far better than its composer, Paul Anka, who struggles against clapped-out backing harmonies.

"True Love Ways" has been in the UK charts four times—Buddy Holly (25, 1960), Peter and Gordon (2, 1965), Cliff Richard with the London Philharmonic Orchestra (8, 1983), and David Essex and Catherine Zeta Jones (38, 1994). One of the best versions comes from the Mavericks and there is some curious high-pitched balladry from Michael Crawford.

Despite the presence of "Peggy Sue" on *Billy Fury Sings A Buddy Holly Song Plus Other Demos And Rarities* (2001), I am 99% certain that it is not Billy Fury as it doesn't even sound like him. His slowed-down "I'm Gonna Love You Too" and his low-key "Well…All Right" are worth checking out, but turning "Maybe Baby" into a Dave Clark-styled stomper doesn't work.

Over to Manchester, and **Allan Clarke (460)** of the Hollies: "We were doing a gig one night late 1962 and we were looking at the possibilities of getting a good name because we had a feeling that things were going to happen. Because it was near Christmas and we were fans of Buddy Holly, we called ourselves the Hollies."

Freddie Garrity (461) from Freddie and the Dreamers: "I loved his songs and the simplicity of the music and the fact that he wore glasses made me identify with him. I used to sing all his songs in the late 50s. I regret that I didn't see him but communication wasn't as good back then and I don't remember anyone telling me that he was coming to town or even seeing a poster."

"Heartbeat" was the opening track on Herman's Hermits' first album. **Peter Noone (462)**: "Herman's Hermits was originally called Pete Novac and the Heartbeats because we were like a tribute band to Buddy Holly and the Crickets. I thought that I did his songs really well. I wore glasses to look like Buddy Holly when I sang them, and someone in a pub said, "You don't look like Buddy Holly: you look like Sherman from *The Bullwinkle Show*" and that led to Herman. I bought every one of Buddy Holly's records and we could play them all. I could go on stage tonight and do a complete Buddy Holly set. My daughter is 21 and she could too as she is into Buddy Holly as well. It is very good pop music: it is like country and western and rhythm and blues mixed together and his records are perfect. And I always felt that 'Can't You Hear My Heartbeat' was the perfect song for us—it was Buddy Holly meets 1965."

The heartwarming Yorkshire TV series, *Heartbeat,* about a London policeman now based on the North Yorkshire moors, starred Nick Berry from *EastEnders*. Unlike many TV series set in the past, it prominently used old hits on its soundtrack and there were best-selling albums of music from the series. The title song was Holly's and when the lead actor, Nick Berry, issued his own version in 1992, his record reached Number 2.

In 1969, an early supergroup, Blind Faith (Steve Winwood, Eric Clapton, Ginger Baker, Rick Grech) recorded an excellent "Well…All Right"..

Gary Murphy (463): "We've done the Blind Faith version of 'Well...All Right' in concert. It was structured slightly different and it was more modern as it brought his sound more up to date. It rocked the solo up with the same chord structure. Maybe that is how Buddy Holly would have sounded today. I used more distortion on my guitar and various effects, whereas the Crickets had very little effects—it was just a Fender and a Vox amp. We have the technology to make it sound bigger or better or whatever we want."

"Well...All Right" gives scope for different interpretations and more recently, it has been recorded by Nanci Griffith with the Crickets. She said that when she grew up, she wanted to be a Crickette

Billy Butler (464): "My all-time favourite Buddy Holly cover version is Nanci Griffith's 'Tell Me How'. She had heard Bobby Vee slow down 'Tell Me How' and then she did it herself and it is wonderful. She could make a great album of Buddy Holly covers."

"Everyday" is beloved of the folk-based rock performers such as John Denver and James Taylor, with Don McLean's version making the UK Top 40 in 1973. **Frankie Connor (465)**: "Phillip Goodhand-Tait did a wonderful slow version of 'Everyday', a great version on the piano. You can play 'Rave On' as a ballad: you can do so much with his music. A lot of them are just three chords, but the melodies are so strong."

During the 1960s, Carolyn Hester recorded "Rave On" with Norman Petty in Clovis, but he was uncomfortable about it, feeling that it wasn't a woman's song and he refused to pass the tape over to Dot Records for release.

Michael Cox (466): "I did 'Rave On' with the Checkmates for Joe Meek and I thought it sounded good. Joe put it out in Sweden as I was having hits there but he had equalised it so much that it sounded like it was recorded in a cupboard. That was it with Joe: You put down great tracks and he couldn't leave well alone."

In 1966, the singer/songwriter Tom Rush recorded an album of his favourite songs, *Take A Little Walk With Me*. He included a very rhythmic but not very exciting version of "Love's Made A Fool Of You". He said in the sleeve notes, "The whole debate about folk musicians not being allowed to play electric music was pathetic, an almost retarded way of thinking."

This debate came to a head in April 1970 when the political singer/songwriter, Phil Ochs, performed in a gold lamé suit for a concert in New York in a deliberate act of audience provocation. He was, I suspect, trying to out-Dylan Dylan but the audience didn't warm to his rocked-up "Mona Lisa", which was copying Conway Twitty, his Buddy Holly medley of six songs or the Elvis Presley one of seven. I would guess that he chose to package the songs so that there would be fewer pauses and hence, fewer places for the audience to jeer, but jeer they did. There was five minutes of solid booing after the Holly medley (reduced for the album) and he told the audience, "Let's not be narrow-minded Americans. You can be a bigot from all sides. You can be a bigot against blacks: you can be a bigot against music. I think what we're doing up here is music, and I think it should be heard." Perhaps wisely he then chose one of his most poignant compositions, "Pleasures Of The Harbour". The concert, *Gunfight At Carnegie Hall*, was eventually released in 1975, and Ochs himself was so incensed by the reception that he put his fist through a plate glass door, which meant he couldn't rock'n'roll for a while anyway.

His brother, **Michael Ochs (467)**: "I didn't go to that concert and I was against it even though I was such a rock'n'roller myself. I thought it was dumb because Phil Ochs stood for original songwriting and original ideas, and this was recycling the past. The idea, though, was clever. He thought that the only way we could get any radical change in America was to combine the intelligence of a Che Guevera with the merchandising of an Elvis Presley. If he could have got Elvis to have come out against the war, it might have ended a lot sooner. That was a great idea, but I didn't like the execution."

Buddy Holly's songs are well suited to folk singers, and now at a folk club, nobody would turn a hair if a floor singer performed a Buddy Holly song acoustically. Indeed, it shows the strength of the songs that they work in that setting, but that is also how they were written. In recent years, Carolyn Hester, the folk singer with the best credentials to sing Buddy Holly, has made several UK appearances and she recorded an excellent "Lonesome Tears" in 1996. However, being a folkie, she can't resist adding a few words of her own.

In 1972, the cream of the British folk-rock fraternity as the Bunch recorded an album of their favourite rock'n'roll songs, *Rock On*, for Island Records. With Sandy Denny on lead vocals and Richard Thompson on lead guitar, they perform "That'll Be The Day", "Learning The Game" and "Love's Made A Fool Of You". It's ragged and they sound as though they have had too many sherbets. If the producer, Trevor Lucas (Eclection, Fotheringay) had knocked them into shape, this could have been an important album instead of an odd curio: indeed, it is among the most disappointing albums I have purchased. However, it is significant that three of the songs are Buddy Holly's, which suggests that he was one of the fathers of folk/ rock.

In the same year, another label specialising in folk-rock, Peg, released a compilation, *Clogs*, and one of the new tracks was a one-minute acappella workout of "Rave On" from Steeleye Span. That one minute was better than the whole of the Bunch's album. **Martin Carthy (468)**, then with Steeleye Span: "There's no big deal about it being acappella: it's just that we couldn't play rock'n'roll, no matter how much we would have liked to. We used to sing 'Oh Boy!' for fun in the car and we recorded it in the same way."

Maddy Prior (469): "I was brought up on Buddy Holly, great stuff and it doesn't date for me at all. We were singing 'Rave On' in the car one day and we thought we would surprise Ashley Hutchings with it at the gig that night."

In May 1975, Mud had a Number 1 for two weeks with "Oh Boy!". **Les Gray (470)**: "We stole the idea completely from Steeleye Span. They had recorded an acappella version of 'Rave On' which we loved. We felt we could do something like that as a relief from all the rock'n'roll stuff on our albums. One of the lads suggested another Buddy Holly song, 'Oh Boy'. We were on a roundabout on the A1 and we sang it and took harmonies, we knew instinctively what our parts should be."

Nicky Chinn (471), who produced the record with Mike Chapman, comments, "It just shows that you can do Buddy Holly songs in any number of different ways. He is one of my all-time favour-

ite performers. Who knows where he would have gone if he hadn't died?"

Les Gray (472), the lead singer of Mud: "We had finished our deal with RAK and we were moving to Private Stock, and Mickie Most said that 'Oh Boy!' was going to be our last single. I said, 'You're trying to destroy us just because we're leaving. That's not a single; it's just a change on the album.' It was released on a Friday and the following Tuesday, it was Number 2 and the next week it was Number l. Mickie Most knew a wee bit more about the business than I did."

Leo Sayer had a Top 30 hit with "Raining In My Heart" in 1978 and followed it in 1980 with a Top 10 single with the Crickets' "More Than I Can Say". **Leo Sayer (473)**: "I've always loved 'Raining In My Heart' and I could sing it over and over and never tire of it. I was doing an album with Richard Perry and we were looking for things in a country/ folk direction. This seemed ideal and I also played harmonica on the track. The song was written by Boudleaux and Felice Bryant and I did another of Boudleaux's songs, 'Love Hurts'."

Among the more unlikely covers are "Rock Around With Ollie Vee" (Shakin' Stevens), "Down The Line" (excellent version from neo-rockabilly performer, Darrel Higham, in 2006), "I'm Gonna Love You Too" (Blondie), "That'll Be The Day" (Freddy Fender in Spanish, Pat Boone, Pure Prairie League), "Well…All Right" (Santana), "Midnight Shift" (Commander Cody and his Lost Planet Airmen), "Maybe Baby" (as a ballad by Wee Willie Harris in 2000), "Oh Boy!" (Jackie DeShannon, Nitty Gritty Dirt Band), "Crying, Waiting, Hoping" (Wreckless Eric) and "You're The One" (Billy Swan). Best to avoid Pat Boone doing "That'll Be The Day" on an album called *Great! Great! Great!,* but you know that anyway. Boone takes it far too fast and sounds like a cheerleader at a holiday camp.

Oh, and then there's Billy Connolly's take on "Oh Boy!":

"All of my life I've been kissing
Your left tit
'Cause your right one's missing."

Family Connections

In 1980, the Holley family released an LP, *Holly's House—A Family Album*, primarily the work of Larry, but also featuring his children, Sherry and Randy Buddy, and his other brother, Travis. It was beautifully packaged with a booklet of family photographs and reminiscences. Unfortunately, most of the music is plonkety-plonk country music and some vocals are grim, notably Travis Holley's "Just Out Of Reach". Larry Holley pays a special tribute to his young brother with "The Buddy I Knew" and sings a tribute written by two fans, "Buddy Holly And The Crickets".

In1992, Sherry Holly released an album, *Looking Through Buddy's Eyes*, with a cover photograph in which she held up his glasses: a Yoko Ono moment. I wanted to like this album so much but sadly, she misses so many notes that it is hard going. This is especially noticeable on the slow songs. Sherry can just about get through "True Love Ways" because it is a wonderful song, but "I Guess I Was Just A Fool" meanders on forever. As well as 12 Holly covers, Sherry has written "Kiss The Blues Goodbye" and "The Cost Of Loving You".

Tommy Allsup has had a rich and varied career, working with Snuff Garrett at Liberty Records for many years. He did the music and Buzz Cason the voices for *The Chipmunks Sing The Beatles' Hits* (1964) and, in 1969, Zager and Evans recorded their Number 1, "In The Year 2525" in his studio. He made several albums in the 70s with Asleep at The Wheel. For several years, Tommy was working for Epic Records and recording with Charlie Rich, Tammy Wynette and George Jones. He has owned clubs in Fort Worth and Dallas—the Heads Up Saloon—and was in the Clint Eastwood film, *Honkytonk Man*. Even now, in his 70s, he plays for the Texas Playboys. He told me a joke,

"What's thirteen deep and has blue hair?" "The front row of a Texas Playboys concert."

Each year the Buddy Holly Centre in Lubbock holds a symposium honouring Buddy's music and influence. Old-time musicians gather together and the fans love it. The 2004 album, *Stay All Night—Buddy Holly's Country Roots,* came out of that, produced by Tommy Allsup and Scott Porter. Tommy had two bands for the album, the Texas Playboys and the Stay All Night Studio Band (including Allsup, Al Perkins from the Burritos, Robert Reynolds from the Mavericks, and Carl Bunch). It's good to hear Jack Neal doing the Webb Pierce favourite, "There Stands The Glass" and Larry Welborn with "Drivin' Nails In My Coffin" and "Statue Of A Fool". Larry and Travis Holley sing "Remember Me", a T. Texas Tyler song that Travis had learnt in the navy, the hymn, "Softly And Tenderly", a favourite hymn of their father's, and "When My Blue Moon Turns To Gold". Jack Neal offers both the 1953 version and a 2004 version of "I Saw The Moon Cry Last Night".

Norman Petty's studio had not been used commercially since 1969 and he had died in Clovis of leukaemia in 1984, his mother still being alive. He had recorded the music for his funeral service as well as the sounds of his wind chimes. During the service, he was likened to Michelangelo and Beethoven. He had recorded around 1,500 tracks at Clovis and the equipment lay dormant. **Kim Fowley (474)**: "Norman Petty did one great thing: he recorded the music for his funeral before he died. I have my own music selected and it has all been recorded too."

In 2006, some 50 years after it opened, a new CD, the first, was made there. It was *That'll Be The Day,* produced by Tommy Allsup and Scott Porter. Jack Neal and Larry Welborn were on hand and also Gary and Ramona Tollett and David Bigham, who sang with the Roses. Jack Neal does his song, "Modern Don Juan", although he sounds a bit old for the lyric! Good to hear Tommy Allsup doing "Raunchy". At long last there's a version of "Down The Line" from John Mueller in which you can make out the words.

12

WHAT'S GONNA BECOME OF ME?

"Hollywood History is different. The final product gleams, and it sears the imagination. For many, Hollywood History is the only history."
("Past Imperfect—History According To The Movies", Mark C Carnes)

The Buddy Holly Story

As a feature film lasts two hours, any biographical story has to be condensed for the screen and in order to concentrate on the plot, incidental characters have to be dropped or amalgamated, and sometimes, for legal reasons, renamed. A so-called biopic cannot be factually accurate but in its distillation, it may reveal some truths about the character. Some filmmakers deliberately distort history or present a skewed version of the facts, but most want an accurate depiction of the subject matter. When they do it well, Hollywood histories become the recognised view. If I say "Ghandi", don't you think of Ben Kingsley and "Patton", George C. Scott?

There are problems in making biopics, especially about entertainers where drinks and drugs are rife. They can add drama to the story but they can be box-office poison. *Lady Sings the Blues* (1972) was explicit, and no doubt accurate, about Billie Holiday's drug addiction, but it hardly added up to a good night out at the cinema. The Oscar-winning films, *Ray* (2004), with Jamie Foxx as Ray Charles, and *Walk The Line* (2005) with Joaquin

Phoenix as Johnny Cash, did not gloss over the more unsavoury elements of their lives. They are cautionary tales about the price of fame. Redemption is a favourite theme of Hollywood films, but how often does it happen in real life?

Rock'n'roll stars have been badly served by the cinema and there has yet to be a decent film about Elvis Presley. In *Elvis* (1979), Kurt Russell decides that the most important thing to do when he takes possession of Graceland is to display his gold records. *Great Balls Of Fire!* (1989) conveys Jerry Lee Lewis's manic energy but the result is an animated cartoon that gives no indication of his extraordinary talent. It skirts the very serious issue of paedophilia and, similarly, no film about Presley has touched on this issue, largely because it wouldn't get an audience. There has yet to be a biopic about Chuck Berry, but from the DVD extras for the concert film, *Hail! Hail! Rock'n'Roll* (1987), we can see that Chuck is in denial about many events in his life or at least has put his own spin on them.

The first biopic of a rock'n'roll star was of a performer who had never appeared in a film, *The Buddy Holly Story*, in 1978, and it has turned out to be amongst the best music biographies. A film about Holly had been mooted for years. In 1975, Jerry Allison had acted as advisor on a script, *Not Fade Away*, to be directed by Jerrold Friedman. Twentieth Century Fox agreed the finance but they closed down the shooting after two weeks. Nobody had looked closely at the script and the producers realised that this wasn't the bright rave-up they'd been expecting. It concentrated on the tour that the Crickets had made with black performers in 1957 and it reflected the tensions on both sides. It was a brave idea and it's a pity that the film was not completed or that the shot footage has not been seen.

Joe Ely (475): "Jerry Allison had written a script that 20th Century Fox had picked up on called *Not Fade Away*. I'd been playing around Lubbock and Jerry mentioned the possibility of me playing Buddy Holly. I told him that I wasn't an actor but I'd like to see the script. It was a real intimate thing, seen from their perspective and there was an early tour with black artists where the promoter didn't know what he was getting into. They split the audience, blacks on one side and whites on the other, and it led to strange feelings between the stars and there was a fist fight between LaVern Baker and Buddy Holly in front of the buses. I guess the script was a little too real and Fox wanted a more romantic picture and it was never made."

Just prior to *The Buddy Holly Story*, there had been a very good film about a crucial week in Alan Freed's life, *American Hot Wax*. There was much about the city fathers and concerned parents wanting to end his influence, and there is one wonderfully inaccurate, and clearly deliberate, moment where Chuck Berry says that he will do a concert for free.

The producers of *The Buddy Holly Story*, Ed Cohen and Freddy Bauer secured the rights to John Goldrosen's well-researched biography of the star, but their budget was only $2m and by way of contrast, the abysmal film of *Sgt Pepper's Lonely Hearts Club Band*, starring the Bee Gees, was made around the same time with a budget of $12m. The director of *The Buddy Holly Story* wanted the Crickets to pass dancing bears on their way to the stage on *The Ed Sullivan Show*, but to save money, the bears were mentioned rather than shown. As it happens, the tight budget and

lack of big production values helped to give the film the feeling that it had been made in 1959.

Gary Busey, who had played Jerry Allison in the aborted *Not Fade Away*, was a superb choice for Buddy Holly. He was a musician, having worked as the drummer Teddy Jack Eddy for Leon Russell, and he was a good actor, having played Kris Kristofferson's road manager in *A Star Is Born* (1976). *The Buddy Holly Story* was his first lead role and it was wisely decided that he would perform his own music, often in front of live audiences. The opening scene where he performs "Rock Around With Ollie Vee" is dynamite and tells you that is going to be a highly energetic and vibrant film. Busey handles all of Holly's music and although Holly never had an orchestra with him on the *Winter Dance Party*, I can see the logic as it would have come.

Because of the possibility of *Not Fade Away* being completed, both Allison and Mauldin did not want their names to be mentioned in *The Buddy Holly Story*. So, the complaint that the correct Crickets aren't mentioned is not down to the filmmakers but the obstinacy of the Crickets themselves. Instead we had Don Stroud (Allison) as Jesse Charles and Charles Martin Smith as Ray Bob Simmons (Mauldin), which might have been a good thing as the script called for Jesse Charles to make racist remarks. Stroud had only played bongos before but he learnt the drums quickly and well. All three were too old with both Busey and Stroud being in their mid-30s, but who cares? Wasn't Dustin Hoffman the world's oldest graduate? Norman Petty is not mentioned in the film, but this was because he was refused script control. He, apparently, had a script for a TV movie, which was never made.

Maybe this is biased, but **Jerry Allison (476)** told me: "They didn't have the rights to use our names in *The Buddy Holly Story* so they called me Jesse and Joe B. was Ray Bob. Apart from that, I hated it. Nobody who was involved in it knew what really happened. They took a book and even got that wrong, so the movie was pretty disappointing to me."

Buddy Holly is depicted as rebellious, determined to pursue his music despite the opposition of his parents, the church, record producers and anyone else you care to mention. It made for a good, if clichéd, story, and the truth, as this book shows, was very different. Buddy Holly had no more supportive fans than his parents and his brothers, who are also not shown in the film. The 1950s itself is captured well with Buddy viewing a 3-D film and an amazing selection of American cars, but there is nothing of Holly coming to England. He is portrayed as opportunistic and there is little about his friendship with other musicians. Joe B. Mauldin told me that Buddy was much smarter than the character in the film, and that his pants always reached his feet!

Sonny Curtis (477): "The movie, *The Buddy Holly Story*, wasn't true to life. For one thing, there are no mountains in Lubbock. It depicted Buddy's parents as being opposed to him doing rock'n'roll, but not only were they 100% behind Buddy, they were 100% behind all us boys. They were real good people, they were great and they loaned us the car all the time. The movie portrayed Buddy as a sloppy dresser and Buddy was not like that at all, man. He always had tapered, crisp jeans and moccasins: nice-looking glasses too. He always looked as though he'd stepped out of the bandbox. They didn't even acknowledge that I existed or even Norman Petty. The worst thing was depicting J.I. as a racist. That was a terrible thing to do when it wasn't true at all." Curtis put his feelings about the film in his song, "The Real Buddy Holly Story".

Alan Robinson (478): "In *The Buddy Holly Story*, one of the most conspicuous errors for me is that the headstock on the Fender Stratocaster that Gary Busey plays is from the 1970s, not the pre-CBS, 1950s headstock. That always jars with me, which gives you some idea of how tediously anally retentive I am!"

Although Buddy punches Owen Bradley in the film, that never happened and also, it was not the Nashville version of "That'll Be The Day" that was the hit. The songs are performed out of sequence but that hardly matters as they also have to underline events in the story. Maria Elena was one of the advisors on the film and as a result, their romance is handled well. There are no groupies and because Holly was clean, no drugs. You may wonder: where's the story and, surprisingly, the producers decided not to show the plane crash and they end on a high after a performance on

the *Winter Dance Party*, which according to the awning was on 3 February 1959. A caption says what happened next, but still leaves Maria Elena pregnant. Not showing the crash was curious, but it could be down to economics.

Gary Busey was nominated for an Oscar for his role as Buddy Holly, and the film did win an Oscar for the best adaptation of original material, which effectively meant that Buddy Holly won an Oscar. *The Buddy Holly Story* had used John Goldrosen's book as source material, but he was disappointed with the film and blocked the book of the film.

Mr and Mrs Holley filed a $300,000 suit against the filmmakers for showing them as unsupportive of their son. I don't know how it was settled, but Mr Holley must have regretted pointing at Gary Busey on the screen at the Dallas opening and exclaiming, "That's my boy." Certainly, he had the right mannerisms and this could have come from working with Jerry Allison on the aborted *Not Fade Away*.

Since then, Marshall Crenshaw has played a cameo as Buddy Holly in the biopic about Ritchie Valens, *La Bamba*. Holly was portrayed by Joe Warren Davis in *Mr Rock'n'Roll: The Alan Freed Story* (1999) and Frankie Muntz did the honours in the Johnny Cash spoof *Walk Hard: The Dewey Cox Story* (2007).

Marshall Crenshaw (479): "I was experiencing my short period of near fame and I was asked to be in *La Bamba*. The film producers were looking for people who were on the contemporary scene who bore some resemblance to the 50s rock stars, and I was one of those people. There was also Brian Setzer as Eddie Cochran and Howard Huntsberry as Jackie Wilson. About a month before I filmed the scene, I went in the studio with Garry Tallent and Max Weinberg from the E Street Band. The director wanted 'That'll Be The Day' and so we recorded that. Then the producer of Warner Bros Records wanted us to do 'Well…All Right' and we did that too. Garry wanted to do 'Cryin', Waitin', Hopin'' and I said, 'There's no point as it wasn't released when Buddy Holly was alive and he didn't do it live.' We did a drum heavy version of it and lo and behold, the film producers heard that and that was the one they wanted."

For the opening credits of *Peggy Sue Got Married* (1986), Francis Ford Coppola, used Buddy's undubbed, acoustic version of "Peggy Sue Got Married" and it sounded stunning. The time travel story, highly derivative of *Back To The Future*, was about a disillusioned 43-year-old Kathleen Turner, who goes back to 1960 and meets her sweetheart, Charlie, played by Nicolas Cage. This was shaped into a West End stage musical with Ruthie Henshall in 2001 with an original score from Bob Gaudio and although it had plenty of charm, it coincided with 9/11 and soon closed.

There is a steady flow of Holly songs in movies and television productions. The David Essex film, *That'll Be The Day* (1973), and the Hugh Laurie comedy, *Maybe Baby* (1999) used Holly titles, and "Maybe Baby" was performed on the soundtrack by Paul McCartney. In addition, the long-running TV series, *Heartbeat,* made a star of Nick Berry and gave him a Top 10 hit single in 1992. "Rave On", for example, was on the soundtrack of *Cocktail* (1988), "It's So Easy" was in *Brokeback Mountain* (a 2005 film showing that it wasn't easy at all) and the acoustic "Dearest" on the teen movie, *Juno* (2007). It didn't sound out of place at all.

The novelist Nigel Hinton has written three books for teenagers in the Buddy series—*Buddy* (1983), *Buddy's Song* (1989) and *Buddy's Blues* (1997), Buddy in this case being the son of Teddy Boy and 50s rocker, Terry Clark. Following a TV series on the first book, *Buddy's Song* was filmed in 1991 by Claude Whatham, the director of the David Essex and Holly-titled film, *That'll Be The Day*. **Chesney Hawkes (480)**: "I had my wisdom teeth out when I was 17 and as I was coming round, Roger Daltrey was on TV, talking about his search to find someone of my age who could sing and play guitar and piano and also looked a bit like him as he would be playing his son. I hadn't done acting but I had done some gigging and played piano in wine bars, and so a week later, I did an audition and got the job."

Nigel Hinton (481): "When I was planning the first book in the series I came up with the idea of a Teddy Boy from the 50s still living the rock 'n' roll lifestyle and I knew that he would have named his son after one of his heroes. In the end it came down to Elvis or Buddy. They were

also both my personal heroes but I chose Buddy because he was less obvious than Elvis. His music was subtler and more inventive and he wrote much of his own material, so in many ways he was more original and off-beat. There's also something about Buddy's voice that is totally open and honest and speaks to the heart. It's indefinable, but it is as though his music is the medium through which his spirit is conveyed directly to the listener—the transparency of great art. The other astonishing thing about him is how timeless and undated the music sounds. I am delighted to say that the books in my *Buddy* trilogy have often prompted many of my young teenager readers to start listening to Buddy Holly and they often comment on how fresh and alive it sounds."

Exactly what **Chesney Hawkes (482)**, the son of Chip Hawkes, of the Tremeloes, found. "My dad is a rock'n'roller at heart and so I grew up with rock'n'roll and I have always loved Buddy Holly. A lot of those records were only two minutes long but they are masterpieces; so simple, so well crafted and so crisp. A lot of the great rock'n'roll records sound dated because the sound quality isn't too good, but the sound on Buddy Holly's records is outstanding. I love the feel of records like 'Oh Boy!' and 'Peggy Sue' and they could have been made yesterday."

And the film led to a Number 1 hit. **Chesney Hawkes (483)**: "Roger Daltrey was a mentor to me and he loved the character he was playing. He would walk around the set all day long in that costume with his hair done up. It was quite a gritty film as it dealt with a lot of family issues. I loved the story and it has became part of the school curriculum. My dad found the song, 'The One And Only', and he championed for it to be in the film from the beginning. Nigel Hinton has written a sequel, *Buddy's Blues*, so there could be another film sometime. It's about someone who dies in their late 20s but I could get way with it as long as they don't leave it too late."

Nigel Hinton (484): "For the third book, I went to Lubbock and checked out his schools and all the places associated with Buddy Holly. I ended up, like many pilgrims, at his grave. I was surprised at how moved I was to be there and how full of gratitude my heart was for the joy and beauty he had brought me ever since I first heard him back in the grey old England of 1957."

Buddy

Andrew Lloyd Webber notwithstanding, stage musicals with new scores are scarce, largely because of the enormous costs and the possibility that the musical may flop dramatically. Commercially successful new musicals are now exceedingly rare. They have been replaced by juke box musicals, a derogatory term to be sure, but describing entertainments like *Mamma Mia!* or *We Will Rock You* which have proven hits at their foundation—and maybe 20 of them at that. Audiences go for a good night out and the musicals invariably end in a rave-up with everybody out of their seats. The current publicity for *Buddy* describes it as "Still the best party in town."

The juke-box musical started with Jack Good's *Elvis,* which was staged shortly after Presley's death in 1977. The biggest hits have been *Buddy* (the music of Buddy Holly), *We Will Rock You* (Queen) and *Mamma Mia!* (Abba) and a current favourite is *Jersey Boys (*Four Seasons). There have also been musicals based on the catalogues of Roy Orbison, Billy Fury, Jerry Lee Lewis, Rod Stewart, Blondie and Take That, while Jack Good told his own story in *Good Rockin' Tonite!* The songs of Jerry Leiber and Mike Stoller were featured in *Only In America* and *Smokey Joe's Café,* and Ellie Greenwich and Jeff Barry's in *Leader Of The Pack.* Some musicals combine a fictitious story with a score of oldies such as *A Slice Of Saturday Night.*

Generally, the plots are flimsy and almost have to be. A musical is two hours long and effectively the writer only has one hour to tell the story, and if they are all-singing, all-dancing musicals, a lot of characters may end up as ciphers. Why bother with a plot at all? Easy: there are rules relating to the royalties on songs used in a musical and if the show is more than 50% music, the rate for the songwriters rises and by the same token, the rate for the dramatist falls. Hence, most dramatists keep the music at the 49% level.

Buddy was not the first stage musical about Buddy Holly as there had been *The Adventures Of Buddy Holly*, which opened in Dallas in 1980.

This was about a professor establishing there were no redeeming features in rock'n'roll, and Billy C. Farlow (from the Commander Cody band) proved him wrong.

Looking back in time, you might think *Buddy* was an obvious runaway success. The songs are very catchy and familiar (even to someone who has not heard them before) and the problem was how to make this a goodtime musical when the protagonist died when he was 22. Like *The Buddy Holly Story,* the musical covered Buddy Holly's professional career and again like the film, it did not depict the crash.

The musical ends with "Rave On" at the *Winter Dance Party*: then the song is cut off in mid-verse and the curtain lowered. A single spotlight picks out an empty chair with an acoustic guitar against it. The guitar strap bears the name "Buddy Holly". The curtain opens again and the whole cast rocks through "Johnny B. Goode" with Buddy Holly doing a Chuck Berry duckwalk. Some have queried why it should be "Johnny B. Goode" but Sonny Curtis told the producers that Buddy did this song and demonstrated how he did it as well.

The West End impresario and rock'n'roll fan (he subscribes to *Now Dig This*), Laurie Mansfield had the concept for a musical about Buddy Holly. He had seen how inaccurate the film was and he wanted to create a stage musical which wouldn't play fast and loose with the facts. The musical was written by TV dramatist Alan Janes (*Grange Hill, Minder*), directed by Rob Bettinson (*The Fifteen Streets, Jolson*) and great care was taken with the script: for starters, both Jerry Allison and Joe B. Mauldin were named (although, was Joe B's drinking a contributory factor in the break-up of the Crickets?) and both Norman and Vi were characters. Buddy's romance with Maria Elena was handled well, although Maria Elena is seen, quite correctly, as a forceful character.

Laurie Mansfield (485): "It was the film of *The Buddy Holly Story* that inspired me to do the stage musical, *Buddy*. The film was inaccurate but Gary Busey was marvellous and got an Oscar nomination, but there were no Crickets, no Norman and Vi Petty in the story, and I was very grumpy about all this. I thought I would put the record straight and I discovered that the Crickets weren't in it because they had refused permission because they wanted to do their own movie, *Not Fade Away*. Norman and Vi had wanted to read the film script first and the producers wouldn't let them see it. I had blamed the film unfairly, but I thank them for the inspiration."

I thought that the musical wouldn't fail as presumably Paul McCartney had bankrolled the show. **Laurie Mansfield (486)**: "Not at all. Paul was very supportive as a Buddy Holly fan, but moneywise, no. He still has the first pound he has ever earned. (Laughs)."

The first production of a show is all-important, and in this case, a major factor was finding the right person to play Buddy Holly. **Paul Hipp (487)**: "I was 24 and I'd been playing rockabilly since I was 12 and I'd always liked Buddy. I was working in Carole King's band and writing with her and we played the Royal Albert Hall on a Thursday. I had done a reading for the play and the producers wanted to see me again. The next day we went to the Liverpool Empire and as the opening act didn't turn up, Carole asked me to do an opening set. I included 'Oh Boy!' as I thought that might be good karma. I told the producers that I would be back in London on Monday morning at 9.30 but I was flying out at noon and could only give them 20 minutes. Fortunately, that was enough. I'd never even thought I looked like Buddy Holly and then I put on the glasses and thought, 'Wow, that's it.'"

Laurie Mansfield (488): "Paul Hipp has been the template for every other Buddy Holly in the show. We were holding auditions and Paul was playing bass for Carole King at the Royal Albert Hall. His London agent heard about the auditions and suggested that he went along. He came on stage and sang 'That'll Be The Day' and it was like *The Producers* when they found their Hitler! The three of us who produced the show knew then that we were going to be all right. He was electrifying in a rehearsal room on a wet afternoon."

Buddy was previewed out of town. **Laurie Mansfield (489)**: "We opened in Plymouth and then we went to the Victoria Palace and we opened in October. We thought, 'If we can run to Christmas, this will be brilliant.' People say that Cole Porter and George Gershwin wrote great songs, but to our generation it was Buddy Holly

and the Crickets. I was convinced that there was an enormous audience which would want to see something on Buddy Holly in the legitimate theatre. This was for us, and that has turned out to be the truth." You cannot come out of that show without thinking, 'God, we've had a good time.'"

And he was right. **Paul Hipp (490)**: "We had a party after the first night of *Buddy* and about one in the morning, someone came in with the first edition of *The Sun*. It had the headline, 'Buddy Brilliant', so we were off to a good start."

Alfred Marks' son, Gareth, had a superb cameo as the Big Bopper, and Enzo Squillino Jr (from Sheffield) was almost as impressive as Ritchie Valens. Bruce Welch from the Shadows was the music consultant and Rick Price from the Move and Wizzard was in charge of sound.

Mick O'Toole (491): "Buddy Holly could rock'n'roll extremely well but he wasn't very exciting to look at. If I was compiling a list of Top 10 rockers, he would be about 8 or 9. When I saw the stage show, *Buddy*, I thought that the guy playing him was far more animated than Buddy Holly ever was."

Buddy was staged by the Theatre Royal, Plymouth in October 1989 and soon moved to the Victoria Palace, the former home of the Crazy Gang and *Buddy*'s home for several years. Since then, it has been in and out of London and there have been very successful touring productions. It transferred to Broadway very successfully, initially with Paul Hipp, and there have been further touring productions around the world. The musical's success depends on getting Buddy Holly right and among the other Buddys have been Joe Warren Davis, Stephen Gray and Billy Geraghty, who later played in a stage musical of Jerry Lee Lewis. *Buddy* was a phenomenon but when the same production team staged a musical of *Jailhouse Rock*, it failed to last, largely because they couldn't use the songs that were in the film.

Paul Hipp (492): "Buddy had a temper but it only came out when somebody messed with his music such as when Decca wanted to change him into a country singer. He didn't dislike country music, but it wasn't where his heart was. Other than that, he was a real Texas country gentleman. There is a line in the play where Hi Pockets Duncan says, 'Buddy, you're about the nicest guy in the world until it comes to that music of yours and then, boy, you're the most stubborn critter I've met in my life.' Buddy is about the triumph of someone who has a dream and won't let it be compromised."

Ellis Amburn (493): "Both *The Buddy Holly Story* and the *Buddy* musical present an idealised view of Buddy Holly—neither is dealing with the terrible time that he had with Norman Petty."

Laurie Mansfield (494): "There is no doubt that Buddy and Norman fell out and there is no doubt that Norman withheld royalties, which forced him to go out on that fateful last tour, all of that is in the show. We show what happened as near as we can tell how it happened. We had no real knowledge of the business dealings which went deeper than that. We would have laid ourselves open for a law suit had we got it wrong. We do show that Norman persuaded the Crickets to stay in Lubbock whereas Buddy wanted them to go with him to New York."

Criticising the play may be nit-picking. You have to make concessions. **Gordon Payne (495)**: "*Buddy* was really good and entertaining but they did mess up the facts, but then the film makers always do. They did a good job and the first half had me laughing."

Joe B Mauldin (496): "I thought that the guy who played me had watched all the clips that are available and did a great job of recreating what he had seen."

Jerry Allison (497): "The drinking didn't have anything to do with the split, but they've got to show conflict in a play, and that's what they do in *Buddy*. The truth is that Buddy, Joe B. and me sat in Buddy's new car and we agreed that he would live in New York and we would work as the Crickets and see how things worked out. We weren't mad at each other at all."

Since the success of *Buddy,* there have been scores of juke box musicals, including some with little or no play content. *Rock'n'Roll Heaven* (2002) was about "where the legends never die". It gave the impression that heaven was a big rock'n'roll concert featuring Elvis Presley, Eddie Cochran, Roy Orbison, Del Shannon, Ricky Nelson and Buddy Holly. If that were the case, my dear old dad would be hoping that he went below.

There have also been tours by Buddy Holly and the Cricketers, which is a cheek as the Crickets are still a working unit. They performed *Holly At Christmas* close to me, but the endorsements on the tacky poster from the Falmouth Arts Centre ("The house rocked!") and the *Crawley News* ("Superb") didn't entice me to go, but then I wasn't writing this book at the time. I'm now intrigued to know how they made Holly's repertoire seasonal; the only thing Christmassy about Buddy Holly was his name.

When an IRA bomb exploded in London on 20th February 1996, pictures of the destroyed bus were on the news bulletins and in the papers. The only thing that hadn't been damaged on the bus was the advert for the stage musical, *Buddy.* No-one commented on this because it would have been appalling taste, but a headline could have been "Buddy Holly survives".

Buddy On The Box

The front cover picture for *Radio Times* is, more often than not these days, something to do with *Doctor Who*, but back in 1989, it was an honour to be on the cover, and for the week of 28 January, the cover picture was of Buddy Holly with the inevitable caption, "The day the music died". To remember the thirtieth anniversary of his death, there was to be a new TV play, *Words Of Love*, by Philip Norman. It was a clever drama that contrasted Buddy's final hours with a fan of his, effectively Norman himself, growing up in the Isle of Wight: from Clear Lake to Ryde Pier. Gary Kemp was going to play Buddy Holly and would have been good but for the fact that he could not be made to look sufficiently like him. Buddy was therefore played by a Texas actor, Pancho Russell. He did not sing as he mimed to Holly's records. Charlie Creed-Miles played Philip Norman (here Ivor) and Tom Bell was his father and Liz Smith his gran.

Philip Norman was also the presenter of a Channel 4 *Without Walls* special on Buddy Holly. This iconoclastic series was known for its controversial opinions—Da Vinci couldn't paint: John Lennon was intolerable—but it didn't have much to say about Holly. Norman said that he lacked business acumen, but which of the rock'n'rollers knew their worth? Chuck Berry perhaps, but only after he had been ripped off himself and studied accountancy in jail. The programme revealed that Holly could suck his own willy: had *Without Walls* being talking to Little Richard? I have no idea whether this is remarkable or not: I can't do it myself.

Despite its lack of sensationalism, the noted soul writer Dave Godin felt obliged to write to *Radio Times* about the "stomach churning" programme. He wrote, "Buddy Holly, like Elvis and many others, simply appropriated the music of black America secure in the knowledge that their whiteness would always ensure that they would get preferential media exposure over the black originals they plagiarised. How about a *Without Walls* programme entitled *The Musical Theft Of The Century*?" Sounds like Godin was touting for business and was being more iconoclastic than the original programme.

The BBC's arts programme, *Arena*, has occasionally featured rock artists—Eddie Cochran, the Everly Brothers—and in 1985, they broadcast a 65 minute special on Buddy Holly. An extended, 90 minute version, *The Real Buddy Holly Story*, was released on videotape, but this omitted Maria Elena as well as adding more interviewees and Paul McCartney performing a complete "Words Of Love". As a spin off and using some of the same material, *Arena* made a programme on *Peggy Sue* in the 1993 series, *Tales Of Rock'n'Roll*. The documentary pressed the right buttons and had some revealing clips including Jerry Allison's tips on how to play a cardboard box.

In the television version, Maria Elena says that she encouraged Buddy to become an actor and he became interested after seeing an Anthony Perkins' film. I guess this would be the 1958 film, *Desire Under The Elms*, which was based on a play by Eugene O'Neill and also starred Sophia Loren and Burl Ives. It's easy to imagine Buddy following Perkins' style and giving nervy, edgy performances: perhaps he could have played Norman Bates in *Psycho*. If biopics were being made in the early 60s, Perkins could have been great as Holly.

Although Universal has not released a CD box set, there is the DVD/CD package, *The Music Of Buddy Holly And The Crickets—The Definitive Story* (2005). This feature length film concentrates on the music (no Maria Elena!) and contains new interviews with the Crickets, Jack Neal, Sonny West, Peggy Sue and many more, with bonus additions of the full interviews of many of the participants. The picture quality of the *Ed Sullivan* clips is the best I've seen. The *Jukebox Gallery* is pointless: a selection of songs with photographs.

From Lubbock To Liverpool

For a long time, there was little acknowledgment of Buddy Holly in Lubbock itself. Strangely, it was the Hollywood representation of Buddy Holly in *The Buddy Holly Story* that changed that. Lubbock's city elders realised that they had a tourist attraction here, but their efforts to promote it fall well behind Memphis or Liverpool. Prior to the film, there was only the cemetery: Buddy's grave is easy to find and he is buried alongside his mother, father and a nephew. Then came the Buddy Holly Recreation Area, but that was no more than a few trees (admittedly, a rarity in Lubbock) and a picnic area. Sorry, first off, was the cemetery:

Jimmie Dale Gilmore (498): "In the mid-60s, Buddy had been gone for a while and he had been forgotten by the general public in Lubbock, although the musicians remembered him. The first recording that I did in a studio was paid for by Buddy's father. We had met through an English journalist in Lubbock who was doing some research on Buddy Holly, and a girl that I was going with in Lubbock met him on a train and introduced us and he introduced me to Buddy's father. I organised a band and it was the first time Joe Ely and I had done any music together. Buddy's father had some contacts but he really didn't know the ins and outs of the business. It didn't come to anything and I don't think that those tapes exist anymore."

Lubbock, whose population is still rising and is now around 250,000, has attractions devoted to windmills, wineries, space research, ranching, prairie dogs and, at last, Buddy Holly.

The funds for a statue were raised by tribute concerts in Lubbock featuring Bo Diddley, Roy Orbison, Waylon Jennings and the Crickets, and the eight and a half foot bronze, made by Grant Speed from Utah, was erected in September 1980. It was the first statue anywhere for a rock'n'roll star and it is a good likeness. It captures him accurately and shows how he kept time with his heel.

Alongside the statue is the Walk of Fame with bronze plaques for musicians from the area like the Crickets, Mac Davis and Waylon Jennings but it soon ran of out of locals and included nearby celebrities such as Roy Orbison and Tanya Tucker. When Joe Ely was inducted, he looked over to the jail he was thrown into for being drunk.

The Crickets included Niki Sullivan when they were put into the Walk of Fame. He occasionally played at Holly tributes but mostly he worked for Sony Electronics. He kept memorabilia in his music room and his granddaughter was named Holly. In 2004, he was playing golf one day and he died the next.

The Buddy Holly Centre, housed in old railway buildings, opened in 1999 and has caught the vibrancy of his music. It includes a stage jacket, a Fender Strat and his wallet from the crash site.

For a time, there was also a minor league baseball team in Lubbock, the Crickets, but they disbanded after winning their league championship in 1995. Various events and streets had been named after Buddy Holly—Avenue H became Buddy Holly Avenue—but following a disagreement between Maria Elena and the authorities in 2007, his name can no longer be used. How do you solve a problem like Maria?

The problem started when Maria Elena, who had been paid $30,000 for the use of the name for a Buddy Holly Symposium, wanted money for the continuation of the Buddy Holly Terrace, the Buddy Holly Walk Of Fame and the Buddy Holly Plaza. Her argument was that she could make $150,000 on a commercial. She said, "This is a business and I'm not going to give anything for free" and she had even stopped a performer from wearing lookalike glasses. Buddy's brother, Travis Holley, commented, "As a proud citizen of Lubbock, I am ashamed that Maria lives in Texas and uses my brother's name as her own. After all, she is more recently widowed by another man.

Let's hope she doesn't try to charge a fee to visit Buddy's grave in Lubbock cemetery as his name is on the headstone."

When Paul McCartney acquired the publishing rights to Buddy Holly's music, he established an annual series of events, known as Buddy Holly Week, starting in 1975 and usually in London. Instead of remembering the day he died, he centred them around the day he was born, 7 September. By and large, there was a concert, often at the Mermaid Theatre in London, which the Crickets and artists connected to Holly would perform, and Paul McCartney would get up for a few Holly numbers at the end. There were public competitions for the best tribute song, the best rock'n'roll dancers, the best Holly painting, the best Holly poem and the best lookalikes as well as rock'n'roll quizzes.

Bob Montgomery (499): "Like Buddy, I love England. Paul McCartney did the Buddy Holly shows every September on Buddy's birthday and I did one of them. It was the first time I had been on stage in 25 years and it was nerve-racking. I was up half the night trying to make sure I got the chords to the songs right. I had to perform a couple of songs at the Odeon, Hammersmith. The British fans are the best in the world as they were shouting out songs that I'd forgotten about."

There have been tribute events too in Lubbock, Clovis and the Surf Ballroom. Again, the Crickets are regular performers and the name acts have included Bo Diddley, Roy Orbison, Del Shannon, Jimmy Gilmer and the Fireballs, Tommy Roe and Bobby Vee. In 2003, the Rock And Roll Hall Of Fame And Museum in Cleveland, held a special event, *Rave On: the Life And Music Of Buddy Holly*, with the usual suspects performing. Nearly all the events are well attended, even in Clear Lake in February. The UK company, Dead Great Tours, organises rock'n'roll pilgrimages, which take dedicated fans on tours of Buddy Holly and Elvis Presley sites.

Dave Williams (500): "There are a lot of Holly fans in America now and some of them are very young. The *Buddy* show has helped a lot. I love going there and meeting all the fans. We wrote down once how many people we had met and got friendly with and there was more there than here. It has been marvellous."

On 20 March 2008, 50 years to the day since he played the Philharmonic Hall in Liverpool, a tribute concert was held there, performed by Liverpool artists and organised by David Crosby, a lead singer from the 60s band, the Tabs, The show was directed by the former Granada TV producer, Johnnie Hamp, and the result was superb with the music being performed by a wide range of artists.

After Anthony John Clarke sang the opening verse of "American Pie", Holly's repertoire was opened by two guests from America, Johnny Rogers and Tommy Allsup, performing "Oh Boy!" with local band, Juke Box Eddies. Johnny, a Hollyalike, played the guitar behind his head—a real showman. Another American guest was Kevin Montgomery, who commented "I don't know what I'm doing here. My wife thinks I've gone for cigarettes", before doing his father's songs, "Love's Made A Fool Of You" and "Heartbeat".

Ian McNabb of Icicle Works did "Rave On", with a slowed-down intro, while Pete Wylie ran "Real Wild Child" (singing "Buddy Holly was a real wild child") into "Peggy Sue". Hambone performed an eccentric "Brown Eyed Handsome Man"—I say, eccentric because Brian Farrell is like an Otis Lee Crenshaw tribute act. Jade Gallagher was stunning on her acoustic "Tell Me How" and she teamed up with TV talent show finalists, Eton Road, for "True Love Ways". Kenny Johnson was with the Britannia Bluegrass Quartet for "Learning The Game" and "Love Is Strange". Tim Harvey Jazz gave "Take Your Time" a new look, while the 80-strong West Kirby Light Operatic Society performed "Moondreams" and "Raining In My Heart". The highlight for me was Jack Roberts with Andy Steele on cardboard box doing "Fool's Paradise".

Other performers were Phil Jones, Liverpool Express, Connie Lush, Beryl Marsden, the Merseysippi Jazz Band, the Quarry Men, Michael Snow and the Undertakers. Maria Elena joined the whole cast for a rocking finale of "Not Fade Away".

The success of *The Buddy Holly Story* and *Buddy* has prompted a new interest in Buddy Holly and he is now accepted as one of the most important musicians of the rock'n'roll era. In 1993, he had the ultimate accolade as he was depicted on a US postage stamp.

13

THE CRICKETS AND THEIR BUDDIES

"So many years ago, so many beers ago"
(Jerry Allison)

To the public at large, the Crickets might be viewed as the first tribute band, recreating the hits of their former leader, Buddy Holly. There is an element of that as they cannot appear anywhere without doing "That'll Be The Day" and "Oh Boy!", but they have also continued to chirp on, making numerous singles and albums, and there has been a steady stream of new members, some of whom have transformed the band. If they chose to release a "best of" collection with none of their Holly material, it would still be an impressive collection with several familiar songs.

When Buddy Holly left the Crickets, he left the group without a vocalist, without a guitarist and without an image: just a drummer and a bass player. They responded to the challenge remarkably well although a lot of people didn't take them seriously. They took their music forward and got surprisingly close to what became Merseybeat.

After Buddy Holly's death, Ronnie Smith, Tommy Allsup, Waylon Jennings and Carl Bunch had been performing as the New Crickets on the *Winter Dance Party*. When they returned to New York, they found the (old) Crickets there as well—their line-up was now Jerry Allison, Joe Mauldin, Sonny Curtis and Earl Sinks. **Bill Dees (501):** "The first time I heard Earl Sinks was in a drive-in. He had a great voice, just like Elvis when he wanted to be, and his job was singing to the people in the cars. He was really good at it, and a good songwriter too. He wrote a very pretty song for Roy Orbison, 'Big As I Can Dream', around 1965."

Naturally, Irving Feld felt that there were too many Crickets. He supported Jerry Allison's group, but with Tommy Allsup for Sonny Curtis, and the New Crickets disbanded. Sonny took Jerry's old Chevrolet and drove Waylon, Carl and Ronnie back to Lubbock. However, the new line-up of the Crickets only existed in photographs. Within a few weeks, Jerry Allison had tired of Feld's organisation and Sonny Curtis replaced Tommy Allsup. So, one line-up of the Crickets only exists in a photograph.

Norman Petty had held onto the tapes that the Crickets had recorded in Clovis, confirming the suspicion that he only regarded the Crickets as a lever to get Holly back. As soon as he heard that Holly had died, Petty sent the tapes of "Love's Made A Fool Of You" and "Someone, Someone" to Coral. This made commercial sense but the Crickets lost whatever respect they had for him. The single, which was excellent, made the UK Top

30 and in 1964, Norman revived 'Someone, Some-one' on a single for Brian Poole and the Tremel-oes, which made Number 2. More than anything, the Crickets' single demonstrated that they could make valid music without Buddy Holly.

That single marked the last time that Petty would work with the band and the next sessions were in the Bell Sound Studio in New York with Jack Hansen producing. The follow-up, "When You Ask About Love", with Earl Sinks on lead vocal, also made the UK Top 30 and the B-side was another good ballad, "Deborah", both songs being written by Sonny and Jerry. Deborah was Peggy Sue's young niece and the following year Jerry wrote "My Little Kim Ruth", so family names were coming in useful. The British rocka-billy band, Matchbox, went to Number 4 with "When You Ask About Love" in 1980.

Sonny Curtis (502): "J.I. and I wrote 'When You Ask About Love' at Peggy Sue's. They were teen songs—'Don't cry on my shoulder, Rely on someone who's older.' I certainly can't get my head back in that space. I wish I could, sometimes. I was quite pleased with 'infatuation': it's a good rhyme for 'summer vacation'. I can still sing it but then a song is a song and anybody can sing it. That's just a happy little song like 'Oh Boy!' which has real teenage lyrics: (sings) 'All my love, all my kissing / You don't know what you've been missing.'"

Jerry Allison (503): "When we wrote 'When You Ask About Love', we needed another rhyme for 'graduation' and 'summer vacation' and we could only think of 'infatuation'. After I got mar-ried, someone had told me that I was never in love with Peggy Sue, I was just infatuated, which was a little late to discover."

Sonny Curtis took the lead vocals on "More Than I Can Say" and "Baby My Heart" and both sides made the UK Top 40 in their own right. "More Than I Can Say" went to Number 4 for Bobby Vee in 1961, and was then a US and a UK Number 2 for Leo Sayer in 1980.

Jerry Allison (504): "Sonny Curtis and I were in a 58 Chevrolet driving to New York City from Lubbock, Texas. We were writing a song but we couldn't come up with a first line, so we were going 'Whoa-ah-whoa-ah, yea, yea' and we meant to write words there. We just never got round to it. Bobby Vee recorded it after us but I don't think

there was anyone else until Leo Sayer cut it in 1980 and it helped to pay for my farm."

Geoff Taggart (505): "A lot of the early hits do have very simple chord sequences like 'All I Have To Do Is Dream', 'Move It!' and 'Wild Thing'. 'A Teenager In Love' has an extra chord in there but it is also very simple. When Alan Tarney did 'More Than I Can Say' for Leo Sayer, he didn't follow the chord sequence of the original song and it is typical of his productions."

Leo Sayer (506): Alan Tarney and I were work-ing on the *Living On A Fantasy* album and on TV at lunchtime, we saw a commercial for Bobby Vee's *Singles Album*. He was singing 'More Than I Can Say'. We went to a record shop, bought the record and I had it recorded by midnight. There wasn't much discussion about it: we just did it. There is a vocal loop that we used for the solo and I also put it on my answer phone message, I was singing, 'There's nobody in right now'. When I was promoting the single in 1980 in Nashville, I got a phone call at a radio station from Sonny Curtis who said, 'I love you Leo: you've just bought me a new tractor.'"

A little-known cover version from Jim Habers of Asleep At The Wheel with Chris O'Connell has an additional verse ("You're my sparkling star at midnight, Love you more than I can say").

Earl Sinks, who wanted to stay in Texas, left the group and joined an up-and-coming band, the Omegas before signing with one label after another as a solo artist. The Omegas recorded "Froze" with its memorable line, "Your love is colder than an Eski-mo's nose". Earl Sinks appeared as a character called Snake Richards in the film *Girl From Tobacco Road* (1965), and decided that this was a better name for himself: why? Earl Sinks is as distinctive as they come, but this guy is uncomfortable with his name. He was Sinx Mitchell and Earl Henry for a while, and then, as Earl Richards, he had small run of US country chart entries in the 1970s. He became a producer in Nashville and married another singer, Rita Faye. He is a talented singer ("Lookin' For Love") and writer ("Two Of A Kind" for Sue Thompson; "Love And Learn" for Brenda Lee; "That's What You Do To Me" for the Everly Brothers, all with Bob Montgomery). He left the music business to run the Racehorse Inn, Kentucky, and since then, he has acquired a chain of abattoirs.

The album, *In Style With The Crickets*, showed Sonny, Joe B. and Jerry on the cover, and Joe B. was largely playing the electric bass. As well as previously released tracks, the album included a fine version of Huey "Piano" Smith's "Rockin' Pneumonia And The Boogie Woogie Flu", the Clover's "Ting-A-Ling" (excellent Earl Sinks vocal which rivals Buddy's) and a new Sonny Curtis composition, "I Fought The Law". The album made Number 13 on the UK album charts, but Coral had missed the boat. "I Fought The Law" should have been issued as a single in the US and pushed hard. The song became a Top 10 hit for the Bobby Fuller Four in 1966 and an anthem for the Clash.

The Shadows recorded "Baby My Heart" on their Number 1 début album, *The Shadows*, in 1961. **Bruce Welch (507):** "The Crickets made a fine album without Buddy Holly. I can't remember why we picked 'Baby My Heart' but I'm glad we did."

John Rostron (508): "I thought every track on that album, *In Style With The Crickets*, was a classic. I was intrigued by 'Love's Made A Fool Of You'. As Buddy had written it, it seemed obvious that his version must be around somewhere. I loved the Crickets when they moved to Liberty, and 'My Little Girl'/ 'Teardrops Fall Like Rain' is one of the best singles ever. I have watched many concerts and been lucky to have been on the road with them on at least five occasions, I treasure their songs, their sounds and their friendship."

The Crickets' new album and singles didn't make the US charts and they took work where they could. Both Allison and Curtis worked with the Everly Brothers, and Allison's drumming was a strong component feature on their million-selling "'Til I Kissed You". He was working alongside Chet Atkins, Floyd Cramer and Lightnin' Chance, and Don Everly had wanted to capture the character of "Peggy Sue". It was unusual to hear rolling tom-tom licks on a Nashville session and it is hard to imagine the single without them. They are also used on the B-side, "Oh What A Feeling". Jerry Allison played on their English version of a Gilbert Becaud song, "Let It Be Me".

Jerry and Sonny accompanied Eddie Cochran in January 1960 on his final session before he went to the UK on tour. They recorded "Three Steps To Heaven", "Cherished Memories" and "Cut Across Shorty". During the session, the label executive Sy Waronker thought that they were rushing songs and brought in a metronome. Jerry disabled it as soon as Waronker left.

Jerry Allison (509): "We cut 'Three Steps To Heaven', 'Cut Across Shorty' and 'Cherished Memories' just before Eddie's English tour. Snuff Garrett was there but we didn't really have a producer who said 'Play this' or 'Play that'. That's why Eddie wanted us. He liked what he played and he knew what he wanted."

Sonny Curtis (510): "The acoustic guitar at the beginning of 'Three Steps To Heaven' is Eddie Cochran himself and I'm playing electric. He was a tremendous musician, innovative and full of ideas and I loved his style. He had a lot of drive, but you can't compare him to Buddy Holly because Buddy was the only guitarist on most of his hit records. He had all the responsibility and he had to make every stroke count. Eddie had other guitarists and so had more freedom."

Unbilled, the Crickets backed the Everly Brothers on their tour of Australia and the UK, and they met up with Cochran who was in the midst of his UK tour. He was homesick and said, "If I knew you guys were coming, I'd have asked you to bring me a bottle of American air." They were in England at the time of Cochran's death in a road accident on 17 April 1960.

The Crickets welcomed the chance to come to the UK. It enabled them to determine what they were going to do next and it helped them come to terms with the tragedy. They backed the Everly Brothers for a year.

Vince Eager (511): "About two weeks before he died, Eddie was asked about his favourite clothes and his favourite movies. When he was asked about his best friends, he said, 'Vince Eager and Buddy Holly'. There was chemistry between us and I was going to the States with him for five weeks. We were going to stay on his ranch in California and I was going to record with him. If the tragedy hadn't happened, I think I would have been very successful because Eddie Cochran would have written stuff for me."

Jerry Allison told the *NME*: "If people had seen the Crickets billed to appear, then they'd have rightly expected us to do an act on our own.

That wouldn't have been right because this was Phil and Don's tour." The music papers reported that Joe B. had just married Sherry and their first child, a daughter, Melody, was due later that year. There is a clip of the Everly Brothers backed by the Crickets on *youtube*, taken from an ITV *Startime* show, hosted by Alma Cogan. The 10 minute sequence includes Alma Cogan singing "'Til I Kissed You" on a ukulele.

During the tour, Sonny Curtis received his call-up papers. He went into the forces as soon as he returned to the States, and spent most of his duty in France. On a weekend pass, he sang the Everly Brothers a new song, "Walk Right Back".

Sonny Curtis (512): "I can't remember why I wrote 'Walk Right Back'. I was into Cole Porter and Don Gibson at the time and 'Walk Right Back' may be a combination of the two. I got the idea when I was over here picking with the Everly Brothers. During that tour, I was drafted into the United States Army. When I got back, my mother said, 'The army's been looking for you.' I got into trouble because I was late reporting. When I got to basic training in California, I'd go down to the dayroom and play an old beat-up guitar that somebody had. I wrote the first verse to 'Walk Right Back' and I got a three-day pass and went to Hollywood to see the Everly Brothers. They were studying acting for Warners although nothing came of it. We had a few laughs and I sang 'Walk Right Back' to them. They said they'd record it if I wrote another verse. I was trying to think of another verse but the army keeps you pretty busy. I had nine days right after basic training and I wrote the second verse then. I put it in the mail but the next day I got a letter from J.I. saying that the Everlys had cut it. I knew that they hadn't had time to get my verse and it turned out that they sang the first verse twice."

Sonny and Jerry wrote a lesser-known but excellent song for the Everlys, "This Is The Last Song I'm Ever Going To Sing". Jerry had started it as comedy number but Sonny was quick to spot its potential. It was recorded by the US country performer, Joe Carson, who was produced and managed by Tommy Allsup. Carson died in a motor accident in 1964. Sonny and Jerry recorded "The Ballad Of Batman" for Cameo-Parkway as the Campers.

Jerry Allison moved to Los Angeles and found work with Snuff Garrett, who was now producing for Liberty Records. Jerry Allison, in particular, became a very popular session drummer, working with Bobby Vee, Johnny Burnette and Buddy Knox.

Snuff Garrett (513): "Tommy Allsup became my right hand guy. I made him head of the country department. Joe Allison was doing the country stuff, and Tommy replaced him and cut all those early sides with Willie Nelson. We all had a lot of good times."

Willie Nelson would sing behind the beat and Tommy would tell the musicians not to listen to him or they would break time. He came to an agreement with Willie: he wouldn't tell him how to sing, and Willie wouldn't tell him how to produce. The recording sessions may have been difficult enough, but Tommy ran a booking agency with him. One night a jealous husband, annoyed to see his wife flirting with Willie, split Willie's head open with a car jack and put him in hospital. Willie shrugged it off: it was the price you paid for working the night life.

Tommy Allsup (514): "I did a lot of work on Ben Weisman's songs, cutting demos for Elvis. Dick Glasser used to do the vocals and he had a great voice. I never managed to get in on the sessions as he brought in his own guys, but I did put down a lick for 'Little Sister' on the demo and when the record came out, they had used it."

And the sessions mounted up. **Tommy Allsup (515):** "I've done more that 6,000 sessions over the years. There is a system where 10% of the fee is withheld to go towards a pension fund but there were many times when someone would come into town with a bundle of cash and we would get paid with no official record of the work."

While Sonny was doing his military service, Jerry and Joe B. kept the Crickets going with a new vocalist. **Snuff Garrett (516):** "Jerry Allison is one of my closest friends. We were with each other a lot and I loved him. I got the idea for the *Bobby Vee Meets The Crickets* album, but they didn't have a lead singer. I knew a guy in Dallas who was a good singer and I suggested that we flew out this guy. He and Jerry didn't hit it off the way I imagined. After a few months, it was over and the guy started playing clubs around LA. I did demos with him and took them to my boss, the president of Liberty, and he said, 'You've got enough of your friends signed to the label. You've signed the Crickets and Buddy Knox and they're not doing much business, and this guy can hardly speak English.' I said, 'Well, I think he's going to be something.' 'Okay,' he said, 'Drop one of the acts that you've got and you can sign him.' I said, 'Forget it.' A year later, he was an international star and his name was Trini Lopez. Just because I was doing good didn't mean I could do just what I wanted."

Trini Lopez (517): "About two months after Buddy Holly was killed, I got a call from Lubbock. A disc jockey friend said that the Crickets wanted me to go to Hollywood to be their new lead singer. They sent me the money and I drove myself there. I had $200 in my pocket and I was there partying for a month. I asked their agent if he could find me a little job until they decided what they were going to do. There was a new night club, like an English pub, opening in Beverley Hills, the Ye Little club, and I was there for two weeks, and they liked me a lot. The manager asked me to stay for two more weeks. In the end, I stayed there a year and the Crickets never really did anything. After that I went to another place called P.J's and you know what happened then: Frank Sinatra saw me and I had hit records."

Jerry Allison was impressed by David Box, who had been recommended by his mother. He gave a song he had written with Ernie Hall, "Don't Cha Know", and they recorded it on his 17th birthday with Hall on drums and Allison on guitar. He's a good vocalist and he includes a Buddy Holly hiccup, but the middle eight is stolen from "Dream Lover". The other side was a fast version of "Peggy Sue Got Married" in which they demonstrated that the song could be played as a continuation of "Peggy Sue". The Searchers recorded "Don't Cha Know" on their Top 5 album, *Sugar And Spice*, in 1963.

David Box had been born in Sulphur Springs in 1943 and raised in Lubbock. It was to be his only single with the group. He then did some solo work and his single, "Little Lonely Summer Girl" was doing well regionally in 1964 when a small plane he was travelling in crashed outside of Houston in 1964.

Mauldin returned to Texas and set up his own trucking company. Peggy Sue preferred life on the west coast so Allison formed a little unit with Tommy Allsup (guitar) and Joe Osborn (bass), which was available for session work. Snuff Garrett was pleased with their expertise and thought that Jerry should record as the Crickets: only problem was—he didn't have a group.

With some session men including Tommy Allsup on guitar and Earl Palmer on drums, Jerry Allison sang his own song, "He's Old Enough To Know Better", with Bobby Vee on harmony vocal, and "I'm Feeling Better" (Vee's song and vocal) for a single. Norman Petty commented, "Jerry Allison is one of the best rock drummers in the whole business and it's something of a mystery to me why he has to sing."

"He's Old Enough To Know Better" was inspired by the Everly Brothers' "Poor Jenny", and it was the final Liberty release to be issued in the UK on the Decca's London-American label. After that Liberty would have its own imprint through EMI. Indeed, the A-side was included on their introductory LP, *The Stars Of Liberty*. The song was covered in the UK by the Brook Brothers. The Brook Brothers' single, which was produced by Tony Hatch with an enormous kettledrum sound, made the UK Top 40.

Ravin' On—From California To Clovis, a selection of unissued recordings was put out by Rockstar in 1991. It included Sonny Curtis's own versions of "Don't Breathe A Word" and "Lookin' All Over Town", which had been recorded by Ricky Nelson and Vic Damone, respectively. There are demos of previously unknown songs ("Fell In Love With A Face", "Never Ever Told Me", "There's No Beter Way To Die") but just who are the vocalists? Are these simply songwriters' demos or were the Crickets auditioning potential lead vocalists? If so, Glen D. Hardin wouldn't get the job as his vocal on "A Harlem Girl" doesn't compare to his piano playing. The Crickets' new lead vocalist was Jerry Naylor. The good looking Jerry Naylor had star quality: he was a fine writer and singer and one of the tracks, which was surprisingly left on the shelf was his ballad, "Break It Easy".

Bobby Vee and Jerry Allison worked on some rock'n'roll sessions which became the album, *Bobby Vee Meets The Crickets*. In reality, it was

Bobby Vee and Jerry Allison meet session musicians. Joe B. flew from Lubbock to Los Angeles for the cover photograph, although he didn't play on the album. The highlights included Earl Palmer and Jerry Allison drumming together on "Keep A Knockin'", and Tommy Allsup playing his guitar riff on "Well…All Right". The album did especially well in the UK where it climbed to Number 2 on the album charts. The only single that the Crickets had in the US Hot 100 without Buddy Holly was "Someday" with Bobby Vee, which got to Number 99.

Bobby Vee (518): "The album I made with the Crickets was a very natural process. Snuff Garrett, my producer, was a good friend of the Crickets and he worked with them in Los Angeles. The Crickets and I were living in the same apartment building and we became good friends—playing cards, making music and we had friends in common. We thought it would be a good idea to revisit the 50s with that album."

Allison thought that he should rebuild the Crickets and he brought in an up and coming session guitarist, Glen Campbell, for the next recordings. Bobby Vee passed them a new Carole King and Gerry Goffin song, "Don't Ever Change", and, in the summer of 1962, it went to Number 5 in the UK. The quaint lyric criticises the girl in the song for always wearing jeans "except on Sunday". The Beatles used to perform the song live and their 1963 recording is on *Live At The BBC*. The B-side was another good Allison song, "I'm Not A Bad Guy", which has a guitar solo from Glen Campbell. The song was performed by several Merseybeat bands.

Mark Lewisohn (519): "'Don't Ever Change' suited the Beatles well: Gerry Goffin and Carole King were their favourite composers in that period, and it's a nice tune with perfect scope for, unusually, George and Paul's vocal harmonies. They also had no problems with its country tinge, and it was one to which Pete could drum. Spring 1962 to spring 1963 was the Beatles' hot Goffin and King period, and three cheers for that, I say: without Goffin and King those early Lennon-McCartney songs would not have been nearly so wonderful."

Glen D. Hardin had been born on 18 April 1939 and his father was a horse-wrangler. When the creek started to rise and the snakes were coming in the house, Hardin's mother said that she was moving into town and so the family came to Meadow, Texas when Glen D. was five. He had met Buddy Holly when he was in his teens and Holly was impressed that he could ride his bicycle without holding the handlebars.

Glen D. Hardin had been raised in Meadow and had known Sonny Curtis for many years. At first, he had little time for rock'n'roll as he had wanted to see the world in the navy, enlisting in 1957 when he was 17. It was Glen D. who first called Jerry Allison "J.I.", really because Jerry was a popular name and Jerry Naylor had come into the band. Jerry Allison's grandfather, John Isaac Allison, was also a "J.I."

Bobby Vee and the Crickets were twinned for a UK tour but this time it was Allison who couldn't come as he found himself on emergency call-up because of the Cuban missile crisis. The Crickets that toured this time were Sonny Curtis (now back from the forces), Jerry Naylor and new boy, Glen D. Hardin, on piano and also a gimmicky, new Fender instrument, the piano bass. They added a British drummer from Mike Berry's Outlaws, Don Groom, the first British Cricket. He had played in Hamburg with the Wild Ones and then done session work for Joe Meek, his first hit single being John Leyton's "Son, This Is She" (1961). He worked with Mike Berry and Mike had recommended him to the Crickets. The tour went well and Naylor was a popular lead vocalist, working with a microphone on a long lead. Vee, Berry and the Crickets mixed with each other on stage. Vee and Crickets appeared on the most unlikely TV programme of all-time, *Kingsley Amis Goes Pop*, hosted by an ill-tempered writer with little time for teenage culture. Well, it worked for Ed Sullivan.

In January 1963, all four Beatles signed a letter to the Crickets thanking them for the interest shown in their work while they were in the UK: "We'd just like to say that we take this as a great compliment and appreciate it very much." In the *Melody Maker* poll for 1963, the top three vocal groups were, in order, the Four Seasons, the Beatles and the Crickets.

The Crickets made their own album for Liberty, *Something Old, Something New, Something Blue, Something Else!!!!!!* and the sleeve note told of the difficulty of getting the group together—"Jerry is stationed at March Air Force Base in Riverside, only about 75 miles from Los Angeles, so the group gets a chance to get together once in a while." The line-up, according to the notes, was Curtis, Naylor, Hardin and Allison, but Hardin, now in the navy, was missing from the group photograph. Still, for all these changes in personnel, the group was making consistently good records. The tracks included "What'd I Say", "Love Is Strange" and "Blue Monday".

The follow-up to "Don't Ever Change", was a delightful Gerry Goffin and Jack Keller song, "Little Hollywood Girl" and a Sonny Curtis song, performed by Curtis and Naylor, "Parisian Girl", inspired by his military service and which he hoped the Everly Brothers would record. The arrangement of "Parisian Girl" is very similar to Bobby Vee's "Please Don't Ask About Barbara". "Little Hollywood Girl" had been intended for Bobby Vee but the Crickets grabbed it as he was out of town.

They reverted to rock'n'roll for Sonny Curtis' "My Little Girl", which was backed by another group original, "Teardrops Fall Like Rain"., one of the shortest singles ever released as the total playing time is 3 minutes 45 seconds. "My Little Girl" was never one of Jerry's favourites: "That's just the 'Peggy Sue' lick again and I've played it a million times." However, you can easily see how Sonny Curtis' guitar parts influenced the Searchers' "Sugar And Spice".

The Crickets had a strong UK fan base, led by John Beecher, and they bombarded the BBC's request programmes especially *Saturday Club* for their records. It helped to get "My Little Girl" into the Top 20. The Crickets performed both sides of the single in the British pop film, *Just For Fun*, which starred Mark Wynter and Cherry Roland. When Jerry Allison remarked, "Sonny, Glen D. and Jerry Naylor did that movie as I was fighting against Fidel Castro at the time", Sonny Curtis added, "J.I. was guarding the USA, and I felt a lot safer for it."

John Firminger (520): "I've always been interested to see how bands continue and evolve, which was originally brought about by following the Crickets. After Buddy's death, we all thought it would be the end of the Crickets but it was great to see the band emerge and enjoy renewed success in the 60s. This success has held them in good stead through the years and contributed towards their longevity. They've also had a continuous flow of really talented people in the band and managed to record some quality music along the way. My favourite track is 'My Little Girl' which recaptures their early sound with Jerry Naylor's Hollyesque vocal whilst also demonstrating both Sonny Curtis' songwriting talents and superb Chet Atkins-like guitar picking with a more familiar 'Peggy Sue' beat."

The Crickets followed "My Little Girl" with a country ballad, "Don't Try To Change Me", a decent enough song from Sonny and Jerry but its title was too like "Don't Ever Change" to be successful. It scraped into the Top 40, and the B-side was "Lost And Alone", curiously credited to Jerry and Peggy Sue. This was followed by a Jackie DeShannon and Sharon Sheeley song, "Right Or Wrong", which was recorded by Bobby Vee on his album with the Ventures.

As the early Beatle records owed so much to the Crickets, it was no big deal for them to cover the songs but the album, *California Sun/ She Loves You*, was as clumsy as its title. There were five Beatle songs plus "Money" and they recorded "Slippin' And Slidin'", a new Sonny Curtis song, "A Fool Never Learns", which became a hit for Andy Williams, and the Beatle-like "You Can't Be In Between", which Jerry wrote with the group's new producer, James "Buzz" Cason. Jerry sometimes played a claviette: you blow it like a harmonica and it comes out like a keyboard. The best track was their rocking version of Doc Pomus' song for Ray Charles, "Lonely Avenue", now given a "Bo Diddley" beat. It could have done well but Liberty rush-released "From Me To You" as a single, which was rock'n'roll suicide. The UK B-side of "Lonely Avenue" was an early David Gates song, "Playboy".

Unlike Jerry Allison, Joe B. had not done much session work but he had toured with Johnny Burnette. One day they drove away from Oregon and noticed a terrible smell in the car. They opened the hood and found a dead cat cooking on the radiator. They assumed that some jealous boys had done it. Joe B. managed the Club Larue in Lubbock and then got into transporting lumber and grain. He remarried in 1963 and sold his interest in the Crickets to Jerry Allison, so that it was totally his group.

Joe B. Mauldin (521) had also been called up. "I thought I could get out of the services very easily. I had a letter from my doctor saying I was unfit to participate but sure enough, when I did my physical, they said, 'You're great. We've got lots of doctors here who'll take care of you.' I had to go in. I tried to make the best out of it that I could and I did have a lot fun in Germany. It was always hard to get the Crickets together. There was always somebody away or missing."

On his return to military life, Joe B. worked in publishing for the west coast office of George Pincus. He was involved with "I Saw Her Standing There", "Misery", "There's A Place", "From Me to You", "She Loves You", "I Wanna Be Your Man", "A Taste Of Honey" and "I Like It".

Buzz Cason was a versatile musician who had worked with the Statues and then had a US hit, "Look For A Star", as Gary Miles. He spent a couple of years backing Brenda Lee. He could play guitar, piano and drums and was a useful guy to have around, at first producing the Crickets and then playing with them. The Crickets had Chan Romero, the writer and original recorder of "Hippy Hippy Shake", on bass for a short while.

One of the Crickets' strangest records, and also one of their best, was their attempt at putting a Merseybeat spin with surfing lyrics on a Mexican song, together with references to "Hippy Hippy Shake" and "Twist And Shout". This was a new arrangement of Ritchie Valens' "La Bamba", devised by Jerry Allison and Buzz Cason with an arrangement from Leon Russell, and it is a rare occasion when money was spent on making a Crickets' record.

The B-side, "All Over You", was the Crickets doing Merseybeat, but doing it badly. The single made Number 21 in the UK in the summer of 1964 and was the last time that the Crickets had new material on the charts. They are introduced by Dennis Wilson of the Beach Boys and mimed to the record in the film, *The Girls On The Beach*. I don't know how well they're doing it as they can hardly be seen over the heads of the dancers. They are also backing Lesley Gore with Jerry Allison on guitar. The movie is so cheesy, you could sell it at

the deli, but as it's full of girls in bikinis, I don't want to criticise it too much.

Buzz Cason (522): "The Crickets are wonderful guys—J.I, Sonny, Joe B. and Glen—and we are still friends. We did well in England. I produced 'La Bamba' at Goldstar with Larry Levene, a sweetheart of a guy, as the engineer. I was banging on the drums and J.I. was playing guitar on that. It's the same chords as 'Twist And Shout', 1,4,5,4, and Leon Russell did the horn arrangement and is playing piano. When we kicked that song off on *Ready Steady Go!* the power went off and it was nothing but me and J.I. that you could hear for the first few bars. There wasn't a publicity machine behind the Crickets but we sure had a great time in England. My best record with the Crickets was 'Lonely Avenue' with Jerry Naylor singing lead, which was the first record I cut in California."

A UK tour with the Crickets had been arranged, but as Jerry Naylor suffered a heart attack (mostly as a result of taking drugs), Buzz Cason, wearing Holly-styled glasses, took his place. The group appeared on a big beat festival at the Royal Albert Hall and did *Ready Steady Go!* but most of the tour was low-key with venues like the Plaza at Widnes.

Buzz and Jerry also wrote "Surfin' Special", or rather adapted "Midnight Special", but it was not completed as they wanted to add more voices. They updated "My Bonnie" as "Bring Back My Surfboard". In 1964, Jerry Allison was at the Bel Air Hotel for the wedding of record executive, Lou Adler and singer/ actress, Shelley Fabares (US Number 1 with "Johnny Angel", 1962.) The all-star group at the wedding featured Sam Cooke, Johnny Rivers, Phil Everly and Jerry Allison.

Sonny Curtis was taken with Merseybeat and he released a charming album, *Beatle Hits—Flamenco Style*, and even now, he will include one of those arrangements in concert. From the sublime to the cor blimey, Sonny recorded a jokey single, "A Beatle I Want To Be". **Sonny Curtis (523)**: "I was sitting around the apartment one night, playing 'All My Loving' fingerstyle on the guitar. Snuff Garrett said, 'I like that. Let's do a whole album like that.' The next day I was in the studio so I didn't have time to arrange anything and was groping for something to play. *Beatle Hits, Flamenco Style* is a nice album though, not earth-shattering, but pretty good for what it is."

The liner notes for the album, *The Crickets—A Collection*, in the spring of 1965, said that the Crickets (Allison, Curtis, Hardin) had split up. Curtis joined the Everly Brothers, while Hardin became part of the backing band on Jack Good's US TV series, *Shindig*. Hardin was a good but occasional writer having success with "Count Me In", a million seller for Gary Lewis and the Playboys, the son of comedian Jerry Lewis.

Sonny Curtis (524) also wrote for Gary Lewis and the Playboys. In 1966, Snuff Garrett wanted a B-side for "My Heart's Symphony", which Glen D. has written: "I wrote a song called 'Tina' and it was understood that we would split this four ways, I'd get 25% and Snuff, Gary and the arranger Leon Russell would also get 25%, and Snuff would get the publishing. I did it willingly as it made good business sense. 25% of the back of a hit single could be a substantial amount of money for an afternoon's work. If the A-side sold a million copies, the song on the flip side made just as much money as you can't buy one side without the other. Of course, you don't get as much performance royalties and radio play. At the time, we're talking about a cent a record split four ways, but it was $2,500 for an afternoon's work." The single didn't quite sell a million but it did make the US Top 20.

Bob Montgomery (525): "Composers have the best deal in the industry. There are no overheads, other than a guitar and a pencil, and you can work wherever you are."

Given a few months, Jerry Naylor, now recovered, went with Jerry Allison and Buzz Cason to, of all places, Norman Petty's studio in Clovis, although Buzz Cason was producing. As Jerry Allison and the Crickets, they recorded "I Think I've Caught The Blues" and "Now Hear This", which was influenced by the Kinks. George Tomsco of the Fireballs played lead guitar, so it was good to have him on the original session for a Crickets record. This was their last session in Clovis: Norman hadn't got his name on the songs but he did manipulate publishing income by pushing songs at them including "I Think I've Got The Blues".

Back in Texas, Jerry and Peggy Sue tried to save their marriage and Jerry worked as the Crickets with three other Lubbock musicians, Larry Trider,

Doug Walding and, another friend from the past, Larry Welborn. There is a recording of them at the Panther-A-Go-Go in Fort Worth, Texas, but say no more. "I'd get some shitty gigs," Jerry recalls, "Someone would say, 'Do you want to be a Cricket for a night?' and I'd say yes. Sometimes I would be with guys I'd never worked with before. If they had a black suit and knew a few of the songs, they'd be a Cricket for a night." By then, Jerry and Peggy Sue's marriage was as precarious as the group, and both fell apart. Jerry went on the road, playing drums for Roger Miller for two years. Jerry found it simple work, but thought Roger Miller was a very funny guy, both on and off stage.

Allison moved to the west coast and managed Elf Records, which was owned by Buzz Cason and Bobby Russell. In1968, he did a spell with the Everly Brothers and met his second wife, Joanie, while they were working in Florida. He is on the Everlys' evocative recording, "Lord Of The Manor". He worked with Lee Dresser and is on his albums, *El Camino Real* and *To Touch The Wind*, the latter with Albert Lee.

In 1968, Sonny Curtis, Jerry Allison and Glen D. Hardin got back together for a single, "Million Dollar Movie" and "A Million Miles Apart", but because Sonny had a solo contract with Viva Records, which was owned by Snuff Garrett, Glen D. sang the lead vocals. Sonny's vocals wouldn't have saved such dreary songs, and there is a clicking percussive effect throughout "A Million Miles Apart" that is especially annoying. The label, Music Factory, went bankrupt a week after the single's release.

Undaunted, the Crickets accepted UK dates, but the tour had to be delayed as the hapless Allison was on the reserve list for Vietnam. Jerry, Sonny and Glen D. played 12 dates including five different venues in Manchester. Both Jerry and Sonny were wearing hippie shirts and beads, a little inappropriate as both were balding, and during "Don't Ever Change" at Manchester's New Century Hall, Glen D. lost his way and Sonny said, "Don't worry, catch us up in the middle eight." The promoter, Roy Tempest, failed to capitalise on the rock'n'roll revival as both "Peggy Sue" and Bill Haley's "Rock Around The Clock" had returned to the charts. The rockabilly movement had collected new young fans, who were fed up with synthesiser pop. There were few original practitioners of the double-bass around and Joe B., and hence the Crickets, should have tapped into this.

Back in Los Angeles in 1970, Jerry and Sonny supplied backing vocals on Eric Clapton's first solo album, *Eric Clapton*, and they were on albums by the likes of Delaney and Bonnie, Leon Russell, Billy Preston and Johnny Rivers. In 1971, Jerry, Sonny and Glen D. got together with Delaney Bramlett for a Crickets album for Andy Williams' label, Barnaby. Williams hated doing old material himself, but that was all he wanted from the Crickets and the result was disappointing, as ill conceived as its title, *Rockin' 50s, Rock'n'Roll*. They reworked their 50s hits, but the title track was original. Sonny Curtis knew that he was more suited to mellow material, ballads and country songs, and the best track is his version of "True Love Ways". Although uncredited, Eric Clapton played lead guitar on the title track and "That'll Be The Day".

In 1972, the Crickets returned to the UK with Richard Roman Grech, better known as Rick Grech, who was born in Bordeaux on 1 November 1945. He had been in Family, Blind Faith and Traffic and Rick had been brought into the Crickets by Glen D. after they had met on some recording sessions for Gram Parsons. Rick knew about playing rock'n'roll as he had been on Chuck Berry's *London Sessions* (uncredited) and would appear on Jerry Lee's. He joined the Crickets on bass, but he was a player used to huge Marshall speakers. The chicken-in-a-basket tour must have been a culture shock but he loved playing solid rock'n'roll. The Crickets promoted their new Phonogram single, a Kenny O'Dell song, "My Rockin' Days" and a revival of Hank Williams' "Lovesick Blues".

The Crickets completed a new album in the UK, *Bubblegum, Bop, Ballad And Boogies*, which was produced by Bob Montgomery, and Pete Townshend played lead guitar on the Dennis Linde song, "Can I Make You Feel It". Even though it had echoes of the *Something Old* LP, the title was ridiculous—who wants bubblegum from the Crickets?—the pop-art cover looked silly and the photographs on the back were appalling, possibly the darkest publicity shots ever taken. The packaging was a disgrace but the music wasn't

bad with a strong version of Tony Joe White's "I've Got A Thing About You Baby" and Sonny Curtis writing two good songs, "Destiny's Child" and that favourite Crickets theme of being on the road, "Day Gig".

Bob Montgomery (526): "That was a fun project. We did it in London and Albert Lee was with them. They live close to me in Nashville and so we are often in touch. I loved the album that I did with Buddy Knox. I loved his voice. I thought he had one of the most pleasant, listenable voices in the whole world."

"Hayride", a catchy Buzz Cason song which had been recorded by Gary Lewis and the Playboys, was released as a single. Maybe that's the reason for *Bubblegum* in the album's title. There's too much echo on "Rockin' Pneumonia And The Boogie Woogie Flu", but the old-time revival of "Lovesick Blues" is excellent. There's a wistful, romantic song, "Wasn't It Nice In New York City" and a funky J.J. Cale composition, "Outside Looking In". On the whole, though, the album was bland. There is a comment on the sleeve, "The Crickets appeared through the courtesy of the Middlesbrough Constabulary".

During their time in the UK, the Crickets met up with the lightning fingered guitarist from Heads, Hands And Feet, Albert Lee, and so the Crickets, for the first time ever, were a five piece. However, the line-up returned to four as Glen D. Hardin's principal job, working with Elvis Presley, took precedence.

Hardin worked for Presley from February 1970 until the end of 1975. Among his arrangements were "The Wonder Of You", "American Trilogy" and "Burning Love". He also arranged Kenny Rogers and the First Edition's "Ruby, Don't Bring Your Love To Town". He was with Emmylou Harris's band from November 1974 and he decided to go on the road with her and subsequently left Presley, but at one stage he was in three bands at once—Emmylou's, Elvis' and the Crickets. His piano playing is showcased on Emmylou's "Together Again".

The Crickets secured a contract to make a new album in Nashville for Mercury Records with Bob Montgomery producing. This became *A Long Way From Lubbock,* which with slightly different tracks was called *Remnants* (hardly an inviting title) in the US. One track, "Rhyme And Time", featured Albert Lee and had Rick on violin. Grech's friend, Gram Parsons, asked about taking part, but this was turned down, although they did record his song, "Ooh Las Vegas". The sessions might have saved his life as he died of a drug overdose at Joshua Tree.

Albert Lee (527): "Buddy Holly had given Sonny Curtis one of his jackets. I was at his parents' house and I don't think his mother was very pleased about it. She'd been looking after the jacket for years and all of a sudden, this stranger walks in and Sonny gives him the jacket. It's a real cool jacket and I'm very pleased to have it. In the breast pocket is a piece of a serviette with a 'phone number or a car number on. I feel very fortunate in having things like this. I have been given a number of wonderful things over the years and I feel like the custodian. I don't feel that they are mine to do with as I like."

In 1973 Jerry Allison wrote a country hit for Del Reeves, "Trucker's Paradise". The Crickets played UK dates in 1974 and then Albert Lee left to work with Joe Cocker and Rick Grech to work with Johnny Rivers. As there were upcoming gigs, Sonny and Jerry completed the tour with Steve Krikorian, who had been writing songs for them and is now the rock artist, Tonio K.

In the mid-60s, Stan Ross had asked Joe B. Mauldin if he wanted to be a recording engineer and he spent three years at the Gold Star studio. He worked on albums by Leon Russell and Herb Alpert, and helped Phil Spector with the backing tracks for John Lennon's rock'n'roll album. A proposed vocal album with James Burton was cancelled but he spent a long time sifting through the concert tapes for a live album from the Association. He became involved in music publishing and he wrote "A Prophecy Of Love" for the Midnight String Quartet. Joe B. rarely performed but he kept his double-bass in a wardrobe and brought it out for Paul McCartney's Buddy Holly week. Then he moved to Nashville and opened a studio with Bobby Russell, who wrote "Honey" and "Little Green Apples", called Malrus. They recorded the music tracks for the first 26 episodes of *The Dukes Of Hazzard* including the title song by Waylon Jennings.

In 1976, both Sonny and Jerry bought farms outside Nashville, and they were reunited with

Joe B. who had moved there from California. They decided to reform for a concert at the Kilburn Gaumont for the second Buddy Holly Week in 1977. John Beecher produced a single for his Rollercoaster label, "Cruise In It"/ "Rock Around With Ollie Vee" (amazing how often this song crops up and it was easily the better side.). "Cruise In It" is about Jerry's model Studebaker from the 50s and they cruised in it to the Hi-D-Ho and McKenzie Park: "It ain't brand new but it was owned by an undertaker." The song included references to the drag racing and to Peggy Sue.

In 1978, Waylon Jennings, now at the helm of outlaw country, invited his three old friends to join him on tour. They loved playing with Waylon as they had large audiences and after years of guest houses and cheap hotels, they liked his philosophy, "If you can't go first class, don't go." For once, Jerry didn't haul his own drums around. The Crickets worked as Waylon's opening act for five years, and they recorded a medley of hits with him for the album, *I've Always Been Crazy*. When Waylon's lifestyle got the better of him, the Crickets returned to weekend gigs.

Duane Eddy produced some further tracks of Waylon with the Crickets and they include "Lady Of The Harbour" and "That'll Be The Day". What would Buddy think of Waylon as a country superstar? Jerry Allison says, "I told you so." Waylon, in some ways, is a continuation of Buddy Holly as a lot of that hard rhythm comes from Holly.

Jerry Allison (528): "I loved Waylon Jennings, he was a good ol'boy and he would never lie to you. Whatever he said was good. Waylon was a long time in cutting 'Lady In The Harbour', which I wrote with Sonny Curtis. We wrote him a letter one time to remind of the song, and he told us that he was going to cut the letter too. He did the song on a Waylon and Willie album, which was fine by us."

In 1985, Sonny Curtis left the group to further his solo career and he was replaced by Gordon Payne, an excellent musician from Tulsa, Oklahoma with a high-pitched singing voice who had been part of Waylon Jennings' band. He had sat in with them when they were with Waylon and he had called himself "an auxiliary roach". The new Crickets returned to rock'n'roll with an album of new songs for Roller Coaster, *Three Piece*, in

1978. The cover photograph implied that the group was a joke with Jerry apparently sharing the same tailor as George Melly. On the title track, Gordon Payne sang: "We cut it back to a three piece, Overheads down and money's increased."

And would Glen D. ever play with them again: "No piano player bangin' on the keys, Play what you want in a three piece."

Jerry Allison (529): "There are lots of advantages in being a three piece: you don't have to split the money so many ways, for starters. You can all fit into one car or one train compartment."

Joe B. was given solo vocals. He supplied the bass voice for "Summertime Blues" and sang a verse of "Brown-Eyed Handsome Man". In 1991, he sang a complete vocal on "Last Night".

In 1986, the first ten entrants were named for the Rock And Roll Hall Of Fame. Their suitability depended upon your definition of rock'n'roll and although it was good to see Buddy Holly there, it was mean-spirited not to induct the Crickets at the same time.

The Crickets agreed to record the winning song in the songwriting contest for Buddy Holly Week in 1987. This was no hardship as the winning entry was a very witty song written by a publican, Jim Imray's "T-Shirt". They recorded it at Paul McCartney's studio in Sussex and Paul producing, playing piano and singing backing vocals. As well as an album track, "T-Shirt" was released on 7 inch and 12 inch singles and, although it wasn't a hit, it could have been. There was talk of Paul producing a whole album for them but he was too busy: the Crickets told him that they could wait but it hasn't happened. Yet.

The album, *T-Shirt*, was released in 1988 (their first CD!), but, apart from the title track, the rest of the tracks had been *Three Piece*. It was good material, mostly of a country bent. Gordon Payne does very well on the love song, "The Weekend", written by Randy Sharp. There is a punning song written by Jerry Allison that was called "Mulholland Drive" on *Three Piece* and "Holly Would" on *T-Shirt*. It has also been recorded by Christine Lakeland (J.J. Cale's partner) as "Billy Mulholland".

John Firminger (530): "'Forever In Mind' is a superb track, which features Gordon Payne, who played a major role in the band's continuance, both as a performer and songwriter. This track

demonstrates the band's versatility and superb choice in material."

Starting in the late 70s, Sonny Curtis made three solo albums in quick succession: *Sonny Curtis* (1979), *Love is All Around* (1980) and *Rollin'* (1981). There was a 1979 single on Elektra of "The Real Buddy Holly Story" and on the second LP, he included the full version of "Walk Right Back" as well as a song for his daughter, "It's Not Easy Being Fifteen". After a gap of some years, there was *Spectrum* (1987), a live cassette, *Ready, Able And Willing* (1988) and *No Stranger To The Rain* (1990).

Sonny Curtis (531): "I have a real good friend who is a producer at Capitol Records and when we needed a couple of tracks to finish off an album, he suggested 'True Love Ways'. We used a mandolin and a marimba, and a gut-string classical guitar as well. It turned out real well."

Sonny wrote the theme for *The Mary Tyler Moore Show*, "Love Is All Around" and the Country Music Association's song of the year in 1989, "I'm No Stranger To The Rain", which was a hit for Keith Whitley. "Walk Right Back" is a standard, topping the charts for the Everly Brothers and being recorded by Perry Como and Anne Murray, and so in its own way is "I Fought The Law" (Bobby Fuller Four, the Clash, Roy Orbison, Hank Williams Jr, and Green Day on *Superbowl*). Bing Crosby recorded "The Straight Life" and Shakin' Stevens has sung "Rock Around With Ollie Vee". His other songs include "Why Did You Say I Do To Me (When You Still Meant To Do It With Him)" for John Schneider and "Party Of The First Part" (Tammy Wynette, Bobby Bare). Sonny played on some of the LPs in the series, *The 50 Guitars Of Tommy Garrett* (Snuff, naturally) albums, and he wrote a lyric for one of the tunes, "Gypsy Man", then recorded by J.J. Cale.

There is so much mix and matching in the Crickets' story. **Bob Montgomery (532)** has produced Waylon Jennings. "One album that I love was with Waylon and Willie, *Clean Shirt*, in 1991—it didn't do much commercially but it was a really good album. Merle Haggard is probably the greatest country singer who has ever lived. He is just incredible. Unfortunately, the album that I got to do with him was a live album. I didn't have much input into it. It was an okay album but not one of Merle's best."

Just as Sonny wrote "Walk Right Back", **Bob Montgomery (533)** has written a classic standard, "Misty Blue". "If you have a really good title, the song writes itself and it leads you where you need to go. I usually know when I've got a good song, but it is amazing when a song like 'Misty Blue' proves to have a life of its own. I've written other songs that I have liked as much but for some reason the public hasn't latched onto them. The trick really is to tell the story in a few words. Some of the huge copyrights don't use a lot of words. There aren't many words in 'White Christmas' and I could draw up a very long list of songs like that."

In 1990, the Crickets released an EP, *Back Home In Tennessee*, on Rollercoaster. The lead song was "Blackmail", written by Gordon Payne, an excellent track very much in the tradition of Tony Joe White.

The *T-Shirt* album was followed in 1993 by another Rollercoaster album, *Double Exposure,* which featured new versions of 20 of their hits, both with and without Holly. The three piece had some guest musicians including Sonny Curtis, Glen D. Hardin and, on sax for "True Love Ways", Bobby Keys. It was recorded in Jerry Allison's Branch Studio at his home in Lyles, Tennessee, and the small combo arrangements of "It Doesn't Matter Anymore" and "True Love Ways" work very much. Gordon Payne then left because he needed a more regular income as the Crickets only worked sporadically in the States.

In 1996, the Crickets made a new record in Nashville, *Too Much Monday Morning*, an excellent but restrained album with a nondescript cover. It was produced by Stuart Colman, known for his work with Shakin' Stevens and Cliff Richard. This time it was Jerry, Sonny, Joe B. and Glen D. with some guest musicians including Nanci Griffith on the playful "Do You Wanna Be Loved" and the accordion player, Fats Kaplan. There were new songs from the band as well as Billy Swan's "Betty Sue's Still Breaking Jimmy Lee's Heart" with its evocative feel of southern life and Paul Kennerley's Buddy Holly-fashioned "Letter Of Love". Sonny and Jerry's "I Gotta Pass" opens with "When I get enough Texaco to get me to Mexico."

Ian Higham (534): "Following Buddy's demise, the Crickets were blessed with some great sing-ers, all having different styles yet still turning out memorable material. Of these, 'Don't Cha Know' (David Box), 'A Sweet Love' (Earl Sinks) and 'Lonely Avenue' (Jerry Naylor) rate highly with me. Even as late as 1997 on the *Too Much Monday Morning* album, there is a wonderful track 'Letter Of Love' featuring J.I. on lead vocal."

Mike Jones (535): "It was a great thrill, almost forty years later, to see the Crickets at the Cavern. I could sing every word of every song, so memorable are his lyrics and melodies. This raises a question about 'memorability' and music: pop is still often dismissed for being trivial and, of course, nursery rhymes are easy to remember, but what struck me about Holly's songs that night was how contemporary they sounded—not like museum pieces but so essential to the very fabric of pop music itself that they sounded as if they had been written *that day*. He was a great writer and I marvel at how someone so young could have produced music that has lasted so effortlessly."

Jerry Naylor was working for several years on a *Rockbilly Legends* project and, in 2005, it was eventually completed—the full package consisting of a beautifully designed, full colour, hardback book, with a one hour DVD; one 3½ hour DVD; four CDs of new performances featuring Jerry Naylor and Carl Perkins's son, Carl Stanley Perkins; eight CDs of vintage tracks; a CD of archive interviews; and a CD of performances on *Louisiana Hayride*. Its scope is impressive and the new performances are very good, but the book is let down by some elementary mistakes (Gene Vincent never appeared in a movie called *Woman Love*) and unclear definition: just what is rockabilly? Some obvious names are omitted, while others are in, clearly because Jerry Naylor knew them. The tribute CD to Carl Perkins is especially recommended as it contains an acoustic performance of "Blue Suede Shoes" with Carl Perkins telling how it came about, plus Carl performing his tribute to Bill Monroe, "Mr Bill".

In 2005, Mike Berry and the Crickets recorded an album, *About Time Too!*, at Jerry Allison's studio, which was produced by Chas Hodges, formerly one of Mike Berry's Outlaws. It was released on Rollercoaster with its usual, superb packaging. The album mixed rock'n'roll with pub singalong, as might be expected from Hodges.

With a couple of exceptions, the album concentrated on lesser-known songs from rockabilly and rock'n'roll artists such as Jerry Lee Lewis's "I'm Feeling Sorry", Bobby Darin's "Bullmoose" and Buddy Holly's "I'm Gonna Set My Foot Down". Entering Jimmy Buffett territory, the Mexican song, "Cozumel", was excellent. There is the two verse version of "Walk Right Back", a solo "Don't Think Twice, It's All Right" from Sonny Curtis, and Jerry Allison on "Summertime Blues". But why is Mike playing Don Everly's acoustic guitar? Where was Don Everly?

This led to a spin-off album by Chas Hodges and Jerry Allison as Chas & J.I. and called *Before We Grow Too Old*, released in 2007. The only other musician on the session was Jack Clement on dobro: he'd been Jerry Lee Lewis and Johnny Cash's producer at Sun Records. Chas wrote additional lyrics to Billy Swan's "Lover Please" and to Laurel and Hardy's "Honolulu Baby". It's a good-time album and its lack of quality is part of its charm. "Tell Me How" sounds like two old boozers on a night out. They give "Tell Me How" a New Orleans feel and the title track is associated with Fats Domino. When J.I. suggested that they did the Clovers' "One Mint Julep", he brought out his original 45: it had "13" on it to show that it was 13th record he had ever bought.

For some time, the Crickets were working on tracks with celebrity guests including Paul McCartney, but contractual problems kept delaying the album's release. It came out, *sans* Paul McCartney, as *The Crickets And Their Buddies*, in 2004, and "Heartbeat" with Nanci Griffith was issued as a single. This was produced by Greg Ladanyi, who had a Norman Petty approach to recording: as long as it takes. The Crickets for this project were Jerry, Sonny, Joe B., Glen D. and Albert Lee. While testing the microphones, Albert Lee did a slow, haunting "Learning The Game" on piano, which led to its inclusion on the album.

The CD is a mixed bag but it hits far more often than it misses and the only disaster is a terrible version of "I Fought The Law" with a rasping vocal from Vince Neil of Mötley Crüe. How did this guy get a recording contract? He makes John Prine sound like a schoolboy. Even then, you could argue that it was valid, that he sounds like someone who has fought the law.

In 1974, Eric Clapton had considered making an album with the working title, *Buddy's B-sides*. It never materialised but it indicated that he recognised the depth of his work and he did perform "It's Too Late" on stage with Derek and the Dominoes. When this project was mooted, he suggested "Someone" and Jerry at first thought he meant "I'm Lookin' For Someone To Love": he was surprised when it turned out to be "Someone, Someone", the B-side of "Love's Made A Fool Of You". It is an excellent version which brings out the quality of the song.

Phil Everly and his son, Jason, whip their way through "Rave On". They sound good together but the track is too hurried, reminding me of the Everlys' shows in the 1960s. On the other hand, there is a delightful version of "Blue Days—Black Nights" with Bobby Vee, recorded at Jerry Allison's studio, where Jerry sat outside with the cows, banging his cardboard box.

The other guests are Rodney Crowell ("That'll Be The Day"), Tonio K. ("Not Fade Away"), J.D. Souther ("Everyday"), Waylon Jennings ("Well…All Right"), Graham Nash ("Think It Over") and Johnny Rivers ("Love's Made A Fool Of You"). The Crickets promoted the album by appearing with Brian May and Ronnie Wood at Wembley Arena at a charity concert to celebrate the 50th anniversary of the Fender Stratocaster. They returned later for a short tour with Nanci Griffith. On most of their visits to the UK, the Crickets have included a charity performance in Southport for osteoporosis.

Joe B Mauldin (536): "Our music is fun. We have fun playing the tunes and the audiences enjoy hearing them. It's easy for us to play them and we do them like the original recordings as that's what people want to hear. It's a shame that Buddy's not with us but he's here in spirit. We were very lucky to have him for a lead singer."

Jerry Allison (537): "We don't have to play the old songs but we like to do it. We enjoy playing them and it is what people want to hear and what we get paid for. We like those songs and we could play them a million times if we had to. We don't have to force ourselves to play them and we can still improve on them. The tighter we get, the better we like it. I suppose I'm trying to recapture my youth, but is there a better way?"

14

NOW AND FOREVER TILL THE END OF TIME

"The music you'll love forever—the man you'll never forget." (Strapline for The Buddy Holly Story)

Those Who Really Care

Record Mirror journalist, **Norman Jopling (538)** speaks for millions, including myself, when he says: "The music of Buddy Holly was imprinted on me so deeply during my adolescent years that, even now, hearing his familiar unique voice with its youthful confidence and great artistry gives me a lift and touches my heart."

But it's more than nostalgia. Bob Dylan said, "The singers and musicians I grew up with transcend nostalgia—Buddy Holly and Johnny Ace are just as valid to me today as then." Dylan was being as mysterious as ever. Why didn't he say Buddy Holly and Chuck Berry or Buddy Holly and Little Richard? Why instead did he bracket Buddy with a relatively unknown performer, Johnny Ace, who had little effect on the generation that followed? Most likely, Johnny Ace came to mind as another singer who had died early, in his case, at the age of 25 on Christmas Day, 1954 and probably as a result of playing Russian Roulette with his girlfriend. There has been talk that it was a Mob killing, made to look like an accident. Good subject for a book, providing you don't want to go on living.

Buddy Holly's, though, was the first rock'n'roll death, a death that echoed that of another teenage star, 24-year-old James Dean, in 1955, the rebel without a cause. Buddy Holly, in contrast, was a rebel with a cause. He was committed to his music and determined not to rest on his laurels and be as innovative as possible in conjunction with a punishing work schedule. A major act today works a three year cycle: a year making an album, a year touring on the back of it, and a year's holiday to spend the proceeds. Buddy Holly, like a bagatelle ball, was ricocheting from one location to another and because he was based in Lubbock, he was travelling much more than a star from New York.

Michael Lydon (539): "Buddy Holly was the first singer-songwriter. It's hard to remember now, after decades in which rock'n'roll music has been recognised as a legitimate art form, that in the 1950s even its fans didn't take it seriously. Early rockers were considered to be all body and no brains, musical slobs with slamming drums and crude guitar riffs. Everybody loved Chuck Berry songs, but no one thought of him as a 'lyricist'. White middle class kids did not consider rock'n'roll a possible career choice--it was something that was fun but stupid, something for the teen years only. Buddy Holly changed all that. Holly was a highly intelligent kid, bursting with musical talent, who saw that rock'n'roll could be truly good music. He listened to everything with open ears, and from all the sounds of early rock-- the Everly Brothers, Bo Diddley, Ray Charles, Little Richard-- he put together his own sound, clear and strong enough to be heard through the electric din of 50s pop music."

Tommy James (540): "I was struck by the first generation of rock'n'rollers—Buddy Holly, Elvis and Eddie Cochran. They broke the ice. I was playing a ukulele at that point which my grandfather had given me. I was 9 when I saw Elvis on television for the first time, and I knew I had to get a guitar. I got an acoustic guitar for $17 and I began by playing along with whatever I heard on the radio and then two years later, I got an electric guitar. I was picking up things from Gene Vincent and Buddy Holly and I was copying everything I could do. I had my first band when I was 12. We played any place that would have us, VFW halls and American Legions and YWCAs and so forth. It seemed then that being a rock'n'roller was a job opportunity. You could consider doing it after graduation, and I did."

We can say that Buddy Holly created a series of firsts, although most of them need qualification— the first singer/ songwriter of the rock'n'roll era (what about Chuck Berry, Carl Perkins, Charlie Gracie, Buddy Knox?), the first to have the lead/ rhythm / bass/ drums line-up (Buddy Knox again, and Buddy's outfit was soon reduced to a three piece), the first to use studio trickery such as double-tracking (Les Paul), the first to have strings on a rock'n'roll record (okay), the first to use the Fender Stratocaster (Carl Perkins, who switched to Gibson: Paul Burlison from Johnny Burnette's group used a Fender Telecaster) and the first rock'n'roll star to wear glasses (Bo Diddley plus others like jazz pianist Dave Brubeck and TV host Steve Allen all did their bit for Specs-Lib). Not that this retro-gazing means much—by general acknowledgment, Bill Haley and his Comets made the first rock'n'roll record—certainly the first truly successful one—but what Haley

did was totally surpassed by Elvis Presley a few months later and the poor bloke was bin-bagged. Does it even matter that Buddy Holly was the first geek star? Well, Bill Haley, Bo Diddley and Gene Vincent hardly traded on their looks, and really in that department, it was really Elvis versus everybody else.

Justin Hayward (541): "In the fifties the BBC rarely played 'pop' music, records were the only way to hear it, if you could find someone with a record player! Most of us carried our 45s and 78s around to parties looking for a Dansette or a radiogram, as the posh ones were called, because we all had records, but few families could afford a player. Our records were our whole lives, and Buddy's are still my favourites. At the time of course, Elvis was the King, but Buddy was the one who really did play the guitar on the records, who wrote his own brilliant songs and sang within a great group. He didn't pose out front as he didn't have to, and for me he was the true Number 1. He showed us all the way, and when he was taken so early there was a chill emptiness in our lives that was only warmed eventually by the arrival of the Beatles. He made the world a better place."

Harvey Andrews (542): "In 18 months, Buddy Holly achieved an incredible amount. One or two of his songs are like root songs, like contemporary folk songs. You could walk into a folk club now and do a floor spot with them. He was writing songs that worked with just an acoustic guitar. You put together Buddy Holly and Woody Guthrie and you've got Bob Dylan. The tree grows."

Billy Bragg (543): "Buddy Holly is the original singer/songwriter. The things that he was doing in the 50s laid the groundwork for people writing their own songs. He showed that white guys with specs could make great rock'n'roll music. He was a huge inspiration to the Beatles and a lot of the early British bands. It does seem to me travelling around the world that it was the Brits who really got Buddy Holly. The Americans don't hold him in such reverence. They just see him as one among many."

Perhaps Buddy should be acknowledged as rock'n'roll's first great all-rounder, the Ian Botham of rock'n'roll. He should be recognised for all his talents: singer, songwriter, instrumentalist, bandleader, arranger and producer and he could perform ballads, country and rock'n'roll with a winning personality—and he was good at everything. No other rock'n'roll star possessed all these attributes, although Eddie Cochran was coming up fast. Chuck Berry ticked most of the boxes but he possessed no team spirit.

Tim Whitnall (544): "Any artist who was that talented has three or four sections to their career: in his case, the Nashville stuff, the Petty recordings, the orchestral tracks, and the songs that he recorded alone in his apartment. Like Eddie Cochran, he'd been using strings and sounding glossier, and maybe they were realising that they would have to reinvent their careers to stay on top. It would be interesting to know what Buddy Holly would have done with Rick Rubin, you know, just a man and his guitar and an odd instrument or two. Buddy would have done it brilliantly, I'm sure. His voice and his song would have carried it as those *Apartment Tapes* are fantastic."

Tommy Allsup (545): "Buddy Holly had more ideas that anyone I've ever known. He would have remained a big star and I could see him living in England. He liked the people very much."

Richard Hawley (546): "When I was a kid, Buddy Holly and the Crickets' music was always around the house, either via the records or my Mum and Dad playing the songs. I learned a lot about guitar playing from listening intently to those records—'Mailman Bring Me No More Blues', 'Words Of Love', 'Crying Waiting Hoping' and 'Blue Days—Black Nights' were some of the first songs and guitar riffs that I ever learned to play. His music had, and still has, a magical hold on me: he covered so much ground in such a crazily short space of time. He was a huge influence on every songwriter of his day and many after including Lennon and McCartney and Joe Meek, and I humbly submit myself in amongst those lofty ranks influenced directly by Buddy. When I was a young lad wanting to learn how to write, record and produce my own music, he was a light in the dark for me because he did all of those things and more."

Glenn Skelhorn (547): "As a kid, the early-80s *Arena* documentary and *The Buddy Holly Story* got me hooked on Buddy Holly. I memorised his greatest hits, listening to the *Buddy Holly Lives* collection on loop in the family car. I can still

remember the running order and become a little annoyed when I hear a Holly song now and it's not followed by what's supposed to come next. The simplicity of songs like 'Oh Boy!', which, against all odds, defy embarrassment, and the gripping sense of personal emotion invoked, sometimes naïve but always sincere, in luscious tracks like 'True Love Ways', struck a chord with me. That and his ability to play out-and-out rock'n'roll backed by a killer rhythm section with balls that belied his gawky exterior: I can never resist the hillbilly-punk rocker, 'Rave On'."

Maria Elena might disagree, but the one thing that Buddy couldn't be was sexy. Both he and Elvis play with their voices on "Baby I Don't Care", but Elvis sounds provocative while Buddy is childlike and playful. What girl could have resisted Elvis' pleas on "Don't", but Buddy singing the same song would have been comical. However, even this worked in Buddy's favour. It may be subconscious but one reason why he has so many male fans is because he is asexual and unthreatening. Male anxiety is a regular theme of his songs—for example, "Maybe Baby" and "Learning The Game".

Paul Hipp (548): "Buddy was one of the first guys to write his songs and play lead guitar. They still speak to people today because he wrote about human emotions and they never change. The world changes but his songs don't."

Richard Hawley (549): "My kids enjoy the music just as much as I do and I am sure something in that music will appeal to the human race forever because its subject matter and delivery is so soulful. It's something we all need to help us along."

Buddy Holly was a maverick in the best sense of the word—an independent minded person who knew how to get others on his side.

Michael Lydon (550): "Buddy Holly was something new, a white kid who knew he was an artist who borrowed from everybody but who, like all true artists, transformed what he borrowed into a unique, and uniquely appealing, style. His independent stance, the freedom with which he picked up colours and themes and sounds from other artists, his brainy approach to music making—we've seen these qualities again and again in the Beatles, Bob Dylan, Van Morrison, Elvis Costello, Billy Joel, Bruce Springsteen and so many more."

Glenn Skelhorn (551): "I wonder what would have become if Buddy had lived through the 60s—some no doubt reckon he'd have been swept aside by more progressive artists. I prefer to imagine that the seeds of his own rebellious originality would have bore all kinds of weird and wonderful fruit, feeding off the Beatles and Jimi Hendrix *et al*. Alas, it wasn't to be, but it's lucky that we're left with the music he did record, which constitute the finest slices of pop music you're ever likely to hear."

Peter Carlin (552): "Buddy Holly was only 22 when he died. He would not be sophisticated when he died: who is at 22 and so where would he have gone? Holly had just gotten married and so his relationships were becoming more complex. Romance isn't a fantasy but a real day-to-day thing. Who knows how that would have affected his work? He could have been doing something completely different in even four months' time. Look at Brian Wilson. His abstract songs about

girls are the happiest—'California Girls' is just saying what could be better than a chick in a bathing suit? When he got to know girls well, it fell to pieces. 'Caroline No' and 'Wendy' are tragic and tormented."

Joe Mauldin (553): "Buddy would have gone on and on because he was such a creative person. He was very sure of himself and when he made his mind up to do something, he did it, never mind about the expense."

Maria Elena Holly (554): "I am so happy that people still want to listen to his music and remember him. He would be glad that this has happened. Buddy was so versatile and his music made people happy, and no two songs are alike either. As fast as I met him, I lost him too but his fans have kept his music alive. I think of him as gone but people are remembering him all the time. He is still around for me. That's my consolation."

Phil Everly (555): "From time to time, I see girls wearing Buddy Holly T-shirts. Buddy would have loved that sort of notoriety."

What If...

(1) Buddy makes an album with Ray Charles. Buddy loved Ray Charles, but, according to his autobiography, Ray wasn't impressed by rock'n'roll. The album is on Charles' terms and has a bluesy feel, but includes "That Makes It Tough". It is a rare recording collaboration between a black and a white artist. Holly's career is nearly destroyed through mass burnings of his records in the South. The Klan tell him, "This year the record, next year you."

(2) Buddy gives up touring after his friend Eddie Cochran is killed while touring in England. He records a song about it, "The Day The Music Died";

"April showers make me shiver,
And as I stare into the river,
I can't remember if I cried,
The day the music died"

—but he knows it doesn't quite sound right.

(3) In 1960, Buddy Holly opens his new recording complex in Lubbock, but he records too many old friends who have no chance of selling records and he is soon declared bankrupt.

(4) Bob Dylan befriends Buddy, who helps him on his first album when they duet "Pretty Peggy-O", the third song in the "Peggy Sue" trilogy. Buddy becomes immersed in the folk music played in coffee-houses in Greenwich Village and later they record an album of oldies, *Self Portraits*. Dylan's *Lubbock Skyline* is recorded at Buddy's home studio and includes a duet of "Midnight Shift".

(5) Buddy's career gets a welcome boost with the advent of the Beatles and he opens for them at Shea Stadium. John Lennon says, "Everyone forgets the white guys who created rock'n'roll."

(6) His rock'n'roll days over, Buddy follows Conway Twitty, Carl Perkins, Jerry Lee Lewis and Rick Nelson into country music. He grows long hair and wears a bandana and some guy called Willie thinks, "That's a good idea." Eventually, his country music friends play tribute with an album, *notfadeaway*.

(7) Fans start a "Buddy Holly Is Dead" campaign and claim that he died in a plane crash on 3rd February 1959. Among the clues: his biggest single was "That'll Be The Day When I Die", he recorded "Not Fade Away", and the single before his "death" was "It Doesn't Matter Anymore". A splinter group says that Buddy Holly was so disfigured by the crash that a wannabe has taken his place, is singing his songs and has fallen in love with his "widow": Andrew Lloyd Webber gets an idea for a musical.

(8) Buddy Holly sues Norman Petty for songwriting royalties and demands the correct songwriting credits on his records. He becomes interested in music publishing. Years later, a wealthy man, he buys Paul McCartney's catalogue. Every September, he holds a Paul McCartney week in Lubbock.

(9) Holly forms a new company, Tex-Specs, which favours spectacles over the new contact lenses. Hank Marvin, John Lennon, Elvis Costello and Jarvis Cocker are recruited to follow Holly's example.

(10) Buddy Holly, Ritchie Valens and the Big Bopper reunite for a 50th anniversary tour, playing the same itinerary as the famed *Winter Dance Party*. On 2 February 2009, they play the Surf Ballroom in Clear Lake. The snow is snowing and the coach is cold, so they decide to take a plane to the next gig…

And if only the pilot in 1959 had said, "I'm sorry, guys, the weather's awful and I'm not qualified to fly in these conditions."

15

Appendices

BUDDY HOLLY AND THE CRICKETS
U.K. DISCOGRAPHY

The licensing of the hit singles in particular has been so widespread that a full discography would be a book in itself. This discography concerns itself with the first appearance of each of Buddy's recorded performances in the UK, and other significant releases.

Following Holly's death, titles originally under the Crickets' name have frequently been issued under Buddy Holly's.

Chart placings are from *Guinness Book Of British Hit Singles And Albums*.

Singles

Blue Days—Black Nights/ Love Me (Brunswick 0.5581, 45/78rpm, 1956)
The 45 is rare and mint copies are worth around £800.

That'll Be The Day/ I'm Lookin' For Someone To Love (Crickets, Vogue Coral Q 72279, 45/78rpm, 1957, No 1: soon reissued under Coral imprint.)

Peggy Sue/ Everyday (Vogue Coral Q 72293, 45/78rpm, 1957, No 6; quickly reissued under Coral imprint.)

Oh Boy!/ Not Fade Away (Crickets, Coral Q 72298, 45/78rpm, 1958, No 3)

Listen To Me/ I'm Gonna Love You Too (Coral Q 72288, 45/78rpm, 1958, No 16)

Maybe Baby/ Tell Me How (Crickets, Coral Q 72307, 45/78rpm, 1958, No 4)

Rave On/ Take Your Time (Coral Q 72325, 45/78rpm, 1958, No 5)

Think It Over/ Fool's Paradise (Crickets, Coral Q 72329, 45/78rpm, 1958, No 11)

Early In The Morning/ Now We're One (Coral Q 72333, 45/78rpm, 1958, No 17)

Real Wild Child/ Oh, You Beautiful Doll (Jerry Allison as Ivan, Coral Q 72341, 45/78rpm, 1958)

It's So Easy/ Lonesome Tears (Crickets, Coral Q 72343, 45/78rpm, 1958)

Heartbeat/ Well...All Right (Coral Q 72346, 45/78rpm, 1958, No 30)

It Doesn't Matter Anymore/ Raining In My Heart (Coral Q 72360, 45/78rpm, 1959, No 1)

Midnight Shift/ Rock Around With Ollie Vee (Brunswick 0.5800, 45/78rpm, 1959, No 26)

Peggy Sue Got Married/ Crying, Waiting, Hoping (Coral Q 72376, 45/78rpm, 1959, No 13)

Heartbeat/ Everyday (Coral Q 72392, 45/78rpm, 1960, No 30) (Extremely rare on 78rpm, but copies do exist!)

True Love Ways/ Moondreams (Coral Q 72397, 45rpm, 1960, No 25) (On some copies, the title was shown as 'Moonbeams')

Learning The Game/ That Makes It Tough (Coral Q 72411, 45rpm, 1960, No 36)

What To Do/ That's What They Say (Coral Q 72419, 45rpm, 1961, No 34)

Baby I Don't Care/ Valley Of Tears (Coral Q 72432, 45rpm, 1961, No 12)
Both titles were listed on the chart.

Look At Me/ Mailman Bring Me No More Blues (Coral Q 72445, 45rpm, 1961)

Listen To Me/ Words Of Love (Coral Q 72449, 45rpm, 1962, No 48)

Reminiscing/ Wait Till The Sun Shines, Nellie (Coral Q 72455, 45rpm, 1962, No 17)

Brown Eyed Handsome Man/ Slippin' And Slidin' (Coral Q 72459, 45rpm, 1963, No 3)

Bo Diddley/ It's Not My Fault (Coral Q 72463, 45rpm, 1963, No 4)

Wishing/ Because I Love You (Coral Q 72466, 45rpm, 1963, No 10)

What To Do/ Ummm Oh Yeah (Coral Q 72469, 45rpm, 1963, No 27)

You've Got Love/ An Empty Cup (Coral Q 72472, 45rpm, 1964, No 40)

Love's Made A Fool Of You/ You're The One (Coral Q 72475, 45rpm, 1964, No 39)

Maybe Baby/ That's My Desire (Coral Q 72483, 45rpm, 1966)

Peggy Sue/Rave On (MCA MU 1012, 1968, No 32)

True Love Ways (MCA MCA 1302, 1988, No 65)
There have been many other reissues besides these, and the most attractive package was a box set of 10 singles in 1984, but wouldn't it have been cheaper and more convenient to buy *20 Golden Greats*?

Extended Plays

LISTEN TO ME (Coral FEP 2002, 1958, No 12)

Listen To Me/ Peggy Sue/ I'm Gonna Love You Too/ Everyday
The original cover, showing Holly without glasses, is worth £400 in mint condition. It was reissued very quickly and the better known cover of the EP is only worth £50.

THE SOUND OF THE CRICKETS (Crickets, Coral FEP 2003, 1958)

Oh Boy!/ Not Fade Away/ Maybe Baby/ Tell Me How

RAVE ON (Coral FEP 2005, 1958, No 9)

Rave On/ Take Your Time/ Early In The Morning/ Now We're One

IT'S SO EASY (Crickets, Coral FEP 2014, 1959, No 18)

It's So Easy/ Lonesome Tears/ Think It Over/ Fool's Paradise

HEARTBEAT (Coral FEP 2015, 1959, No 13)

Heartbeat/ Well...All Right/ Baby I Don't Care/ Little Baby

THE BUDDY HOLLY STORY (Coral FEP 2032, 1959)

It Doesn't Matter Anymore/ Heartbeat/ Raining In My Heart/ Early In The Morning
Most odd: why wasn't this EP on the EP charts while the next one, featuring pre-hit titles, was?

BUDDY HOLLY NO 1 (Brunswick OE 9456, 1959, No 18)

You Are My One Desire/ Blue Days—Black Nights/ Modern Don Juan/ Ting-A-Ling

BUDDY HOLLY NO 2 (Brunswick OE 9457, 1959)

Girl On My Mind/ Love Me/ I'm Changin' All Those Changes/ Don't Come Back Knockin'

THE LATE GREAT BUDDY HOLLY (Coral FEP 2044, 1960, No 4)

Look At Me/ Ready Teddy/ Mailman Bring Me No More Blues/ Words Of Love

FOUR MORE (Coral FEP 2060, 1960, No 7)

Last Night/ Send Me Some Lovin'/ You've Got Love/ Rock Me My Baby
What an inspired title!

THAT'LL BE THE DAY (Coral FEP 2062, 1960)

BUDDY—BY REQUEST (Coral FEP 2065, 1964)

THAT TEX-MEX SOUND (Coral FEP 2066, 1964)

WISHING (Coral FEP 2067, 1964)

SHOWCASE, VOLUME 1 (Coral FEP 2068, 1964)

SHOWCASE, VOLUME 2 (Coral FEP 2069, 1964)

BUDDY HOLLY SINGS (Coral FEP 2070, 1965)

GOOD ROCKIN' TONIGHT (Rollercoaster RCEP 104, 1986)

Albums

THE CHIRPING CRICKETS (Vogue Coral LVA 9081, 1958, No 5)
(Quickly reissued on Coral LVA 9081)
Oh Boy!/ Not Fade Away/ You've Got Love/ Maybe Baby/ It's Too Late/ Tell Me How/ That'll Be The Day/ I'm Lookin' For Someone To Love/ An Empty Cup/ Send Me Some Lovin'/ Last Night/ Rock Me My Baby

BUDDY HOLLY (Vogue Coral LVA 9085, 1958) (Quickly reissued on Coral LVA 9085)
I'm Gonna Love You Too/ Peggy Sue/ Listen To Me/ Look At Me/ Valley Of Tears/ Ready Teddy/ Everyday/ Mailman Bring Me No More Blues/ Words Of Love/ Baby I Don't Care/ Rave On/ Little Baby

THE BUDDY HOLLY STORY (Coral LVA 9105, 1959, No 2)
Raining In My Heart/ Early In The Morning/ Peggy Sue/ Maybe Baby/ Everyday/ Rave On/ That'll Be The Day/ Heartbeat/ Think It Over/ Oh Boy!/ It's So Easy/ It Doesn't Matter Anymore
On the LP charts for three years.

THE BUDDY HOLLY STORY, VOLUME 2 (Coral LVA 9127, 1960, No 7)
Peggy Sue Got Married/ Well...All Right/ What To Do/ That Makes It Tough/ Now We're One/ Take Your Time / Crying, Waiting, Hoping/ True Love Ways/ Learning The Game/ Little Baby/ Moondreams/ That'sWhat They Say

THAT'LL BE THE DAY (Ace Of Hearts AH3, 1961, No 5)
You Are My One Desire/ Blue Days, Black Nights/ Modern Don Juan./ Rock Around With Ollie Vee/ Ting-A-Ling/ Girl On My Mind/ That'll Be The Day/ Love Me/ I'm Changin' All Those Changes/ Don't Come Back Knockin'/ Midnight Shift

REMINISCING (Coral LVA 9212, 1963, No 2)
Reminiscing/ Slippin' And Slidin'/ Bo Diddley/ Wait Till The Sun Shines, Nellie/ Baby Won't You Come Out Tonight/ Brown Eyed Handsome Man/ Because I Love You/ It's Not My Fault/ I'm Gonna Set My Foot Down/ Changin' All Those Changes/ Rock-A-Bye Rock
Good marketing here as this was hardly a commercial selection.

SHOWCASE (Coral LVA 9222, 1964, No 3)
Shake Rattle And Roll/ Rock Around With Ollie Vee/ Honky Tonk/ I Guess I Was A Fool/ Ummm Oh Yeah (Dearest)/ You're The One/ Blue Suede Shoes/ Come Back Baby/ Rip It Up/ Love's Made A Fool Of You/ Gone/ Girl On My Mind

HOLLY IN THE HILLS (Coral LVA 9227, 1965, No 13)
I Wanna Play House With You/ Door To My Heart/ Baby It's Love/ I Gambled My Heart/ Memories/ Wishing/ Down The Line/ Soft Place In My Heart/ Queen Of The Ballroom/ Gotta Get You Near Me Blues/ Flower Of My Heart/ You And I Are Through

(Due to an error, 'Reminiscing' played instead of 'Wishing' on an early pressing.)

BUDDY HOLLY'S GREATEST HITS (Ace Of Hearts AH 148, 1967, No 9)

GIANT (MCA MUPS 371, 1969, No 13)
Love Is Strange/ Good Rockin' Tonight/ Blue Monday/ Have You Ever Been Lonely/ Slippin' And Slidin'/ You're The One/ Dearest/ Smokey Joe's Café/ Ain't Got No Home/ Holly Hop

BUDDY HOLLY'S GREATEST HITS, VOLUME 2 (Coral CP/CPS 47, 1970)

REMEMBER (Coral CPS 71, 1971)

LEGEND (Coral CDMSP 802, 2LP, 1974)

RAVE ON (Music For Pleasure MFP 50176, 1975)

THE BUDDY HOLLY STORY (World Records SM 301-5, 5LP, 1975)

THE NASHVILLE SESSIONS (Coral CDLM 8038, 1975)

WESTERN AND BOP (Coral CDLM 8055, 1977)

BUDDY HOLLY LIVES—20 GOLDEN GREATS (EMI EMTV 8, 1978, No 1)
When I first saw this listed as Buddy Holly Live I thought it was going to be a discovered concert, but no, it was a greatest hits collection and a superb one.

THE COMPLETE BUDDY HOLLY (MCA Coral CDMSP 807, 6LP box set, 1979)
At last a six album box set, although we know now (and knew then) that it wasn't complete, but it was still comprehensive and superbly packaged with a book of press cuttings. Very well annotated by John Beecher and Malcolm Jones. It was retailing at £12: a fantastic bargain.

HEARTBEAT (Marks & Spencer IMP 114 2188 3008, 1980)
Marks & Spencer's venture in record retail didn't work out, making this compilation with only three hits highly collectable.

BUDDY HOLLY (Pickwick SSP 3070, 1980)
Going down market with some of Buddy's best tracks.

ROCK ON WITH BUDDY (Music For Pleasure MFP 50490, 1980)

LOVE SONGS (MCA MCF 3117, 1981)

FOR THE FIRST TIME ANYWHERE (MCA MCM 1002, 1983)
Rock-A-Bye Rock/ Maybe Baby/ Because I Love You/ I'm Gonna Set My Foot Down/ Changin' All Those Changes/ That's My Desire/ Baby Won't You Come Out Tonight/ It's Not My Fault/ Brown Eyed Handsome Man/ Bo Diddley

BUDDY HOLLY AND THE CRICKETS (Cambra CRT 123, 2LP, 1984)
Hit and miss compilation which includes three post-Holly Crickets' titles.

BUDDY HOLLY'S GREATEST HITS (MCA DMCA 109, CD, 1985)
Buddy Holly makes shiny.

GOLDEN GREATS (MCA MCM 5003, 1985)

FROM THE ORIGINAL MASTER TAPES (MCA DIDX 203, 1985)

SOMETHING SPECIAL FROM BUDDY HOLLY (Rollercoaster ROLL 2013, 1986)
Outtakes starting to surface with three takes each of Gone and Have You Ever Been Lonely

TRUE LOVE WAYS (Telstar STAR 2339, 1989, No 8)

WORDS OF LOVE (Polygram TV 5144872, 1993, No 1)

BUDDY HOLLY AND THE PICKS: THE ORIGINAL VOICES OF THE CRICKETS (Magnum Force CDMF 088, 1993)

THE VERY BEST OF BUDDY HOLLY (Dino DINCD 133, 1996, No 24)

THE VERY BEST OF BUDDY HOLLY AND THE CRICKETS (Universal TV 1120462, 1999, No 25)

GOTTA ROLL: THE EARLY RECORDINGS 1949-1955 (Rev-Ola CR REV 174, 2006)

MEMORIAL COLLECTION (Geffen/Universal B001G9LV91, 3CD, 2009)

DOWN THE LINE—RARITIES (Geffen/Universal B001G9LV98, 2CD, 2009)

At last an official 3CD package of the best-known Buddy Holly tracks with a 2CD addition of rarities. Great to have Buddy and Bob tracks and the Apartment Tapes on CD without additional accompaniment, but there is some duplication. I'd have gone for a 4CD box set but this is progress.

THE CRICKETS (WITHOUT BUDDY HOLLY)—U.K. DISCOGRAPHY
Singles

Love's Made A Fool Of You/ Someone, Someone (Coral Q 72365, 45/78rpm, 1958, No 26)

When You Ask About Love/ Deborah (Coral Q 72382, 45/78rpm, 1959, No 27)

Baby My Heart/ More Than I Can Say (Coral Q 72395, 1959, No 33)
More Than I Can Say also made an appearance at No 42.

Peggy Sue Got Married/ Don't Cha Know (Coral Q 72417, 1960)

I Fought The Law/ A Sweet Love (Coral Q 72440, 1960)

He's Old Enough To Know Better/ I'm Feeling Better (London HLG 9486, 1961)

Don't Ever Change/ I'm Not A Bad Guy (Liberty LIB 55441, 1962, No 5)

Little Hollywood Girl/ Parisian Girl (Liberty LIB 55495, 1962)

My Little Girl/ Teardrops Fall Like Rain (Liberty LIB 10067, 1963, No 17)

Don't Try To Change Me/ Lost And Alone (Liberty LIB 10092, 1963, No 37)

Right Or Wrong/ You Can't Be In Between (Liberty LIB 10113, 1963)

Lonely Avenue/ Playboy (Liberty LIB 10145, 1964)

(They Call Her) La Bamba/ All Over You (Liberty LIB 55696, 1964, No 21)

I Think I've Caught The Blues/ We Gotta Get Together (Liberty LIB 10174, 1965)

Now Hear This/ Everybody's Got A Little Problem (As Jerry Allison and the Crickets, Liberty LIB 10196, 1965)

April Avenue/ Don't Say You Love Me (Liberty LBF 15089, 1968)

My Little Girl/ Lonely Avenue (Liberty LBF 15089, 1968)

Rockin' Fifties Rock'n'Roll/ True Love Ways (CBS 2672 061)

Don't Ever Change/ Playboy (United Artists UP 35457, 1972)

My Rockin' Days/ Lovesick Blues (Philips 6006 269, 1973)

Hayride/ Wasn't It Nice In New York City (Philips 6006 294, 1973)

Rhyme And Time/ Ooh Las Vegas (Mercury 6008 006, 1974)

Rock Around With Ollie Vee/ Cruise In It (Rollercoaster RRC 2001, 1978, issued in two different sleeves)

T-Shirt/ Holly Would (CBS TSH 1, 1988)

T-Shirt/ Forever In Mind / Holly Would (CBS TSH T 1, 12", 1988)

T-Shirt/ Forever In Mind/ Holly Would (CBS CD TSH 1, CD, 1988)

Extended Plays

THE CRICKETS (Coral FEP 2053, 1958)
When You Ask About Love/ Deborah/ Love's Made A Fool Of You/ Someone, Someone

DON'T EVER CHANGE (Coral FEP 2064, 1961)
More Than I Can Say/ Baby My Heart/ Peggy Sue Got Married/ Don't Cha Know
There was no Trade Descriptions Act back then but if there were, this EP would surely have been withdrawn. Don't Ever Change wasn't included and it was an attempt by their previous label to cash in.

JUST FOR FUN (Liberty LEP 2084, 1963, No 1)
Soundtrack EP featuring two Crickets songs (My Little Girl and Teardrops Fall Like Rain) and two by Bobby Vee.

STRAIGHT—NO STRINGS (Liberty LEP 2094/ SLEP 2094, 1963)
Willie And The Hand Jive/ Summertime Blues/ Searchin'/ What'd I Say

BOBBY VEE MEETS THE CRICKETS (Liberty LEP 2116/ SLEP 2116, 1963)
Someday/ Bo Diddley/ I Gotta Know/ Peggy Sue

BOBBY VEE MEETS THE CRICKETS, VOLUME 2 (Liberty LEP 2149, 1963)
Peggy Sue/ Well…All Right/ Lookin' For Love/ Lucille

COME ON (Liberty LEP 2173, 1964)
Slippin' And Slidin'./ A Fool Never Learns/ Come On/ Money

MILLION DOLLAR MOVIE (Rollercoaster RRCEP 0001 and then RCEP 101, 1978)
Million Dollar Movie/ A Million Miles Apart/ Rock'n'Roll (I Gave You The Best Years Of My Life (Sonny Curtis solo)/ My Momma Sure Left Me Some Good Old Days (Sonny Curtis solo)

BACK HOME IN TENNESSEE (Rollercoaster RCEP 111, 1990)
Blackmail/ I Can't Hold On/ (For a while) We Helped Each Other Out/ Back Home In Tennessee

Albums

IN STYLE WITH THE CRICKETS (Coral LVA 9142, 1961, No 13)
More Than I Can Say/ Rockin' Pneumonia And The Boogie Woogie Flu/ Great Balls Of Fire/ Ting-A-Ling/ Just This Once/ Deborah/ Baby My Heart/ When You Ask About Love/ Time Will Tell/ A Sweet Love/ I Fought The Law/ Love's Made A Fool Of You

BOBBY VEE MEETS THE CRICKETS (Liberty LBY 1086/ SLBY 1086, 1962, No 2)
Peggy Sue/ Bo Diddley/ Someday/ Well…All Right/ I Gotta Know/ Lookin' For Love/ Sweet Little Sixteen/ When You're In Love/ Lucille/ Girl Of My Best Friend/ Little Queenie/ The Girl Can't Help It

SOMETHING OLD, SOMETHING NEW, SOMETHING BLUE, SOMETHING ELSE! (Liberty LBY 1120/ SLBY 1120, 1962)
What'd I Say/ Searchin'/ Willie And The Hand Jive/ Love Is Strange/ Don't Ever Change/ Little Hollywood Girl/ He's Old Enough To Know Better/ Parisian Girl/ Pretty Blue Eyes/ Blue Blue Day/ Summertime Blues/ Blue Monday

THE CRICKETS—A COLLECTION (Liberty LBY 1258, 1965)
(They Call Her) La Bamba/ All Over You/ Everybody's Got A Little Problem/ I Think I've Caught The Blues/ We Gotta Get Together/ Playboy/ My Little Girl/ Teardrops Fall Like Rain/ Right Or Wrong/ Don't Try To Change Me/ Lost And Alone/ I'm Not A Bad Guy

ROCKIN' FIFTIES ROCK'N'ROLL (CBS 64301, 1971)
Rockin' Fifties Rock'n'Roll/ That'll Be The Day/ True Love Ways/ Well…All Right/ Peggy Sue/ Oh Boy!/ Rain-

ing In My Heart/ It's So Easy/ (Medley) Everyday—Think It Over—Maybe Baby

ROCK REFLECTIONS (Sunset SLS 50207, 1971)
Compilation of Liberty tracks

BUBBLEGUM, BOP, BALLAD AND BOOGIES (Philips 6308 149, 1973)
Can I Make You Feel It/ Hayride/ Wasn't It Nice In New York City/ Rockin' Pneumonia And The Boogie Woogie Flu/ Lovesick Blues/ My Rockin' Days/ I've Got A Thing About You Baby/ On The Outside Looking In/ Keep A Knockin'/ Day Gig/ Destiny's Child

A LONG WAY FROM LUBBOCK (Mercury 6310 007, 1974)
An American Love Affair/ Lay Lady Lay Down / Decoy Baker/ He's Got A Way With Women / Rhyme And Time/ I've Got A Thing About You Baby/ (Medley) You Make It Way Too Hard—Ain't Protestin'/ Bony Moronie/ Ooh Las Vegas/ Find Out What's Happening/ I Like Your Music/ Now And Then It's Gonna Rain

RARE ITEMS, 1959-1960 (Germany, MCA Coral COPS 7335)
Alternative takes of post-Holly Coral tracks.

BOBBY VEE MEETS THE CRICKETS (Sunset SLS 50357, 1977)

Reissue

BACK IN STYLE (MCA Coral MCFM 2710)

THE COMPLETE CRICKETS (Charly CR 30266, 1984)

THE CRICKETS FILE, 1961-1965 (See For Miles SEE 79, 1987: reissued on CD See For Miles CD SEE 79 in 1990)

THREE PIECE (Rollercoaster ROLL 2014, 1987)
Your M-M-Memory Is T-T-Torturing Me/ Cruise In It/ The Weekend/ Three Piece/ Rockin' Socks/ Forever In Mind/ Mulholland Drive/ That's All She Wrote/ Don't Tell Me That You Can't Come Out Tonight/ Let's Do It Again

T-SHIRT (CBS 462876-1, LP, 1988)

T-SHIRT (CBS 462876-2, CD, 1988)
Your M-M-Memory Is T-T-Torturing Me/ Rockin' Socks/ The Weekend/ Holly Would/ T-Shirt/ Forever In Mind/ Cruise In It/ Three Piece/ Don't Tell Me That You Can't Come Out Tonight/ That's All She Wrote

THE BEST OF THE CRICKETS (EMI EMS 1318, LP, 1989)

THE BEST OF THE CRICKETS (EMI 791757-2, CD, 1989)

BOBBY VEE MEETS THE CRICKETS (EMI CDP 7960542, 1991)
Original album plus two takes of Lonely Weekends and It's Too Late as well as Come On Baby, Mountain Of Love, No One Knows, Shanghaied, Keep-A Knockin' and Vee's Buddy Holly medley.

THE LIBERTY YEARS (EMI CDP 7958452, 1991)

RAVIN' ON—FROM CALIFORNIA TO CLOVIS (Rockstar RSRCD 002, 1991)

STILL IN STYLE (Bear Family BCD 15599, 1992)
Crickets' recordings from 1958 to 1960.

DOUBLE EXPOSURE (Rollercoaster RCCD 3006, 1993)

IN STYLE WITH THE CRICKETS (MCA MCLD 19243, 1994)

A COLLECTION/ CALIFORNIA SUN—SHE LOVES YOU (BGO BGOCD 251, 1995)
A clumsy title for a twofer of US albums.

TOO MUCH MONDAY MORNING (Carlton 30360 00332, 1996)

BOBBY VEE MEETS THE CRICKETS / I REMEMBER BUDDY HOLLY (BGO BGOCD 413, 1998)
Reissue of the Vee / Crickets album with Vee's 1963 tribute LP

TOO MUCH MONDAY MORNING (Castle Select SEL CD 589, 2001: reissue of Carlton CD with different insert)

THE CRICKETS AND THEIR BUDDIES (Cooking Vinyl COOKCD 328, 2004)
The Real Buddy Holly Story/ More Than I Can Say plus That'll Be The Day (with Rodney Crowell)/ Rave On (with Phil and Jason Everly)/ Not Fade Away (with Tonio K and Peter Case)/ Someone, Someone (with Eric Clapton)/ Everyday (with J D Souther) / Heartbeat (with Nanci Griffith)/ Blue Days, Black Nights (with Bobby Vee)/ Learning The Game (with Albert Lee)/ Well…All Right (with Waylon Jennings)/ Think It Over (with Graham Nash)/ Oh Boy! (with John Prine)/ I Fought The Law (with Vince Neil)/ Love's Made A Fool Of You (with Johnny Rivers)
Paul McCartney's anticipated contribution was not included.

BUDDY HOLLY AND THE CRICKETS— U.S. DISCOGRAPHY

The licensing of the hit singles in particular has been so widespread that a full discography would be a book in itself. This discography concerns itself with the first appearance of each of Buddy's recorded performances, and other significant releases. Chart placings are from *Billboard* magazine.

Singles

Blue Days—Black Nights/ Love Me (Decca 29854, 45/78rpm, 1956)

Modern Don Juan/ You Are My One Desire (Decca 30166, 45/78rpm, 1956)

That'll Be The Day/ I'm Lookin' For Someone To Love (Crickets, Brunswick 55009, 45/78rpm, 1957, No 1)

Words Of Love/ Mailman Bring Me No More Blues (Coral 61852, 45/78rpm, 1957)

Rock Around With Ollie Vee/ That'll Be The Day (Decca 30454, 45/78rpm, 1957)

Peggy Sue/ Everyday (Coral 61885, 45/78rpm, 1957, No 3)
On the rival Cash Box chart, Peggy Sue was listed at No 2 and Everyday at No 51.

Oh Boy!/ Not Fade Away (Crickets, Brunswick 55035, 45/78rpm, 1957, No 10)

Love Me/ You Are My One Desire (Decca 30453, 45/78rpm, 1958)

Listen To Me/ I'm Gonna Love You Too/ (Coral 61947, 45/78rpm, 1958, No 56)

Maybe Baby/ Tell Me How (Crickets, Brunswick 55053, 45/78rpm, 1958, No 17)

Rave On/ Take Your Time (Coral 61985, 45/78rpm, 1958, No 37)

Think It Over/ Fool's Paradise (Crickets, Brunswick 55072, 45/78rpm, 1958, No 27)
Fool's Paradise made the US charts in its own right, reaching No 58.

Ting-A-Ling/ Girl On My Mind (Decca 30650, 45/78rpm, 1958)

Early In The Morning/ Now We're One (Coral 62006, 45/78rpm, 1958, No 31)

It's So Easy/ Lonesome Tears (Crickets, Brunswick 55094, 45/78rpm, 1958)

Real Wild Child/ Oh, You Beautiful Doll (Ivan, Coral 62017, 1958 : Jerry Allison, lead vocal)

Heartbeat/ Well…All Right (Coral 62051, 45/78rpm, 1958, No 82)

It Doesn't Matter Anymore/ Raining In My Heart (Coral 62074, 45rpm, 1959, No 13)
Raining In My Heart made the US charts in its own right, reaching No 88.

Peggy Sue Got Married/ Crying, Waiting, Hoping (Coral 62134, 45rpm, 1959)

True Love Ways/ That Makes It Tough (Coral 62210, 45rpm, 1960)

Baby I Don't Care/ Valley Of Tears (Coral 62283, 45rpm, 1961)

Reminiscing/ Wait Till The Sun Shines, Nellie (Coral 62329, 45rpm, 1962)

Bo Diddley/ True Love Ways (Coral 62352, 45rpm, 1963, No 116)

Brown Eyed Handsome Man/ Wishing (Coral 62369, 45rpm, 1963, No 113)

Rock Around With Ollie Vee/ I'm Gonna Love You Too (Coral 62390, 45rpm, 1964)

Maybe Baby/ Not Fade Away (Coral 62407, 45rpm, 1964)

What To Do/ Slippin' And Slidin' (Coral 62448, 45rpm, 1965)

Rave On/ Early In The Morning (Coral 62554, 45rpm, 1968)

Love Is Strange/ You're The One (Coral 62558, 45rpm, 1969, No 105)

Extended Plays

THE CHIRPING CRICKETS (Crickets, Brunswick EB 71036, 1957)

THE SOUND OF THE CRICKETS (Crickets, Brunswick EB 71038, 1958)

THAT'LL BE THE DAY (Decca ED 2575, 1958)

LISTEN TO ME (Coral EC 81169, 1958)

THE CHIRPING CRICKETS (Crickets, Brunswick EB 71036, 1957)

THE SOUND OF THE CRICKETS (Crickets, Brunswick EB 71038, 1958)

THE BUDDY HOLLY STORY (Coral EC 81182, 1959)

PEGGY SUE GOT MARRIED (Coral EC 81191, 1962)

THE CRICKETS (Coral EC 81192, 1963)
Includes one Holly track, 'It's Too Late'

BROWN EYED HANDSOME MAN (Coral EC 81193, 1963)

THE CRICKETS LIVE (BHMS, BHMS 100, no sleeve)
Oh Boy!/ Maybe Baby/ Well…All Right/ That'll Be The Day

MY TWO TIMIN' WOMAN + 3 (Holly House, no number, no sleeve, 1986)
My Two Timin' Woman/ I'll Just Pretend/ Don't Come Back Knockin'/ Brown Eyed Handsome Man

Albums

THE CHIRPING CRICKETS (Crickets, Brunswick BL 54038, 1957)

BUDDY HOLLY (Coral CRL 57210, 1958)

THAT'LL BE THE DAY (Decca DL 8707, 1958)

THE BUDDY HOLLY STORY (Coral CRL 57279/ 757279, 1959, No 11)
Over three years on the chart.

THE BUDDY HOLLY STORY, VOLUME 2 (Coral CRL 57326, 1960)

REMINISCING (Coral CRL 57426/ 757426, 1963, No 40)

SHOWCASE (Coral CRL 57450/ 757450, 1964)

HOLLY IN THE HILLS (Coral CRL 57463/ 757463, 1965)

GIANT (CRL 757504, 1969)

BUDDY HOLLY RECORDED LIVE (Cricket C 001000, 1977)
Interviews and London Palladium show bootleg

BUDDY HOLLY IN PERSON (Cricket C 002000, 1977)
Newscast of the plane crash, session work and Mike Berry's tribute.

THE COMPLETE BUDDY HOLLY (MCA 6-80000, 1981)

FOR THE FIRST TIME ANYWHERE (MCA MCA 27059, 1983)

FROM THE ORIGINAL MASTER TAPES (MCA MCAD 5540, 1985)

LEGEND (MCA MCA2 4184, 1986)

HOLLYBILLY: BUDDY HOLLY 1956 (El Toro ETCD 1012, 2CD, 2006)
Spanish album.

THE CRICKETS (WITHOUT BUDDY HOLLY)—U.S. DISCOGRAPHY
Singles

Love's Made A Fool Of You/ Someone, Someone (Brunswick 55124, 1959)

That'll Be Alright/ Frankie Frankenstein (Ivan, Coral 62081, 1959)

When You Ask About Love/ Deborah (Brunswick 55153, 1959)

More Than I Can Say/ Baby My Heart (Coral 62198, 1960)

Peggy Sue Got Married/ Don't Cha Know (Coral 62238, 1960)

He's Old Enough To Know Better/ I'm Feeling Better (Liberty 55392, 1961)

Don't Ever Change/ I'm Not A Bad Guy (Liberty 55441, 1962)

I Believe In You/ Parisian Girl (Liberty 55492, 1962)

Little Hollywood Girl/ Parisian Girl (Liberty 55495, 1962)

My Little Girl/ Teardrops Fall Like Rain (Liberty 55540, 1963)

Don't Say You Love Me/ April Avenue (Liberty 55603, 1963)

Lonely Avenue/ You Can't Be In Between (Liberty 55660, 1964)

Please Please Me/ From Me To You (Liberty 55668, 1964)

(They Call Her) La Bamba/ All Over You (Liberty 55696, 1964)

I Think I've Caught The Blues/ We Gotta Get Together (Liberty 55742, 1964) (As "Jerry Allison and the Crickets)

Now Hear This/Everybody's Got A Little Problem (Liberty 55767, 1965)

The Ballad Of Batman/ Batmobile (Parkway 974, 1965) Under the name of the Camps.
Reissued the following year as the Campers with the same number: go figure.)

Real Wild Child/ That'll Be Alright (Ivan, Coral 65607, 1967)

Million Dollar Movie/ A Million Miles Apart (Music Factory 415, 1968)

Rockin' Fifties Rock'n'Roll/ True Love Ways (Barnaby 2061, 1972)

Hayride/ Wasn't It Nice In New York City (MGM 14541, 1973)

T-Shirt/ Holly Would (EPIC 34-08028, 1988)

Extended Plays

None

Albums

IN STYLE WITH THE CRICKETS (Coral 57320 / 757320, 1960)

BOBBY VEE MEETS THE CRICKETS (Liberty LRP 3228/LST 7228, 1962)

SOMETHING OLD, SOMETHING NEW, SOMETHING BLUE, SOMETHING ELSE! (Liberty LRP 3272/LST 7272, 1964)

CALIFORNIA SUN—SHE LOVES YOU (Liberty LRP 3351/ LST 7351, 1964)

I Want To Hold Your Hand/ California Sun/ She Loves You/ A Fool Never Learns/ Slippin' And Slidin'/ I Saw Her Standing There/ Lonely Avenue/ Please Please Me/ Money/ From Me To You/ You Can't Be In Between/ Come On

ROCKIN' FIFTIES ROCK'N'ROLL (Barnaby Z 30268, 1970)

REMNANTS (Vertigo VEL 1020, 1973)

Find Out What's Happening/ Lay Lady Lay Down/ Rock And Roll Man/ I'm Gonna Ruin Your Health/ Rhyme And Time/ Decoy Baker/ Losin' Streak/ Atmore/ The Truth Is Still The Same/ Hitchhike Out To Venus/ Ooh Las Vegas/ Draggin' Chains

BUDDY HOLLY'S CRICKETS (Koala KOA 14206, 1980)

That'll Be The Day/ Maybe Baby/ Quando Quando Quando/ Everyday/ Keep A Knockin' / Welcome To The Country/ Well … All Right/ Doin' Like Elvis/ Oh Boy!/ I've Got To Be Me

T-SHIRT (Epic FE 44446, 1988)

T-SHIRT (Epic EK 44446 CD, 1988 issued in long box)

THE LIBERTY YEARS (EMI CDP 7 95845 2, 1991 issued in long box)

BOBBY VEE MEETS THE CRICKETS (EMI CDP 7 96054 2, 1991)

THE CRICKETS AND THEIR BUDDIES (Sovereign Audio CD 1952 -2, 2004)

SOME BUDDIES—DISCOGRAPHY
Singles

Mood Indigo/ Petty's Little Polka—Norman Petty Trio (UK, HMV 7M 274, 1954)

A UK release for Norman Petty's first US success.

The Great Tragedy—Hershel Almond (ACE NS 48, 1959)

Tribute To Buddy Holly—Mike Berry and the Outlaws (UK, HMV POP 912, 1961)

Three Stars—Ruby Wright (Parlophone R 4556, 1959)

American Pie—Don McLean (United Artists UP35325, 1972)

I Feel Like Buddy Holly—Alvin Stardust (UK, Chrysalis CHS 2784, 1984)

Buddy Holly—Weezer (UK, Geffen GFSTD 88, 1995)

Whatever Happened To Peggy Sue? Bobby Vee and the Vees (UK, Rockhouse, CD single, no number, 2002)

Bobby Vee and the Vees

Albums

I REMEMBER BUDDY HOLLY—BOBBY VEE (UK, Liberty LBY 1188, 1963)

THE BUDDY HOLLY SONGBOOK—TOMMY ALLSUP (UK, London HA-U 8218, 1964)

BUDDY'S BUDDY—JIMMY GILMER (Dot DLP 3577, 1965)

SKEETER DAVIS SINGS BUDDY HOLLY (US, RCA LSP-3790, 1967)

BUDDY HOLLY—THE HOLLIES (UK, Polydor POLTV 12, 1980)

HOLLY'S HOUSE (US, Cloud Nine (no number), 1980)

Larry, Travis, Sherry and Randy pay tribute to Buddy. Excellent booklet from Larry, but the singing talent in the family surely went to Buddy.

BUDDY'S BUDDYS (UK, Connoisseur VSOP 175, 1992)

25 track compilation of Holly covers.

BUDDY HOLLY DAYS (US, FR 1007)

30 obscure soundalikes.

EVERYDAY IS A HOLLY DAY (France, ROSE 175)

Double 10" album. 22 artists sing 20 Holly covers and 2 tribute songs.

LOOKING THROUGH BUDDY'S EYES—SHERRY HOLLY (US, Cloud Nine 451-04, 1993)

Covers and tribute songs from Buddy's niece.

notfadeaway (Remembering Buddy Holly) (UK, MCA MCD 11260, 1996)

The Mavericks, Los Lobos and Waylon Jennings. Buddy Holly, unbeknownst to him, teams up with the Hollies for Peggy Sue Got Married.

THE LEGACY OF THE BIG BOPPER—THE BIG BOPPER JR (FMG Records, no number, 1997)

A fine tribute album with many guests including the Crickets, James Burton, the Coasters and Johnny Preston.

DIFFERENT VIEWS (Germany, Edel 0058812 ERE, 1999)

Buddy Holly covers and tributes (Weezer's "Buddy Holly").

DOWN THE LINE—BOBBY VEE (UK, Rollercoaster RCCD 3046, 2000)

A selection of Buddy Holly covers covering Buddy's career and some unlikely selections

BIBLIOGRAPHY
Books

Buddy Holly—Dave Laing (Studio Vista, 1971)
An academic, Dave Laing has written on popular music for 40 years and this study of Holly's music, although short, was the first, and indeed, among the first rock books. Laing packs plenty into his text, with a good chapter on the structure of Holly's songs. According to Laing, Holly's exuberance comes from "his enjoyment of his own craftsmanship."

Buddy Holly…A Biography In Words, Photographs And Music—Elizabeth And Ralph Peer (Peer International, 1972)
Attractively presented book of sheet music with an 8,000 word biography, a discography and many photographs. The list of cover versions entertained me the most—the Unchained Mynds doing "Everyday", Little Caesar and the Consuls "It's So Easy", Esquerita "Maybe Baby" and Françoise Hardy "That'll Be The Day", and Pat Boone recording for a label called Agoom Agooc. I'd have welcomed some commentary on these versions but I suppose if you're a music publisher, you just want artists to record the songs.

The Buddy Holly Story—John Tobler (Beaufort, 1979)
This is an affectionate study of Holly by the best-known UK rock writer of the time, but it was written to tie in with *The Buddy Holly Story*, which distorts the book's balance.

The A-Z of Buddy Holly—Alan Mann (The Sound Of Tex-Mex, First Edition 1994)
The A-Z of Buddy Holly—Alan Mann (Aurum Press, Second Edition 1996)
If you use the word "legendary" to describe Ray Campi, how are you going to describe Buddy Holly? Too many vague entries too: what's the point of telling us that Jerry Allison went to see *Buddy* if we're not told what he thought of it? That said, compiling an encyclopaedia should be relatively easy as you follow the route the standard encyclopedias take or, quite simply, "Think of the user." Alan Mann, however, steers his own course and under "D" you will find "John Denver And

Other Folkies", which includes Carolyn Hester and Tom Rush without a cross-reference. Not as wayward as Bill Harry's Beatle encyclopedias but that's no compliment. Alan Mann is rewriting and expanding his book for 2009 publication.

What A Wonderful World—Bob Thiele as told to Bob Golden (Oxford University Press, 1995)
Coral's chief executive and record producer, Bob Thiele presents colourful anecdotes about the New York record industry and he pulverises a songwriter, Don George, who wrote unfavourably of an album Duke Ellington made with Thiele's wife, Teresa Brewer. He describes how inaccurate George's comments were and yet neither he nor his ghost writer, Bob Golden, appear to have done any serious research. For example, it wasn't Sonny Curtis who wrote "Sugartime" and Thiele didn't write "Mailman, Bring Me No More Blues" especially for Buddy. He makes a big deal of his song, "What A Wonderful World" being the follow-up to "Hello Dolly!" but they were recorded three years apart. Great shame as this book had potential. Oh, and dig the "publicity photograph" on page 91; if you look like an ageing bouncer, why do you bother with publicity shots?

Remembering Buddy: The Definitive Biography—John Goldrosen and John Beecher (GRR/Pavilion, 1987: updated by Omnibus, 1996)
This book has been issued in several editions, usually with updates and different illustrations. Both men have made researching Buddy Holly their life's mission so their collaboration makes this book a very attractive proposition. Sometimes though, they make references in the first person singular and you wonder just who is talking. The 1987 edition has photographs the size of postage stamps, but the text is excellent.

Buddy Holly; The Real Story—Ellis Amburn (Virgin, 1996)
Ellis Amburn does an Albert Goldman as Buddy Holly, in a nightmarish story is portrayed as a randy delinquent, desperate to earn big money. He likes fighting and loses his virginity in a gangbang. None of this is impossible, however, but we know that because of his ulcer, Buddy didn't drink much, and Amburn writes, "Buddy's inability to navigate himself home indicates he was black-

ing out which Alcoholics Anonymous identifies as the sign of a drinking problem." More 'Now Throw Away' than 'Not Fade Away'.

Rave On: The Biography Of Buddy Holly—Philip Norman (Fireside, 1996)
Philip Norman, a noted biographer of the Beatles, the Rolling Stones and Elton John, wrote a series of features, *The Secret Buddy Holly*, for the *Daily Mail* in 1994. They jumped to conclusions and the feature on Holly's alleged paternity reached, in my view, unjustifiable conclusions. Norman locates and interviews Holly's English girlfriend, and is an experienced researcher, but there are too many hyperboles for the book to work well. He describes Holly's death as "the most famous tragedy in rock history" and now he has written a biography of John Lennon, which presumably has to be the second most famous tragedy in rock history. Listen to me, Philip. Think it over. Over whose lost heartbeat should we be reminiscing?

The Day The Music Died: The Last Tour Of Buddy Holly, The Big Bopper And Ritchie Valens—Larry Lehmer (Schirmer, 1997)
Superbly researched account of the *Winter Dance Party* and the resulting crash.

Buddy Holly, Day By Day—Bill Griggs (Five volumes, Rockin' 50s, 1997)
These five magazines were published by the noted Holly researcher, Bill Griggs and desperately needed a good editor, or even a half-good one. Utterly trivial facts are alongside important ones, and even details about Griggs himself appear in the chronological run-through. However, Griggs has had access to a vast amount of new research material—for example, Jerry Allison's receipts from the 1950s—and it's a shame that he has written such an annoying work.

The Winter Dance Party Murders—Greg Herriges (Wordcraft of Oregon, 1998)
Buddy Holly lives in this spoof crime novel in which rock's big calamities are not what they seem. The book's narrator finds out where Buddy is being kept after the crash: "Buddy turned around to look at me. I guess he was expecting the doctor. You could still see that he looked like Buddy in a way. The way an egg still looks like an egg if you scramble it." Tasteless, but with some

good industry jokes: "So let's get it straight—rock and roll is a very masculine lifestyle. Ask anyone who's ever lived it. Except maybe Little Richard. Or Elton. Or Bowie." If you want a clue to help you solve the mystery, spell the publishing company, Stek-Circ, backwards.

Elvis & Buddy: Linked Lives—Alan Mann (Music Mentor, 2002)
Natal charts and star signs—not for me at all, and I remain unconvinced. Credit to the author for trying something different, but no marks at all for the result.

Buddy Holly And The Crickets: The UK Tour—Jim Carr (Holly International Publishing, 2005)
This satisfying paperback, limited to 1,000 copies, neatly and concisely tells the story of the 1958 UK tour with a comprehensive photo selection of the entourage, the venues, the coach driver, hotel bills and the contracts, and written by an author, the editor of *Holly International*, deeply in love with his subject.

Buddy Holly And The Crickets: Musical History In Australia—Roderick Jordan (Soft back First Edition 2007)
A privately published 251 page examination of the Australian tour, limited to 250 copies.

Whatever Happened to Peggy Sue?—Peggy Sue Gerron and Glenda Cameron (Togi Entertainment, US, 2008)
With a love so rare and true, indeed: Buddy Holly wanted to divorce Maria Elena, and Peggy Sue wanted to divorce his drummer, Jerry Allison, and together the two would marry and run a recording studio in Lubbock, Texas. Was this really their future and if so, why has Peggy Sue kept quiet for so long? For all that, *Whatever Happened To Peggy Sue?* is entertaining, well-written and candid, but, despite Gerron's assurances that everything is true, I have reservations about some of these conversations. Did Peggy Sue really have premonitions of Buddy's death in a plane crash and warn him accordingly? Did she tell him that his music would last forever? Did she say that it is about time that a rock group played Carnegie Hall? The book is based upon her extensive diary entries, but despite the many illustrations, I would have liked a photograph of at least one page of the

diaries to substantiate her claims. Unsurprisingly, Maria Elena has dismissed the book as fiction and as she is depicted as permanently bad-tempered, you wonder how anyone could have married her, let alone the effervescent Buddy Holly. Classic on-stage quote from Sonny Curtis: "Peggy Sue is still around. She is just not around us anymore."

Buddy Holly And The Crickets: Musical History In Australia—50th Anniversary Edition—Roderick Jordan (Hardback Second Edition 2008)
A privately published 468 page examination of the Australian tour, limited to 262 copies. Completely revised and expanded edition with comprehensive Australian discography.

Academic Papers

Pity Peggy Sue—Barbara Bradby and Brian Torode (Popular Music 4, Cambridge University Press, 1984)
The authors are sociologists based in Dublin and they point out the childlike features of "Peggy Sue", both in the lyrics ("Pretty pretty pretty pretty Peggy Sue") and in Holly's vocal, which has three performance modes: normal, falsetto and deep.

Oh Boy! (Oh Boy!): Mutual Desirability And Musical Structure In The Buddy Group—Barbara Bradby (Popular Music, 21:1, Cambridge University Press, 2002)
Roughly speaking, I read a minute a page, but this slowed me down to five minutes. The paper is a complex analysis of "Oh Boy!" looking at it from several angles: a comparison with the Five Satins' "In The Still Of The Night": the use of nursery rhymes in writing popular songs (the first line of "Oh Boy!" is "This Old Man", and "A little bit of lovin'…" is "The king was in his counting house"); not to mention the homoerotic subtext ("The continual echoing of the singer's 'Oh Boy!' allows for a literal hearing of cries of mutual desire and admiration between two men."); and the reason Holly sounds so excited is because he is about to lose his virginity. (The song is set in the evening and he's looking forward to the night.) These 30 pages of long-winded analysis have little to do with the people who made the music. Indeed, the author doesn't appreciate that the songwriter, Sonny West recorded the song

first and that it is not just a single male, backing vocalist on "Oh Boy!" If she had, the paper might have reached even more outrageous conclusions. Still, it's food for thought.

Magazines

Crickets File
(5 Springwell Gardens, Doncaster, DN4 9AH)
John Firminger's quarterly fanzine has been published since 1979 and is an invaluable source of information, concentrating just as much on the Crickets and their current activities as Buddy Holly. Anyone who has even been a Cricket may be featured so that gives the magazine a wide brief. It reprints articles, old and new, and judging by the amount of anecdotes, you'd think that Buddy Holly had a year long residency in Yorkshire.

Holly International
(PO Box 1436, Doncaster, DN11 9YQ)
Jim Carr's A4 fanzine looks better than *Crickets File,* has colour photographs, and is full of information you don't normally come across. Unusually for a fanzine, the layout makes good use of white space. Many of the illustrations come from Ian Higham's extensive collection

Reminiscing and *Rockin' 50s*
Both of Bill Griggs' magazines are no longer published, but they contain masses of information about Buddy Holly, often involving considerable research in Lubbock. *Reminiscing* was Hollycentric, *Rockin' 50s* was a spin-off publication dedicated to rock'n'roll but in every issue, it is self-evident where the editor's main interest lies. The publications are hampered by wayward spelling, appalling grammar and excessive use of superlatives, but that's the world of fanzines for you: *Crickets File* and *Holly International* also fall down in this respect. Griggs is a good-natured soul: I know several UK fans have contacted him and he has shown them around Lubbock.

Websites

www.buddyhollylives.com
The fabulous worldwide collection of Buddy Holly memorabilia, owned by Ian Higham

www.buddyhollyonline.com
Started in 1997, this has been an increasingly comprehensive site of Holly news and memorabilia.

CONTRIBUTORS

All the quotes from my interviews in *Everyday: Getting Closer To Buddy Holly* have been numbered and this is a guide to the speakers and where you can find their contributions.

Tim Adams (276) (299) is an authority on American cars and motorcycles.

Chloë Alexander (349) is an artist, radio DJ and book designer: she designed *The 1,000 UK Number One Hits* (Omnibus, 2005).

The Searchers' front man, **Frank Allen (112) (124)**, has been working on the group's biography for the past five years and it's going to be good.

As a qualified architect, noted artist and singer/songwriter, **Terry Allen (2) (4)** is Lubbock's Renaissance man. His 1978 double-album, *Lubbock (On Everything)*, is about his love/ hate relationship with Lubbock, mostly hate. His companion song to "Peggy Sue", "Peggy Legg", is about a one-legged dancer and is typical of his off the wall but wholly engaging songwriting.

Jerry Allison (45) (46) (56) (57) (68) (72) (77) (84) (88) (105) (108) (109) (118) (121) (131) (135) (137) (140) (175) (187) (192) (203) (220) (222) (225) (273) (327) (341) (377) (476) (497) (503) (504) (509) (528) (529) (537) plays drums for the Crickets.

Guitar supremo, **Tommy Allsup (279) (281) (285) (286) (342) (347) (353) (366) (369) (371) (372) (373) (378) (379) (387) (392) (398) (514) (515) (545)** can be said, in that dreadful cliché, to be 76 years young. "I'm going to see Les Paul when I get back from this tour," he told me in 2008, "and he's 92."

Ellis Amburn (25) (82) (96) (116) (177) (211) (290) (329) (351) (370) (381) (401) (493) has written biographies of Roy Orbison (*Dark Star*) and Buddy Holly (*Buddy Holly—The Real Story*).

Birmingham's **Harvey Andrews (53) (106) (336) (380) (542)** has recorded several albums of his own songs and written his autobiography, *Gold Star To The Ozarks*, in 2008.

Until a few months ago, **Craig Baguley (90)** was the long-standing editor of *Country Music People*.

Anton Barbeau (150) is an American singer/songwriter based in Oxford. His most recent album is *The Automatic Door* (2007).

Now the producer of Katie Melua, **Mike Batt (422)** wrote "Bright Eyes" (1979) and "I Feel Like Buddy Holly" (1984).

Dave Berry (251) had several 60s hits including "The Crying Game" (1964) and "Little Things" (1965) and has recorded "Maybe Baby".

Mike Berry (418) (431) had hits with "Tribute To Buddy Holly" (1961), "Don't You Think It's Time (1963) and "The Sunshine Of Your Smile" (1980). He remains popular with rock'n'roll revival shows and you can book him, if you wish, to perform a tribute set to Buddy Holly. He's as good as they come.

Singer/ songwriter **Eric Bibb (178)** is an engaging, blues-based entertainer who has introduced the music to a new generation.

The image of his father, **Big Bopper Jr (354) (355) (356) (376)** is producing a film about him.

Alan Blakley (245) was a member of the Tremeloes and they recorded "Everyday".

Although he has an extensive catalogue, the Bard of Barking, **Billy Bragg (332) (543)** is associated with political songs.

Will Bratton (274) is the son-of-law of the songwriter, Doc Pomus.

Mike Brocken (100) (120) (156) (337) (445) is a university lecturer who has written *The British Folk Revival* (Ashgate, 2003) and a biography of Burt Bacharach, *Maestro!* (Chrome Dreams, 2003).

John Broven (205) (395) is a British music writer based in America. His study of New Orleans rhythm and blues, *Walking To New Orleans* (Blues Unlimited, 1974) is a definitive text.

American singer/ songwriter **Stephen Bruton (436)** can be seen with Kris Kristofferson in *A Star Is Born*.

In the 1960s, Liverpool DJ and personality, **Billy Butler (338) (464)** was part of the *Spin-A-Disc* panel on ITV's *Thank Your Lucky Stars*.

Trevor Cajiao (86) (132) (199) is the editor of the best of all rock'n'roll magazines, *Now Dig This*.

Raphael Callaghan (113) (114) is among the UK's leading blues harmonica players.

Peter Carlin (157) (552) wrote a biography of Brian Wilson, *Catch A Wave* (Rodale, 2006) and is now concentrating on Paul McCartney.

Martin Carthy (468) is a stalwart of English folk music.

The composer of "Everlasting Love", **Buzz Cason (522)** is a performer and record producer, who did his time in the Crickets during the 60s.

With Mike Chapman, **Nicky Chinn (471)** formed the songwriting/ producing team, Chinnichap, and had hits with Mud, Sweet and Suzi Quatro.

Now retired (you see, some rockers do give up!), **Allan Clarke (460)** was the lead singer of the Hollies.

Terry Clarke (424) is a country-based singer/ songwriter from Reading with several albums to his name.

Stuart Colman (103) (179) (237) (456) is a record producer who has worked with the Crick-

ets, Connie Francis, Shakin' Stevens and Cliff Richard.

Radio DJ, **Frankie Connor (66) (297) (465)** was part of the Liverpool band, the Hideaways, and writes and records with Alan Crowley and Billy Kinsley as the Class Of '64. 'Do It Right Now' is their Holly song and they have also recorded a short tribute, 'Thank You'.

Michael Cox (466) had a hit with "Angela Jones" (1960).

Singer/ songwriter **Marshall Crenshaw (195) (408) (479)** has released several albums as well as writing the *Encyclopaedia Britannica* entry for Buddy Holly and the Crickets.

David Crosby (405) organised the Buddy Holly tribute in Liverpool in 2008

Sonny Curtis (32) (33) (35) (36) (40) (47) (50) (55) (64) (65) (76) (79) (87) (99) (144) (196) (214) (328) (382) (435) (477) (502) (510) (512) (523) (524) (531) played with Buddy Holly in his early years and has been in and out of the Crickets since 1958.

Bob Davis (258) saw Buddy Holly and the Crickets in Woolwich.

Bill Dees (321) (501) was part of Roy Orbison's band and co-wrote "It's Over" and "Oh, Pretty Woman".

Rock'n'roll would not be the same without **Bo Diddley (122)**.

Dion (344) (360) (362) (365) (367) (374) (386) and the Belmonts grew up in the Bronx and had their first hits with "No One Knows" (1958) and "A Teenager In Love" (1959). Dion's solo successes include "Runaround Sue" and "The Wanderer", both 1962.

Andrew Doble (155) (317) is an authority on Brill Building songwriters.

Bryan Dodson (449) was the drummer for Liverpool Scene.

Former editor of *Record Collector*, **Peter Doggett (67)** is the author of *Are You Ready For The Country?* (Viking, 2000).

Lonnie Donegan (256) kicked off the skiffle craze with "Rock Island Line", and his own career lasted much longer than the music did.

With his poetic lyrics and whimsical personality, **Donovan (400)** is unique (if a bit irritating) and his many hits include "Catch The Wind" (1965) and "Sunshine Superman" (1966).

Vince Eager (511) was one of the UK's first rock'n'roll singers and established himself on BBC-TV's *Drumbeat*.

Tom Earley (267) was a member of the Merseybeat group, the Valkyries.

Instrumentalist **Duane Eddy (307)** was known as the Man with the Twangy Guitar.

Bobby Elliott (413) (455) is the drummer with the Hollies.

Joe Ely (3) (12) (16) (21) (475) came to prominence in the mid-70s and had the potential to be country music's next big star. Instead, he opened for the Clash and ever since, he has followed his own path rather than adopt some marketing strategy. Joe ran away from home to join the circus and returned to Lubbock with a llama.

Paul Evans (153) (204) (384) is a New York songwriter who wrote the Kalin Twins' Number 1, "When" (1958), and had his own successes with "Seven Little Girls Sitting In The Back Seat" (1959) and "Hello This Is Joanie" (1978).

Phil Everly (62) (320) (555) is the younger half of the Everly Brothers.

Charlie Feathers (151) was a Sun recording artist, known for such rockabilly sides as "Tongue-Tied Jill", "Defrost Your Heart" and "Uh Huh Honey".

Narvel Felts (385) is a 50s rockabilly performer, who is still rocking with authenticity. As a mark of his success, he lives on Narvel Felts Avenue in Malden, Missouri.

John Firminger (166) (169) (246) (252) (520) (530) plays drums for Dave Berry's Cruisers and is the editor of the fanzines, *Crickets File* and *Looking Back*. His book with Martin Lilleker, *Not A Proper Job* (Juma, 2001), is the story of popular music in Sheffield.

Neil Foster (185) (243) (345) edited the rock'n'roll magazine, *Not Fade Away*, and has written the novel, *Cradle Of Rock* (Top F, 2004).

Looking even geekier than Buddy Holly, **Kim Fowley (474)** is one of rock's great characters, producing B. Bumble and the Stingers' "Nut Rocker" (1961).

Pete Frame (51) is famous for his informative and attractive *Rock Family Trees*. He won a Sony award for his radio documentary about Buddy Holly.

The Texas Jewboy, **Kinky Friedman (11) (28)** has turned to crime fiction, but his early songs include "Sold American", "Asshole From El Paso" and "They Ain't Makin' Jews Like Jesus Anymore". This is the true Alt. Country.

Goldmine contributor, **Gillian Gaar (440)** has written books on the Beatles and Green Day as well as a history of women in rock, *She's A Rebel* (Seal Press, latest edition 2002).

Snuff Garrett (17) (60) (197) (322) (346) (419) (429) (513) (516) was a DJ in Buddy Holly's time who went on to produce hit records by Johnny Burnette, Bobby Vee, Gene McDaniels and Gary Lewis and the Playboys.

Freddie Garrity (461) was the lead singer of Freddie and the Dreamers.

Bob Gaudio (226) was a member of the Four Seasons and wrote many of their biggest successes. He wrote the score for the stage musical, *Peggy Sue Got Married*.

Former girlfriend and wife of Jerry Allison, **Peggy Sue Gerron (39) (71) (134) (136) (191) (326) (331)** was the subject of "Peggy Sue".

Birmingham's **Steve Gibbons (182) (253) (298) (312) (425)** played with several groups, the Uglys, Balls and the Idle Race, before forming the Steve Gibbons Band. He had a Top 20 single with Chuck Berry's "Tulane" in 1977. Now tours with his band or as part of the Dylan Project.

In August 2008, I interviewed **Jimmie Dale Gilmore (7) (14) (18) (20) (27) (340) (498)** on the day he was recording a song with a Buddy Holly influence which had been written by his son. Jimmie, Butch Hancock and Joe Ely work together as an occasional outfit, the Flatlanders.

The songwriter **Geoff Goddard (209) (417) (432)** worked for Joe Meek and wrote "Tribute To Buddy Holly" (Mike Berry) and "Johnny Remember Me" (John Leyton).

Phillip Goodhand-Tait (128) (201) (394) (450) wrote hit songs for Love Affair (including "Bringing On Back The Good Times") and has released several albums of his own work.

Keith Goodwin (249) was a key reporter for the *New Musical Express*.

Hans Olof Gottfridsson (444) is a meticulous researcher of Beatle history, writing the gigantic *The Beatles From Cavern To Star-Club* (Premium Publishing, 1997).

Les Gray (470) (472) was the lead singer of Mud.

Michael Gray (13) (49) (451) is a leading authority on Bob Dylan and the author of *Song And Dance Man* and *The Dylan Encyclopedia*.

The country singer, **George Hamilton IV (61) (176)** had his first successes with the pop hits, "A Rose And A Baby Ruth" (1956) and "Why Don't They Understand" (1957).

TV producer, **Johnnie Hamp (235) (247)** has written his autobiography, *It Beats Working For A Living* (Trafford Publishing, 2008).

Starting with *West Texas Waltzes And Dust-Blown Tractor Tunes* on his own Rainlight Records in 1978, **Butch Hancock (6) (10)** has been a prolific singer/ songwriter, usually writing about the environment around Lubbock. His best-known song, "If I Were A Bluebird", has been recorded by Emmylou Harris.

Chesney Hawkes (480) (482) (483) starred in *Buddy's Song* in 1991 and had a Number 1 single with "The One And Only".

Dale Hawkins (189) wrote and recorded the rock'n'roll classic, "Susie-Q".

Highly acclaimed singer/ songwriter **Richard Hawley (546) (549)** often writes about his working class roots in Sheffield.

Justin Hayward (91) (149) (183) (541) is a Moody Blue and he wrote "Nights In White Satin".

Mike Heron (275) was part of the Incredible String Band.

The singer/ songwriter **Carolyn Hester (170) (171) (221) (236) (323)** has been recording since the 1950s and has had both Buddy Holly and Bob Dylan as session musicians. She appeared at the Edinburgh Festival in 1962 and toured Russia the following year, sponsored by the UK government.

The 50s rock'n'roll singer, **Ben Hewitt (194)**, recorded "I Ain't Givin' Up Nothin' (If I Don't Get Somethin' From You)" and "Patricia June".

Ian Higham (19) (83) (213) (534) is a staunch collector of Buddy Holly memorabilia.

Nigel Hinton (481) (484) wrote the teenage novels, *Buddy, Buddy's Song* and *Buddy's Blues*.

Paul Hipp (487) (490) (492) (548) was the first person to play Holly in the stage musical, *Buddy.*

Giving us some rabbit, **Chas Hodges (238)** is half of Chas and Dave.

Barry Holley (111) (287) writes for *Now Dig This* and has determined, much to his chagrin, that he is no relation.

Maria Elena Holly (291) (292) (293) (294) (295) (296) (302) (303) (310) (324) (334) (352) (375) (399) (415) (442) (554) moved to Florida in 1968 with her three children. Her first son, Carlos, is Spanish for Charles and so is named after Buddy. Now lives in Dallas.

In the 1960s, **Frank Ifield (212)** topped the UK charts with "I Remember You", "Lovesick Blues", "The Wayward Wind" and "Confessin'".

Tony Jackson (168) was a founder member of the Searchers.

Backed by the Shondells, **Tommy James (165) (540)** recorded the 60s classics, "Hanky Panky" and "Mony Mony".

The Mexican accordionist, **Flaco Jiminez (23) (357)** established himself when he worked with Ry Cooder (notably, "He'll Have To Go") and as well as being an excellent session musician, he has made many albums and toured in his own right.

A popular folk club performer, **Robb Johnson (158) (233)** is at the cutting-edge with songs about contemporary life and world affairs.

Mike Jones (406) (535) is the lyricist for the hit-making Latin Quarter.

Norman Jopling (257) (409) (410) (411) (412) (538) was a key journalist on *Record Mirror*.

One of the world's leading guitarists, **John Jorgenson (446)** was with Elton John's band for many years.

As well as owning Del-Fi Records, **Bob Keane (434)** produced Sam Cooke, Ritchie Valens, Chan Romero and the Bobby Fuller Four.

Stand-up comedian, **Mark Kelly (234) (421)** writes for Jo Brand.

Paul Kennerley (350) (448) is a British songwriter who cracked Nashville, writing for the Judds, Johnny Cash, the Everly Brothers, Marty Stuart and his former wife, Emmylou Harris.

Norman Killon (24) (101) is a Liverpool DJ, noted for his time at Eric's and the Sink.

The rockabilly singer, **Buddy Knox (42) (98) (277) (388) (420)**, recorded with his Rhythm Orchids.

Born in Smackover, Arkansas in 1935, **Sleepy LaBeef (78) (123)** is a big-voiced, powerfully built rockabilly singer.

Denny Laine (443) has been a member of the Moody Blues and Wings.

Albert Lee (527) is the fastest guitarist in the world and one of the best. Catch him with Hogan's Heroes or Bill Wyman's Rhythm Kings.

Mark Lewisohn (107) (263) (447) (452) (454) (519) is the world's leading authority on the Beatles, more so than Paul and Ringo, I would say, and is currently working on a mammoth three-volume biography.

Trini Lopez (198) (517) scored with his singalong version of "If I Had A Hammer" in 1963.

A founding editor of Rolling Stone, **Michael Lydon (539) (550)** wrote *Ray Charles—Man And Music* (Payback, 1999).

Underrated singer/ songwriter, **Don McCalister (31)** has a western swing band and *Brand New Ways* (1993) is particularly good.

Paul McCartney (63) learnt Holly's songs, copied his songwriting tricks and then bought the publishing catalogue.

Actor and musician, **Joe McGann (154)** has been touring the UK in *Fiddler On The Roof.*

British songwriter, **Tony Macaulay (397)**, has written "Baby, Now That I've Found You" (Foundations), "Let The Heartaches Begin" (Long John Baldry) and "Lights Of Cincinnati" (Scott Walker).

Theatre impresario, **Laurie Mansfield (485) (486) (488) (489) (494)** had the concept of staging *Buddy* and saw it through.

Ernie Maresca (361) (363) (364) wrote "No One Knows" (Dion and the Belmonts), "Runaround Sue" (with and for Dion) and "The Wanderer" (Dion).

Neville Marten (143) plays with Marty Wilde's Wildcats and is one of the UK's leading authorities on guitars. (Gosh, I've been talking to a lot of guitarists!)

Joe B. Mauldin (117) (188) (215) (227) (240) (254) (284) (289) (300) (325) (383) (496) (521) (536) (553) plays upright bass with the Crickets.

Record producer **Huey P. Meaux (104)** is best known for the 1965 million-seller, "She's About A Mover" for the Sir Douglas Quintet.

Chris Montez (358) (359) had hits with "Let's Dance" (1962) and "The More I See You" (1966).

Bob Montgomery (29) (34) (37) (38) (43) (48) (52) (58) (59) (74) (97) (278) (282) (283) (343) (390) (407) (499) (525) (526) (532) (533) and Buddy Holly developed their playing styles together. Although Montgomery was never a

Cricket, he wrote "Heartbeat" and "Love's Made A Fool Of You".

The son of Bob Montgomery, **Kevin Montgomery (54)** is among the best Americana singer/ songwriters of today and he performed at the 2009 tribute in Clear Lake, Iowa to Buddy Holly.

Johnny Moore (193) was the longest-standing lead singer of the Drifters and he can be heard on "At The Club" and "Saturday Night At The Movies".

Gary Murphy (115) (139) (147) (463) is an experienced Merseyside musician who has presented shows about guitar heroes and staged concert versions of *The War Of The Worlds.*

Graham Nash (414) is associated with the Hollies and Crosby, Stills and Nash.

Jerry Naylor (26) (30) (41) (44) (110) (223) became the lead singer of the Crickets and was featured on their hits, "Don't Ever Change" and "My Little Girl". In recent years, he has put together the vast *Rockabilly Legends* project, which is a combination of book, DVDs and CDs.

Jim Newcombe (190) (265) (270) (393) (428) is a songwriter from St Helens, now living in Canada, who has written for Rayburn Anthony, Ben Hewitt and Charlie Gracie.

Peter Noone (462) was the lead singer of Herman's Hermits.

Noted rock biographer, **Philip Norman (439)** has written both a biography (*Rave On*) and a TV play (*Words Of Love*) about Buddy Holly.

Comedian **Des O'Connor (241) (250) (255) (272)** was the compère on the Crickets' UK tour in 1958.

Mick O' Toole (491) is an authority on rock'n'roll.

Brother of Phil, **Michael Ochs (467)** owns the key photographic agency for rock'n'roll performers.

Gary Osborne (159) (333) wrote the lyrics for what is now known as Jeff Wayne's musical version of *The War Of The Worlds*. His many songs with Elton John include "Blue Eyes" (1982) and he also wrote the English lyric for Kiki Dee's "Amoureuse".

Larry Page (184) (239) managed both the Kinks and the Troggs.

A former member of Waylon Jennings' band, **Gordon Payne (495)** joined the Crickets as lead singer and guitarist in 1978 and stayed 15 years. He has written a novel about a tornado, *The Hail And The Fury* (WordWright, 2008).

Dominic Pedler (129) (138) (216) (218) (280) (308) (314) (318) (441) wrote *The Songwriting Secrets Of The Beatles* (Omnibus, 2003).

Mike Pender (244) (266) (271) was a founder member of the Searchers and now runs Mike Pender's Searchers.

With "24 Hours From Tulsa" and "I'm Gonna Be Strong", **Gene Pitney (458)** was among the most successful singers of the 60s.

In preference to the Beatles, **Brian Poole (248) (433)** and the Tremeloes were signed to Decca and had a run of hit singles including "Twist And Shout" (1963). and "Do You Love Me" (1963).

Maddy Prior (469) is the lead singer with those English folk/ rockers, Steeleye Span

John Repsch (210) (416) wrote the biography, *The Legendary Joe Meek* (Woodford House, 1989).

Tim Rice (152) has been knighted for his contribution to musical theatre.

Tim Riley (167) is an academic writer with books on the Beatles and Madonna. He wrote *Fever: How Rock And Roll Transformed Gender In America* (St Martin's Press, 2004).

Music writer **Alan Robinson (478)** owns the PR company, Indiscreet.

Tommy Roe (430) had hit records with "Sheila" (1962), "The Folk Singer" (1963) and "Dizzy" (1969).

John Rostron (262) (396) (508) is a Southport dentist who has staged charity concerts with the Crickets. He and his wife have taken a holiday on the Orient Express with the Allisons.

Peter Sarstedt (133) topped the UK charts with "Where Do You Go To, My Lovely?" in 1969.

Noted rock journalist, **Jon Savage (217)** wrote the definitive study of punk rock, *England's Dreaming* (St Martin's Press, 1991).

Among the many hits by **Leo Sayer (231) (473) (506)** are revivals of "Raining In My Heart" (1978) and "More Than I Can Say" (1980).

Canadian singer/ songwriter **Ron Sexsmith (348)** has released several albums of his own material. Some critics say that his wimpish looks count against him: now, where have I heard that before?

In the early 70s, **Martin Simpson (316)** from Scunthorpe emerged from the British folk scene and is now a highly acclaimed singer and guitarist.

Glenn Skelhorn (547) (551) runs the Liverpool neo-punk band, the Gutterfighters.

Pirate DJ **Keith Skues (206)** became a mainstay of Radio 1 and Radio 2 and is about to complete 50 years in broadcasting.

Gerry Standard (264) (269) saw Buddy Holly and the Crickets in Liverpool.

Bob Stanley (161) writes on popular music for *The Times* and is part of the chart band, Saint Etienne.

Back in the 60s, **Alvin Stardust (259) (260) (261) (423)** had hit records as Shane Fenton. Alvin had a Top 10 hit with "I Feel Like Buddy Holly" in 1984.

With "Rock With The Caveman" (1956) and "Singing The Blues" (1957), **Tommy Steele (69) (70) (426)** was Britain's first rock'n'roll star.

Singer/ songwriter **John Stewart (125)** wrote "Gold" and "Daydream Believer" and was also one-third of the Kingston Trio.

As well as working with Kris Kristofferson's band, **Billy Swan (75)** had an international hit with "I Can Help" in 1974. He was in Black Tie, who recorded "Learning The Game" (1990).

St Helens' guitarist **Geoff Taggart (505)** has written for Shakin' Stevens and the Shadows.

The name says it all: **Jesse "Guitar" Taylor (15)** is a fine guitarist from Lubbock, who has been part of Joe Ely's band.

Formerly with Fairport Convention, **Richard Thompson (181)** is a highly acclaimed folk-based songwriter.

Johnny Tillotson (228) is best known for "Poetry In Motion" (1960).

John Tobler (186) (232) (288) is possibly the most prolific of all the UK rock writers. My files bulge with features he wrote in the 1970s. Among his many books is a biography of Buddy Holly and he also has an intriguing record label, Road Goes On Forever, whose artists include Carolyn Hester.

George Tomsco (89) (304) (305) (402) (403) (404) was lead guitarist with the Fireballs.

Bobby Vee (126) (141) (315) (389) (391) (457) (518) was one of the best-selling acts of the 60s,

his hits including "Take Good Care Of My Baby", "Run To Him" and "The Night Has A Thousand Eyes".

Simon Warner (313) is a Senior Teaching Fellow at the School of Music at the University of Leeds. His book, *Text, Drugs And Rock'n'Roll*, will be published in 2010.

Terry Wayne (200) (230) was one of the UK's first rock'n'roll performers, making an impact on *Six-Five Special*. When Jerry Lee Lewis' 1958 UK tour was in disarray, Terry Wayne was recruited to replace him and did surprisingly well.

Julian Lloyd Webber (130) is among the world's leading cellists.

UK guitarist, **Bert Weedon (146)** played on hundreds of 50s records and made the Top 10 with "Guitar Boogie Shuffle" in 1959.

Bruce Welch (102) (119) (127) (142) (145) (229) (242) (309) (330) (437) (507) is one of the Shadows.

Sonny West (92) (93) (162) (163) (164) (207) (208) (301) (306) (453) wrote "Oh Boy!" and "Rave On".

BBC Radio York's **Chas White (Dr Rock) (73) (85) (173) (174)** has written authorised biographies of Little Richard and Jerry Lee Lewis.

Scottish blues singer **Tam White (219)** had his moment of glory with "What In The World's Come Over You" (1975).

Singer/ songwriter **Tony Joe White (311)** devised his own form of swamp rock and has written "Polk Salad Annie" (Elvis Presley), "Rainy Night In Georgia" (Brook Benton) and "Steamy Windows" (Tina Turner).

If you're staging a rock'n'roll musical, look no further than West End actor, **Tim Whitnall (5) (81) (94) (148) (172) (202) (224) (335) (339) (544)**, who has played both Elvis Presley and Eddie

Cochran and been a part of *The Rocky Horror Show*.

Andy Wilkinson (9) (22) (160) (459) is a singer/songwriter and playwright based at Texas Tech. His album, *Texas When Texas Was Free* (1990), includes a song about 40 inches of snow in Lubbock. He has written a song from the pilot's point of view, "Leave It In The Hands Of Fate".

Dave Williams (80) (180) (268) (368) (500) was with the Merseybeat band, Dale Roberts and the Jaywalkers, and has made pilgrimages to Lubbock and Clear Lake.

In 1967, **Mark Wirtz (95)** wrote and produced the hit single, "Excerpt From A Teenage Opera".

Bob Wooler (438) was the DJ at Liverpool's Cavern Club.

The well-travelled **Richard Wootton (1) (8)** owns a PR company which looks after many visiting American rock and country artists.

Johnny Worth (427) wrote many of the biggest UK hits of the early 60s including "What Do You Want" (Adam Faith) and "Well I Ask You" (Eden Kane).

Robert Wyatt (319) was part of Soft Machine and Matching Mole and has made several experimental albums.

saf publishing

SAF Publishing

Buy Titles Online

www.safpublishing.co.uk
info@safpublishing.co.uk

All SAF titles are available from the SAF Publishing website.
You can browse the full range of rock, pop, jazz and experimental music books we have available. You can also keep up with our latest releases and special offers.

Also visit our eBay shop, where there are a large number of new and old, rare and out-of-print books, as well signed editions and rock memorabilia, CDs and DVDs. The stock is constantly changing, so come back regularly to the address below:

www.theflyingpiranha.co.uk